In the Whirlwind

In the Whirlwind

GOD AND HUMANITY IN CONFLICT

Robert A. Burt

HARVARD UNIVERSITY PRESS

CAMBRIDGE, MASSACHUSETTS

LONDON, ENGLAND

2012

Library of Congress Cataloging-in-Publication Data

Burt, Robert, 1939–
In the whirlwind : God and humanity in conflict / Robert A. Burt.
p.   cm.
Includes bibliographical references (p.   ) and index.
ISBN 978-0-674-06566-6 (alk. paper)
1. God—Righteousness.   2. God—Omnipotence.
3. God—Goodness.   I. Title.
BT130.B877   2012
296. 3–dc23   2011050231

And the Lord answered Job from the whirlwind and He said:
Who is this who darkens counsel in words without knowledge?

JOB 38:1

Contents

Preface

My father's father was a *kohen*. This meant he was a member of a priestly caste in Jewish ritual practice that traced its origins directly to Moses's elder brother Aaron. The status is passed from father to son, and one of the prerogatives of this caste membership is the authority to recite a specially sanctified blessing over the members of the synagogue congregation. Immediately after my bar mitzvah, which signified that I had become an adult for all Jewish ritual purposes, I went with my father to my grandfather's *shul* and the three of us—all the eldest sons in our generations—stood together to deliver this ceremonial blessing. A member of the congregation had washed our feet—this, too, was part of the *kohenim* prerogative—before we emerged, barefoot, on the dais to recite the blessing. As ritual practice prescribed, we each placed a prayer shawl over our heads so that the congregants could not see our faces as we blessed them. And thus, I imagined, we could communicate directly with God, like the ancient high priests who alone were authorized to enter the inner sanctum, the Holy of Holies, in the Jerusalem Temple.

My grandfather took immense pride in his priestly status. He had come to America from a village near Kiev in 1901, when he was around eight years old. Near Newfoundland, his ship sank; and though everyone on board was rescued, he and his family lost all their meager belongings. Within two years of their arrival, his father died, and my grandfather suddenly became responsible for supporting his mother and young siblings. Somehow he accumulated the resources to buy a horse and wagon and became an itinerant seller of fruits and vegetables.

This might have been the beginning of an American success story. But it was not for my grandfather. He was a physically slight and temperamentally shy man, an unworldly man. When he married my grandmother, he traded his horse and wagon for a small grocery store attached to their living quarters and barely scratched out a living for the rest of his life.

I remember the grocery store, located in a poor, mostly African-American neighborhood in South Philadelphia. I remember the interminable Passover seders in the dining room of the attached house, and especially my grandmother's quickly opening and then slamming shut the front door to the house when it was time to admit the Prophet Elijah to drink from his wine goblet on the seder table—time enough, my grandmother made sure, to admit Elijah but without enough time for her to see any passersby, who, by Jewish law, would be entitled to join the seder dinner. These long hours when my grandfather presided over the Passover rituals were the only memory I have of his appearing comfortable, at home, in charge, in his house.

But in the synagogue, he was a different man. When he sat in the synagogue, he seemed to expand; he spread himself out as if to occupy several seats. When he stood to pray, he seemed elevated, transported. The few times my father took me to this *shul*, I luxuriated sitting next to my other-worldly grandfather. Occasionally, but furtively, I would look up toward the small balcony in the rear of the synagogue where the women were crowded into their separate quarter and see my grandmother—a large-boned, imposing woman who towered over my grandfather everywhere except here.

My grandfather's life, his stature, his meaning, was in that synagogue. Everywhere else, it seemed to me, he was a beaten-down man.
But not in the synagogue. Not where he was a *kohen* who was authorized to speak directly to God on behalf of the congregants.

When I joined the ranks of the *kohenim* at my grandfather's congregation and stood barefoot with my prayer shawl covering my face, I
didn't know what I was supposed to do. I hadn't rehearsed the required
prayer, and I told my father that I didn't see how I could make the
proper ceremonial gesture with my hands, support the *tallit,* or prayer
shawl, over my head, and read from the prayer book. "It doesn't matter," my father said. "Just hold up the *tallit* and mumble. The congregation won't hear you and your grandfather will pray loudly enough for
all of us." I did as my father said. But I felt like a fraud.

My father had a vexed relationship with his father. I now see in retrospect that this was typical between immigrant parents and their
American-born children. But as I grew up witnessing the tension between my father and his father, I didn't put their relationship in any
sociological perspective. They seemed to me simply locked in continuous, muted, and mysterious warfare.

My grandfather died when I was sixteen, and my father subsequently
told me, "I rebelled against his religion, but I had the religion to rebel
against. I didn't give that to you. And I feel that I failed in educating
you as a Jew." Years later, after I had become a tenured law professor,
and just months before he suddenly died (at the young age of fifty-
nine), my father told me that my grandfather had always wanted him
to become a rabbi, and now he would have been very proud that I had
become a rabbi. I replied that I was a law professor, not a rabbi. My father said, "I've read what you've written in your law review articles. You
are a rabbi."

And so I come to writing *In the Whirlwind.*

The overarching theme of this book is the relationship between God
and humanity in the Hebrew Bible as it evolved from complete har-

mony at the outset, even before God created the Garden of Eden, to a mutual struggle over authority on both sides, with God insisting on unconditional obedience to his commands and humanity insisting that God keep his promises to them or else they would withhold obedience. This narrative extends beyond the Hebrew Bible and is equally central to the Christian Bible, which begins with an appeal for unconditional love between God and all mankind but ends with an assertion of God's authority to destroy sinners and even sin itself.

I suppose it is no surprise that my book, which had its origins in a generational struggle between fathers and sons, should divine a pattern in the Hebrew and Christian Bibles of initial harmony that became transposed and distorted into mutual recriminations over who is authorized to control whom. I do believe that this narrative sequence is in the biblical texts and is not simply a projection that I am imposing on it derived from my professorial concerns about the origins and legitimacy of legal authority or my personal grappling with unresolved Oedipal issues. Projection is, of course, inevitable. But these concerns and struggles are not unique to me, and it seems plausible enough, and even likely enough, that the biblical texts speak to these common issues of generational conflict and the relationship of love and obedience to authority.

I am not a theologian nor a member of the profession of biblical scholars. And my reading of the biblical texts departs in many ways from conventional accounts. I may be trying to protect myself against accusations that I was faking it, as I had done in my grandfather's *shul*. But I do believe that support for my reading can be found in the biblical texts, even though contradictory readings can also be supported with equal plausibility. In my view, the presence of contradictory meanings is an essential aspect of the narrative strategy of the Bible, reflecting its underlying theme of extolling unconditional obedience to God's will at the same time that the text raises questions—at first tentatively and ultimately (in the book of Job) loudly and insistently—about the legitimacy of God's authority in demanding obedience.

This progression is not identified as such in the Hebrew and Christian Bibles. It is instead embedded in thick narrative accounts of the extended relationships between God and specific human beings. The goal of this book is to draw out the underlying issues about God's authority from these narratives. Approaching this goal requires often close attention to the details, and especially small and easily overlooked details, of the relationships. If I succeed in my goal, examination of these details will illuminate the overall pattern of the progression that I see.

In these details, we will see God trying out different strategies for obtaining what he wants in his relationship with humanity. We will also see God, as he repeatedly encounters difficulty in getting what he desires, doubting whether he wants any continued relationship with humanity. When he first created man and woman together in his image, God and humanity appeared to see a fundamental harmony between them. But this harmony quickly vanished and was succeeded by God's punitive commandments and humanity's disobedience. After the Flood, when God destroyed almost all of humanity because of its apparently inbred evil, God tried a new tactic with Noah—not simply rescuing him from the Flood but also making promises to him about God's future protective intentions. These promises to Noah applied to all of humanity, but when God subsequently turned to the patriarchs, Abraham, Isaac, and Jacob, he offered a variation—a special relationship with them and their progeny. God promised a more intense, more protective, but also more demanding relationship. As attractive as this offer appeared to the patriarchs, God's promise was also met with considerable, though often masked, skepticism.

This skepticism grew exponentially during the Israelites' four centuries of enslavement in Egypt, and it hardly abated during their forty years of wandering in the Sinai desert. During this time, God escalated the number and complexity of the observances that he demanded from the Israelites as a condition for his continued protection. God ultimately capped these obligations with a commandment that the Israelites not simply obey but also love him. This commandment, conveyed by Moses in his final address to the Israelites, contains a considerable paradox: "love me or I will punish you" hardly seems an appealing basis for a relationship between a lover and his beloved. God's embrace of this unattractive demand suggests that he was still trying to accomplish what he had sought all along from the first moment of creation—a fundamental unity, an unquestionably loving relationship with humanity.

In God's last appearance in the Hebrew Bible, in the book of Job, his command for unconditional love seems to explode with primal force and destructiveness. But then, in the Christian Bible, God seems to speak in a different voice. Through the presence on earth of his Son, Jesus Christ, God seems to offer love and to invite a reciprocal response rather than to command love. By subtle degrees in the Gospel accounts of Jesus's ministry, however, God seems to edge more toward a relationship based on command and punishment—a demand that erupts in the book of Revelation with the same punitive force and destructiveness that we see in the book of Job.

This in quick strokes is the overall narrative pattern for the development of the idea of authority that I see in the biblical texts. The full force of this pattern will emerge in close attention to the details of the biblical portrayals of the relationship between God and specific, successive human beings. I offer this account not simply to tell a good Bible story—though I see it as a very good story, as a collection of richly engrossing, psychologically acute, beautifully rendered portraits of the variety of relationships between God and humanity. I offer this reading also to show the relevance of the biblical portrayal of God's authority to modern secular accounts of political relations between State and

Subjects. I see a political theory about what differentiates legitimate from illegitimate authority embedded in the narratives of the Hebrew and Christian Bibles. By explicitly drawing this theory out from these narratives, we can see some valuable lessons for secular political theory in its various efforts to identify principles that establish the legitimacy of authority relationships.

This book will not satisfy readers who are looking to debunk religion. As I have worked closely with the biblical texts in writing this book, I have been awestruck by their moral profundity, their psychological acuity, and their literary grace. In this, I am my grandfather's grandson.

But neither will this book satisfy readers who want to view God as wholly admirable and entirely deserving of humanity's worshipful love. I find much to admire in God as he is portrayed in the Hebrew and Christian Bibles. But I find even more to admire in the ambivalent portrait of God that emerges in the clear-minded, courageous criticisms of God's conduct and character that human beings repeatedly offered to him. In this, I am my father's son.

In the Whirlwind

CHAPTER ONE

In the Beginning

No authority, whether divine or secular, deserves automatic obedience. All authority must justify itself by some extrinsic standard of justice or righteousness. This is the core claim of modern, secular Western political theory. This theory defines itself as fundamentally different from the demand for unquestioning obedience to God's authority that is supposedly embedded in the Hebrew and Christian Bibles.[1] According to this account, the biblical God deserves obedience simply because he is God, not because he is righteous or just as judged by some external standard.

I believe that this conventional view is based on a misreading of the biblical texts. It ignores the fact that God's specific claims to absolute authority are regularly, if for the most part indirectly, denied in the Hebrew and Christian Bibles themselves. The biblical texts almost never openly challenge God's authority. But the challenges are there, sometimes buried and sometimes on the surface of the biblical accounts of interactions between God and human beings.

Contrary to modern secular claims, there is a political theory that underlies the account of God's authority in the Hebrew and Christian Bibles, and this theory attempts to answer the three questions that are the core inquiries in any normative account of political authority:

1. Why should anyone obey God? In other words, are God's claims for authority based on anything more than his raw power to coerce humanity?
2. If God claims that his authority is based on standards of righteousness and justice, does this mean that humanity is entitled to make independent judgments of God's specific exercise of his authority? In other words, does God owe any obligations to humanity?
3. If God does owe obligations to humanity, in light of the vast difference in raw power between him and us, how do we humans enforce these obligations?

Both the Hebrew and the Christian Bibles wrestle with questions about the legitimacy and extent of God's authority as strenuously as the most skeptical modern political theorist challenges state authority. The challenges are there within the texts, waiting to be seen if only we have eyes to see. But these challenges can only be brought into visibility by a carefully detailed unraveling of the biblical narratives.

We must begin at the beginning, with the account of God's creation of the universe in the first two chapters of Genesis. These opening chapters present two apparently inconsistent accounts of creation itself—and it is in these inconsistencies that the basic groundwork is established for the political theory of the Bible.

In the first chapter of Genesis, God's creative acts move progressively—dividing Day from Night on the first day; dividing Heaven from Earth on the second day; dividing the earth between dry land and seas and planting seeds for grass, trees, and fruit on the third day; creating the sun, moon, and stars on the fourth day; creating animals on the fifth day; and finally, on the sixth day, creating humans—male and female together—"in the image of God." At successive steps of this creation, the biblical narrator relates that God "saw that [his creation] was good." Finally, after creating humanity, God looks over his entire effort and concludes, "Behold, it was very good."

There is a small suggestion in this first chapter of Genesis that God had in mind standards of "goodness" that he was applying to his own conduct—though this is only the barest hint. The biblical account gives no content to the idea of "good" that God was invoking, and it may be that this chapter of Genesis provides no extrinsic standard on the grounds that whatever God wants must be considered by that fact alone to be "good."

After chapter 1 concludes with God's supremely self-satisfied evaluation of his creation as "very good," chapter 2 of Genesis begins as an apparently natural extension. On the seventh day, we are told, God rested from all the work he had done. But then the chapter 2 narrative takes a strange swerve. Without any explanation or any acknowledgment of inconsistency, we are suddenly thrust back to the third day of creation, after God had made the earth and the heavens but before there were any plants or animals or humans; on the eighth day following creation, after God rested, there was only barren dust in the universe. From this dust, God then formed man and breathed life into his nostrils. This man (*adam* in Hebrew) was initially created all alone on the earth, unlike in the first chapter, where animals had preceded humanity and male and female humans were created at the same time.

After this solo appearance of man in the second chapter, God plants a garden in Eden. But unlike the events in the first chapter, in which the entire earth abounded in plants and trees and fruit to feed both animals and humans, this Garden of Eden in the second chapter is a circumscribed place surrounded by the barren earth. God then places Adam alone in the garden and immediately issues his first negative commandment: God says to Adam, you may eat from every tree in this garden except for one, and if you eat fruit from the tree of the knowledge of good and evil, "on [that] day . . . you are doomed to die."

Here is another difference from the first account of creation. In the first chapter, after creating the animals God told them, "Be fruitful and multiply." God then created humans, male and female together, and gave them the identical instruction, "Be fruitful and multiply." In this first chapter, it is as if God were saying, "I have given you the potential to procreate, it's in your essential nature, now go to it." This is more an instruction and encouragement than a negative commandment. Most notably, God attaches no punishment to this injunction. The implication of his directive is that humans as well as animals might need God's prompting about the desirability of procreation, but that once clearly informed, they will readily understand that fecundity will be its own reward.

In the second chapter, God's coupling of his command to Adam with a threat of punishment for disobedience is vastly different in its implications. In this chapter, God relies on a distinctive "command and punish" mode for exercising his authority. From this point through the entire corpus of the Hebrew Bible, God predominantly relies on this "command and punish" mode. But though this mode predominates in the Hebrew Bible, it is not exclusive; on a few notable occasions, as we will see, God returns to the style of authority that he displayed in the first chapter—encouragement more than command, an appeal to his addressees' own self-understanding rather than threatened punishment as an inducement for compliance. In the Christian Bible, as we will see, this initial mode becomes predominant (though not exclusive).

These different approaches to exercising authority are not the only difference between the first and second chapters of Genesis. There is yet another apparent inconsistency. Immediately after God forbade Adam to eat from that one tree, God said, "It is not good that the man should be alone; I will make him a helper fit for him." In the first creation chapter, everything that God created, everything that he touched, was explicitly recognized as "good" or ultimately as "very good." But suddenly in the second creation chapter, something appears that was "not good"—and, indeed, nothing in the second chapter was described as "good."

After recognizing this specific shortcoming regarding Adam's solitude, God immediately set out to remedy it. According to Genesis, God created a virtual zoo of every beast and bird and brought them to Adam for naming. But nonetheless, the Genesis narrator observes, "for the man there was not found a helper fit for him."

This is a striking admission in the second creation chapter. God avowedly created all the beasts and birds to "make [Adam] a helper fit for him." But after his vast zoological efforts, it was clear that God had not yet succeeded in his chosen task. Surely an omniscient and omnipotent God would have been able to solve any problem as soon as he had identified it as such. In the first creation chapter, God made no apparent wrong turns; he did indeed seem omniscient and omnipotent. Does the second creation chapter reveal some shortcoming, some weakness in God that had not appeared before? Does this revelation imply some standard of conduct, or at least of efficacy, against which the biblical narrator is measuring God's performance?

Having failed to accomplish his goal by creating animals to keep Adam company in the second chapter, God now takes a different tack. He anesthetizes Adam and extracts a rib from which he fashions a woman. When Adam awakes and sees Eve, he says, "This at last is bone of my bones and flesh of my flesh."

These were the first words directly ascribed to Adam since his appearance in Genesis. A literary convention is employed throughout the entire text of the Hebrew Bible that the first words spoken by any actor are especially revealing of his or her essential character.[2] If we apply this convention to Adam's first quoted words, Adam is revealed as a person who had been very lonely, who had shared God's evaluation that it was "not good" for him to be alone. And more than this, as God paraded one animal after another before him, Adam seems to become increasingly impatient, maybe even increasingly despairing, until finally God figured out that what Adam really needed was a helper. "This one *at last*," Adam said. Adam thus appears to be a lonely and needy man who is not completely confident that God will adequately respond to his loneliness and neediness.

In Adam's reaction to God's creation of Eve, we can see the first hints of human presumption to evaluate God. It is not as if Adam saw himself as having authority to judge God or as having capacity to punish God, for example, by disobeying his orders. But Adam's impatient welcoming of Eve conveys the barest suggestion that he is prepared to assess God's conduct with reference to his own needs and wishes. These are the first seeds for human claims to judge God, and they progressively grow, as we will see, in subsequent narratives in the Hebrew and Christian Bibles.

In juxtaposing the two creation accounts in the first and second chapters of Genesis, we have thus seen three themes that will recur, and will become increasingly important—the presence in the biblical text of substantive standards by which God's conduct might be judged, the claim of human beings to exercise those judgments, and different modes by which divine (and human) authority can be exercised. Moreover, another difference between these two chapters points to a further theme of vast significance in the biblical texts. This difference is signaled by the opening sentence in the first chapter of Genesis.

The traditional translation of this first sentence is "In the beginning God created the heavens and the earth." This translation reaches back at least to the King James version of the Bible in the seventeenth century. But this is not the only possible translation of the biblical Hebrew. Robert Alter, a professor of Hebrew and Comparative Literature at the University of California, Berkeley, has recently offered an important variation. He translates opening words of the first sentence as follows: "When God began to create heaven and earth, and the earth then was welter and waste and darkness over the deep ..." There is an important difference here. The traditional translation seems to imply that God created the heavens and earth from nothing, that nothing at all existed before this initial moment. Alter's translation, by contrast, makes clear that something existed before God created the heavens and earth. That something was "welter and waste and darkness over the deep," but it was not nothing.

Neither Alter's translation nor the traditional version is obviously correct; both are grammatically permissible readings of the Hebrew. And if we read the second sentence in the traditional translation with close care ("The earth was without form and void, and darkness was upon the face of the deep") we can find the same implication—that something (that is, "darkness") existed before God said, "Let there be light." But Alter's more direct translation gives us a handle for understanding the apparent contradictions between the first and second accounts of creation that we don't get from the traditional translation. If something existed before God created heaven and earth, that something was chaos—"welter and waste and darkness." And God did not create something from nothing; he created order out of chaos.

This is the implication of God's entire creative effort in the first chapter of Genesis—he differentiates light from darkness, day from night, the heavens from the earth, dry land from the sea on the earth, and so on. If we understand the Genesis account of God's creation as imposing order on chaos, then we can read the Genesis account of the second creation in a different light. After God finished the six days of the first creation, on the seventh day he rested, but after this rest period in chapter 2, God seems to resume work almost all over again. Now, however, we can see that something might have happened at some time during the seventh day: that while God rested, the forces of chaos might have returned and unraveled much of what God had done, rolling us back to the third day of the initial creation when the earth was nothing but barren dust, with no plants, animals, or human beings.

Chapter 2 of Genesis does not say this explicitly. But if we read this possibility into the text, then many things in the second creation account become clear that are otherwise inexplicable. Why, for example, was there one forbidden tree in the Garden of Eden? If God didn't want Adam to eat the fruit of this tree, why was it in the garden? Did God put it there or, if not, why didn't he remove it?

Several possible answers seem plausible. First of all, God may not himself have planted this forbidden tree. The tree may have sprouted like a noxious weed that God did not invite and perhaps even could not control—like the primordial chaos that persisted notwithstanding his creative efforts.[3] God's command to Adam against eating from the tree of knowledge of good and evil could be, from this perspective, his attempt to control chaos—or at least to control Adam and to keep chaos away from him even if he could not entirely eradicate chaos. (Perhaps by this hortatory effort, God meant to protect Adam against infecting himself by ingesting the noxious weed that God could not— or chose not to—exterminate on his own.)

Even if God did himself plant the forbidden tree, we could understand this planting and his negative command to Adam as God's testing his capacity to control the human he had created. In his first creative efforts, in chapter 1 of Genesis, God had seen no need to test his command of any part of the universe that he had made. God had simply assumed that his powers were so vast that he controlled all that he saw. For this reason, God was able to survey all of his creation at the end of the first chapter and declare that it was "very good." In the second chapter, by contrast, God never bestows any praise on his new creative efforts. To the contrary, in the second chapter, God's only evaluation of his handiwork was in the negative, when he stated that it "was not good that [Adam] should be alone."

I've noted that after God made this observation, it took him a long time to remedy this error, this design flaw, running through all the animals before he finally realized that Adam needed Eve to keep him company, and I stated that this long search process, which Adam impatiently endured, implicitly raised some question about God's omnipotence and omniscience. If we now surmise that chaos had returned to unravel God's initial ordering of the universe, we can see an even stronger reason that God himself would question his own power, and why he would be moved the second time around to test the extent of that power, which he had previously taken for granted.

We can also see why the redactors of the Bible would have purposefully omitted this missing link in the account of the second creation, the link that chaos had reasserted itself while God rested. To openly acknowledge that God's powers might be limited was, at the least, disrespectful, if not sacrilegious; but even more, this acknowledgment would be unwelcome and even exceedingly distasteful to the general audience for whom the redactors were compiling the biblical text. If God could not conclusively control chaos, how could he be depended upon to protect the human beings that he had created?

The redactors' silence about the stubborn force of chaos can be understood as an attempt to pursue the same goal that God had sought when he tried to bar Adam from eating from the tree that would give him knowledge of "good and evil." I read this juxtaposition of "good and evil" as equivalent to the distinction between order and chaos, and so long as Adam knew nothing about the persistent existence of evil—about the irreducible force of chaos—then he could sleep comfortably in the conviction that God would protect him no matter what. Adam could confidently and without self-consciousness believe what King David explicitly prayed for in Psalm 121: "My help comes from the Lord, who made heaven and earth . . . Behold, he who keeps Israel will neither slumber nor sleep." The sad (but inadmissible) fact is, however, that God did "slumber" in the opening chapters of Genesis: he rested after making heaven and earth, and his work was almost undone by the apparently persistent force of chaos.

As it turned out, of course, notwithstanding God's command, Adam did gain knowledge of evil, and with this knowledge, Adam lost his innocence. This loss was not just Adam's sin, his guilt and shame, at disobeying God's commandment but also his loss of naïveté. As a consequence of this lost innocence, the two humans were expelled from Eden into the desolate earth that always had lurked outside this garden. They were left to fend for themselves against the barrenness of the earth. With their knowledge of the existence of evil, they were now consigned to struggle endlessly against the forces of chaos. They were in this sense like God himself—not his mirror image like the original couple, but led by the persistent forces of chaos to disobey him. Adam and Eve, this second human couple, thereby differentiated themselves from God at the same time that they ensnared themselves in the very difficulty that God had failed to overcome in his effort to eradicate chaos.

This interpretation of the first two chapters of Genesis leads us to an overarching theme that pervades the Hebrew Bible. Not just in Genesis but throughout the entire text of the Hebrew Bible we see an endless struggle by God to control humanity, and human beings in turn sometimes resisting this control but nonetheless endlessly trying to induce God to protect them against evil, against the forces of darkness, against destruction and death. The fact that this theme pervades the Bible is what gives plausibility to the interpretation I have offered regarding the apparent conflict between the two creation accounts in the first and second chapters of Genesis. I certainly can't prove that mine is the only possible interpretation of this apparent conflict. But in the same way that the multiple meanings of each word in the spare vocabulary of ancient Hebrew can only be interpreted based on the context of the sentence or paragraph in which the word is used, so also in interpreting every episode in the narrative of the Hebrew Bible we must rely on the full context in which that narrative is embedded in order to make sense of any portion of it.[4]

This interpretive method does not, however, yield single-minded determinative results. The narrative interpretation that I have offered for explaining the strange contradictions between the first and second creation accounts still presents a puzzle. Perhaps I have appropriately grasped the bind that the redactors faced and that led them to reticence about directly acknowledging God's inability to conclusively defeat the forces of chaos, of evil in his universe. But the fact remains that the immediate juxtaposition of the contradictory accounts can suggest more than reticence. It can suggest that the redactors intended to convey an inexplicable puzzle.

One explanation for the apparent contradictions between the first and second chapters of Genesis has been offered by philologists or historical scholars who, beginning in the mid-nineteenth century, concluded that the unified biblical text as we have it today is essentially a compilation from four different sources (labeled P, J, E, and D) that were originally written by different authors at different times during the eighth to the sixth centuries BCE. The scholarly basis for these different authorial attributions rests on internal comparisons—some portions of Genesis, for example, use Yahweh to designate God (the J source, based on the German pronunciation of the letter "J") while others used Elohim (the E source). Additional differences mark the "P" source (for Priestly) and "D," which refers to the entire Book of Deuteronomy. Scholars disagree about the exact datings of these various portions, but there is widespread agreement among scholars that there were four sources and that they were drawn together by a group of so-called redactors into one canonical text sometime during the sixth century BCE, possibly led by one man, Ezra the Scribe. (Ezra is credited with instituting public readings of the biblical text for the Judeans returning from the so-called Babylonian Exile, where they had been taken from Palestine by military force.[5])

The philologists or historical scholars see the contradictions between the first and second chapters of Genesis as the result of different versions of the same events among the four original sources. They argue that the redactors essentially did a "cut-and-paste" job in compiling what we now have as the single canonical text, and that the redactors were unwilling to resolve any of the inconsistencies but simply preserved them out of piety toward the venerable original sources.[6]

This may be an adequate explanation for the contradictions. But even granting the existence of different sources pasted together by the biblical redactors, there is another way to understand the redactors' intention that is consistent with the overall narrative pattern of the Hebrew Bible—not an alternative but an additional interpretation that deepens the narrative in a way that is also intrinsic to the text. This addition builds on the narrative interpretation that I have offered—that God is unable to exert definitive control over the universe but that the redactors are reluctant to admit this possibility.

In the overall narrative of the Hebrew Bible, it is clear that God himself is reluctant to admit the possibility that he is incapable of universal control. Notwithstanding all the accumulated experience in the Hebrew Bible that testifies to the truth of this proposition, God persistently attempts to exert control over the humans he created, if not over the entire universe, and he repeatedly fails. As we will explore in succeeding chapters, God tries different strategies for exercising control, and he occasionally succeeds in imposing order. But this imposition is always temporary; his efforts always ultimately fail. In his relations with humanity, this failure sometimes appears to originate with us, with our stubborn refusal to accede to God's will. Other times the failure appears to originate with God, as he seems to repudiate the previous conditions of an ordered relationship with us, his explicit promises to us (most notably, as we'll see in the book of Job—but also, though less ostentatiously, in his relations with Noah, Abraham, and Moses).

There are, in effect, two interlocked puzzles here. The first is why God's effort at imposing order regularly fails, and the second is why he persists in the attempt despite the repeated evidence of its futility. The redactors do not presume to answer these puzzles. Instead, I would say, they represent the puzzles as such—and this is the deeper narrative sense in the opening passages of the Hebrew Bible, in the patent contradictions between the creation accounts in chapters 1 and 2 of Genesis. The juxtaposition of these two chapters conveys that at the outset, God achieved perfect harmonious relationships in all aspects of the universe, including his relations with humanity, and he saw that it was all "very good." This harmonious order was immediately shattered, however—perhaps by some extrinsic force, perhaps by some element intrinsic to God's creation, perhaps by who knows what. From this disruption, God tries to recreate order by his commandment to Adam, but this fails. And so the extended, repetitive underlying narrative of the Hebrew Bible begins.

This theme is at the core of what I consider the political theory of the Bible. The complete harmony between God and humanity and among all elements of the universe corresponds to a state of perfect justice in the lexicon of modern, essentially secular political theorists. Chapter 1 of Genesis portrays a world in which the core problem of politics has been solved—the problem, that is, of scarcity, which necessarily demands some allocation of resources among competitive constituents. There is no need for competitive allocations—no need for a political theory about the relationship among constituents—at the outset of the Hebrew Bible. Its universe is a place of boundless fecundity, of self-renewing vegetation and fruit that satisfy all the nurturance needs of animal life, including humans. Indeed, the very idea of competition is incoherent in the terms of chapter 1. Competition depends on a conception of separateness among component parts, but the harmony in chapter 1 extends beyond mere agreement. The constituents of chapter 1, especially God and humanity, are identical to each other. As chapter 1 described it, God made "a human in our image, by our likeness" and he created "male and female" together "in the image of God."

This fundamental harmony, this unity, was not present in the universe of chapter 2. The earth was barren when the first human appeared, and though God immediately planted a garden for him in Eden, the problem of scarcity was not absent nor irrelevant from the outset but only ameliorated by God's post-creation act. Eden was not all-encompassing nor endlessly available. The memory traces of a universe without Eden remained in the fact that Eden was a bounded territory in "the east," surrounded by persistent barrenness. Moreover, God's critical observation in chapter 2 that the human "was alone" would have been incoherent in the universe of chapter 1. The unity of God, male, and female described in chapter 1 is the antithesis of solitude on the part of any one of them. For man to be "alone" as he is described in chapter 2 depends on a conception of his separateness that has no grounding in chapter 1.

God's remedy for Adam's solitude in ultimately creating Eve was inevitably incomplete because it was a remedy that required affirmative action rather than an inevitable feature, an a priori state, of existence. After Adam's joyful welcoming of his newly created companion, "this one at last," there is an authorial interjection in the chapter 2 narrative—"therefore does a man leave his father and his mother and cling to his wife and they become one flesh." This interjection in itself conveys that some human effort is required to attain unity between male and female, that it is not a natural state as it had been in chapter 1, but is instead a remedial action. One might say that man's leaving his parents and becoming "one flesh" with his wife in chapter 2 was an effort to recapture the fundamental state of seamless unity between man, woman, and God that had obtained effortlessly (so far as the humans were concerned) in chapter 1.

In the overall narrative arc of the entire Hebrew Bible, the puzzling juxtaposition continually recurs between the first and second creation accounts in the opening chapters of Genesis. Over and over again, both God and humanity strive to re-enter the boundlessly harmonious world of the first account; again and again, God and humanity—sometimes in unison and sometimes separately—believe that this seamless universe has been recaptured. But again and again, in the narrative ac-counts of the relationship between God and humanity, this unity is broken. On God's side or humanity's or both, this repeated breach raises the question whether the effort to recapture the universe of Gen-esis chapter 1 is futile, not worth the effort. But notwithstanding these recurrent doubts, the effort is repeated—sometimes on one side, some-times on the other, sometimes on both. And then failure repeats it-self—a puzzling failure, given the intensity of the wish on both sides to succeed.

In this repetitious narrative, we can see an underlying parallel with the deepest theme of modern political theory. Modern theory presents itself in wholly secular terms as attempting to solve the problem of so-cial relations among human beings—and most particularly the prob-lem of devising an appropriate calculus for the allocation of scarce re-sources. God may hover in the background for some modern political theorists, but relations between God and humanity are not center stage in the modern era. (Indeed, the brutal religious wars from the sixteenth century onward led the modern theorists to seek intellectual pathways that put aside religious concerns in their search for organizing princi-ples of secular political relations.) Nonetheless we can see the same narrative arc in modern political theory that I have identified in the Hebrew Bible—that is, a persistent search for perfectly harmonious re-lationships, typically presented as a search for a just regime, and an equally persistent failure to identify a satisfactory, internally coherent set of principles on which a regime of just relationships can be solidly grounded.

This is not simply a practical failure. The biblical treatment of these breaches of relationship points to a deeper problem—the problem that there is no satisfactory, internally coherent overarching principle that is available to govern relations between God and humanity. This is a failure of principle—mirrored in practical failures but analytically dis-tinct from them.

The parallels that I see between biblical and modern political theory have recently been diagnosed with great acuity by Amartya Sen in his book *The Idea of Justice*.[7] According to Sen, the central characteristic of the dominant strand of Western political philosophy—beginning with Hobbes and extending to Locke, Rousseau, Kant, and Rawls—has been the quest for "what it identifies as perfect justice," focusing on what Sen calls "transcendental institutionalism," that is, concentrating on designing institutions that would yield "perfect justice." "The characterization of perfectly just institutions," Sen maintains, "has become the central exercise in the modern theories of justice."[8] Sen argues that this quest has always failed and always will fail, notwithstanding the intensity and ingenuity of the efforts devoted to it. The reason for this inevitable failure, as Sen portrays it, is that the "diagnosis of perfectly just social arrangements is inherently problematic" because "theorists of different persuasions, such as utilitarians, or economic egalitarians, or labour right theorists, or no-nonsense libertarians, may each take the view that there is one straightforward just resolution that is easily detected, but they would each argue for totally different resolutions as being obviously right. There may not indeed exist any identifiable perfectly just social arrangement on which impartial agreement would emerge."[9]

This conclusion leads Sen not to abandon the pursuit of justice but instead to recast the inquiry toward avoidance of injustice as revealed in the particularities of lived experience of peoples' comparative "freedoms and capabilities."[10] In this recasting, Sen draws inspiration from a classical distinction in Indian jurisprudence between "two different words—*niti* and *nyaya*—both of which stand for justice in classical Sanskrit." He characterizes the terms respectively as "organizational propriety and behavioral correctness" compared with "a comprehensive concept of realized justice."[11] In exemplifying the difference between these two concepts, Sen invokes a Western figure, "Ferdinand I, the Holy Roman emperor [who] famously claimed in the sixteenth century: 'Fiat justitia, et pereat mundus', which can be translated as 'Let justice be done, though the world perish.'" Sen comments:

> This severe maxim could figure as a *niti*—a very austere *niti*—that is advocated by some (indeed, Emperor Ferdinand did just that), but it would be hard to accommodate a total catastrophe as an example of a just world, when we understand justice in the broader form of *nyaya*. If indeed the world does perish, there would be nothing much to celebrate in that accomplishment, even though the stern and severe *niti* leading to this extreme result could conceivably be defended with very sophisticated arguments of different kinds.[12]

My explorations of the Hebrew and Christian Bibles in this book serve the same purpose as Sen's invocation of classical Indian jurisprudence—as a template for understanding two conceptions of justice, an identification of the differing social consequences that follow from each, and ultimately a normative foundation for choosing between them. In particular, we can see the difference in Sen's terms between *niti* and *nyaya* in the different roles in the Hebrew Bible of presentations of abstract principles for governing relations between God and humanity on the one hand and the elaborate narrative accounts of the actual lived conflicts between God and humanity on the other. In these conflicts, abstract principles are frequently invoked by one or both participants. The narrative details of the conflicts between God and humanity in their lived relations, however, point to the incommensurate nature of the demands that each makes of the other and the consequent limitations of the abstract principles invoked in these conflicts as satisfactory instruments for conclusively resolving their disputes.

The contradictions between the two creation accounts present a template for this juxtaposition. Throughout the Hebrew Bible, God repeatedly demands unconditional obedience from humanity, though the specific justifications for his demand vary from generation to generation. At the outset, God demands obedience simply because his authority appears "natural"—in the inherent nature of things—essentially because he was the creator of all things. In reaction to unsatisfying responses from humanity over succeeding generations, God alters this claim (or adds to it) with demands based on his services rendered (for example, I saved you from the Flood that engulfed the rest of humanity, or I made you the progenitor of a great nation, or I rescued you from enslavement in Egypt) or on obligations freely accepted by humanity (for example, at Sinai, you agreed to follow my commandments).

Subsequent chapters will explore the reasons for these shifting accounts of God's authority, the shortcomings that he sees in the earlier modes that lead him to different strategies for commanding control, and the consequences from God's perspective of these new strategies. In this exploration, we will see the repetition of the narrative framework established by the two contradictory accounts of creation at the outset of Genesis. We will see, that is, clear preference on the part of God and humanity for the first account, in which harmony was so complete between God and humanity that the question of authority itself was a moot issue. Although this complete harmony often seems within reach for God and humanity—and thereby promises a return to the conditions of the first creation account—the destruction of that harmony, as in the second account, repeatedly recurs with seeming inevitability.

This failure, this destruction of harmony, in turn leads God to devise different strategies for returning to the original state of his unquestioned authority in Genesis chapter 1. But even when it appears that the new strategy succeeds in this goal, once again this success is only fleeting, and the harmony is destroyed as if to re-enact the narrative succession between the first and second creation accounts.

As we identify this theme in successive generational narratives, we will also see that Emperor Ferdinand's impulse to destroy the entire world in order to attain perfect justice is not simply an incidental possibility but, in the biblical account of God's deployment of his authority, a recurring and apparently unavoidable consequence of his pursuit of unquestioned legitimacy, of perfect justice. Thus we will see harmony between God and humanity repeatedly exploded. Just as the second creation account exploded the perfect harmony of the first, the initial harmony between God and humanity is continually undone—when Noah suspects that he will not survive the Flood, notwithstanding God's apparent promise; when Abraham progressively loses confidence that God will protect his progeny (capped by God's command that Abraham sacrifice Isaac); when Moses is barred from entering the Promised Land (or even earlier, in a brief but jarring passage in Exodus when God seeks to kill Moses immediately after he had accepted God's charge to lead the Israelites from Egypt); and when God destroys Job's family and fortune despite the fact that Job, according to God himself, was "innocent, upright, and God-fearing."[13]

When we then turn to the Christian Bible, we will be able to see it as not so much a "new" testament but as another variation on this same old theme—God and humanity trying yet another strategy for attaining perfect harmony and failing yet again. From our exploration of these repeated narratives, we will see some possible explanations that arise from the biblical accounts of this recurrent pattern—a pattern that was reflected in Emperor Ferdinand's dictum that the pursuit of perfect justice can readily express itself as a willingness and even as an obligation to destroy the entire world.

CHAPTER TWO

The Appearance of Authority

THE FIRST STRATEGY that God devised to restore the harmony that he had initially enjoyed with humanity was to issue a specific command that would bring about this result—a command that Adam should not eat from "the tree of knowledge [of] good and evil." So far as humanity was concerned, all the universe was "very good" when God created us, male and female, in his image. But though we were the beneficiaries of this condition, we were not conscious of its goodness as such. We had no basis for comparison with anything else. God's goal in the second creation account was not to devise a new state of affairs but to keep us in ignorance about the very existence, and therefore even the possibility, of evil.

There was, however, a new element in God's plan. Whereas in the first creation account, God assumed that the perfection of his creation would persist, he now took affirmative action intended to ensure this result. He issued a negative commandment joined with a threat of punishment. If Adam had been alert to the implications of this novelty, he would have seen that God's explicit commandment implied the possibility that Adam could disobey if he were willing to risk the threatened consequences. In other words, God's very commandment to avoid knowledge of good and evil implicitly conveyed the idea that disobedience to God's will was possible, though "not good." (Adam was a bit dense on this score; it took the combined efforts of the snake and Eve to show him this possibility. But this was not the last time in the biblical narratives that mankind was oblivious to some clear, if implicit, meaning of a communication from God.)

In the first creation account, the issue of disobedience never arose on either side of the transaction, whether from God's perspective or humanity's. The entire earth was teeming with fecundity before humans appeared on the scene. In the second creation, Eden was a circumscribed garden surrounded by barrenness, but in the first creation, all the world was Eden, and it was all available to the humans for the satisfaction, even for the anticipation, of their every possible wish or need. This first account seemed to depict humanity as living in a state of utter satiation, of virtually self-contained omnipotence as the reflection of our status in the likeness, the image, of God. By contrast, the second creation implied a dramatic diminution of humanity's status.

Adam's act of naming all the animals in the second account is conventionally understood as the exercise of human dominion over all other living things. In one sense it is this, albeit a less complete dominion than humanity had in the first creation. In the first account, though God spoke to both humans and animals, there is no indication that any of them spoke to him or to one another or that they even had capacity for speech. This apparent muteness might seem like a disability, but it is not that in the context of the world of the first creation. In that account neither humans nor animals had any need for communicative speech; the world gave them what they might want or need without any exertion on their part, not even the exertion of speaking or calling or asking. In the second creation, Adam named the animals at his pleasure, but this was an exertion, a conscious shaping of the world to meet his wishes and needs rather than a world that yielded effortlessly to him.

In the second creation, moreover, God initially placed Adam alone in Eden and only afterward provided first animal and then human companionship for him. Perhaps these provisions should have been enough to slake Adam's hunger. But would he not retain a memory nonetheless of the experience of loneliness, neediness, and incompleteness, an experience that had been entirely absent from the first creation? The ultimate denouement of the second creation—Eve and Adam eating from the tree and their punitive expulsion from the garden—was in its essence already prefigured by Adam's prior experience of loneliness. His expulsion from the garden intensified this loneliness since he could no longer rely on God's assistance; Adam was now on his own, relying only on the sweat of his brow to extract food from a hostile environment. The bountiful fecundity of the first creation was even more graphically ended for Eve, who was on her expulsion condemned to painful childbirth. And with this unaccustomed human pain and struggle came death itself—"dust you are and to dust shall you return." The unambiguous blessings of the first creation had been transformed into a set of curses by the end of the second.

Of these many inflictions, the most interesting for our purposes is the clear appearance by the end of the second creation of the idea of hierarchical authority. The first creation hinted at a hierarchical relationship between humanity and the rest of animate creation; indeed, part of God's blessing was for humans to "hold sway" over fish, fowl, and every beast that crawls upon the earth. It was not clear, however, exactly what this hegemony implied, since God followed this grant with the instruction that all animate life, including humans, was exclusively vegetarian, and vegetable life itself appeared effortlessly self-renewing without any human or animal activity.

In the second creation, authority makes a more direct appearance in two guises. God's hierarchical authority over Adam was implicitly conveyed by his negative injunction and threat of punishment for eating from the tree of knowledge. Hierarchy is first made explicit, however, in relation to Eve. The punishment for her infraction against God's command was her subordination not to God but to her husband. The exact terms of Eve's submission to Adam are, moreover, quite intriguing. Unlike God's previous grant to all humanity of dominion over other creatures, God did not simply announce that man shall "hold sway" over woman; instead, he said, "for your man shall be your longing, and he shall rule over you."[1] God thus made Eve the instrument of her own subjection because she will "long" for the man—need him, it appears, more than he needs her—and by this asymmetry, man effectively controls woman.

I stress this detail because it illuminates an essential underlying question about the source of authority—that is, whether the exercise of authority rests on a claim of legitimacy or merely on a claim of brute force to exact compliance. This is the central issue for all political theory, modern and ancient, secular and divine. In the biblical account, hierarchy appears to arise without any clearly visible exertion of force by the hierarchical superior. Authority appears assumed rather than asserted, and accordingly seems to be an expression of a "natural order." The key to this development is in the Genesis depiction of woman's longing for man as the implied source of his authority over her.

According to the second creation, however, "longing"—that is, awareness of unsatisfied neediness—was not restricted to woman. The depiction of Adam's loneliness has exactly the same import. Adam's longing for a companion was not, moreover, quickly or easily satisfied. God paraded all of animal life before Adam. When God finally hit upon the expedient of creating woman, Adam's first words reflected his prolonged experience of neediness: "This one at last . . ."

As Eve's longing for Adam explicitly translated into his authority over her, it is similarly plausible that his need for her implicitly established her influence over him—an influence that she appeared to exercise in leading him to eat the forbidden fruit. And God's instrumental role in responding to Adam's neediness, however delayed in its performance, can equally be understood as the source for Adam's deference toward God. An implicit threat lies behind God's response to Adam's neediness: that he could punitively withhold assistance if he chose to do so. But in the biblical account of the second creation, to all appearances God was eager to assist Adam; he kept trying, notwithstanding that it took him some time to hit upon an adequate response. The attitude toward authority that emerges from this account is more gratitude than fearful submission; the coercive implications of authority are, in this sense, virtually invisible in the biblical account of the origins of the relationship between God and man.

It is true that when God issued his commandment to Adam about abstaining from the fruit of the tree of knowledge, he explicitly joined it with a threatened punishment for violation. But this threat does not necessarily establish itself as legitimate; it might only be based on God's superior brute force and invite efforts to counter God's power, if not by direct combat then by deception. The serpent in effect treated God's command in this mode—as entirely without intrinsic legitimacy and easily bypassed. The serpent lured Eve into disobedience by assuring her that the threatened punishment would not occur because, upon eating the forbidden fruit, "you will become as gods knowing good and evil"—as if to say that Eve would have power equal to God's and so sufficient to countermand his punishment. In the event, the serpent was proven wrong, yet this in itself demonstrated not the legitimacy of God's command but only his possession of superior force.

The legitimation of God's authority was revealed by the fact that Adam and Eve were afflicted with shame in response to their transgression—and they experienced this shame before God himself discovered their disobedience. Before their sin, Genesis tells us, "the two of them were naked . . . and they were not ashamed."[2] Their subsequent awareness and their efforts to cover themselves—first by sewing fig leaves into loincloths and then by hiding from God as he sought them in the garden—were motivated, so Genesis says, not only by shame but by "fear." (Adam says to God, "I was afraid, for I was naked, and I hid."³) This awareness of nakedness might express nothing more than the couple's vulnerability to God's punishment, their defenselessness against his greater force. But more is implied by the explicit connection between nakedness and shame. God directly acknowledged this larger implication in his immediate response to Adam's self-description as naked. "Who told you that you were naked?" God demanded, and from this he deduced: "From the tree I commanded you not to eat have you eaten?"⁴

God's authority in this account was experienced as legitimate rather than coerced not because of anything that God did or said but because of the attitude toward God that Adam and Eve had themselves internalized. The basis for that internalization was most explicitly revealed in the biblical account of the origins of Eve's subjection to Adam. In this account, man's authority over woman is not imposed on an unwilling subject by an act of force from the outside; man's authority arises from the inside, from within woman's need, from her longing for him. The distinctive character of man's authority is that its force is internally generated by the subject herself. This is coerced subjection, but the coercion comes from the way the woman experiences herself.

Thus does Genesis portray the origins of conscience, the way in which norms of right conduct become experienced as internalized commandments rather than as impositions from outside. The concrete, externalized quality of this purported explanation—that the sense of wrongdoing comes from the punitive response of some powerful being—can be read into the biblical story, but it is less psychologically satisfying than the account of the reason Eve is subjected to Adam, namely, that she needed him and that her subordination arises from this need, this longing for him.

According to this account, the figure of authority need not do anything to establish his superiority; it is invested in him by his subordinate. And thus, to both superior and subordinate, the hierarchy is not imposed on the relationship; it does not arise from a struggle for predominance but is the defining character of the relationship from its very inception. Thus man's authority over woman seems offered by her rather than forced upon her. And by parity of reasoning, God's authority over humans seems equally offered by them rather than forced by him. By God's account, Adam's authority over Eve does not arise from any claim of legitimacy, no justification that could persuade an impartial judge evaluating the relationship from an external perspective. But God does not portray this authority as simply in the nature of things, that somehow it is unquestionably self-evident that men should rule over women. If Adam's authority arises from Eve's psychology—that her longing for the man creates his authority over her—this is not a moral justification for Adam's authority, but neither is it simply a brute, mysterious fact. Adam's authority is a consequence of Eve's longing; she submits herself to him because she needs him to respond to her neediness.

But what is the source of Eve's neediness? It is misleading to read the biblical answer to this question as based on some intrinsic quality in Eve—that she is needy because this is in her nature as a vulnerable woman or even embedded in her vulnerability as a human being. By the biblical account in the second Genesis creation, Eve was the answer to Adam's neediness, a sustainer to remedy his loneliness as it appeared both to God and to Adam himself. In this sense, God's creation of Eve from Adam's rib offered Adam a return to the original dual conception of "male and female" together "in the image of God."[5] Thus the second creation ends, following Adam's paean to Eve as the "bone of my bones and flesh of my flesh," with a narrative leap into the future of all humanity, "Therefore does a man leave his father and his mother and cling to his wife and they become one flesh."[6] This unity between husband and wife is thus portrayed as a remedy for loneliness, as a dissolution of separateness, that man can accomplish by leaving his father and his mother, who were not inherently unified but must come together to share in his creation.

This ending of the second creation is thus not inconsistent with the first but instead reaches backward to the unity between male and female that arose naturally in the first. In the first account, no human effort was required to achieve unity between male and female, no leave-taking from a father and mother. Mankind's goal at the end of the second creation was, however, to return to the state of satiation that had obtained effortlessly, naturally, in the first. Mankind's satiated state in the first creation—the fecundity of the entire planet rather than an Eden planted amid barrenness, the absence of any even momentary experience of loneliness for human beings in the first creation because they arrived on earth only after all else had been created for them—did not require effort on their part.

The new substantive element in the second creation is that mankind is aware of its loneliness from the outset and, moreover, is not readily satisfied by God's efforts to remedy that neediness—and God himself knows that because he sensed Adam's dissatisfaction both before and after the parade of animals without any explicit statement by Adam. The new substantive element in the second creation of (potentially remediable) loneliness is not, however, inconsistent with the first creation—it is instead an elaboration, a working out of the premises of that account.

By this reading, the relationship between the first and second creations has a clear narrative connection. The first creation is a vision of utter self-sufficiency: humans "hold sway" over all creatures and plants on earth in the same way that God rules over all creation.[7] But this rule is unopposed; disobedience is an oxymoron in a universe or a world that by its nature is subordinate to divine or human wishes. The enterprise by definition does not raise the possibility of disobedience, of a failure to satisfy the needs and wishes of its beneficiary. Disobedience is impossible not because of the superior coercive force of a ruler, of a Leviathan, but because the very concept of disobedience is unintelligible. If the possibility of disobedience does become plausible, then it

also becomes plausible in retrospect to imagine the early state of satiated self-sufficiency as an exercise of omnipotent authority. But this is
a retrospective, anachronistic conception that distorts the absence of
any conception of authority as such in the original state. The world of
the second creation was not effortlessly satisfying—and it raises the
conceptual possibility not only that human wishes might not be fulfilled but that God's wishes also might encounter some resistance. This
is the implication, the negative predicate, of God's explicit commandment to Adam. The commandment is coherent only on the premise
that God's wishes might be disobeyed. In the first creation, there was
no need for God to issue a negative injunction. The first biblical "thou
shalt not" appears in the second creation because it was only in the
second creation that disobedience to God's will became a comprehen-
sible possibility.

The second creation does not endorse this possibility. But it does
acknowledge it—not only in the form of a forbidden tree amid Eden's
bounty but also in the person of the wily snake who tempts Eve into
sin. A God truly intent on, or capable of obtaining, an iron-clad assurance of obedience to his will would not have made disobedience possible, much less so tempting. Two possibilities follow from this recognition: either God did not want automatic obedience but instead
wished for freely offered deference, or the inherent nature of a world
separate from himself necessarily entailed the possibility of disobedience in that world, and God acknowledged this at the same time that
he took steps against it.

God's command to Adam was, however, relatively modest and easily honored. In the midst of a bountiful Garden of Eden, God marked
only one tree as off-limits; everything else was fair game. But that
modest limitation as such seemed to be an irresistible lure for Eve and
Adam. Indeed, Eve is described as "lusting" to taste the fruit of the tree
with the same apparent intensity as her "longing" for her man.[8]

Adam and Eve's transgression was only the beginning of eruptions not simply of disobedience but of murderous rage against God's clear but minimal demands for abstention. Thus when Cain was visibly angered at God's favoritism toward Abel, God warned him that "sin crouches and for you is its longing but you will rule over it."[9] But Cain nonetheless killed Abel. Adam and Eve may have been ashamed at their violation of God's injunction and, to this extent, may have internalized his authority as legitimate; Cain may have felt shame and longing when God condemned him to permanent exile and Cain cried that his "punishment is too great to bear [now that] I must hide from your presence."[10] But these internalized attitudes were evidently at war with, and weaker than, the humans' impulse to resist God's authority. The possibility of disobedience that initially appears in the second creation turns out to become a self-fulfilling prophecy. Disobedience is not just possible for humans but positively attractive.

This impulse arises from resentment; it gathers force from the memory, however vaguely recalled, of an earlier and entirely different experience of instant, constant satiation—from the recollection of the first creation. Here are the roots of longing for a remembered idyllic state and of a conviction that there is something wrong, something incomplete and undesirable, in the world of the second creation where that idyll exists only as a fantasy. From this conviction of wrongfulness, it is a short step toward blame—whether attached to those who should by rights be perfect, instant nurturers or to those whose blameworthy conduct has disqualified them from obtaining the perfect, instant nurturance for which they long.

Why, however, does this longing become gendered in the second creation, so that Eve subjects herself to her husband's rule but he is not reciprocally subject to her? From a psychological perspective, a twofold answer appears. First, Adam's longing for his woman is even more clearly acknowledged in the text than Eve's longing for him; he knew what it was like to be alone and unsatisfied until she "at last" arrived. She, by contrast, needed instruction from God to recognize her longing for her husband. Second, Adam's longing for a wife was, from his perspective, a way to return to the experienced self-sufficiency and wholeness of the gestational womb; thus, as the end of the second creation instructs, "does a man . . . cling to his wife and they become one flesh." For Adam to acknowledge his dependency on Eve's willingness to cling to him would, however, be inconsistent with his underlying desire to recapture self-sufficiency. This acknowledgment would be, as psychologists put it, cognitively dissonant.

Thus Adam responds to the dissonance by suppressing one pole of an inherently contradictory thought. But the suppression, as with all cognitive dissonances, cannot entirely succeed; some trace of the contradictory thought necessarily persists. In the second creation, this contradictory pole emerges in the account of Adam's gullible acceptance of Eve's invitation to eat the forbidden fruit—his self-subjection to her notwithstanding the specific contrary directive that he had received from God.[11]

But despite this clear account of Adam's longing for and self-subordination to his wife, God speaks only to Eve about her longing and self-subordination to her husband. As the Genesis account makes clear, this is only half the story. The psychological consequence of this half-truth is that Adam is able to maintain his hope for re-attaining self-sufficiency by denying the outstanding obstacle to that attainment—that is, by denying his dependence on Eve.

God played an enabling role in this gendered charade. Why might he have done this? It is plausible to conclude that God chose to mask Adam's dependence on Eve by emphatically subjecting her to Adam's ruling authority because he was intent on masking the derogations from his own authority. This derogation inevitably arose from the breach in his own self-sufficiency when he chose to create a universe separate from himself. God thus bolsters Adam's authority over Eve to protect his own authority over all humanity, and this very effort betrays some doubt about the solidity of that authority.

The derogation of God's authority could have arisen from the force of the syllogism at the heart of his punishment for Eve, that she would long for her husband and, therefore, "he shall rule over you." The syllogism would apply equally to God if he wanted a relationship with humanity that we were free to deny him—if he, that is, might want our companionship more than we want his. Genesis recounts that God was "walking about in the garden in the evening breeze . . . and called to the human and said to him, 'Where are you?'" and Adam then confessed that he had hidden from God because he was afraid and naked. As we have already seen, God immediately construes this confession as an admission that Adam had eaten from the forbidden tree. The implication of this irenic prelude to Adam's confession is that God was seeking a companion for his garden stroll in the evening breeze and that Adam had not reciprocated but instead had hidden from him. Even if we indulge in the conventional assumption that God is omniscient and already knew about Adam's breach before his confession, it is still plausible to conclude that God was disappointed in the distance that Adam had put between himself and God. God may not have "longed" for Adam's companionship with the same intensity that God ascribed to Eve. But even an unreciprocated wish is enough to establish an asymmetry and a power differential between God, who wanted companionship, and Adam, who hid from this possibility. Adam might have disqualified himself from a relationship with God because of his disobedience. But it would be an easy step for God to conclude that although Adam might have wanted a relationship with God, he wanted even more to taste the forbidden fruit.

In this early encounter, God could see that however much he wished for a relationship with humans, to that extent he had ceded power to them. If he was intent on maintaining absolute power over humans, he could do so only by having zero investment in obtaining any pleasure from them. We will see, as we trace the narrative progression of God's relationship with us, that periodically God acts on this premise—by destroying almost all of us in the Flood, by threatening to destroy all of his chosen people, the Israelites, as they wandered in the Sinai desert, and even more emphatically by absenting himself from any relationship with us as he did for the four centuries of the Israelites' enslavement in Egypt.

It is clear from this narrative that God does not consider himself obliged to sustain any relationship with humanity. But the difficulty for God is that, if he wants a relationship, he will have subjected himself to humanity's power over him. No wonder, then, that he portrays Eve's longing for her husband as the basis for a curse, that her husband shall rule over her. From Eve's perspective, this may not have seemed to be a punishment because she embraced her longing for Adam. But from God's perspective, this was an apparent asymmetry of desire, and it seemed to constitute a curse to him—or, by projective identification, a curse on him. Thus we can see that the biblical account of Eve's internally generated attitude toward Adam's authority over her—her "longing for him," a desire that he alone can satisfy—is an unacknowledged mirror of Adam's attitude both toward her and toward God. Moreover, Adam and Eve's attitude toward their authority over each other is an even more buried but nonetheless recognizable portrait of God's wish for, and his potential dependence on, humanity's longing for him. In the first creation account, longing on humanity's side was inconceivable, redundant. But God might have longed for human companionship, as evidenced by the fact that he exerted considerable effort in the first creation account to bring into being the universe and us within it. If, however, God made humans—male and female together—in his own image, this would appear to be an effective expedient to ensure that his access to human companionship would never be in doubt. He and we were the same, seamlessly united; it was accordingly inconceivable that he or we would ever "long" for each other. We were each other.

In the second creation account, this unity was destroyed. The intensity of God's wish for its resurrection can be seen in details in his creation of Adam that differed from the account of his relationship to humans in the first creation account. Consider the mechanics of the second account: "The Lord God fashioned the human, humus from the soil, and blew into his nostrils the breath of life, and the human became a living creature." In this account, there is an intimacy, even an erotic quality, to God's engagement with Adam, blowing "into his nostrils the breath of life." The first creation account depicted no physical contact in God's creation of either man or woman. In the first account, it seemed that God might have conjured man and woman in his own mind, in the same way that his declaration of intention "let there be light" in itself produced the light. In the second account, God did much more than creatively imagine Adam; he actively shaped him and shared his own vital breath with him.

Unlike in the first creation account, moreover, in which God created male and female at the same time, in the second account Adam was alone with God for a considerable time—for ten verses in Genesis chapter 2, which recounted that God created the garden in Eden and placed the human there among beautiful and nutritious trees. It was only after this considerable activity on God's part—apparently intended to shape a comfortable, even bounteous, home for Adam—that God announced, "It is not good for the human to be alone." Even then, God spent considerable time trying to rectify this apparent solitude by creating animals and birds before providing another human as company for Adam.

Strictly speaking, however, it was not true that Adam was alone when God embarked on the parade of the animals. God was with Adam, and not simply in a spiritual sense but in an intensely physical way. Why then did God conclude that his company was insufficient for Adam? Why was it "not good for the human to be alone"? Perhaps God had intended Adam to be only the first of an entire race of humans that should inhabit the planet, as he had suggested in the first account by

his invitation to the original human couple that they should "be fruitful and multiply." But if God wanted more humans, he could have satisfied this wish in the same way that he brought forth Adam—that is,
he could create them himself. Indeed, God's long delay before creating
Eve, his extensive attempt to remedy Adam's aloneness with birds and
beasts, strongly suggests that God was not concerned with finding a
reproductive partner for Adam.

Moreover, it was clear from the narrative progression in the second
account—from Adam's solitary creation and residential placement in
Eden before God observed that he should not be alone—that the creation of other creatures besides Adam was not part of God's original
plan. It appears, that is, that God was responding to what he saw in
Adam—that Adam seemed lonely, notwithstanding the luxury of the
garden and the prospect of God's presence there with him. Adam's response when Eve finally appeared, "this one at last," confirms that it
was Adam, and not God, who was initially concerned about his loneliness.

Is it possible that God was disappointed when he saw Adam's loneliness, that God regretted that he was not all that Adam wanted? We
know from the subsequent extended narrative in the Hebrew Bible of
God's interactions with humanity that he described himself as a "jealous God" and that he wanted a special relationship with Israel in addition to recognition by the rest of humanity of his superior brute power
over all other gods. In this extended narrative from Genesis into Exodus, God appears fully self-contained, very much in control of himself
and of humanity. In his first encounter with humanity, in the first creation account in Genesis, God similarly appears self-contained and in
full control; this is the implication of his creation of humanity as a
mirror image of himself. In the second creation account, however, the
human seems different. He is not described as created "in the image of
God" but seems instead to differ from him in important ways. Thus

God found it necessary to instruct Adam about what he could and could not eat in the garden; there was no automatic unity between them, no mirroring or identity of purpose.

Some scholars have suggested that God created humanity so that he could attain self-knowledge, which was impossible for him when he was alone in the universe.[12] This is plausible, but only based on the second account of creation. In the first account, it appears that humanity was identical to God, indistinguishable from him; this is the implication of the creation of humanity in the image of God. It is only in the second account that man appears as different from God, as other than God—in a way that could lead God to a clear conception of a distinct "self."

Whatever God's reasons for creating humanity, or for taking a different course when his first creative efforts were undone and he started over again, his creation of Adam alone and his subsequent revision of this plan suggest that God was reluctant to give up his exclusive claim on Adam. God's extensive effort to satisfy Adam without giving him a human companion appears to confirm his reluctance, his jealousy at the prospect that Adam might want a relationship with his own kind— whether in preference to or simply in addition to the exclusive relationship with God that was originally offered to him. Perhaps we can read God as a shy lover, reluctant to admit the full extent of his feelings toward his beloved Adam but revealing it nonetheless by his extended efforts to keep Adam for himself.

In the event, Eve did interfere with the relationship between Adam and God. It was she who tempted Adam to disobey God's command. God's response to this disobedience—not only expelling the couple from Eden but also heaping pain and suffering on them—might seem excessive, disproportionate to the offense. Adam and Eve were, after all, inexperienced and swayed by the wily serpent; and, as is common with all children, the very fact of the prohibition heightened the allure of the forbidden act. God might have been more temperate in his response. The enraged punishment that God inflicted is more like the response of a betrayed lover than a judge of all the earth.[13]

The idea that God needed human beings more than we needed him is never openly avowed in the Hebrew Bible. There are, however, occasional hints of this possibility. For example, when the elders of the Israelites informed the prophet Samuel that they wanted a king to rule over them, "like all the nations," God told Samuel not to be offended, "for it is not you they have cast aside but Me they have cast aside from reigning over them. Like all the deeds they have done from the day I brought them up from Egypt to this day, forsaking Me and serving other gods, even so they do as well to you." On this occasion, God did not react punitively to this breach that he perceived; he said only that Samuel should acquiesce in the people's choice "though you must solemnly warn them and tell them the practice of the king that will reign over them."[14]

We can see here a glimpse of God's wistfully hurt pride rather than his customary explosive anger at being abandoned by his specially favored wards. In Genesis itself, there is a confirmation of this wounded attitude on God's part toward Adam's wish for a human companion. Immediately after God built Eve from Adam's rib and Adam responded with great pleasure and relief, a different narrative voice suddenly intrudes: "Therefore," this third-person narrator explains, "does a man leave his father and his mother and cling to his wife and they become one flesh."[15] Therefore, we might also say, Adam left God, his father and mother, to cling to his wife. This was not the last time in recorded history that parents have felt abandoned when their only son leaves home to take a wife; this first time, however, God also seems to have experienced some sense of loss and abandonment.

The majestic authority of the God of the Hebrew Bible is not typically portrayed this way. But the political theory of the Hebrew Bible, its conception of the sources and legitimacy of God's authority in relationship to humanity, cannot be fully understood without keeping in mind the possibility that God had unsatisfied needs that humanity failed or even refused to fulfill—at the same time that God adamantly refused to acknowledge any dependence on us whatsoever.

The problem that God confronted, however—and that he could not completely solve—was that the more explicitly that he tried to assert control over us, the more he betrayed his need for our deference to him. Put another way, if he did not much care whether we existed or not, he would not have bothered to exert any energy to keep us in line. In the narrative progressions that follow, we will see many occasions when this thought did indeed occur to God, and he envisioned dispensing with us altogether as a way of finally achieving complete mastery over us. But something kept holding him back.

CHAPTER THREE

God Gives, God Takes Away

*W*HATEVER ITS EFFECT might have been, God did not conceive his first avowed command as a temptation toward disobedience. But his unhappy experience with Adam and Eve led him to devise increasingly elaborate tests of humanity's inclination to give him unquestioning obedience. As he learned through these tests that his direct commands were regularly disregarded and that threats of negative punishments were insufficient to overcome humanity's unruly impulses, God increasingly added promises of positive benefits as incentives toward obedience. In offering these promises, God appeared to go beyond attempting to impose limits on human conduct; he now seemed willing to impose limits on his own conduct in order to secure humanity's allegiance.

God's underlying goal for these novel tests of, and promises to, humanity was reparative—that is, to restore the relationship with humanity to its earlier state of perfect harmony. This reparative purpose is a central marker for the difference between the political theory of the Bible and the programmatic goal of the dominant modern school of Western political theorists. In the Bible, there is no conception of a state of nature outside political relationships; even if the modern theorists saw this asocial state as a heuristic device rather than as a historical reality, their goal of creating a regime of perfect justice was most aptly embodied by imagining a world in which social relations were constructed from nothing. The biblical account contains a memory of a broken relationship—a reminder even from the beginning of the reparative effort that a state of prior perfection had been destroyed and by implication that the breach could occur again. The modern account, however, imagines a blank slate conveying an optimism that is alien to the biblical account. The greater sobriety, even pessimism, in the biblical account explicitly arises from the puzzling juxtaposition of the two creation stories at the outset—the absence of any explanation for the destruction of the original harmony of the world, and the further puzzle, equally consequential from humanity's perspective, about why Adam and Eve were unable to comply with God's minimal commandment and were thus expelled from the almost-paradise of Eden.

God's original commandment to Adam was not necessarily understood as a test. The first test, avowed as such by God, was aimed at Adam and Eve's eldest son, Cain. This test, moreover, was openly provocative, as if God himself were playing the wily serpent's role. God's initial provocation was his blatant preference for Abel's offering of sheep from his flock over Cain's offering of home-grown fruit. God said nothing to explain this preference, but according to the Genesis account, Cain immediately "was very incensed, and his face fell." God then said to Cain, "Why are you incensed and why is your face fallen?" To this obviously obtuse and infuriating question, God appended a warning: "[W]hether you offer well, or whether you do not, at the tent flap sin crouches and for you is its longing but you will rule over it." Cain didn't bother to answer God's challenge. Instead he turned to his brother Abel, invited him to "go out to the field," and killed him.

God then immediately asked Cain, "Where is Abel your brother?" This seems to be a direct echo of God's question to Adam and Eve, "Where are you?" Perhaps God already knew the answer to both questions. But perhaps not. It may be that God was genuinely unsure where he might find Adam, Eve, or Abel. Whatever the explanation for God's conduct—and specifically for his role as instigator in the misdeeds of Eve, Adam, and Cain—it seems clear that something was troubling God about the humans he had created. Thus he found it necessary to test whether something was missing in them or in his relationship with them. When Cain revealed by his murderous act that he, too, was an unreliable companion, God imposed the same consequences that he had done with Cain's parents: he shattered his relationship with Cain. God exiled Cain: "A restless wanderer shall you be on the earth." The devastating impact of this sanction was immediately expressed by Cain, who after all had originally sought to please God with his offering and was impelled to fratricide by Abel's greater success in this effort. "My punishment is too great to bear," Cain cried out. "Now that ... I must hide from Your presence, I shall be a restless wanderer on the earth and whoever finds me will kill me." Notwithstanding this plea, God did not relent, but he slightly softened the edge of his abandonment by setting "a mark upon Cain so that whoever found him would not slay him."[1] This was a protective gesture similar to God's parting gift to Cain's parents: "skin coats for the human and his woman, and He clothed them," presumably to protect them against the harsh elements outside of Eden.[2] But in both cases this was only a gesture, not a promise of any possibility of a restored relationship.

After these unhappy encounters, God came increasingly to doubt whether he wanted any continuing relationship with humanity. His doubts hardened into a firm conviction ten generations after Adam's birth, when God "regretted having made the human on earth and was grieved to the heart." Only Noah and his immediate family seemed exempt from God's condemnation, on the apparent ground that "Noah was a righteous man, he was blameless in his time, he walked with God."[3] Thus it seems that God was still seeking a walking companion from among humanity and for this reason protected Noah against the Flood that destroyed all other living creatures. And after the Flood subsided, God promised Noah that "never again shall all flesh be cut off by the waters of the Flood, and never again shall there be a Flood to destroy the earth."[4]

In retrospect, this appears to be a comforting story for Noah and all of his progeny, that is, for all of humanity alive today. But when we closely examine the details of the Flood story, comfort vanishes. In fact, the Flood story is a continuation of the narrative arc that we have been tracing from the first creation account to the resurgence of chaos in the second account and God's efforts to reassert his control over the universe and humanity within it. Discomfort intrudes into the Flood story because, closely examined, it reveals that God seemed to have second thoughts about whether he wanted to exempt Noah from universal destruction—whether Noah would betray his hopes for a righteous companion as Adam, Eve, and Cain had betrayed him. Noah himself perceived God's irresolution and increasingly doubted whether God would keep his promises either during the Flood or afterward.

The Flood story introduces a new element to the account of God's relationship with humanity. Thus far we have seen God working to restore his initial harmony with humanity, despite the possibility that disharmony, disobedience, had intruded into their relationship. The new element introduced by the Flood account is the possibility that God might conclude that the harmony he desires can never be achieved, no matter how diligently human beings try to conform themselves to his wishes, no matter how exceptionally "righteous" or "blameless" any one human being such as Noah might appear in his own eyes or in God's.

At the end of the Flood story, God tries to reassure Noah by making explicit promises to him. God's willingness to make promises to humanity is a new element of critical importance for understanding the political theory underlying the Bible. It is equally important, however, to see that God might view his promises as an excessive derogation of his own authority and that he might choose to retract them regardless of humanity's reliance on them, simply to assert his superiority. Before Noah, God had made only implicit vows to humanity—that if Adam or Eve or Cain obeyed him, then they would not suffer punishment. With Noah, God made this promise explicit. But just as the serpent lured Eve into believing that God would not punish as he had promised, so Noah's experience during the Flood led him to fear that God would not honor his promises to withhold punishment, notwithstanding his apparent commitment to do so.

Noah was the tenth patriarch after Adam. Though the genealogical listing in Genesis, chapter 5, doesn't say this explicitly, it provides clear enough information about dates of birth and death to calculate that Methuselah, the last surviving patriarch who was born during Adam's lifetime, died in precisely the year that the Flood came. According to the Genesis genealogy, Adam died 930 years after his birth; Methuselah, Noah's grandfather, was born 687 years and died 1,656 years after Adam's birth (and just 5 years after Noah's father, Lamech, died); Noah was born 1,056 years after Adam's birth, and the Flood came when Noah was 600 years old.

The identical correspondence between the death of all Noah's paternal ancestors and the beginning of the Flood cannot be coincidental. In the richly imaginative world of Genesis, the correspondence suggests not only the possibility of a new beginning following the destruction of all the patriarchs who lived during Adam's lifetime. This narrative also conveys the sense that after almost a millennium in which death did not touch any of the patriarchs—930 years from Adam's birth and more than 800 years after his expulsion from Eden—the second millennium after Adam's birth was marked by a cascade of patriarchal deaths, as if to anticipate the final inundation of the entire human race. The shortest-lived patriarch in this listing was Enoch, who was born 622 years after Adam's birth and died only 365 years later—a mere stripling among the patriarchs both before and after him. But Enoch was uniquely described in this listing as one who "walked with

God and he was no more, for God took him." Only Noah was also graced with this same description, as "walking with God." We know that Adam didn't walk with God but hid from him in the garden; he and the other patriarchs presumably died without being taken by God.

Adam had survived for a considerable time after his expulsion from Eden. God had initially told him that "on the day you eat [the forbidden fruit] you are doomed to die," but this fated death didn't finally appear until Adam was 930 years old (some 800 years after his third son, Seth, was born). Thus Adam remained alive until 56 years after the birth of Lamech, Noah's father—long enough to have been around when Lamech boasted to his wives that he had exceeded Cain's vengeful killings by tenfold. The Genesis report of Lamech's boast appears inserted in chapter 4, between the accounts of Cain's killing of Abel and Adam's fathering of Seth.

This juxtaposition of Cain and Lamech appears to support God's conclusion that "the evil of the human creature was great on the earth and that every scheme of his heart's devising was only perpetually evil."[5] This was God's reason for regretting his creation of humanity and bringing on the Flood. God might have deduced from this bleak conclusion that he should destroy the entire human race and begin again. But he did not do this; he exempted Noah on the apparent ground of his blamelessness. Noah appeared to be God's chosen instrument for restoring some vestige at least of the harmonious relationship that had previously existed between him and humanity.

There is an interesting connection here between Noah as God saw him and Noah as his father, Lamech, saw him. When Noah first appeared in the Genesis genealogy, an explanation was provided for the derivation of his name; Lamech, we were told, "called his name Noah, as if to say, 'This one will console us for the pain of our hands' work from the soil which the Lord cursed.'"[6] (*Nahem,* the Hebrew word for "console" or "consolation," is a sound-play on the name Noah—a typical instance of the use of phonetic association in biblical narrative.[7])

The report that Noah "walked with God" suggested that God also found consolation with him for the loss he experienced when, "walking about in the garden in the evening breeze," he had sought out Adam and Eve only to find that they had betrayed his trust. Noah, moreover, was the first of the genealogical line of patriarchs born after Adam's death. With the curse of mortality finally enacted against Adam, Noah's subsequent birth might have seemed to God as offering an opportunity to undo Adam's curse and to begin again—perhaps even as Lamech himself saw possible consolation in Noah as an opportunity to escape the resentment, the murderous rage, and the consequent curse that had gripped Cain and escalated in Lamech's boasts.

God's orchestrating of the Flood itself evokes Eden: the ark as a haven for a single human family and representatives of all other species of animals, protected in the middle of a desolate world. But just as the presence of the serpent in the original garden implied some disharmony, some doubt in God's mind about the goodness of this creation, so even more powerful doubts intrude in the Flood narrative of God's effort to cleanse the earth of human wrongdoing.

The doubts initially appear in the chronology of the Flood. The commonplace account is that the Flood lasted forty days and forty nights. This is an erroneous reading of the plain meaning of the text, but this error is understandable. After God directed Noah to construct the ark, he told him, "I will send rain upon the earth forty days and forty nights; and every living thing that I have made I will blot out from the face of the ground." Sure enough the rains came and stopped after forty days. But the Flood waters did not subside and Noah could not leave the ark until some time after the rains stopped. From the Genesis account, moreover, it is very difficult and confusing to calculate this time lapse.

This calculation is especially complicated if you don't have the actual text of Genesis in hand so that you can flip back and forth in the narrative. As the redactors of the Bible well knew, oral recitation of the text was the only way that most people in ancient times received it. These listeners would be very confused about chronology, just as we are confused and are about to be confused even more. (But bear with me, please; there is a reason for this confusion.) Thus, in chapter 7, verse 17, the narrator stated, "The flood continued forty days upon the earth." Then in verses 23 and 24 of the same chapter, the narrator said, "And the waters prevailed upon the earth a hundred and fifty days." Where, you might well ask, did this 150 days duration come from? What happened to forty days and forty nights?

We readers are not the only ones who are confused at this point. Chapter 8, verse 6, subsequently declared that "at the end of forty days," Noah opened the window and sent out a raven, apparently to search for dry land. But if you read it closely, it seems that this mention of forty days refers to the time span after the ark had come to rest on a mountaintop and not to the end of the rainfall. Genesis doesn't tell us the time lapse between this end and the first reappearance of land. Moreover, the sudden mention of the 150 days seems entirely disconnected from the rest of the narrative.

Apparently Noah did realize that something was amiss when the raven didn't come back. Noah subsequently dispatched a dove, who soon returned to the ark. But Genesis doesn't tell us how much time elapsed between this event and Noah's release of the raven. We are told that seven days after the dove's expedition, Noah sent it out again, and this time it returned with a "freshly picked olive leaf [in its mouth]; so Noah knew that the waters had subsided from the earth." The narrator then tells us that Noah waited another seven days and dispatched the dove again; this time the dove did not return. So now we're up to twenty-one days with the dove, but we still don't know how many days or months or maybe even years elapsed between the time that Noah had sent out the raven who never returned and the dove who came back twice and then disappeared.

Then suddenly the narrator shifts the time calculus on us. After the dove disappeared, the narrator tells us, "In the six hundred and first year, in the first month, in the first day of the month, the waters were dried from off the earth." But then, the narrator adds, it was not until "the second month, on the twenty-seventh day of the month," that the earth was totally dry so that Noah and his passengers could finally disembark. What does this time sequence mean? We now know that the passengers left the ark 601 years, 1 month, and 27 days after . . . what? After they had entered the ark, after the Flood had begun, and after it had rained forty days and forty nights, did they spend 601 plus additional years on the ark? That would have been some long trip.

With the written text of Genesis at hand, we could find the answer to these questions by flipping back from chapter 8, verse 13, to chapter 7, verse 6, when the narrator told us that Noah was "six hundred years old when the flood of waters came upon the earth." When we first encountered this number, it looked like a casual aside with no special meaning, but when we reach chapter 8, verse 13, and the narrator refers to 601 years, 1 month, and 27 days, it is apparent that this refers to Noah's age. Even so, the narrator doesn't tell us this; we must deduce it for ourselves. But with this deduction, we can finally calculate that the earth had not dried so that the passengers could disembark until 1 year, 1 month, and 27 days after the rain first fell and the Flood had begun.

This is a long and circuitous route to calculate the duration of Noah's cruise trip. And I am sure that you are confused—that any reader of or listener to the text of Genesis would be confused. But that, I believe, is the point of the narrative. We are so confused because Noah himself was hopelessly confused about when, or whether, the Flood waters would ever recede—about whether he and his passengers would survive.

When God warned Noah about the impending Flood and instructed him to build the ark and bring the animals on board, God said only that it would rain forty days and forty nights. At the end of forty days, Noah dispatched the raven, and it thereby seems clear that he thought that his ordeal had ended and that some safe harbor had emerged somewhere. This turned out to be a false hope, and we can only imagine Noah's surprise and disappointment when he reflected back on God's statement and realized that God had promised only that the rain would end after forty days and nights but had said nothing about when or whether dry land would appear. As it turned out, Noah and his passengers spent almost fourteen months on the ark—and during this prolonged voyage, they had no knowledge when or whether it would end. The dizzying numerical confusion of the narrative is a literary device, as I read it, to put us in the shoes of Noah and his passengers, to help us feel their anxiety and confusion.

The extended length of their voyage points to another question raised by yet another numerical confusion in the Genesis account of the Flood—a confusing inconsistency about the number of animals on board the ark. In chapter 6, when God first instructed Noah to take his immediate family and one male and female pair of every kind of animal, he added this injunction: "Also take with you every sort of food that is eaten and store it up; and it shall serve as food for you and for them." But how much food was needed to sustain them all? This obviously depended on the length of the voyage. It wasn't until chapter 7 that God mentioned that the rain would last forty days and nights, and it was in this chapter that he increased the animal count to seven clean pairs and one unclean pair. This addition of animal passengers obviously increased the amount of food that Noah should load into the ark, but notwithstanding this increase, God seemed to leave Noah with the impression that he should pack for a forty-day voyage.

And here the puzzle of the numbers begins to darken. Until the Flood, both humans and all animals were exclusively vegetarian in their diets. This was clearly God's intention in chapter 1 of Genesis, where he told the humans that they should "have dominion" over all the fish and animals but that everyone should have seed-bearing plants for food. In chapter 2, God repeated that in the Garden of Eden, hu-

manity might "freely eat" from every tree (with a significant exception).[8] After the Flood had ended, God changed this permissible menu
for humans. In chapter 9, he said, "Every moving thing that lives shall
be food for you; and as I gave you the green plants, I give you everything."[9] God then added a crucial detail to the "dominion" over the
animals that he had previously given to humanity. He blessed Noah
and his sons and said to them, "The fear of you and the dread of you
shall be upon every beast of the earth [and birds and fish]."

Thus something had happened in the interval between creation and
the end of the Flood to transform the relationship between humans
and the rest of animate life—from peaceful co-existence to a domination based on "fear and dread." The most plausible account is that
something happened on the ark itself. I would say that as the voyage
unaccountably lengthened and Noah's food supply dwindled, the humans on board turned to slaughtering the animals for food—and the
seven pairs of clean animals gave the humans leeway to eat six pairs
and still have preserved one pair for future reproduction when—and
if—the Flood waters ever receded.

From the animals' point of view, imagine the betrayal that this turn
of events represented. So far as they knew—assuming that they knew
anything—they had been invited onto the ark for their safety, to shield
them from the devastation that was about to fall on all the rest of creation. But now it turned out that they were on board to serve as the
food supply—that they should die so that the humans could survive.
Was there a time on the ark when the animals realized that their human hosts were not benign? Did the animals try to revolt? After the
forty days and nights of the voyage had elapsed, did mayhem and murder overtake the ark? Or did the animals line up complacently, with
misplaced confidence, like the proverbial lambs to the slaughter? Genesis doesn't tell us; all we know is that after the Flood the relationship
between humans and animals was transformed from an essentially be-

nign domination to a domination based on fear and dread. This is what the confusion about the numbers tells us, if we read it carefully.

God appended to the new dietary regime two restrictions, that humans should not eat "flesh with its lifeblood still in it"—the first iteration of what ultimately became an elaborate set of dietary laws—and that humans should not kill one another. This latter rule was not new; it had been the basis for Cain's punishment. But God's reiteration of this rule in tandem with his permission for interspecies killing may have arisen from some recognition that the bloodletting that had already occurred on the ark had an expansive psychological dynamic that must be specifically arrested, if mankind were indeed to be fruitful, to multiply, and to fill the earth.

The experience of the Flood thus had two implications for the biblical portrayal of relationships of authority and subjects. The first was not only that the authority has brute power to destroy subjects, but also that this power can be wielded in unpredictable ways without any necessary connection to the welfare or interests of subjects. The second follows from the first, that subjects will regard authority predominantly with "dread and fear." These implications and their novelty are clearest in the post-Flood relationship explicitly portrayed between humans and other animals. For relations between God and humans, the destructive potential was always there, but it remained latent rather than directly acknowledged. Even God's curse that Adam must die remained only an abstraction until just sixty-six years before Noah's birth. This was the first clear sign in Genesis of God's willingness to deploy destructive power against humans. Even so, Noah lived for six hundred years until God decided to destroy all the rest of humanity in the Flood, which was an unmistakable sign even to the most obtuse that God was willing to use his powers against humanity.

Even if Noah and his family were not thinking of God in a fearful, mistrusting way, Genesis gives us good reason to think that God himself was thinking in terms that, if they had known it, would have inspired dread and fear among all the passengers on the ark. After the Flood waters had receded and Noah and all his passengers had left the ark, Genesis records that "the Lord said in His heart, 'I will not again damn the soil on humankind's score. For the devisings of the human heart are evil from youth. And I will not again strike down all living things as I did.'"[10] This is on its face a puzzling rationale for God's vow. He had originally decided to "wipe out the human race" on the ground that its "evil . . . was great" and only Noah seemed exempt because he alone was "a righteous man . . . blameless in his time." God, moreover, directly confided in Noah that "the end of all flesh is come before me, for the earth is filled with outrage by them."

Did God's subsequent conclusion that the human heart is evil from youth exempt Noah—who was, after all, the son of Lamech, the most flagrant evildoer in Genesis to that point? Or did God find himself having doubts about Noah's blamelessness as the Flood wore on and on? God, after all, had brought the Flood because he had changed his mind about his prior creation of mankind ("the Lord regretted having made the human on earth and was grieved to the heart"[11]). Might he now regret his exemption of Noah, perhaps in witnessing the carnage on the ark as the human passengers slaughtered and ate the others despite God's original instruction in Eden that mankind should eat only vegetation?

Genesis tells us that on the 150th day of the Flood, "God remembered Noah and . . . sent a wind over the earth and the waters subsided."[12] The use of the verb "remembered" is echoed in Exodus where God "remembered His covenant with Abraham, with Isaac, and with Jacob" after the children of Israel had suffered 400 years of Egyptian slavery.[13] In both instances, the ambiguity of this verb is striking—suggesting either that God had always remembered and remained faithful to his assurances to Noah and his covenant with the later patriarchs or that God had forgotten those promises and only belatedly recalled them.

The doubts about God's faithfulness during the Flood were amplified by his direct statement to Noah after he had brought the ark to dry land. God announced that he would establish a "covenant" with Noah and his descendants that "never again shall there be a Flood to destroy the earth." This statement is followed by a repetition of the formula "And God said." In his splendid commentary to his translation, Robert Alter notes that the biblical narrative conventions regarding this repetition indicate that God's first words were met with silence on Noah's part. Alter says, "The flood-battered Noah evidently needs further assurance, so God goes on, with a second formula for introducing speech, to offer the rainbow as outward token of His covenant."[14] The specific promise has an odd, and not entirely reassuring, aspect to it, however. "When I send clouds over the earth, the bow will appear in the cloud," God said. "Then I will remember my covenant, between Me and you and every living creature of all flesh, and the waters will no more become a Flood to destroy all flesh."[15] The rainbow thus appears to be not simply a signal for God's subjects but a mnemonic for God himself—as if he might forget his promise without some automatic prompting.[16]

If, moreover, Noah had managed to eavesdrop on God's earlier conversation with himself—if he could hear what the narrator and we readers have already heard—he might notice a disquieting variation between God's internal musings and his specific covenant with Noah. To himself, God said, "I will not again strike down all living things as I did."[17] But to Noah, God said, "I will establish my covenant with you, that never again shall all flesh be cut off by the waters of the Flood, and never again shall there be a Flood to destroy the earth."[18] Was God thus reserving the possibility that he might destroy everything by some other means (perhaps by a fire next time, as he later deployed to destroy Sodom and Gomorrah)? Might Noah have learned from his apparent initial misunderstanding of the Flood's duration that God's promises sometimes contain less than meets the eye and must be scrutinized with lawyer-like precision for loopholes and unacknowledged qualifications?

In the event, Noah said nothing at all to God. He heard the covenant but remained silent in God's presence. Immediately after this encounter, however—as Genesis tells us—Noah planted a vineyard "and he drank of the wine and became drunk, and exposed himself within his tent."[19] This hardly seems the conduct of the Noah who was originally described as "a righteous man, he was blameless in his time, Noah walked with God."[20] In his drunken stupor, Noah was not fit to walk with anyone. And "blameless"? No one had been described as naked in Genesis since Adam and Eve in the garden. Was Noah too drunk to know that he was naked, in which case his nakedness was a sign of his innocence, as in the first days in Eden? Or was it the sign of a guilty conscience, as it was for Adam and Eve after eating the forbidden fruit?

The Genesis account strongly suggests the latter reading. Ham, one of Noah's three sons, entered the tent, saw "his father's nakedness," and told his brothers outside; they in turn put a cloak over their shoulders, backed into the tent, and dropped the cloak over their father so as not to look directly upon him unclothed. Noah then awoke "from his wine and he knew what his youngest son had done to him," and he cursed Ham's descendants, enslaving them to his brothers. Thus Noah ascribed some meaning to his nakedness, unlike Adam and Eve's initial view in the garden. Moreover, if he was not clearly ashamed, he certainly took no pride in being seen naked by his son. But even if it was the vulnerability of nakedness rather than shame that he wanted to mask from Ham, his sense of vulnerability might have come from his lack of confidence in God's promised protection. And this lack of confidence might itself have seemed blameworthy to Noah.

The odd detail that Noah cursed not Ham but only his descendants suggests another ambiguity in Noah's sense of himself. If Ham was the wrongdoer, why should he escape retribution while his unborn descendants were held responsible? Perhaps Noah was thinking of his relationship to his own father's sins. If Lamech had escaped punishment, as it appears from his boastfulness, then perhaps Noah suspected that punishment would fall on him. Perhaps though God had appeared to view him as righteous and blameless, Noah doubted his own merit and feared that God would see his nakedness just as Ham had done. Noah's long—overly long—ordeal on the ark could have amplified those doubts, could indeed have suggested that God was having his own doubts about Noah's worthiness. If Noah had heard God's rueful rumination that "the devisings of the human heart are evil from youth," he would have concluded that God no longer exempted him from blame, and that he was as vulnerable to God's subsequent change of heart as all the other creatures who had been destroyed in the Flood from which Noah barely escaped. No wonder that Noah was driven to drink.

From this description of the interactions between God and humanity in the ten generations from humans' creation, we can see this development in the conception of God's authority. At the outset, God's expectation that humans will obey his wishes appears to need no justification; the expectation seems unremarkable, as much part of the natural order as the daily rising and setting of the sun. Humans, of course, have capacity to disobey God's wishes, but this brute fact does not convey any implication that humans are justified in withholding obedience. This proposition is not rejected; its possibility seems not even conceivable.

And yet even in these earliest interactions, some small doubts about the propriety of God's authority can be seen—doubts that ultimately explode into angry visibility in the main text of Job. The first small doubts appear in Eden itself, with the presence of the forbidden fruit and the tempting serpent as well as the accompanying question why God found it necessary to test human obedience, why he didn't take it for granted that humans themselves would accept his authority as natural and unremarkable. The doubts are amplified in God's inexplicable preference for Abel's offering and his obtuse, even somewhat taunting, response to Cain's disappointment and anger. Why, the question appears, is God not simply testing Cain but even seeming to instigate his violation? These are small doubts; there is no indication that Adam, Eve, or Cain consciously acknowledged them or entertained any question about the legitimacy of God's authority.

With Noah, however, these small doubts increase. From the earlier puzzlement about God's purposes in tempting humanity, a larger mystery grows about God's motives—a sense that God is not reliably consistent in his dealings with mankind. This suspicion does not directly arise from the fact that God comes to regret that he had created mankind; it arises from his dealings with Noah, whom he seemed to exempt from his destructive intentions. Immediately beneath the surface of the Flood story in the Bible—the reassuringly placid surface of the ark, built to God's specifications, safely afloat on the Flood waters—considerable confusion is apparent, even in the very format of the accounts of the time lines for the rainfall and the subsequent emergence of habitable land.

When God "remembers" Noah and makes dry land reappear, it is clear that God himself not only saw Noah's confusion but, more important, vowed to reassure him about God's own future reliability. Noah did not demand this reassurance; if he had done so, this would be the first appearance in the biblical account of human presumption to question the legitimacy of God's authority by demanding that he exercise his authority with some predictability, according to some coherent criteria accessible to human understanding. Noah makes no such claim. But God offers a covenant to Noah, on the apparent premise that it was necessary—or at least desirable—as a basis for his future relations with mankind.

God's covenant did not, moreover, appear to be conditional. He specified some new obligations for mankind—not to eat the flesh of animals with their lifeblood remaining and not to kill one another. But God did not threaten another universally destructive flood if these conditions were disobeyed; he seemed to envision the likelihood of disobedience on the basis of his reflection that mankind is evil from its very youth. Even though Noah had not demanded it, God seemed to anticipate that he could not have the relationship with humanity that he wanted unless he made an explicit promise that Noah's experience would not be repeated. God thus appeared to impose on himself some criterion by which the legitimacy of his actions could be evaluated by mankind—and he added the mnemonic of the rainbow as a constant reminder for both him and us of the standard that he had endorsed. No more floods, he said. Humanity can rely on it.

Some residue of doubt about God's purposes nonetheless remained in the Genesis account of the human reception of this first explicit covenant. There was no rejoicing. Noah in fact remained silent, notwithstanding God's apparent threefold pauses in presenting the covenant, an apparent solicitation of some response from him. The only reported response from Noah was a drunken binge and unseemly nakedness before his sons—hardly a measure of his reassured confidence about God's future intentions toward him.

The patriarch's nakedness before his sons might also be a metaphor for the vulnerability that God had revealed to Noah in promising never again to destroy humanity. Indeed, God's drawing back from his initial, privately voiced inclination that he would "never again strike down all living things" to his more qualified promise to Noah that "never again shall there be a Flood to destroy the earth" suggests that God was having second thoughts about the extent of his authority that he was prepared to cede to the creatures he had sired, to humanity.[21] Noah's younger son had directly gazed upon his father's naked vulnerability. His elder sons more piously averted their glance—but even they could not avoid knowing that their father had revealed his nakedness to them, if only they had chosen to look at it. So, too, we readers of the biblical text can look directly at the evidence of God's vulnerability, of his wish or his need for humanity's continued presence—or we can turn away from acknowledging this evidence and even deny that the evidence exists.

We are given only the barest hint of a reason that God might wish for the continued presence of humanity in his reaction to Noah's first act after leaving the ark: "Noah built an altar to the Lord . . . and offered burnt offerings on the altar. And the Lord smelled the fragrant odor" and then vowed never again to "strike down all living things."[22] But if this sensual pleasure was enough for God to disavow humanity's destruction, it was not enough to allay his concern that humanity might become too powerful and diminish his own capacities.

A genealogic listing of Noah's descendants, known by biblical scholars as a Table of Nations, immediately follows the Flood narrative in Genesis, and the next chapter announces that "the earth was one language" and that all humanity gathered together to build a city and a tower "with its top in the heavens, that we may make us a name." God found no pleasure in this enterprise, no pride in the vaulting ambition of Noah's progeny. To the contrary, God saw their enterprise and concluded, "If this is what they have begun to do, now nothing they plot will elude them." In order to "baffle" them, so they would not understand one another, God deprived humanity of a common language and scattered them all over the earth.

God did not destroy humanity, and to that extent he kept the letter of his promise to Noah. But he drastically curtailed our power so as to eliminate any competition with him. The Genesis narrative had thus traveled a considerable distance from the first creation, when God, with apparent confidence in the good that would result, had invited humanity to be fruitful and multiply. Ten generations later, God saw only evil in humanity's spread, and he did not withdraw this harsh judgment when he overcame his misgivings and decided that Noah would survive the Flood. God's jealous destructiveness at Babel revealed that his relationship with humanity remained ambivalent at best. God viewed humanity with suspicion. Humanity in response must have seen what Noah observed as he tossed endlessly on the Flood waters—that God should be feared more than trusted. If God wanted a continuing relationship with humanity, these were the only terms, the bleak terms, that he appeared to offer.

Even so, one aspect of the Flood experience offered some comfort to humanity beyond the sheer fact that God had refrained from entirely destroying us. This comfort could be found in God's promise that a rainbow would appear whenever he sent clouds over the earth. On its surface, the appearance of the rainbow might have been staged for the benefit of humanity, in case we had forgotten God's promise to us. But in his description of the rainbow, God clearly indicated that he had a different audience in mind—that is, himself. Thus God had said that when the rainbow appeared, "then I will remember my covenant, between Me and you and every living creature ... and I will see it, to remember."[23]

This implicit recognition that God might forget his covenant without the prompting of a mnemonic might not seem reassuring. But the entire transaction that led to God's promise, in fact, if properly understood, offered considerable future advantages to humanity. God's initial decision to bring on the Flood to "wipe out the human race" except for Noah was based on his conclusion that he had made a mistake in creating humanity because "the evil of the human creature was great [and] every scheme of his heart's devising was only perpetually evil." God indeed explicitly acknowledged his mistake: "And the Lord regretted having made the human on earth and was grieved to the heart. And the Lord said . . . I regret that I have made them."²⁴ Yet after the Flood's destruction and Noah's emergence from the ark, God again changed his mind: "The Lord said in His heart, 'I will not again damn the soil on humankind's score. For the devisings of the human heart are evil from youth. And I will not again strike down all things as I did.'"²⁵

God may seem inconsistent here: the reason that he gives for exempting humanity from future damnation appears to be precisely the reason he previously invoked for our destruction. It is, however, more plausible to conclude that after the experience of the Flood, God apparently decided that he had been too harsh in his initial judgment, too unrealistic in his demand that humanity must be entirely cleansed of evil. Recognizing that all humanity—presumably including Noah— was "evil from youth," God saw that he was forced to choose between a world without humanity and cleansed of evil, and a world inhabited by humanity but infested with evil. For whatever reason—perhaps because he was pleased by the fragrance of Noah's burnt offering after the ordeal of the Flood—God opted to retain infested humanity.

This decision was not necessarily comforting to Noah or the rest of humanity. God might yet again change his mind and regret his previous decision. God's marshaling of the rainbow itself signified this possibility in its recognition that he might after all forget his current resolve. Even so, the entire transaction shows a new aspect of God, and this does offer humanity some reassurance.

In the entire transaction before and after the Flood, Genesis for the first time shows us God in a self-evaluative and explicitly self-critical mode. We see him here explicitly applying extrinsic standards to his own behavior, and we also see that once God formulates these standards and applies them to his own conduct, these standards serve him as criteria by which he judges himself in the future. God is thus guiding his own conduct by some internalized authority rather than simply acting on the unexamined assumption that whatever he wanted or did was intrinsically good.

God's invocation of the rainbow is further evidence of his application of extrinsic standards to guide his conduct. With the rainbow, God envisions the possibility that in the future he might be tempted to override his current judgment but that, viewed from his current perspective, this would be a mistake, a lapse in judgment motivated perhaps by a burst of anger at renewed evidence of mankind's inclination toward evil. It thus appears that God establishes the rainbow so that if he gets angry at mankind in the future, he will remind himself of the past time when his anger led him close to destroying all living creatures, an action that he regretted based on his own sober second thoughts.

God's rationale for the rainbow suggests something like a conscience structure in his mind. He is self-reflectively judgmental about his past actions—his regret at having created mankind and then his regret at having almost entirely wiped out all living creatures. At the same time—in establishing the rainbow as a mnemonic device—God is self-reflectively judgmental about the possibility that he might not remember his own resolve in the future.

The rainbow is especially significant because it establishes the pattern for a subsequent, and even more striking, innovation in the Hebrew Bible—the extension of the rainbow function to human beings who give voice to the silent admonition of the rainbow that God should honor his promises and hold steady to his considered judgment of himself. Sometimes, as with Abraham and Moses, God appears to invite humans to take this role; sometimes, as with Moses and Job, human beings assume this function without invitation. But in all events, a new vocabulary emerges by which humans claim to hold God accountable.

CHAPTER FOUR

God's Promises

Abraham, Isaac, and Jacob

*A*FTER THE FLOOD AND his outburst at the presumptuousness of the builders in Babel, God appeared to take a different path for constructing a relationship with humanity. As he had initially attempted with Adam, Abel, and Noah, God decided to choose another favorite in the apparent hope that this would lead to a happier conclusion. This time, however, God did not limit his offer to a single human being; he chose instead human beings whom he promised to make the progenitors of a people, a "great nation," and he also promised to favor their descendants more than other peoples on earth. As we trace God's pursuit of his goal, we will see that he makes repeated promises of protection and good fortune, but at the same time he provides considerable reason for his seemingly favored subjects to mistrust the reliability of his promises. The question that looms over his interactions with the patriarchs, Abraham, Isaac, and Jacob, is why God persistently acted in a way that seemed to undercut his promises at the same time that he solicited a preferential relationship by making those promises. The patriarchs give voice to this question in different ways.

Abraham in Exile

This pattern is evident in God's relationship with Abraham, the first of the patriarchs. The earliest recorded moment in this relationship is at the beginning of Genesis, chapter 12: "And the Lord said to Abram, 'Go forth from your land and your birthplace and your father's house to the land I will show you. And I will bless you and make your name great, and you shall be a blessing.'" Abraham (then known as Abram) instantly complied without any observation, question, or reservation: "And Abram went forth as the Lord had spoken to him."[1] The suddenness of this interchange, on both sides, is quite striking. For all that appears in this narrative, there had been no prior direct exchange between God and Abram. The traditional explanation for Abram's instant acceptance of God's direction is his (presumably habitual) obedience to God's will. On the assumption of God's omniscience, this trait explains why God chose Abram for his blessing. From this seemingly abrupt beginning, God sets a number of tests to Abram—most explicitly and horrifically, his commandment that Abraham (as God had renamed him) should sacrifice his son Isaac. Abraham's silent obedience to this command is traditionally viewed as the final confirming evidence that God sought regarding Abraham's unquestioning self-subjection.

But all this is on the surface of the Genesis story about Abraham. Beneath this surface are numerous indications of Abraham's ambivalence toward God, of some mistrust that lay beneath his silent acquiescence. Noah's silence in response to God's offered covenant revealed misgivings only by implication; the ambivalence beneath Abraham's silences is easier to detect directly from the Genesis narrative. By comparison with Noah, we can see how the relationship as it unfolded between God and Abraham presented a visible step toward the modern experience of pervasive mistrust between ruler and ruled.

To see this step, and to place it clearly in the context of modern political theory, we must examine the Genesis account of God's relationship with Abram/Abraham in considerable detail. The first fruit of this
thorough examination is to call into question the traditional account
that God had no prior direct relationship with Abram before his apparently abrupt offer and Abram's acceptance. This moment of offer
and acceptance at the beginning of Genesis chapter 12 was preceded by
five compressed verses at the end of chapter 11, which provide some
richly significant details about Abram's life before his later encounter
with God. At the end of chapter 11, we are told the following facts about
Abram: (1) He was the eldest of three sons. (2) His youngest brother,
Haran, died in the land of his birth, Ur of the Chaldees, leaving one
son, Lot. (3) Abram married Sarai (later renamed Sarah), and she was
unable to bear children. (4) Following Haran's death, Abram's father
(leaving Abram's second brother behind) took Abram, Sarai, and Lot
away from Ur of the Chaldees toward Canaan but stopped and settled
before arriving there.

These facts are recorded without embellishment. But if we read biblical text—as I believe we must—with the assumption that nothing, no
narrative detail no matter how small, is without significance, then we
are obliged to dig beneath the surface of every detail. And if, as with
this spare recitation of Abram's past, we are given no explicit guides to
deeper meaning, we are entitled, and even obliged, to engage in speculation. Thus I make bold to do so.

Genesis 11 tells us that Abram's relationship with his nephew Lot
took on a greater significance for them both following the death of his
younger brother—a significance that was implicitly heightened by the
fact that Abram's wife, Sarai, was barren. Thus Abram gained a surrogate son from his brother's death. What are we to make of this profit? It
would be especially brazen to speculate that Abram was implicated in
Haran's death. But there are nonetheless hints in the subsequent Genesis narrative that might seem to point in this direction. Thus Abram

states that "the gods made me a wanderer from my father's house" when he explained to King Abimelech why he had passed off Sarai as his sister rather than as his wife.[2] Abram's reason for this ruse was that Sarai was so beautiful that he feared Abimelech's courtiers "will kill me" in order to take possession of her.[3] This was the same fear—that "they will kill me"—that Abram invoked to persuade Sarai to masquerade as his sister in the Egyptian Pharaoh's court immediately after God promised to bless him and make his name great.[4]

Notwithstanding God's promised blessing, Abram's self-depiction exactly corresponds to Cain's condition after he had killed Abel. When God banished him, Cain responded, "I shall be a restless wanderer on the earth and whoever finds me will kill me."[5] God had cursed Cain; with Abram he promises a blessing, and yet Abram responds as if he were—or had been—cursed like Cain.

Could it be that Abram believed that he deserved to be cursed like Cain—not necessarily because he had been responsible for his younger brother's death but nonetheless because he had profited from it? Perhaps Abram had been envious of Haran's good fortune in having a son and a fertile wife. Perhaps Abram felt a tinge of pleasure when his brother's death led to his inheritance of Haran's good fortune—that is, a paternal relationship with Lot.

The possibility of Abram's connection with Cain does not, moreover, end here. Abram is living in Ur of the Chaldees when we first encounter him in Genesis chapter 11, but he was not born there, and we don't learn of his actual birthplace—Aram-Naharaim in the city of Nahor—until much later, in Genesis chapter 24 (after his aborted sacrifice of Isaac and his wife, Sarah's, death) when he sends his servant there to find a wife for Isaac.[6] This detail is significant because of the peculiar light it casts on God's injunction that Abram should "go forth from your land and your birthplace and your father's house" to Canaan. When God delivered this instruction, Abram had already left his land and his birthplace. He was still with his father, but even this was living not so much in a paternal house as in a way-station toward Canaan, their original destination. (Abram much later refers to himself as a "sojourning settler," which seems a more apt description of his father's residence.)[7] At various places in the Bible, God occasionally appears surprised or unknowing, and he may not be as omniscient as conventional interpretations insist. It seems unlikely, however, that at the moment of God's first recorded encounter with Abram, he didn't realize that Abram was already in compliance with the directive that he should leave his land and his birthplace and his father's house.

If Abram was already in compliance with God's directive—if, as seems apparent, Abram had already left his land, his birthplace, and his father's house when God first spoke to him—the real issue between God and Abram at this encounter is not whether Abram will comply with God's wishes. The real issue—from Abram's perspective, at least —is whether God will forgive him and lift the curse of endless, restless wandering. God's first statement, "Go forth . . . to the land I will show you," is, from this perspective, less a command than an opportunity for Abram, a chance to end his punitive exile—something he may have desperately desired long before God offered it to him.

From this reading, it appears that another new element has entered the relationship between God and humanity. We have thus far seen the evolution of this relationship from initial harmony to divinely commanded harmony followed by a breach, to efforts at restored harmony based on God's promise of future protection. The new element makes only a tentative, barely suggestive appearance deduced from the details of Abram's life before God called out to him. This new element is the possibility of forgiveness by God, of remission by him of punishment imposed through breach of relationship. This element is more directly and avowedly restorative than God's actions to this point. From this small allusion, the possibility of God's forgiveness becomes more visible and prominent among his instruments of governance in subsequent biblical narratives. We will see this most notably in Exodus as

Moses urges God to forgive the rebellious Israelites, and in God's contrasting relationships with Saul and with David in 1 and 2 Samuel. Subsequently in the Christian Bible, we will see the possibility of God's forgiveness become central to his relationship with humanity.

With Abraham, to be sure, the implication of forgiveness is well below the surface of God's statements. Even on their surface, God's call appears to be not a command but rather an enticing offer for any young man still living under his father's shadow. Abram was seventy-five when God called to him, a mere youth by biblical standards. Thus Abram's acceptance of God's offer may simply have been a reflection of his ambition for self-advancement rather than a wish for redemption. It seems to me that the Genesis account of the motives for God's offer and Abram's acceptance are so ambiguous that the best course is to assume that both are at work—that God's offer is understood by Abram as both a generous offer of forgiveness and a flattering recognition of his potential for greatness.

However it is viewed, God's offer marks a new turn in his relationship with humanity. In Eden, both the existence and the specific terms of a relationship were essentially taken for granted; God issued only one clear commandment as such and attached a punishment for disobedience. But the punishment was more an abstraction than an experienced reality for Adam and Eve—until, of course, their actions led God to impose it on them. And even then, exile from God's presence was at the core of the experienced punishment—not only for Adam and Eve but for Cain in response to his killing of Abel. It was not until almost a thousand years later, when Adam finally died, that the inevitable fate of human mortality became clear, not simply for those few unlucky enough to encounter a murderous Cain or Lamech but for all humanity. With the coming of the Flood, universal mortality took on an even more draconian implication. Now it was clear that God was prepared to kill everyone who was "evil" in his eyes, not "righteous" or "blameless." God did not prescribe any clear substantive standards for these categories, however; it seemed as if his favor might be dispensed on the basis of arbitrary standards or mere whim. So it appeared to Cain when his offering was rejected, and so it must have appeared to Noah as the Flood waters persisted interminably. God's description to Noah of the post-Flood basis for relations between humans and animals, as now based on the animals' "dread and fear" of the more powerful humans, could readily depict the core human attitude toward God's authority.

God does not appear, however, to welcome this foundation for his human relationships. His stipulation of a covenant with humanity against any new flood, marked by the recurrent appearance of the rainbow, seems designed to allay human dread and fear. But even so, God did not offer the same capacious promise that he had entertained in his private thoughts; his guarantee extended only to floods. A cautious (and lawyer-like) observer, remembering Noah's uncertainty on the ark, might notice God's omission of other disasters from his guarantee and remain locked in dread and fear.

With Abram, God takes a new course. His proffered relationship is not based on a threat of punishment, not "dread and fear." The new relationship would be based on God's promise of great reward, a release from punishment and a prospect of immortality through one's direct lineal descendants. The new element in God's forgiveness is an offer premised on the recipient's previous wrongdoing or sense of guilt. In his approach to Abraham, God did not take for granted humanity's "goodness," as he did in the first creation account. Nor did he command that the subject of his attention avoid evil as a condition of any continuing relationship, as he did with Adam and Cain. Nor did he require some prior assurance of righteousness or blamelessness as he apparently did with Noah. The only basis for a relationship that God offered Abraham was the promise that God would give him progeny and ensure the establishment of a homeland for the great nation born from Abraham's seed. As I see it, God promised Abraham an end to his exile, to his homeless wandering. God did not promise to reward Abraham for past goodness. God promised to forgive him for past trespasses.

And yet this new relationship was vulnerable to the same misgivings that Noah experienced: what assurance was there that God would honor his promises? With Noah, the misgivings were never acknowledged, except indistinctly in Noah's drunken, naked vulnerability, but with Abram, these misgivings come into clear visibility as his relationship with God unfolds over the course of an extended narrative. On the surface of this narrative, God repeats his promises to Abram over and over, and yet as time and circumstances stretch onward it seems less and less likely that the promises will be kept. At one climactic moment, Abraham (just after God changed his name from Abram) "flung himself on his face and he laughed" in response to God's repeated promise that he (now one hundred years old) and his wife, Sarah (now ninety), would bear a child, from whom a great nation would emerge.[8] As Robert Alter observes, Abraham's action speaks to his "disbelief, perhaps edged with bitterness" regarding the reliability of God's promise.[9] Below the surface of this narrative, if we read God's promise not as forward-looking but as redemptive for Abraham's past sin, we can see Abraham as questioning whether he deserves forgiveness, and whether God's repeated, increasingly improbable string of promises was God's way of increasing his punishment rather than simply leaving him alone in his exile.

Abraham's mistrust of God's intentions is apparent from the very moment God made his initial promise. On his journey to God's promised destination, Abraham's first stop is in Egypt. As noted, Abram entreats his wife to pretend she is his sister and to enter Pharaoh's harem or else "they will kill me." Abram takes self-protective action despite the fact that God has just promised to make a great nation of him. Abram was not willing to trust that God would protect his life, much less his capacity to sire a great nation. This masquerade appears in Genesis chapter 12, the same chapter in which God first appears to

Abram. In chapter 20, Abraham repeats this self-protective ruse with his wife in Abimelech's court, out of the same fear that he will be killed, notwithstanding God's repetition of his promise five times in the intervening chapters.[10] On one of those occasions, Abram openly expressed his concern that he "is going to his end childless," and God reassured him, telling him to look to heaven and count the stars, and "so shall be your seed": the Genesis narrator then records that Abram "trusted in the Lord, and He reckoned it to his merit."[11] But Abraham's trust was short-lived; it subsequently failed him in Abimelech's court.

Abraham had good reason for mistrusting the reliability of God's promise to him, even more than Noah had. Noah's mistrust arose from the unanticipated prolongation of the Flood, but he might have reflected that he simply misunderstood God's assurances about its duration and that God had taken enormous precautions, after all, in his directions to build and populate the ark which spoke to his serious commitment to Noah's safety. For readers of the Genesis account, moreover, the existence of, or grounds for, Noah's mistrust are not obvious. If we readers take considerable care to untangle the confusing chronology in the account, the possibility of Noah's mistrusting God's reliability does emerge. But it is easy to overlook, especially if the reader approaches the narrative from a pre-existing attitude of unwillingness to mistrust God's reliability.

Abraham's narrative is strikingly different from Noah's. We repeatedly see unmistakable evidence of Abraham's mistrust. His deceptive, self-protective (and obviously outrageous) ploy with his wife as well as his disbelieving laughter at God's repeated assurance that Sarah will bear a child are the most obvious indications. But more important, God deals with Abraham's children in ways that appear heartlessly inconsistent with his promise that Abraham's direct descendants will outnumber the stars. In responding to these dealings, Abraham does not openly express his mistrust, but the narrative sets out such a strong basis for this attitude that it is difficult for any reader—except the most resolute—to avoid believing in Abraham's disbelief.

The strongest basis for Abraham's mistrust of God's intentions toward him is set out in three climactic chapters of Genesis. Each of these chapters deals with the death of one of Abraham's sons, and each has the same pattern—that God takes a direct hand in commanding these deaths but that Abraham is somehow implicated in the deed, and that Abraham believes each son is in fact killed even though we readers know that God has rescued him. The net result from these chapters is that Abraham believes God has rescinded his promise that he will become a great nation through his progeny and thus ultimately will end his wandering in a new homeland.

In chapter 19, God destroys Sodom and Gomorrah, and so far as Abraham knows, his nephew and surrogate son Lot was killed with all the others. In chapter 21, God tells Abraham to accede to his wife Sarah's demand that Abraham's son Ishmael be expelled into "the wilderness," and Abraham never sees him again. In chapter 22, God directs Abraham to take his son Isaac to Mount Moriah and kill him as a sacrifice; though Isaac is saved at the last moment, Abraham must be forcibly restrained from the killing, comes down from the mountain alone, and never again sees Isaac. Interpolated in these successive accounts, chapter 20 relates a virtual repetition of Abraham's mistrustful, self-protective conduct when God first made his promise; as in chapter 12, Abraham pretends that Sarah is his sister and gives her as a sexual partner to a foreign king to protect his own life.

These chapters are extraordinarily rich in their exploration of the justification for God's authority—the most open exploration that appears anywhere in the Bible except for the book of Job. All of these chapters, and their culminating expression in Job, build on the groundwork that was laid in the Genesis account of Noah and the Flood—that is, the implications for relations between God and humanity of God's readiness to change his mind about the continued worth of the bond. We have already seen God's use of the rainbow as a reminder of his resolve to refrain from destroying humanity, to remain in some relationship with us. God's connection to Abraham can be understood as a continuation of God's own struggle with this issue. His uncertainty about whether he should keep to this resolve is apparent in his continual testing of Abraham, culminating in the command to sacrifice Isaac. At the end of each of these tests, God does nothing more than reiterate the promise he (seemingly) had already made to Abraham. Abraham's perception of God's ambivalence is apparent in his repeated concern for his own safety notwithstanding God's promises, as well as his unseemly resort to self-protection using Sarah as bait to divert his imagined assailants.

This underlying issue arises in a discussion between God and Abraham about whether God should destroy Sodom and Gomorrah. This exchange is the first moment when God appears to ask a human being to serve as judge of God's conduct. Genesis chapter 18 tells us that God had heard about grave offenses committed in these two cities and had said to himself, "Shall I conceal from Abraham what I am about to do? For Abraham will surely be a great and mighty nation . . . [f]or I have embraced him so that he will charge his sons and his household after him to keep the way of the Lord to do righteousness and justice."[12]

This is the first time the words "righteousness" and "justice" appear in the Hebrew Bible. God had already imposed various punishments on human beings. He had expelled Adam and Eve from the Garden of Eden for disobeying his commandment. He had condemned Cain to endless exile for murdering his brother Abel.[13] He had destroyed all humanity in the Flood except for Noah and his immediate family because he had concluded that human beings were irredeemably evil.[14] But God had never explicitly indicated that he was concerned with abstract principles of righteousness and justice or that he was prepared to apply these principles to regulate his own conduct.

God's decision to inform Abraham before destroying the two cities implied that he was not simply prepared to apply his own standards of justice but was willing to listen and perhaps defer to the criteria that a human being might offer to him. The biblical text strongly implies this by observing in the exchange that followed between God and Abraham that God was "standing before Abraham" rather than the other way around. Later scribes copying this text reversed this positioning so that Abraham stood before God, in an apparent effort to avoid the presumptuousness of the original formulation.[15]

The Genesis text doesn't tell us what God said to Abraham, whether he simply declared that "this is what I am about to do" and fell silent, or instead directly solicited Abraham's opinion. Moreover, it is not clear from the text whether God intended to consult Abraham or whether he was already committed in his own mind to destroying the two cities and wanted to use the occasion as an object lesson for Abraham about the demands of "righteousness and justice." Perhaps God intended this advance consultation to be another test by which he would judge Abraham's worthiness to be the progenitor of a "great and mighty nation."

Whatever God's intention in initiating the exchange, Abraham responded with striking boldness. If he had wanted to present himself as entirely obedient to God's will, he might have responded that the decision whether to destroy the cities was entirely dependent on God's own judgment. "Far be it from me," he might have said, to question Divine judgment. But this is not the course that Abraham chose. With God "standing before" him, Abraham "stepped forward and said, 'Will You really wipe out the innocent with the guilty? Perhaps there may be fifty innocents within the city. Will You really wipe out the place and not spare it for the sake of the fifty innocent within it? Far be it from You to do such a thing, to put to death the innocent with the guilty, making innocent and guilty the same. Far be it from You! Will not the Judge of all the earth do justice?'"

God immediately conceded: "Should I find in Sodom fifty innocents within the city, I will forgive the whole place for their sake."[16] God's concession came so quickly that it might seem that Abraham's plea had been no surprise to him, that he had already come to this position in his own mind and that he was indeed testing Abraham rather than accepting guidance from him. But Abraham didn't seem to entertain this possibility. Instead he persisted in his apparent boldness. God had limited his concession to Abraham's suggestion that there might be fifty innocent people in the cities, and Abraham immediately varied his hypothetical, but this time prefaced with a more deferential introduction, "And Abraham spoke up and said, 'Here, pray, I have presumed to speak to my Lord when I am but dust and ashes. Perhaps the fifty innocent will lack five. Would you destroy the whole city for the five?'" Like a clever lawyer—or, even more outrageously in its implication of reversed authority, like a law school professor leading a somewhat dense student into Socratic dialogue—Abraham didn't immediately reveal the basic moral principle at stake, that is, whether the death of even a single innocent person could be justified. Instead he argued by indirection: if you would save the city because of fifty innocent residents, would you destroy the entire city because there were five fewer innocent people?

God again instantly acceded but only in the terms that Abraham specified, only to save forty-five innocents. This interchange continues through four more iterations, with Abraham each time moving downward from forty-five, to forty, to thirty, to twenty, to ten. As before, with each plea, God immediately promised to save the city for the sake of the stipulated number. But Abraham stopped at ten and God volunteered no further self-restraint. The final request that Abraham made, and the last commitment God gave him, is to save the city if ten innocents can be found there.

This is a puzzling conclusion. Why did Abraham stop his pleadings at ten innocents? Why didn't God acknowledge—preferably sooner rather than later, but at some point in this increasingly bizarre bargaining session—that the killing of even one innocent person violated the principle of righteousness and justice that Abraham was invoking, and to which God himself was repeatedly acceding? Perhaps Abraham stopped because he had become increasingly aware of his own presumptuousness in God's presence, notwithstanding his initial boldness and God's instantaneous acquiescence at each step of Abraham's pleading. If we understand their exchange as God's test of Abraham's commitment to righteousness and justice, Abraham's unwillingness to press further than ten innocents might have been a failure in God's eyes.

There may have been, however, a larger question in God's mind than testing Abraham's individual moral mettle. God may have been testing whether any human being could assist him in balancing his own conflicting impulses toward humanity. In God's ambivalence about the Flood, we have already seen the central element of this conflict—from his initial decision to obliterate almost all of humanity (and maybe Noah, too) because of their persistent evil to his regrets at that decision and his vow never again to destroy humanity notwithstanding (and even because of) their persistent evil. God's plan to destroy Sodom and Gomorrah appeared to be a localized version of the cosmic destruction he had unleashed in the Flood. Destroying the cities by fire would not violate his narrowly framed promise to Noah, but it would have apparently violated God's private vow to himself to refrain from destroying humanity by any means.

It thus seemed that God's decision to inform Abraham of his destructive intentions—of what he was "about to do" before he did it—might have been an invitation to a human being to take on the function that God intended for the rainbow after the Flood: to remind him of his vow to himself. God's instantaneous acquiescence to Abraham's insistence that he should not kill innocent people strongly suggests that Abraham was indeed performing the rainbow function—reminding God of his own prior commitment and his deeper sense of his self-

definition as a god committed to righteousness and justice. In this respect, Abraham served like the rainbow as the external embodiment of
God's own conscience—with the notable addition that Abraham was
able to engage in a reasoned interchange with God.

At the same time, the fact that Abraham inexplicably stopped his
advocacy while the possibility of killing ten innocent people remained
open points to a drawback in God's use of a human being as an interlocutor. A rainbow would not have been overawed by God—if this
were the reason that Abraham stopped short in his moral critique. My
own speculation about the reason for Abraham's reticence is even more
troubling. I believe that Abraham stopped at ten innocents because he
was not convinced of his own moral worthiness, whether in God's eyes
or in his own. An inert rainbow would not have encountered this difficulty.

I come to this speculation because Abraham's nephew and surrogate
son Lot lived in Sodom in a household that included Lot's wife, two
daughters, and their husbands, and possibly also two additional un-
married daughters—in other words, a household of six to eight people.
Abraham's stopping at ten innocents left open the possibility that God
would destroy everyone in Sodom, including eight innocent people
whom Abraham knew personally and cared about deeply. Thus Abraham's stopping would have been a challenge to God—a different challenge from his direct plea, "will not the Judge of all the earth do justice?"[17] This second challenge would be whether God was prepared to
forgive Abraham for his unjust acts or thoughts that surrounded his
relationship with Lot, for his gain from the death of Lot's father, Abraham's younger brother.

If Abraham was troubled about his past motives, this possibility puts
his cessation at ten innocents in an especially somber light. Because he
had refrained from extracting a commitment from God and left open
this possibility, Abraham might have seen himself implicated, and thus
blamed himself, if God then proceeded to destroy the two cities not-

withstanding the eight innocents there. And if those innocents were Lot and his family, Abraham might have (unconsciously, at least) invited their destruction in order to wipe out his own ill-gotten gains. Abraham might have hoped that he alone viewed his surrogate parenthood with Lot in this guilt-ridden way—that God did not condemn him as he had condemned himself, or that God might now be willing to rescind his prior condemnation. Viewed from this perspective, it is plausible that Abraham was unwilling to test his hope directly; he might have hoped that God would abstain from killing Lot on his own initiative because this would signify that God both understood and was prepared to lift this burden of guilt from Abraham, a burden that Abraham himself felt but could not allay. God himself might have wanted to test Abraham's sense of his own moral worthiness—and his consequent suitability to serve God as the rainbow had served him—by waiting to see if Abraham would plead for Lot's life, not submerged as part of an anonymous larger group but directly and exclusively.

It is plausible to conclude that Abraham believed that his worst fears, about Lot and about himself, were confirmed as he "hastened early in the morning to the place where he had stood in the presence of the Lord, [a]nd he looked out over Sodom and Gomorrah and over all the land of the plain, and he saw and, look, smoke was rising like the smoke from a kiln." In fact, the next sentence in the narrative tells us that "it happened when God destroyed the cities of the plain that God remembered Abraham and sent Lot out of the upheaval."[18] But there is no record that God told this to Abraham or that Abraham ever saw Lot again, or even knew of his survival. So far as Abraham could tell, God had destroyed his nephew; so far as Abraham could tell, God had not acted mercifully toward him or his surrogate son. This same perspective on Abraham's part persists in his experience of God's subsequent willingness to destroy Abraham's other sons, Ishmael and Isaac.

Immediately after the report of the Abimelech episode, Genesis chapter 21 proclaims that "the Lord singled out Sarah as He had said, and the Lord did for Sarah as He had spoken."[19] Isaac was born, the only son of the centenarian Abraham and his ninety-year-old wife. Whatever doubts Abraham may have had about God's prior commitment were apparently appeased. Abraham had been quite explicit with God about his doubts; fifteen years earlier, he had directly complained to him, "O my Master, Lord, what can You give me when I am going to my end childless . . . Look, to me you have given no seed."[20] At that time Sarah (still named Sarai) responded to Abraham's (Abram's) concern by suggesting that he sleep with her slavegirl, Hagar. Abram did so and Hagar conceived a son, Ishmael. But after Isaac was born, Sarah complained that Hagar was laughing at her, and she demanded that Abraham drive out "the slavegirl and her son, for the slavegirl's son shall not inherit with my son, with Isaac."

Abraham was appalled at this demand: "the thing seemed evil in Abraham's eyes because of his son." But God contradicted Abraham. "Let it not seem evil," he said. "Whatever Sarah says to you, listen to her voice." So Abraham complied. He "rose early in the morning," prepared provisions for Hagar and Ishmael, and banished them to "wandering through the wilderness of Beersheba." For all Abraham knew, he was directly implicated in the death of two more innocents, including his own son. In fact, we readers know that the two came close to death but, as they wept, God "heard the voice of the lad" and rescued them.[21] But Abraham did not know this; he never saw Ishmael again.

The dispatch of Hagar, Abraham's concubine, and Ishmael, his son, was terrible. But worse yet: "And it happened after these things that God tested Abraham. And He said to him, 'Abraham!' and he said, 'Here I am.' And he said, 'Take, pray, your son, your only one, whom you love, Isaac, and go forth to the land of Moriah and offer him up as a burnt offering on one of the mountains which I shall say to you.'"[22] Abraham said nothing in response to this instruction. He "rose early in the morning and saddled his donkey and took his two lads with him, and Isaac his son."

By now we recognize the formula. It was "early in the morning" (in chapter 19) that Abraham rushed to the place where he had spoken with God, watched the smoke rise from Sodom and Gomorrah, and feared that Lot had died in the flames. It was "early in the morning" (in chapter 21) that Abraham rose to make provision and drive Ishmael and his mother into the wilderness. (It was "early in the morning," in chapter 20, that Abimelech rose and confronted Abraham with his death-dealing deception: "What have you done to us . . . Things that should not be done you have done to me.") Now, in chapter 22, Abraham "rose early in the morning" to take Isaac away. When God referred to Isaac as Abraham's "son, your only one," this must have seemed confirmation to Abraham that his older sons, Lot and Ishmael, were indeed dead. Why did Abraham now silently comply with God's demand? Why didn't he invoke the principles of righteousness and justice that he had arrayed before God to avert the killing of innocents in Sodom and Gomorrah? But Abraham had not invoked those principles to protect Lot, and he had mildly protested, but to no avail, on behalf of Ishmael. Abraham, it seems, had given up—perhaps because he had never fully believed that he deserved God's promise to end his wandering and give him an heir and a nation, perhaps because he concluded that God had changed his mind and unilaterally revoked the promise.

The traditional interpretation of Abraham's uncomplaining compliance is that he had faith that God would relent in his demand, as indeed did occur. But so far as Abraham knew, his older sons had already died by God's direct hand or commandment and Abraham himself had been led by God to play a supporting role in those deaths. The conventional interpretation would be plausible only if Abraham retained faith, against all the evidence of his senses, that Lot and Ishmael still lived. But Abraham's silence speaks more eloquently against this interpretation than if he had complained or if, like Job after the death of his children, Abraham had spoken piously, "God gives, God takes

away. Blessed be the name of the Lord." Abraham's unprotesting compliance showed his obedience to God's will. It did not show his belief
that Isaac would ultimately be spared or that God remained committed to his often-repeated promises.

Abraham did not kill Isaac, but he came very close. He and Isaac had
been silent during their three-day journey to Moriah. As they climbed
the mountain together, Isaac spoke for the first time: "Isaac said to
Abraham his father, 'Father!' and he said, 'Here I am, my son.' And he
said, 'Here is the fire and the wood but where is the sheep for the offering?' And Abraham said, 'God will see to the sheep for the offering,
my son.'"

There was an ambiguity in Abraham's response that is not quite conveyed by any English translation; because there are no punctuation
marks such as commas in traditional Hebrew, Abraham's response—
read without the comma—suggested, without saying so, that his son
would be the sheep for the offering that God would see to. But whatever ambiguity might have resided in Abraham's response, it seems to
vanish in the clear implications of his immediately subsequent acts:
"Abraham built there an altar and laid out the wood and bound Isaac
his son and placed him on the altar on top of the wood. And Abraham
reached out his hand and took the cleaver to slaughter his son."[23]

Abraham's murderous intent is unmistakable, to himself and to
Isaac. But suddenly "the Lord's messenger called out to him from the
heavens and said, 'Abraham, Abraham!' and he said, 'Here I am.'" This
address is starkly different from the first time that God called to Abraham in this chapter of Genesis. God called him only once, and Abraham immediately responded (as, indeed, Isaac called him only once
and Abraham immediately responded). This time two calls were necessary to arrest Abraham's attention. There is a traditional interpretation—not, by my lights, distorted by pious wishes—that Abraham required almost forcible restraint to be held back from killing Isaac.
Whatever internal hesitancy might have constrained Abraham from

killing Isaac—his son, his only one, whom he loved—this restraint seemed to have vanished by the time Abraham had taken all the necessary measures to carry out the sacrifice. Abraham acted like a man who had lost all hope and was now entirely consumed by a murderous impulse—like Cain, perhaps, after God had withheld favor from him?

But Abraham was held back. And God then announced, "[N]ow I know that you fear God . . . [and] because you have done this thing, I will greatly bless you and will greatly multiply your seed." Abraham did not directly reply to this renewed promise. But in the middle of God's congratulatory remarks, Abraham intervened to bestow a name on the mountaintop: "YHWH-Yireh, as is said to this day, 'On the mount of the Lord there is sight.'" Abraham's reference to sight here is not clear. It may refer to his assurance to Isaac that God would "see to the sheep for the offering." Or it might refer to something, some epiphany, that Abraham himself saw on that mountaintop. Did Abraham see what Job saw, when in his final speech to God in the whirlwind, Job said, "I knew you, but only by rumor; my eye has beheld you today." But what did Job see in God that he had only heard rumored before? As we will ask about Job, did Abraham's insight lead him to retract any accusations of wrongdoing against God? Did it appall him and make him shudder? Did it comfort him?

As difficult as it is to understand Job's meaning from his last speech to God, we have literally nothing available to us to grasp Abraham's meaning. Aside from proclaiming that someone had seen something on Mount Moriah, Abraham was entirely silent at the end of this event. He was, moreover, surrounded by silence from God, from his wife, Sarah, from his son Isaac. And not just on Mount Moriah. Though Abraham lived for some forty years afterward, so far as Genesis records he and God never spoke again. Abraham never again spoke to Sarah. Immediately after Abraham descended from Moriah, he learned that she had died. (A traditional *midrash*—a rabbinic gloss on the biblical text—posits that Sarah was mistakenly told that Abraham had killed

Isaac and she died instantly of grief.) And Abraham never again spoke to Isaac.

According to the Genesis account, Abraham and Isaac "went together" up Mount Moriah, but Abraham "returned to his lads" alone. This difference was the basis for a rabbinic *midrash* that Abraham had actually killed Isaac and that God subsequently resurrected him.[24] But even if Isaac had not literally been killed, something was sacrificed on Mount Moriah in the relationship between father and son. Perhaps Isaac retained his naive trust in God's protectiveness toward him, as Abraham had apparently urged in his reassurance that God would see to the sheep. But after his father had bound him, put him onto the altar, and raised the cleaver over his body, Isaac must have seen what God's messenger saw in his urgently repeated call. Isaac must have seen that, whatever God's intention, his father was ready to kill him. It is difficult to imagine how this breach of the son's trust in his father could be remedied between them.

Some time afterward, Abraham appeared to have made an effort, a healing gesture toward his son, when he sent his servant to his "land and [his] birthplace" to find a wife for Isaac. When the servant returned with Rebekah, Isaac first saw her from a distance when he had gone "out to stroll in the field toward evening."[25] The "field" is a fateful place in Genesis; it is where Cain lured Abel to kill him, and it is where Joseph's brothers found him wandering and took revenge for their father's favoritism toward him.[26] But Isaac's stroll in the field was a reversal of these experiences. Although this reversal was arranged by his father, Genesis records that after seeing Rebekah from a distance, "Isaac brought her into the tent of Sarah his mother and took Rebekah as his wife. And he loved her, and Isaac was consoled after his mother's death."[27] Perhaps he was also consoled after his father's betrayal.

Isaac might, of course, have taken the lesson from Abraham's conduct that both of them had trusted in God's beneficence and that this trust had been rewarded. This is the lesson that is most evident on the

face of the Genesis narrative, and it is accordingly thus readily available for the readers of that narrative, especially for those inclined toward piety. Without this reassuring reading, God's concluding congratulatory message to Abraham, after he had aborted the sacrifice of
Isaac, would seem starkly out of place. But the resulting mutual silence
among all of the direct actors—God, Abraham, Sarah, and Isaac—suggests that it was more difficult for those who had lived through the experience to draw a reassuring lesson than for those of us who merely
read about it. We readers may take comfort that God rewarded Abraham's trust in him. But if we read the account carefully, it is difficult to
avoid the thought that Abraham himself, after this experience, might
have flung himself on the ground and laughed bitterly, as he had previously done when God had offered an implausible assurance to him.

The silence that apparently engulfed Abraham after his near-murder
of his beloved son Isaac suggests the terrible personal toll that his uncritical obedience to God's command had taken on him. Abraham
might well have concluded that his nephew Lot had died in the general conflagration at Sodom and Gomorrah because he had withheld
any objection to the possible death of ten innocents. Abraham might
equally have concluded that his son Ishmael was dead because, when
God instructed him to acquiesce in Sarah's demand, Abraham abandoned his prior moral conviction that the expulsion of Ishmael and
Hagar would be an "evil."

We don't have certain knowledge of Abraham's personal moral evaluation of God's command that he kill Isaac because Abraham did not
voice any objection and then retreat from it, as he had done regarding
Lot and Ishmael. But faced with God's command about Isaac, Abraham might have reiterated his objection to the killing of any innocent
person. Moreover, God's command was blatantly inconsistent with his
prior promises to Abraham about the great nation that would rise from
his descendants—especially, from Abraham's perspective, because he
believed that Lot and Ishmael were already dead. Before Isaac's birth,

Abraham had protested to God about his apparent failure to honor these promises. But this time, faced with a direct command to sacrifice Isaac, Abraham withheld any objection. In all three instances, Abraham thus had a personal moral objection to the course that God appeared to have chosen, and in all three instances, Abraham overrode his own objection in favor of uncritical acceptance of God's will.

The manifest lesson, on the face of the Genesis text, is that God approved of Abraham's willingness to yield unquestioning obedience to him. But there is a latent message beneath the surface of the text that might seem to contradict this lesson. It is conveyed by the fact that, after each instance of his failure to object to God's intention, Abraham became more deeply implicated in personally violating his own moral position. Abraham did not know that God would actually proceed to destroy Sodom and Gomorrah, thereby killing Lot, because Abraham had stopped his protest at ten innocents. Abraham suspected, but he was not certain, that Ishmael and Hagar would die in the wilderness after their expulsion, and he also knew that he was not directly responsible for the expulsion because Sarah had initiated it and God had instructed him to acquiesce to her wishes. But Abraham had more than a suspicion that Isaac might die in response to God's command. Abraham was prepared to do the killing himself. The latent message in this progression is that Abraham's failure to follow his own moral compass—his sacrifice of his personal integrity in uncritically acquiescing to God's command—led him to increasingly destructive and increasingly direct violations of his own moral code.

This latent critique of the destructive consequences of unquestioning obedience to God's will is further conveyed by the fact that none of the parties involved—Isaac, Sarah, and even God himself—could bring themselves to talk to Abraham after the terrifying, destructive consequences of his willingness to override his own moral convictions had become manifest in the near-killing of Isaac. Perhaps more accurately, in his own willingness to kill Isaac, Abraham was not overriding his moral convictions but was implementing them, on the basis of his secret self-condemnation that he did not deserve to have any sons at all. As it turned out, Abraham became the progenitor of a great nation, as God had promised. But his personal exile never clearly ended.

Isaac Betrayed, Jacob in Pursuit

If we carefully read the Genesis accounts of Abraham's son and grandson, of Isaac and Jacob, we do not find that they confidently trust in God's protective beneficence. In the brief narrative of Isaac's life, there was only one episode in which he initiated action. In all other matters—his conduct on Mount Moriah, his marriage to Rebekah, his paternal blessing to Jacob instead of Esau—Isaac was entirely passive. The one time he did take action was when he traveled to Abimelech's kingdom in Gerar. There Isaac repeated his father's masquerade by claiming that his wife, Rebekah, was his sister. For our purposes, the key similarity in this oddly repetitive episode is the reason given for Isaac's deception; it was the same as Abraham's motive, that is, "fear . . . that the men of the place [will] kill me over Rebekah, for she is comely to look at."[28] Isaac feared this possibility notwithstanding that, immediately beforehand, God himself had directed Isaac to go to Gerar and promised that he would "fulfill the oath that I swore to Abraham your father, and I will multiply your seed like the stars in the heavens."[29] Thus it appears that Isaac, like Abraham, did not trust in the reliability of God's promise and so took independent self-protective action, with potentially deadly consequences to innocent men who might have dallied with his wife.

Isaac's son Jacob—the last of the three foundational patriarchs—was even more overtly mistrustful of God's beneficence than his father or grandfather. At a climactic moment, just after he had deceptively obtained his father's blessing and fled to avoid his elder brother's rage, Jacob saw God in a dream, descending on a ladder from heaven. God identified himself as "the Lord . . . the God of Abraham your father and the God of Isaac," and promised to "bless" Jacob and "guard" him so that his "seed shall be like the dust of the earth and you shall burst forth." When Jacob awoke from this dream, he immediately vowed, "If the Lord God be with me and guard me on this way that I am going and give me bread to eat and clothing to wear, and I return safely to my father's house, then the Lord will be my God. And this stone that I set as a pillar will be a house of God, and everything that You give me I will surely tithe it to You."[30] This carefully calibrated vow—which goes so far as to add items, "bread to eat and clothing to wear," to the list of God's promises—is hardly a model of blind obedience to God. If Abraham's unquestioning acceptance of God's original offer, and even Isaac's passive acceptance of his father's binding, were meant by the Genesis authors to establish a model for humanity's willingly subjugated relationship with God, Jacob's conditional, overtly skeptical bargain does not fit the model.

Jacob's list of conditions for maintaining a relationship with God is the high point in Genesis of mankind's enunciation of increasingly explicit terms for judging the legitimacy of God's authority. Jacob alone spelled out the consequences, the enforcement mechanisms, if God failed to meet his expectations. Jacob virtually announced that if his terms were not met, he would offer allegiance to some other god. Some twenty years after specifying these terms, and after it seemed that God had indeed kept his side of the bargain, Jacob instructed his household, "Put away the alien gods that are in your midst and cleanse yourselves" so that they could accompany him to build an altar "to the God Who answered me . . . and was with me on the way that I went."[31] In retrospect, Jacob's allegiance until then seemed quite tentative.

It may be, of course, that the Genesis authors intended Jacob to serve as a negative model; his repeatedly deceptive and self-promoting actions throughout his life did not establish him as an obviously approved subject for emulation. The Genesis authors may indeed have intended a negative model even in their account of the more limited and less openly avowed skepticism of Abraham and Isaac about God's reliability. We readers of Genesis see much more reason that these patriarchs should have confidence in God's promises than they themselves appeared to see. Abraham, for example, feared that Lot and Ishmael had died and that God would insist on the sacrifice of Isaac, but we know that Lot, Ishmael, and Isaac survived and that God entirely fulfilled his commitment. As a general matter, it is a striking characteristic of the Genesis narratives that we readers are given more information than the actors, and that if they knew what we know about God's actions and intentions, they would trust him with much greater confidence than they actually exhibited.

We cannot understand the political theory underlying the Bible—the attitude prescribed toward, and the justifications offered for, God's authority over humanity—without taking into account the difference between the actions and beliefs of the protagonists in the biblical narrative and the additional information and independent perspective on those actors that we as readers are given. The Bible is clearly not telling stories about interesting characters, human and divine, simply for their entertainment value. All of these stories have a moral purpose; all of them are offered as examples for the audience to emulate or avoid. Thus the fact that the protagonists in Genesis view God as unreliable does not mean that the Genesis authors viewed him that way or intended that we readers concur in the protagonists' fears. From this perspective, it is possible to read all of Genesis as a hymn of praise to God's faithful shepherding of mankind, his unwavering resolve to keep his promises to us, notwithstanding the repeated misgivings and occasionally expressed doubts of our ancestors in their relationship with God.

This reading is one possibility. But a different reading is also possible—that Genesis offers the lesson that our forefathers Abraham, Isaac, and Jacob apparently drew, that God wields his power over us in puzzling and apparently unreliable ways and that, if we should trust his proclamations of protective intentions, this trust should only be tentative and cautiously skeptical. Genesis does not clearly opt for one reading over the other.

It is notable that God never directly reassures Abraham by telling him what we readers know—that both Ishmael and Lot had survived and that God had consistently kept his promises to Abraham both about his elder son's future and about his forbearance from killing any innocent person, even fewer than ten, in destroying Sodom and Gomorrah. It is as if God wanted to keep Abraham, the direct beneficiary of his promises, off-balance while the Genesis narrator nonetheless reassures readers of God's reliability. But this reassurance undermined itself by the continuous evidence that the narrator provides of God's reluctance to keep his promises—his unwillingness, that is, to bind himself indefinitely even though God might choose, on a moment-by-moment basis, to honor his previous commitments.

The basic problem confronting God is that a binding commitment to mankind on any matter is a diminution of his power to do what he pleases when he pleases. Moreover, the basic question that God struggles with in Genesis is whether this diminution is worth its evident costs to him. God never definitively answers this question in Genesis. His persistent ambivalence is, in fact, apparent to his various interlocutors—Noah, Abraham, Isaac, and Jacob—and the basis for their continued uncertainty about the reliability of God's promises to them.

God was apparently pursuing two inconsistent goals: on one side, to reassure mankind and thereby establish a basis for a reliable relationship; on the other side, to preserve his power undiminished. I have construed God's regret about creating mankind before the Flood as evidence of doubts in Genesis about whether he is omniscient; if he were omniscient, that is, he would presumably be able to predict his future wishes as clearly as he knew his current wishes. His apparent inability to do this is the reason he must keep all his options open if he wants to protect his omnipotence. But this goal suggests an inherent limit in God's omnipotence. Is God so powerful that he is capable of pursuing two inconsistent goals at the same time? If God wants not only to avoid any binding commitments to preserve his untrammeled power over mankind but also to enjoy a direct, sustained relationship with mankind that he can achieve only by binding commitments, have we come to the limits even of God's omnipotence?

Genesis suggests this in at least two places. The most overt suggestion is in God's relationship with the third patriarch, Jacob. While Noah, Abraham, and Isaac dealt with their skepticism about God's reliability through silence, Jacob was quite explicit. This is the significance of Jacob's statement, which I previously quoted, setting out specific, detailed conditions that God must meet before Jacob will offer his allegiance.[32] Some twenty years later, Jacob fled with his immediate family from his father-in-law's house and was anticipating an encounter with his brother Esau, who had previously threatened to kill him. Jacob was, as Genesis put it, "greatly afraid, and he was distressed," and—for the first time since his specification of conditional terms for allegiance —he appealed to God for protection and specifically reminded him of his promise to "deal well" with him (a promise God may not actually have made in the sense that Jacob now presented it[33]). That night "Jacob was left alone, and a man wrestled with him until the break of dawn." This mysterious man was, if not God himself, a direct emissary; here is the full account of their nocturnal encounter:

[And] a man wrestled with him until the break of dawn. And he saw that he had not won out against him and he touched his hip-socket and Jacob's hip-socket was wrenched as he wrestled with him. And he said, "Let me go, for dawn is breaking." And he said, "I will not let you go unless you bless me." And he said to him, "What is your name?" And he said, "Jacob." And he said, "Not Jacob shall your name hence be said, but Israel, for you have striven with God and men, and won out." And Jacob asked and said, "Tell your name, pray." And he said, "Why should you ask my name?" and there he blessed him. And Jacob called the name of the place Peniel, meaning, "I have seen God face to face and I came out alive."[34]

Jacob thus succeeded in imposing a condition on this man—he would let go only if the man blessed him. Perhaps Jacob had defeated the man, had "won out" as the man said; perhaps they had fought to a draw, with Jacob injured in the event. But at the least this was not a struggle in which Jacob was defeated; this was a struggle between equals.

It is hardly conceivable that Jacob was physically stronger than God —God who had destroyed his entire creation through the Flood because mankind displeased him; God who had subsequently toppled the tower of Babel because mankind had dared to reach into "the heavens, that we may make us a name."[35] God's struggle with Jacob was not physical but spiritual—or, in an equivalent formulation, psychological. The central question in the struggle was, who will dominate whom? None of his human predecessors had dared to formulate the question in this explicit way. But Jacob brought the question into open visibility.

Jacob thus used force to obtain the blessing he wanted from God —not as obviously unsavory as the fraud he committed on his father Isaac to obtain his blessing, but extraordinarily presumptuous nonetheless. But it was not clear, from Jacob's perspective at least, that these blessings worked to his personal advantage. God seemed to have kept the strict terms of his bargain with Jacob—he was able to return to the land from which he had fled, his older brother Esau whom he had displaced through trickery did not kill him upon his return, he accumulated considerable wealth by which he could clothe and feed himself. But God gave him little more than this; God observed, one might say, the letter but not the spirit of his blessing to Jacob. Near the end of his life, at the age of 130, Jacob offered this retrospective summary,

"Few and evil have been the days of the years of my life, and they have not attained the days of the years of my fathers in their days of sojourning."[36]

He had many grounds for complaint. His father-in-law, Laban, had deprived him of his first choice for a bride (in an ironic replay of Jacob's deception of his father, fraudulently disguising Leah as her younger sister Rachel) and then compounded the breach by lengthening Jacob's term of service to earn the bride whom Jacob had originally chosen. Jacob never got past bitter resentment at Leah, even though she bore him six sons, and his favored wife, Rachel, died young in childbirth. Jacob's grief at Rachel's death was intensified when Joseph, her eldest son (and Jacob's favorite), disappeared—through a fraud inflicted on Jacob by Leah's sons.

Even Jacob's fraudulently obtained precedence over Esau seemed to vanish when the two men encountered each other after a twenty-year separation. Jacob approached Esau fearfully, he "bowed to the ground seven times as he drew near his brother," while Esau "ran to meet him and embraced him and fell upon his neck and kissed him."[37] Jacob offered Esau gifts in order, he said, "to find favor with my lord," but Esau declined, saying, "I have much my brother. Keep what you have." Throughout their encounter, Esau appeared open-hearted, eager to forgive his brother, and entirely contented with his lot notwithstanding his earlier loss of birthright and paternal blessing. Jacob, for his part, appeared apprehensive, reticent, and deferential, as if Esau were his superior. Jacob repeatedly and exclusively referred to Esau as "my lord" while Esau spoke of Jacob only as "my brother."

As the two men parted, never to meet again, Esau made a final gesture that underscored his superior status over Jacob; having declined Jacob's gifts, Esau offered to him, "Pray, let me set aside for you some of the people who are with me"—a display of wealth and generosity that Jacob immediately, but deferentially, declined, "Why should I find such

favor in the eyes of my lord?"[38] Thus Jacob's last recorded words to
Esau were "my lord."[39]

The difference in the brothers' stated rationales for declining gifts is
striking: Esau declined Jacob's gifts because he didn't need them; Jacob
declined Esau's because he didn't deserve them. There is not much satisfaction evident on Jacob's part for his previous, deceptively obtained
precedence over his elder brother. It may be that Esau's displays of
affection were themselves fraudulently offered, more in the spirit of
mockery than forgiveness. But whatever Esau's intent, Jacob emerged
from this briefly renewed relationship more humiliated than trium-
phant.

After his forcibly obtained blessing, God spoke directly to Jacob only
three more times. In the first instance, he directed Jacob to set up an
altar in Bethel "to the God Who appeared to you when you fled from
Esau your brother"—as if God were demanding a specific acknowledgment that he had met the terms that Jacob had initially specified
as the conditions for his allegiance.[40] Immediately thereafter God appeared again to Jacob and not only reiterated his promises to Abraham
and Isaac and renamed Jacob as "Israel" but embellished the promise
to Jacob with the more exalted terms of the first creation: "Be fruitful
and multiply. A nation, an assembly of nations shall stem from you,
and kings shall come forth from your loins."[41] But then—as if to qualify or even mock the grandeur of the promise that God had just made
to Jacob—we learn that as they continued their journey from the site
of this altar in Bethel, Rachel died in childbirth. Jacob now has twelve
sons, enough to ensure that God's promise of a future lineage of kings
will be kept, but Jacob is grief-stricken by the death of his beloved Rachel. What scant pleasure he can take from God's promise is further
undermined when Joseph disappears.

God spoke one last time to Jacob many years later, after Joseph's
lengthy exploits in Egypt and his rediscovery by his brothers, when Jacob was himself on the way to Egypt to see his favorite and now recov-

ered son.[42] In this last encounter, God called twice to Jacob as if to reiterate the difficulty he had in securing Abraham's attention when, by all appearances, God had revoked his promises and abandoned him. Jacob finally responded as Abraham had done, "Here I am." God then identified himself, "I am the god, God of your father"—as if, in their prolonged separation, Jacob might have forgotten who this god was. And though God then reiterated the patriarchal promises, almost immediately thereafter Jacob offered, in an audience with Pharaoh, the pathetic summary of his life, "Few and evil have been the days of the years . . ."

If God wanted a direct, sustained relationship with human beings—if that is the basic reason that he saved Noah from the Flood—and if God embarked upon promises, covenants with human beings, as a way toward establishing this relationship on a more reliable basis than he had experienced before the Flood, it is not at all clear that he accomplished this goal by the end of Genesis. Indeed, after his prolonged, intense engagements with Abraham, God appeared progressively to withdraw from human relationships.

On two occasions, God directly reiterated his promise to Isaac, but they had no other direct interactions.[43] Isaac himself seemed incapable of engaging in a sustained relation with anyone—with God, with his two sons, even with his wife Rebekah, who successfully conspired with Jacob to trick Isaac into depriving Esau of his paternal blessing. Isaac's near-death experience at his father's hand on Mount Moriah may have seemed such a deep breach of trust to him that he was forever disabled from wholehearted engagement in a trusting familial relationship. (Isaac's willful suppression of his suspicions about Jacob's masquerade as Esau—"The voice is the voice of Jacob and the hands are Esau's hands," he said—may have been in the latent service of cheating his son Esau of his blessing as Abraham had cheated him.[44])

God's relationship with Jacob was more sustained than his relationship with Isaac, but also intensely conflict-ridden, and the explicit price that Jacob extracted for maintaining that relationship may have seemed excessive to God. As we have seen, God performed his side of the bargain, but only minimally; he did not "guard" Jacob in the sense of protecting him as fully as Jacob clearly would have wanted. This was not an easy or a happy relationship on either God's side or Jacob's.

For Jacob's children—for Joseph and his brothers—God entirely withdrew from any direct relationship. God was talked about. Many times during his ordeal in Egypt, Joseph, other characters, and the Genesis narrator observed that "God was with him." Joseph himself excused his brothers' conduct, when they had been reunited in Egypt, on the ground that "it is not you who sent me here but God, and He has made me father to Pharaoh and lord to all his house and ruler over all the land of Egypt."[45] But though everyone spoke about God, God himself spoke to no one. He was evidently watching these events; as noted, he did speak directly to Jacob to encourage his travel to Egypt after Joseph's reappearance.[46] But throughout Genesis, God remained silent and distant from Jacob's children.

And then God disappeared. He had anticipated something like this in his early dealings with Abraham when he told him, "Know well that your seed shall be strangers in a land not theirs and they shall be enslaved and afflicted four hundred years. But upon the nation for whom they slave I will bring judgment, and afterward they shall come forth with great substance."[47] In living through the actual event, Abraham's descendants must have felt entirely abandoned—at least those who lived through the four centuries of slavery and affliction. If they had been told of God's promise to Abraham, God gave them no sign of remembering this promise or remaining committed to it. If Noah's faith in God's reliability had been stretched during his unexpectedly prolonged stay on the ark, the faith of the children of Israel in Egypt was pressed seemingly beyond endurance.

CHAPTER FIVE

Loving Power

Moses

*J*UST BEFORE GOD RETURNED to the children of Israel in Egypt after his four-hundred-year absence, an ark reappeared. Pharaoh had vowed to destroy the Hebrew people by killing all their newborn males, but one mother put her baby in a "wicker ark" and launched him into the Nile River—an intimate reenactment of Noah's perilous water voyage with the few surviving members of all humanity.[1] Pharaoh's daughter discovered the tiny ark and bestowed an Egyptian name on its occupant—"Moses," which meant in the Egyptian language "one who is born."[2] The Egyptian princess raised him as her adopted son and unknowingly enlisted the services of his Hebrew mother as a wet-nurse. Thus Moses had a mixed heritage—a child of Israel raised as an Egyptian prince. His allegiance to the God of the Hebrew people was not beyond question.

Notwithstanding his mixed heritage, God chose Moses as the instrument for his re-engagement with the children of Israel—though God did not announce this choice until Moses had reached maturity, had killed an Egyptian overseer who was abusing a Hebrew slave, and had fled from Egypt to avoid Pharaoh's retaliation. Only after narrating these events, Exodus relates that God "heard the moaning" of the Israelites. (Indeed, Moses's first recorded expression in the biblical text was "crying" in his wicker ark—an utterance of some special significance in light of the biblical convention regarding first direct quotations.[3]) Presumably the Israelites had been suffering for a long time and had previously "cried out," but it was not until this moment that "their plea from the bondage went up to God [and] God remembered His covenant with Abraham, with Isaac, and with Jacob. And God saw the Israelites, and God knew."[4]

God then revealed himself to Moses from inside a burning bush. It is not clear exactly what God knew that led him to this self-revelation, but something in the preceding narrative about Moses either reminded God of his long-prior commitment or demonstrated to him that the time had come to honor this commitment. Moses, it seems, was the right man in the right place at the right time. With his appearance, we come to a new phase, a more explicit and bolder phase, in humanity's effort to apply its own norms of good conduct to God. We also see God considering whether to comply with these norms and to treat at least one man, if not all mankind by implication, as his moral equal.

What then was it about Moses that caught God's attention? It was more than his similarity to Noah on the ark, though that may have initially attracted God's notice. There are also some parallels, but even more important differences, between Abraham and Moses. The most striking similarity is revealed in the name that Moses gave his first son, Gershom, which means, Moses said, "A sojourner have I been in a foreign land."[5] As Robert Alter points out, this is the meaning if the name is broken into two parts, *ger* for "sojourner" and *sham* for "there," but the "verbal root of the name *g-r-sh* would appear to refer to banishment."[6] Abraham had referred to himself in the same terms, as a "sojourner and settler," when seeking to purchase a burial site for his wife, Sarah.[7] I speculated earlier that the sparse biographical details that Genesis gives us about Abraham's life before God called him would support the proposition that he saw himself as banished, condemned like Cain to be a "restless wanderer on the earth" because of some responsibility he felt for his younger brother's death, and that God's promise to Abraham involved the possible revocation of his banishment.

Moses had also effectively been banished from his home in Egypt because he had killed a man. In some sense, the Egyptian overseer whom Moses killed was his brother, at least by adoption. But the Exodus narrator clearly described Moses as seeing the overseer "striking a Hebrew man of his brothers." Moses's act suggests two possibilities— that he had made a choice about his essential identity as a brother to the Hebrews rather than to the Egyptians, or that he saw himself as brother to both men (in this sense, to all men) and acted to stop one of his brothers from abusing the other. A second episode immediately followed: "the next day" Moses saw two Hebrew men "brawling, and he said to the one in the wrong, 'Why should you strike your fellow?'"[8] Again, there are two possible interpretations here: Moses may be asserting that brothers have a special obligation not to strike one another, or he may be applying a universalized standard of justice in accusing "the one in the wrong" of striking this man who happened to be his brother, his "fellow."

The conventional reading of these encounters is that Moses was displaying a firm connection with his Hebrew kinsmen, notwithstanding his upbringing and status in Pharaoh's house, and that he intended to protect his kinsmen as such from abuse at the hands of Egyptians and one another. This may be the best reading; it may be anachronistic even to entertain the possibility that a more universal standard of justice lay behind Moses's actions. But the ambiguity that I read in these passages would correspond to an ambiguity in God's purposes in renewing his commitment to the children of Israel—either that he was acknowledging a special relationship with them based on his promises to their forefathers or that he meant to renew this special relationship so that they would become his instrument toward asserting his universal jurisdiction over all of creation. The ambiguity responds, that is, to the question whether God saw himself as a tribal deity or as the sole ruler of the universe. Moses's status as both an Israelite by birth and an Egyptian prince by adoption may have attracted God's attention because God was not interested in answering the pleas of the enslaved Hebrews if his intervention conveyed only a tribal preference, that he had a more exalted idea of himself which Moses was peculiarly well-suited to represent.

Of these two episodes of Moses's response to the Egyptian overseer and the brawl between two Hebrews, his first recorded words occur in the second. In the first account he did not admonish the Egyptian on behalf of the Hebrew slave; he killed the man without a word, and only after looking "this way and that" to make sure that his action was not observed. His first quoted words, upon encountering the two Hebrews fighting in the second episode, were "Why should you strike your fellow?" This exclamation was addressed, as the Exodus narrator tells us, "to the one in the wrong." In the first episode, Moses's wordless action reflects a kinship with Abraham's first recorded words; Moses, that is, was fearful for his own safety should anyone see him killing the overseer, as Abraham's first words had revealed his fear that he would be killed unless his wife, Sarah, pretended to be his sister. Abraham's first words denied his relationship and led to the unjust infliction of punishment on Pharaoh, an innocent party whom Abraham had deceived. Moses's first recorded words distinguished him from Abraham. In this second episode, Moses was seemingly heedless of his own safety; his first words invoked the obligation of just conduct that followed from the existence of a relationship (whether arising from a special tribal connection or from human fellowship).

By his first words, Moses distinguished himself not only from Abraham but even more pointedly from Cain. His question to the wrongful actor—"Why should you strike your fellow?"—is evocative of God's question to Cain, "Where is your brother Abel?" And the brawling Hebrew's retort to Moses's intervention underscored this connection. The

Hebrew responded, "Who set you as a man prince and judge over us?" As the Hebrew brawler intuited, Moses was taking the part that God had played when he challenged Cain's killing of his younger brother. (And, unlike Abraham, Moses himself was the younger brother in his family of origin—Miriam and Aaron were his elder siblings.)

The Hebrew brawler continued in his retort, "Is it to kill me that you mean as you killed the Egyptian?" Moses thus saw that his prior act had been discovered, and the narrator tells us that "Pharaoh heard of this thing and he sought to kill Moses, and Moses fled from Pharaoh's presence."[9] But Moses did not go into exile because he had killed his brother for personal gain; he had killed his Egyptian brother to protect his Hebrew brother, and he had intervened against the brawling Hebrew for the same reason. This is another way that Moses differs from Cain and, as I have suggested, also from Abraham. According to my reading, it is possible that Abraham was never able to persuade himself that he deserved an end to his exile—and also possible that God could never shed his misgivings about Abraham's entitlement, as evidenced by his continual testing of Abraham. But these doubts would not apply to Moses, and God could see that he would not encounter the same difficulties that had appeared with Abraham or Cain. Moses was living in exile, but not because of some wrongful act on his part. Precisely because his banishment from Egypt was unjust, there was no prospect that he could obtain remission from Pharaoh, the perpetrator of the injustice. If Moses wanted to end his status as a "sojourner in a foreign land," he could do so only if he could find a new homeland with a just ruler.

Did God qualify under these criteria? It may seem strange to pose this question. The conventional question for biblical interpreters has been whether God's choice of an interlocutor qualified by his standards. In the Genesis narrative, only Jacob had the temerity to demand that God meet his criteria before he would pledge his allegiance, and the relationship that followed was not a model of success on either side. During the Israelites' enslavement in Egypt, God had removed himself entirely from any protective involvement with Jacob's extended progeny.

With Moses's appearance, God decided to renew his engagement with humanity. But at the outset of their direct relationship, it was not clear that Moses was interested, and his visible holding back carried a strong implication that he was applying his own criteria about the worth of this relationship. Unlike Jacob, Moses did not insist on terms of personal advantage, but unlike God's previous interlocutors —Adam, Noah, Abraham, and Isaac—Moses did not appear unquestioningly to accept God's direction. He visibly kept his own counsel.

If we follow the unfolding relationship between Moses and God, we can see that God had introduced a new turn in his approach to humanity. His initial engagements had rested on the premise that humanity was good—a description that seemed unremarkable and effortlessly deserved in the first creation account and was transmuted in the second account by the command to Adam, Cain, and Noah to be good and avoid evil. With Abraham, God took a different approach. He did not insist on goodness as a prior condition for any relationship but was prepared to extend forgiveness for past wrongdoing as a prelude to goodness. Moses, however, did not appear to need forgiveness for any real or imagined offense. In his relationship with God, if closely examined, the issue appeared to emerge whether God would be forgiven by Moses for his abandonment of the children of Israel during their four centuries of enslavement.

The initial hint of Moses's independent stance toward God appeared in the very first moment of their direct relationship. In all his previous relationships, God had spoken directly to his interlocutors, but he chose to appear in an indirect and mysterious form in his first contact with Moses. As Moses was herding a flock of sheep in "the wilderness," he encountered a bush "burning with fire" and yet "not consumed," and he stopped to investigate this phenomenon. He thought, "Let me, pray, turn aside that I may see this great sight, why the bush does not burn up."[10] It was only then, after seeing that this burning bush had intrigued Moses, that God called to him.

There is an oddity here. It may be that, because of his long absence from interactions with humanity generally or the children of Israel specifically, God believed that Moses would not recognize his voice; but even so, if God was trying to stage a grand reappearance, opening the heavens and shaking the earth might have seemed a more awe-inspiring re-entry than his self-presentation in a burning bush. And though Moses was intrigued by the bush, it nonetheless seemed that God had some difficulty in getting Moses's direct attention. He called him twice, "Moses, Moses!" We have seen this formula before in Genesis—when God had to call Abraham twice to stop him from killing Isaac and when God called Jacob twice in his old age after Joseph had been rediscovered in Egypt. In both of these instances, the two men had reason to think that God had abandoned them after extended prior dealings with him. But Moses had no history of a direct relationship with God.

Moses did, however, respond to God's repetition of his name. "Here I am," he said, in the same formulaic response that Abraham had used. God then instructed Moses to remove his sandals because he stood "on holy ground" and introduced himself as the God of Moses's ancestors, Abraham, Isaac, and Jacob. Moses "hid his face, for he was afraid to look upon God."[11] God then told him that he had "seen the abuse" of his people in Egypt, that he had "heard its pain" and had "come down to rescue it . . . and bring it to a goodly and spacious land, to a land flowing with milk and honey." God instructed Moses to "go . . . to Pharaoh, and bring My people the Israelites out of Egypt."[12]

In this encounter, Moses may have been afraid—but he was not so fearful that he immediately acceded to God's direction. In fact, he repeatedly resisted in the course of an extended interchange with God. At the first direction, Moses responded with apparent humility—"who am I" to do all these things? God responded, "I will be with you." Moses replied that when the Israelites asked him God's name, "what shall I say to them"—an apparently indirect refusal, since only Jacob had previously presumed to ask God's name, and he had been directly refused.[13] But God replied with an incantation, *"Ehyeh-'Asher-'Ehyeh . . .* Thus shall you say to the Israelites, *Ehyeh* has sent me to you." This mysterious name has variously been translated as "I-Am-That-I-Am" or "I-Will-Be-Who-I-Will-Be."[14] Whatever it means, this volunteered name was responsive to Moses's request.

But Moses still withheld his acceptance, saying, "But, look, they will not believe me."[15] God then instructed Moses to throw his staff onto the ground; it immediately became a snake "and Moses fled from it," whereupon God directed him to grasp its tail, Moses did so, and the snake became his staff again. Moses said nothing in response to this—a biblical formula for conveying resistance that we have seen before with Noah and Abraham. God next instructed Moses to put his hand in his bosom, whereupon God turned it white as snow and then restored it to flesh color. If, God observed, the Israelites were not convinced by Moses's re-enactment of "these two signs," then Moses should pour water from the Nile onto dry land and it would turn to blood.

But these displays didn't do the trick for Moses. Instead, he repeated his refusal, emphasizing his own unfitness for the enterprise. "Please, my Lord, no man of words am I, not at any time in the past nor now since You have spoken to Your servant, for I am heavy-mouthed and heavy-tongued." God responded sharply, "Now, go, and I Myself will be with your mouth and will instruct you what to say." But Moses still resisted, "Please, my Lord, send, pray, by the hand of him You would send"—in other words, send someone else.

Finally God got angry: "And the wrath of the Lord flared up against Moses." But even then God drew back and became conciliatory. He immediately reassured Moses, "Is there not Aaron the Levite, your brother? I know that he can indeed speak . . . and I will instruct you both what you should do, and he will speak for you to the people." God then capped this directive with an extraordinary image: he said to Moses, Aaron "will be a mouth for you, and you, you will be for him like a god." At this, Moses offered no further resistance and prepared to return to Egypt to take up God's command.

This prolonged negotiation between God and a human being has only one precedent—the bargaining between God and Abraham about the justifiable circumstances for destroying Sodom and Gomorrah. In that interchange, God told Abraham of his plan and Abraham repeated his resistance to that plan six times, beginning with the hypothetical presence of fifty innocents, then forty-five, forty, thirty, twenty, and finally ten, when he puzzlingly stopped. Moses's refusals are not as easy to enumerate, but if we read the interchange carefully, Moses refused to accede seven times, once more than Abraham. Five of Moses's refusals were stated outright; two others were directly implied by his silence after God's staff-to-snake trick and then again after his blanching of Moses's hand.

Moses did not explicitly invoke norms of justice as Abraham had done. All of Moses's refusals were based on his claimed inability to accomplish the assigned task. Abraham himself had encircled his invocations with acknowledgment of his subordinate status, his awareness of his presumptuousness in challenging God. But just as Abraham's substantive message contradicted his protestations of humility, Moses's humble protestations were at odds with his boldness in refusing God's directive. Moses, moreover, showed a capacity to persist in resisting God that Abraham did not display. Moses resisted at the moment of his first encounter with God, unlike Abraham's first encounter when he accepted God's directive without question or hesitation, as if he were automatically obedient. And even though Abraham had seemed to be a bold advocate for justice in Sodom and Gomorrah, his apparent acceptance of the killing of ten innocent people, his failure to carry through the principle of justice that he had invoked, itself raised questions about his capacity for sustained resistance to God. Abraham resisted six times but stopped when, by the norm of justice he invoked, he should have resisted a seventh time. But Moses resisted seven times. If Abraham's relenting after his sixth iteration was a failure of his moral righteousness—of his willingness to insist that God rigorously observe norms of justice or of his confidence in his moral standing to make this objection—then Moses's readiness to make this seventh iteration was a sign of his superior rectitude.

Was Moses's resistance based on an implicit norm of justice? There was indeed a question of justice hovering over God's interaction with Moses—the righteousness of God's prolonged absence, his apparent disregard for the suffering of the children of Israel, and his promises to Abraham, Isaac, and Jacob that their descendants would be a great nation, living in a land of their own. Though Moses remonstrated with God that he was not a fit instrument for rescuing the Israelites from oppression, there was an unspoken question between them about God's reliability in this enterprise. The objections that Moses ascribed to the Israelites rather than to his own incapacities are virtually explicit on this score. Thus when Moses asked God's name, he said it was for this reason: "Look, when I come to the Israelites and say to them, 'The God of your fathers has sent me to you,' and they say to me, 'What is his name?,' what shall I say to them?"[16] But why would the Israelites demand this extra information unless they no longer recognized the God of their fathers? The name itself, moreover, would be no real assistance in this recognition, since their fathers never knew God's name and only Jacob had even asked (as God himself subsequently acknowledged[17]).

Thus the underpinning of Moses's objection is that the Israelites don't know this God who claims some genetic connection with them. This concern is even more explicit in Moses's subsequent objection, "But, look, they will not believe me nor will they heed my voice, for they will say, 'The Lord did not appear to you.'"[18] In other words, Moses asserted that the Israelites would say, "This Lord whom you claim to have seen has not appeared to us, why should he have appeared to you?" Or, to put it yet another way, "Where has this Lord been all these years?"

God's responses to this question with the three parlor tricks—staff-to-snake, ruddy-to-blanched flesh, Nile water-to-blood—were themselves patently unconvincing. In the event, when Moses had accepted God's mission and confronted Pharaoh by performing two of these tricks and a third bringing an inundation of frogs from the Nile, Pharaoh's sorcerers were able to duplicate them with no difficulty.[19] The God who was powerful enough to create the world surely had inherent capacity to outperform Pharaoh's sorcerers at the outset. Did God hold back from displaying his true strength because of a guilty conscience—or, if that is too impious to imagine, then perhaps because a true display of his awesome power would too insistently raise the question for Moses and the Israelites generally, if God is so strong, why was he so long in coming to our assistance?

Whatever God's reasons for offering inadequate signs of his strength, the ease with which Pharaoh's sorcerers duplicated his special effects surely made a mockery of God's claim to vast powers—and provokes the thought that God himself was inviting this mockery, at least initially. When he finally hit upon a plague that Pharaoh's sorcerers could not imitate—the swarms of lice that infected man and beast—the subject-matter of the plague and its uncomfortable consequences were hardly terrifying or awe-inspiring (though God's ultimate plague, the slaying of Egyptian first-borns, surely qualified on this score).[20]

God thus held himself back from displaying his true might—even from the moment of his first appearance to Moses in a mere bush rather than through explosions of luminous thunder on a mountain-top, as he later would present himself at Sinai, or even as a booming disembodied voice from the heavens, as he had appeared to Abraham, Isaac, and Jacob. Since God could presumably present himself in any way that he wished—as implied by his very name, "I-Will-Be-Who-I-Will-Be"—why would he choose this humble guise in his initial approach to Moses?

The clue to an answer, I believe, is in God's ultimate charge to Moses, his deal-clincher after Moses's seven refusals: "You will be for [your brother Aaron] like a god." Immediately before Moses's first confrontation with Pharaoh, God enlarged upon this designation, "See, I have set you as a god to Pharaoh, and Aaron your brother will be your prophet."[21] The Hebrew word for god in both instances is *'elohim,* which is one way, though not the only way, that God himself is identified in the biblical text. Although its meaning also extends to angelic figures and even eminent humans, this designation of Moses as a god in his dealings with other human beings is itself unprecedented, notwithstanding the eminence of other humans who had preceded him.[22] It is as if God was seeking a human being who would be more of an equal toward him than he had previously obtained with the patriarchs or their predecessors, and God's modest self-presentation to Moses might have been part of this pursuit, his purposefully humbling himself before Moses.

God had tried this course with Abraham in his advance disclosure of his intentions about destroying Sodom and Gomorrah, but Abraham was not able to take full advantage of the invitation. Jacob came closer to this mark in his wrestling match with God; its ending in a draw connoted a kind of equality between the two, and the mysterious man even congratulated Jacob that he had "striven with God and men, and won out." But God's designation of Moses as a god seemed to imply less an endless struggle, as with Jacob, than a cooperative relationship between equals.

With Moses, we can see a further development of God's wishes in his relationship with humans—from easily available companions for his evening strolls in Eden, to Noah whose fragrant offerings pleased him, to the patriarchs whom he blessed but who responded with uncertainty and suspicion to his overtures, toward Moses, whom he treated with more obvious equality. But this development is not a straight path for God. Throughout its course, as described in the biblical text, God remained deeply ambivalent about whether he wanted any relationship at all, notwithstanding his prior dealings with humanity, including his initial acts of creation. The negative side of this ambivalence was clearly predominant (almost to the point of God's entirely dismissing any future relationship) in the Flood and his subsequent doubts about Noah. God's withdrawal from direct interaction with Jacob's sons, followed by his total disappearance during the enslavement in Egypt, testified to the continued strength of the negative pole in him. With this tension in God's very constitution, we might expect some ambivalent response from him following the extraordinary move toward greater intimacy and equality with Moses than he had ever previously allowed any human being. God may have disappointed the reasonable prior expectations of humanity, given his explicit covenants with them. But God remained entirely predictable, entirely true to our expectations that he would be ambivalent about his relationship with Moses as he had been in all his earlier dealings with humanity.

God's ambivalence made a dramatic appearance immediately after he designated Moses as "like a god" in relation to his brother Aaron. Moses then took leave from his father-in-law in Midian to take up God's appointed mission; as Exodus tells us, however, "it happened on the way at the night camp that the Lord encountered him and sought to put him to death." Zipporah, Moses's wife, saved him by circumcising their son and touching the foreskin to the son's or Moses's feet, saying, "Yes, a bridegroom of blood you are to me."[23] Robert Alter observes that "this elliptic story is the most enigmatic episode in all of Exodus."[24] It has inspired reams of commentary, and I do not pretend to have grasped the thread that will unravel this enigma. But it does seem to me unmistakable that God's seeking to kill Moses immediately after convincing him to enter a sustained partnership—not simply instructing him but virtually pleading with him—conveys a deep ambivalence on God's part about the relationship he had just worked so resolutely to establish. It is as if God were reasserting his claim to unquestioned dominance over Moses just moments after he had ceded this claim and had endorsed something closer to equal (or perhaps even subordinate) status.

But as quickly as this ambivalence had appeared, as grimly and mysteriously as it was appeased by the ritual blood-letting, it quickly vanished. We will see it ultimately reappear, I believe, when God ends Moses's life just outside entry into the promised land. But in the forty-year interval between God's initial threat and his ultimate infliction of death on Moses, the most extraordinary relationship between God and man—the closest to a sustained relationship of equals between God and humanity anywhere in the Hebrew Bible—unfolds between God and Moses.

At the outset of their relationship at the burning bush, Moses "hid his face, for he was afraid to look upon God."[25] But by the time Moses had led the Israelites to the Sinai mountain, the Exodus narrator observed that "the Lord would speak to Moses face to face, as a man speaks to his fellow."[26] Still later, when Miriam and Aaron rebelled against Moses's leadership, God rebuked them and emphasized his unique relationship with Moses, saying that if Moses were simply his prophet then only "in a vision to him would I be known, in a dream would speak through him. [But] not so my servant Moses, in all my house is he trusted. Mouth to mouth do I speak with him, and vision, and not in riddles, and the likeness of the Lord he beholds."[27]

What might explain this intimacy, this willingness on God's part to speak directly to Moses, not in riddles, but as "a man speaks to his fellow"? God clearly welcomed this fellowship; indeed, he punished Miriam for challenging Moses's special status by "blanching" her skin "as snow"—precisely the condition he inflicted on Moses as one of his magic tricks when Moses refused to accept God's offer of a relation-ship.[28] But God had previously cultivated a special relationship with Adam, Noah, and Abraham which never attained the intimacy that God ultimately found with Moses. How did this new intimacy come about?

The key to understanding, I believe, is in an interchange between God and Moses immediately before the Exodus narrator first noted their face-to-face relationship as such. Moses had been in God's presence on Mount Sinai for "forty days and forty nights" receiving the stone tablets of the Covenant that God was setting out for the people of Israel.[29] As this time elapsed, "the people saw that Moses lagged in coming down," and—much like Noah at the end of this identical time period—they feared that they had been abandoned. The Israelites then demanded that Aaron make other gods to guide them, "for this man Moses who brought us up from the land of Egypt, we do not know what has happened to him," and the idol of the Golden Calf was erected.[30] God saw this and directed Moses immediately to descend to confront the Israelites with their wrongdoing. "It is a stiff-necked people," God said. "And now leave Me be, that My wrath may flare against them, and I will put an end to them and I will make you a great nation."[31] But Moses did not leave; he remained "in the presence of the Lord" and urged God not to destroy the Israelites.

There are salient differences between Moses's plea and Abraham's pleadings with God against the destruction of Sodom and Gomorrah. God solicited Abraham's views, whereas here he directs Moses to leave his presence; Abraham surrounded his pleadings with elaborate protestations of deference, whereas Moses spoke directly and plainly— "not in riddles" but as "a man speaks to his fellow."

Both Abraham and Moses did invoke an ideal of justice in their pleadings. Abraham relied on the norm that innocent people should not be punished with the guilty, but Moses relied on a different norm, perhaps because he saw that there were no innocents among the idolatrous Israelites. Moses spoke, moreover, at considerable length in making his case: "Why, O Lord, should your wrath flare against Your people that You brought out from the land of Egypt with great power and with a strong hand? Why should the Egyptians say, 'For evil He brought them out, to kill them in the mountains, to put an end to them on the face of the earth'? Turn back from Your flaring wrath and relent from the evil against Your people. Remember Abraham, Isaac, and Israel Your servants, to whom You swore by Yourself and spoke to them, 'I will multiply your seed like the stars of the heavens, and all this land that I said, I will give to your seed, and they will hold it in estate forever.'"

There are two distinct arguments here. The first is an instrumental argument: how would it look to the Gentiles, what kind of reputation would you have if your purported rescue turned out only to be a prelude to your destruction of these people? If you were strong enough to bring them out of Egypt, why weren't you strong enough to extract worshipful obedience from them? This argument bristles with Machiavellian overtones: a ruler must not appear weak or the world will disregard him.

Moses's second argument is more Kantian, a moral claim that God had made a promise to the patriarchs—"You swore by Yourself"—and that promises must be kept. But this moral claim can itself be understood as instrumentally based—an explicit invocation of the implicit criticism that Moses initially put forward about God's reliability after his long inattention to the suffering of the children of Israel. If you purport to rescue this people but then kill them, if you disregard all your prior promises, then who will ever trust you in the future? This may explain why Moses brushed aside God's offer without even acknowledging it—that he disbelieved the reliability of God's offer to start a new lineage with him, to kill the children of Abraham, Isaac, and Israel/Jacob, and then "make [Moses] a great nation." ("God would make me a great nation," Moses might have reflected, "until he changed his mind again and decided not to make me a great nation.")

At the end of Moses's pleading, God immediately "relented from the evil that He had spoken to do to His people."[32] Moses then returned to the Israelites and exploded in anger at them. He destroyed the stone tablets on which he had inscribed God's word and the Golden Calf as well; he berated Aaron for his role in this "great offense"; and he enlisted one of the tribes to exact retribution from the others, as a result of which three thousand men were killed. Moses then addressed the assembled people and did not pretend that all of the wrongdoers had been executed. "You," he said, "you have committed a great offense. And now I shall go up to the Lord. Perhaps I may atone for your offense."[33]

Returning to God, Moses took a different stance. He did not say that he had avenged the insult that the Israelites had inflicted on God or that idolatry had been cleansed from them. This plea had a different tone from his prior argument against their destruction. "I beg You," Moses said. "This people has committed a great offense, they have made themselves gods of gold. And now, if You would hear their offense . . ." At this point the clause is left incomplete, as if Moses could not find words, could not articulate the reasons God should choose to pardon the Israelites' offense. Then Moses continued, "and if not, wipe me out, pray, from Your book which you have written."

This is an extraordinary passage. Why would Moses ask that if God chose to destroy all the children of Israel, this destruction should also fall on him? He was certainly not involved in their idolatry, and he was angry, even vengeful, toward them because of their offense. And yet, as revealed by this passage, he saw himself as so intimately connected to them that he asked God not to exempt him from their destruction. We had seen the seeds of this connection in Moses's first recorded actions—his interventions to protect the two slaves, one beaten by an

Egyptian, the other by a fellow-slave. These actions may have been motivated by an empathic identification with the victims because they
were Israelites or simply because they were vulnerable to the overween-
ing strength of their aggressor, as especially suggested by the second
case. In these instances, however, Moses was cautiously self-protective;
before attacking the Egyptian overseer, he "turned this way and that [in
order to see] that there was no man about," and after interrupting the
Hebrew brawler, he was struck by fear and fled when he learned that
the man knew of his previous assault against the overseer.[34] But when
he spoke to God on Mount Sinai, Moses's empathic identification with
the vulnerable Israelites was virtually complete; no matter what the
risk to his personal safety, he chose to share their fate.

   In making this choice, Moses did more than reject God's offer to
destroy the Israelites and establish him as the progenitor of a new nation. He refused to accept even the benefit of personal survival if the
Israelites were to be killed. Here we can see another possible difference
between Moses and Abraham: if Abraham felt guilt after his younger
brother's death because he gained a surrogate son or perhaps simply
because he had survived, Moses actively chose to avoid any burden of
guilt. But even more than this, Moses's choice meant that the underlying terms of his relationship with God were radically different from
Abraham's. Abraham may have accepted God's offer to become a great
nation because he understood it as a reprieve from the Cain-like curse
that had come to him because of his brother's death; or he may have
accepted the offer because he was ambitious; or he may have accepted
the offer because he was entirely obedient to God's will. But Moses's
rejection of God's offer and his willingness to die instead along with
the idolatrous Israelites reflected none of these motives. Moses had expressed his own independent judgment that God's destruction of the
children of Israel would not be just; if God took this course nonetheless, Moses would not accept any part in it. He was his own man, even
against God's will, even in God's awesome presence.

God might have reacted angrily, as he ultimately did during their first encounter when Moses repeatedly refused to accept his mission. Moses's explicitly enunciated reasons for that refusal were based on his personal shortcomings, although he may have also meant to convey suspicion about God's reliability in keeping his promises. On Mount Sinai, however, Moses was clearly willing to judge God's conduct and to find it morally imperfect.

And God did not respond angrily toward Moses. Quite the contrary: it was at the end of this exchange that the Exodus narrator observed, "And the Lord would speak to Moses face to face, as a man speaks to his fellow."[35] God accepted Moses's implicit but unmistakable claim that he was entitled to judge God's conduct. And even more than this, God then altered his conduct to conform to Moses's moral judgment.

This is apparent in their continued interchange about the consequences of the Israelites' blasphemy in worshiping the Calf. Though God relented from destroying the Israelites, he held onto his rage against them. He directed Moses to return to the Israelites and resume his leadership of them, but he himself refused to remain "in their midst" and instructed Moses to tell them, "You are a stiff-necked people. If but a single moment I were to go up in your midst, I would put an end to you." But Moses implored God to change his mind: "See, You say to me, 'Bring up this people,' yet You, You have not made known to me whom You will send with me. And You, You have said, 'I know you by name, and you have also found favor in My eyes.' And now, if, pray, I have found favor in Your eyes, let me know, pray, Your ways, that I may know You, so that I may find favor in Your eyes. And see, for this nation is Your people."[36]

The basis for this plea went beyond the principle of justice, of promise-keeping, that Moses had already invoked. This was a plea for intimacy: if you will not accompany me, then who will be with me? And if you want to be with me, if I "have found favor in Your eyes," then you cannot favor me alone but must share your presence with "this nation . . . Your people." God was clearly moved by this plea: "My presence shall go, and I will grant you rest. . . . This thing, too, which you have spoken I will do, for you have found favor in My eyes and I have known you by name."[37] God thus acceded for Moses's sake but his accession also conveyed his willingness to resume a relationship with the Israelites generally—not with any intimacy and certainly not with the hint of equal status that he had embraced with Moses, but a relationship nonetheless.

God directed Moses to carve two stone tablets "like the first ones . . . that you smashed" in response to the Israelites' idolatry. When Moses returned to the mountaintop, blank tablets in hand, this extraordinary event followed: "And the Lord came down in the cloud and stationed Himself with him there, and He invoked the name of the Lord. And the Lord passed before him and He called out: 'The Lord, the Lord! A compassionate and gracious God, slow to anger, and abounding in kindness and good faith, keeping kindness for the thousandth generation, bearing crime, trespass, and offense, yet He does not wholly acquit, reckoning the crime of fathers with sons and sons of sons, to the third generation and the fourth."

Moses immediately understood this grand proclamation as God's acceptance of his plea: "And Moses hastened and prostrated himself on the ground and bowed down. And he said 'If, pray, I have found favor in Your eyes, my Master, may my Master, pray, go in our midst, for it is a stiff-necked people, and you shall forgive our crime and our offense, and claim us as Yours.'"[38] The elaborate deference of Moses's response is not a retreat from the intimacy that he and God had shared on Sinai, but it connotes that Moses is seeking more than a personal relationship with God, that the moral criteria he had held out as the basis for evaluating God's conduct should apply not simply to God's relationship with him but to God's conduct generally—at least with his people, the Israelites, and perhaps even more universally.

God's proclamation of his self-image—"compassionate and gra-

cious . . . slow to anger, and abounding in kindness and good faith . . .
bearing crime, trespass, and offense"—had little resemblance to his
initial response to the Israelites' offense with the Calf, and it had no
direct relevance to Moses's personal situation unless his apparent presumption to judge God would be counted as an offense. God embraced
the virtues enumerated in his self-description in response to Moses's
invocation of them, and Moses invoked these virtues not for his personal gain but impartially on behalf of others.

In his first quoted statement in the Bible, Moses had challenged the
Hebrew wrongdoer with the question that echoed God's question to
Cain: "Why should you strike your fellow?" Cain's arrogant retort—
"Am I my brother's keeper?"—did not directly challenge God's authority to judge him, but it was disrespectful at the least. The Hebrew
wrongdoer was directly dismissive of Moses's authority: "Who set you
as a man prince and judge over us?"[39] God answered this question and
more on Mount Sinai; in effect, he said, "I set Moses as a man prince
and judge—and not only over his fellows' conduct but over my own."

The significance of God's proclamation and Moses's role in establishing the norm for judging God's conduct was underscored in a subsequent episode in the Israelites' unhappy wandering in the Sinai desert. After their repeated, bitter complaints, God said to Moses, "How
long will this people despise Me, and how long will they not trust Me,
with all the signs that I have done in their midst? Let me strike them
with the plague and dispossess them, and I shall make you a nation
greater and mightier than they." When God had threatened this destruction after the Golden Calf blasphemy, Moses had responded with
two objections: the Egyptians will view you as vindictive and powerless
to control your chosen people; and you will violate your promise to
Abraham, Isaac, and Jacob. This time Moses repeated the first objection—"And the nations who have heard rumor of you will say, saying,
'From the Lord's inability to bring this people to the land that He swore
to them, He slaughtered them in the wilderness.'"[40] In this objection,

Moses embedded a reference to the promise of a homeland that God had made. But he did not repeat in any direct way the objection that he voiced after the Calf incident, that destroying the Israelites would violate God's promise to the patriarchs.

This time Moses offered an entirely different objection: "Let the Lord's power, pray, be great, as you have spoken, saying, 'The Lord is slow to anger and abounding in kindness, bearing crime and trespass. . . .' Forgive, pray, the crime of this people through your great kindness and as You have borne with this people from Egypt till now." Moses appealed to God's own commitment to the principle of compassion. This was not a promise that God had made to the Israelites, past or present. This was not a promise he had made to Moses, though it arose in response to Moses's pleading. This was a promise that God had made to himself, a vision of himself as a compassionate judge of mankind. More boldly than Abraham, Moses—though uninvited by God—presumed to serve as the mnemonic rainbow for God. Moses was speaking to God's conscience. He was speaking as God's conscience.

Why did God make this promise to himself? It did not arise from any direct coercive threat that Moses made or could have made. The coercion was self-administered, but it arose from a power that God himself bestowed on Moses—a power that Moses could not extract from God but that seemed to arise from some internal compulsion beyond God's power to deny. The internal compulsion was God's wish for some kind of relationship with one man, Moses. God might have created mankind without any expectation of or wish for a continued relationship with anyone among his creation. Indeed, periodically in the biblical saga, God does fall back to this position, seeming to wash his hands of humanity and walk away. But something repeatedly draws him back—and then away again—and then back. His continuous impetus to form a satisfying relationship is as striking as his persistent reluctance to do so.

In this back and forth, God persistently comes up against a problem that he has created for himself: if he wants a relationship with human beings, then he is dependent on their response to him. This dependency exists no matter what kind of relationship God wants, so long as it is some kind of relationship. Even if God tries to reduce his dependency to zero by both threatening and actually exerting the overwhelming coercion that is readily available to him, he can dominate humanity only if it fears the worst that he can impose on it. By inviting God to kill him if he destroyed the Israelite people, Moses effectively informed God that fear would not be the basis for any future relationship between them. Moses was more explicit in setting out his own terms for any future relationship than anyone in the biblical saga with whom God had previously sought contact. God accepted Moses's terms and thus established the basis for a relationship of greater intimacy with mankind than he had ever before achieved.

CHAPTER SIX

Love Offered, Love Commanded

Moses and the Children of Israel

*T*HE INTIMACY BETWEEN God and Moses, as the Bible portrays it, is not simply a domestic love affair between two individuals. It is an aspirational model for God's relationship with the entire people of Israel—an aspiration sought not only by the populace alone but also by God himself.

To modern eyes, this may seem improbable, even bizarre—or terrifying and dangerous. How can one speak of an intimate relationship in which the participants number in the millions, except through a fascist fantasy of the masses' surrendering themselves to the will of one supreme leader? The fascist fantasy can indeed find some grounding in the biblical account. But before we draw out this possibility, we must first grasp the biblical narrative in its own terms, not in the distorted lens through which later commentators have insisted on viewing it.

The relationship that God offered to the people of Israel in the Sinai desert was directly parallel to the relationship that he sought with Moses. He did not present the relationship in identical terms; the simple problem of numbers of participants called for some presentational differences. The offered relationship on its face may resemble a feudal arrangement in which vassals acknowledge the suzerainty of their overlord, but understanding the biblical relationship as impersonal, as a

bureaucratic arrangement like the modern liberal conception of relations between citizen and state, misses a crucial aspect. At its core,
God's offer conveyed an interpersonal intimacy, a loving familial relationship.[1]

Numbers made a difference not only for God and the Israelites but
also for Moses in his relationship to the populace. Just a few months
after the Israelites escaped from Egypt across the Red Sea, Moses's
father-in-law, Jethro, paid a brief visit to their encampment and was
appalled at Moses's expenditure of energy with the masses. "What is
this thing you are doing for the people?" Jethro asked. "Why are you
sitting alone while all the people are poised over you from morning till
evening?" Moses explained that the people came to him with questions and disputes, and "I judge between a man and his fellow and I
make known God's statutes and His teachings."[2] At this time there were
more than six hundred thousand men among the Israelites; Jethro,
sensibly enough, told Moses that he had set himself an impossible
task and urged him to establish a bureaucratic structure for handling
these issues.[3] Moses promptly did so, dividing the population into
nested groups of thousands, hundreds, fifties, and tens with "chiefs" or
"judges" appointed over each grouping, while retaining for himself ultimate appellate authority for the "hard matters."[4]

Immediately after this interlude of domestic politics, God initiated
the drafting of a formal covenant with the people of Israel, using Moses as his intermediary. He instructed Moses to obtain, in effect, a preliminary commitment from the entire populace before proceeding to
the detailed drafting of a formal document—rather like popular endorsement to convene a constitutional convention while reserving the
question of ultimate ratification until later. Thus God instructed Moses to announce these terms to the Israelites: "You yourselves saw what
I did to Egypt, and I bore you on the wings of eagles and I brought you
to Me. And now, if you will truly heed my voice and keep My covenant,
you will become for me a treasure among all the peoples, for Mine is all

the earth. And as for you, you will become for Me a kingdom of priests and a holy nation."[5]

It is important to see what this mandate did say and didn't say. It didn't say to the people of Israel that they were obliged to obey God or to have any future relationship at all with him simply because he had led them out of Egypt. No debt was claimed to be owed for this service rendered. Indeed, in the preceding three months since the Exodus, the Israelites had shown remarkably little gratitude; they had grumbled repeatedly that they were thirsty or hungry or uncomfortable and had implied that rather than owing some duty to God, God owed them a duty of support because he had lured them from Egypt. God had responded by apparently accepting the support obligation, extracting water from the wilderness and sending manna from heaven.[6] When God subsequently offered his covenant, he did not cite these past favors as entailing any obligation to accept his offer. He cited them instead as evidence of his great power to bestow benefits on the people and a reason to trust his capacity to award bountiful gifts in the future.

Even more significant, God did not threaten destruction or even direct punishment if the people refused his offer. He implied, but didn't directly threaten, that the past benefits he had bestowed would dry up in the future—rather like a politician promising future benefits if the populace would vote for him but not threatening to retract past benefits. If some possibility of imposed loss lurked behind this sweet talk, God was nonetheless careful to avoid playing on the fears of the populace. He only accentuated the positive elements in his offer—and the central feature of this offer was a promise of future intimacy: "You will become for me a treasure among all the peoples . . . a kingdom of priests and a holy nation."

The appeal was successful. Moses conveyed God's words to "the elders of the people . . . and all the people answered together and said, 'Everything that the Lord has spoken we shall do.'"[7] But this was only the preliminary; now the hard work of draftsmanship would begin. Moses, still acting as intermediary, brought the people out from their encampment to the foot of Mount Sinai, where they remained as he ascended the mountain, into a cloud of fire, smoke, and trembling earth. God then dictated the Ten Commandments and an extensive series of stipulations that both followed from these initial commandments and extended beyond them. This enormous elaboration of commands—stretching from chapters 20 to 32 in Exodus—is strikingly different from God's prior covenant with Noah after the Flood, which comprised essentially two prohibitions about dietary restrictions and prohibition of murder; it is even more different from the covenant with the patriarchs, which explicitly involved only following God to the land he would show them. The copious details of God's directives in the covenant that he dictated to Moses themselves appeared to reflect the inherent bureaucratic demands of dealing with a huge population. But beneath this extensive statutory superstructure was a simple promissory base—a vow of favored intimacy in return for a pledge of fidelity.

The Israelites could not, however, sustain their initial endorsement of the terms of engagement. Their inability to wait longer than forty days and forty nights directly recalled Noah's plight as the Flood persisted, and their turning to the Golden Calf was as much a response to their sense of abandonment as it was a faithless act in violation of their prior agreement. God reacted with an enraged decision to destroy all the Israelites except for Moses; Moses, after dissuading God from this course, never told the Israelites of God's threat. It was as if he understood, better than God himself, that the kind of relationship God was seeking from the Israelites would be impossible if they feared destruction from him.

Moses agreed with God that the Israelites' turning to the Calf was a breach of the initial covenant that they had entered with him; this was the meaning that he conveyed to the Israelites when he smashed the stone tablets containing God's laws. Moses further understood that if a future relationship were possible between God and the Israelites, it would require a new beginning—and this was the implication of the civil war that Moses then launched among the Israelites: "Moses stood at the gate of the camp and said, 'Whoever is for the Lord, to me!' And the Levites gathered round him."[8] This might be understood as a plebiscite on the issue whether to renew the people's commitment to God's party. It was, of course, a plebiscite fought with weapons not ballots, but an exercise of chosen commitment lay beneath the warfare.

This was not the use of force by God, nor by Moses on God's behalf, to coerce commitment. It was force exerted between those who wanted to renew this commitment and those who opposed this course. In the event, the Levites killed three thousand men, while the great bulk of the populace remained passive. At the end of the open warfare, Moses instructed the rest that they had "committed a great offense [a]nd now I shall go up to the Lord. Perhaps I may atone for your offense."[9] Moses did not threaten to kill all those who had stood by the sidelines in the civil war, exempting only the Levites. Moses did not tell them that God had threatened to destroy all of them; by withholding this information, he implied to them that the issue before God was not whether they would have any future at all but whether God was still willing to have any future relationship with them or would instead cast them off to fend for themselves.

God was indeed willing to have a future relationship with the Israelites—but not, it appears, on the basis of their intrinsic merits nor even of any special attachment to them. It was apparently to preserve his relationship with Moses that God remained engaged with the Israelites. This was the implication of Moses's extraordinary act of atonement; he insisted that if God destroyed the Israelites as he had threatened, then he should also kill Moses. But God valued so much in his relationship with Moses that he was prepared to overlook the flagrant idolatry of the Israelites. The special intensity of this relationship was clearly revealed by the observation in the very next chapter of Exodus that "the Lord would speak to Moses face to face, as a man speaks to his fellow"—the most open expression of intimacy between God and a human being since the second creation, when God breathed life into Adam's nostrils.

God had offered a similar intimacy to the entire Israelite people when they first gathered at the foot of Mount Sinai just three months after leaving Egypt: "You will become a treasure for Me among all the peoples."[10] But unlike Moses, the entire people lacked the capacity to respond to God's invitation. They lacked the self-confidence to sustain the intimate connection when God seemed even momentarily away from them; they lacked what developmental psychologists call "object constancy," that is, the capacity to hold fast to and draw comfort from an internalized image of the nurturing parent when the parent herself is out of sight. But though God was angrily disappointed at the Israelites' incapacity, as revealed in their idolizing the Golden Calf, he did not abandon his wish for intimacy with them. He changed this wish, however, from an invitation to a command.

God's wish for intimacy was embedded and only implicit in the first commandment that he dictated to Moses on Mount Sinai: "You shall have no other gods beside Me."[11] After the trauma of the Calf, when God repeated his dictation, he elaborated the importance of this First Commandment to Moses: "You shall not bow to another god, for the Lord, His name is Jealous, a jealous God He is."[12] This was not an invitation but a demand for intimacy—a demand that God subsequently made even more explicit, as if his self-depiction as Jealous were not enough. Forty years later, when Moses stood before the Israelites as they were poised to cross the Jordan River into the promised homeland without him, Moses delivered an extended valedictory address essentially summarizing the essence of God's commandments. As he gestured across the river to the promised "land flowing with milk and honey," Moses proclaimed, "Hear, Israel, the Lord our God, the Lord is one. And you shall love the Lord your God with all your heart and with all your being and with all your might. And these words that I charge you today shall be upon your heart."[13]

The most notable, and even extraordinary, aspect to this commandment is that it is the first time that the obligation to love God appears in the text of the Bible. Through all of God's interactions with humanity in Genesis and throughout the forty-year course of his dealings with Israelites taken out of Egypt, the only explicit obligation had been that mankind must obey God and must fear him. Why did God wait so long to add the love commandment to this list? Was it because he wanted something different from mankind—perhaps voluntarily offered love—but had finally come to the realization that this would not be forthcoming? Did this realization come because God finally recognized that his raw power was so daunting, so overwhelming, that mankind could not disentangle itself from fear of him, no matter how intrinsically appealing, how lovable, he might seem? Or did God abandon his interest in voluntarily offered love, and shift to the oxymoronic alternative of compelled love, because he was unwilling to accept the possibility of unrequited love and the diminution of his independent power that a request for love necessarily entails?

The biblical text gives no direct answer to these questions. But this much is clear. When God offered his covenant to the Israelites at the foot of Mount Sinai, three months after the flight from Egypt, it was presented in a conditional, not a compulsory, form. "If you will truly heed My voice and keep My covenant, you will become for Me a treasure," God said—which clearly conveyed that he offered love and envisioned the possibility that the offer might be declined. This implication was confirmed by the next action of the entire Israelite people (perhaps speaking through their elders or perhaps directly), proclaiming their acceptance of God's offer: "Everything that the Lord has spoken we shall do."[14] Their subsequent breach with the Golden Calf did not signify that the voluntary terms of the relationship had disappeared;

through Moses's intermediation, they acknowledged the wrongfulness of their broken promise and asked God to renew his offer; God, persuaded by Moses to show kindness and compassion, complied with their request.

What, then, brought God essentially to rescind the voluntary terms of his covenant, to command rather than solicit love? There are hints, but only hints, in the biblical account that God became disenchanted first with the Israelites and then with Moses himself for interrelated reasons. This disenchantment led him to withdraw the promise of intimacy from both of them and replace it with a one-way command for love, a command indicating that God would accept love provided in compliance with his command but would not reciprocally return love.

It is easiest to understand why God would withdraw from the Israelites. From virtually the moment that Moses led them from Egypt, the Israelites complained—as the vernacular aptly would have described it, they bitched and moaned—and repeatedly insisted that they would have preferred to be left enslaved to Pharaoh. Notwithstanding God's forgiveness at Moses's strenuous urging after their abortive shift of allegiance to the Golden Calf, the Israelites' complaints returned and even escalated in intensity. God and Moses agreed that the Israelites were "a stiff-necked people," and ultimately both of them appeared worn down by the Israelites' constant carping. As often happens between parents, their refractory children drove a wedge between God and Moses.

The climactic moment in this falling out came some two years after the Exodus from Egypt, as related in the further account of the Israelites' journey in the book of Numbers. Chapter 11 of Numbers described the recurrent pattern of events: "And the people became complainers of evil in the ears of the Lord, and the Lord heard and His wrath flared ... [a]nd the people cried out to Moses, and Moses interceded with the Lord, and the fire sunk down."[15] But still the Israelites complained, "Who will feed us meat? We remember the fish we used to eat in Egypt for free, the cucumbers and the melons and the leeks and the onions and the garlic. And now our throats are dry. There is nothing save the manna before our eyes."[16]

This complaint is, of course, a stunning example of distorted memory and contemporary ingratitude. The Israelites were hardly starving; they had manna (as the Numbers narrative interjects, "its taste was like the creaminess of oil," and every night following the dew, more manna would descend from heaven[17]). But the Israelites nonetheless complained that their diet was boring and compared its plainness with their recollections of copious feasting "for free" in Egypt—notwithstanding that their feasts, if there had been any, did not descend on them from heaven but were provided by their slavemasters only in exchange for their arduous forced labor. Thus "Moses heard the people weeping . . . and the Lord's wrath flared fiercely, and in Moses's eyes it was evil."

There is some momentary ambiguity here about whether Moses viewed the people's weeping or the Lord's wrath as "evil," but Moses immediately resolves this ambiguity in a direct address to God: "Why have You done evil to Your servant, and why have I not found favor in Your eyes, to put the burdens of all this people upon me? Did I conceive all this people, did I give birth to them, that You should say to me, 'Bear them in your lap, as the guardian bears the infant,' to the land that You swore to their fathers?" Moses thus stated that it was not the weepy Israelites who were evil in his eyes; it was God himself who had "done evil" to Moses.

Moses had continually urged God to show compassion and kindness to the rebellious Israelites; God's repeated anger at them might seem in conflict with Moses's injunction and, on that basis, "evil" conduct by God. But this was not the heart of Moses's complaint here against God. As Moses immediately made clear, the "evil" was not God's anger as such but the fact that in his anger, God had effectively abandoned Moses to deal with the Israelites' complaints on his own. Thus Moses continued his complaint to God: "From where shall I get meat to give to all this people when they weep to me, saying, 'Give us meat that we may eat?' I alone cannot bear this people, for they are too heavy for me."[18]

This can be read as an awe-inspiring clash; it is the Bible's account, after all, of a direct charge of evil-doing aimed at God by Moses himself. But it is difficult to set aside the resemblances here to a standard plot line in a television sitcom: Dad comes home from the office, finds the kids in an uproar and the house unkempt, reacts angrily because he wants nothing more than relaxation after his long day working to keep this family going, and Mom's temper flares at Dad because he had left her alone to cope with these rotten kids.

Moses's anger, his domestic tantrum, then took a nasty, if predictable, turn: "And if thus You would do with me," he said to God, then "kill me, pray, altogether, if I have found favor in Your eyes, and let me not see my evil fate." But God did not return anger with anger; he was markedly kind and compassionate in response. "Gather for Me seventy elders of the people," he said, and "take them to the Tent of Meeting . . . [a]nd I shall come down and speak with you there and I shall hold back some of the spirit that is upon you and place it upon them. And they will bear with you the burden of the people and you yourself will not bear it alone."[19]

As charitable as this response to Moses was, God's anger still burned beneath this sweetly reasonable surface. He immediately continued in his directive to Moses: "And to the people you shall say: 'Consecrate yourselves for the morrow and you will eat meat for you wept in the hearing of the Lord, saying Who will feed us meat? For it was good for us in Egypt. And the Lord will give you meat and you will eat. Not one day will you eat and not two days and not five days and not ten days and not twenty days, but a full month of days, till it comes out of your noses and becomes a loathsome thing to you, inasmuch as you have cast aside the Lord who is in your midst and you have wept before him, saying, 'Why is it we have come out of Egypt?'"[20]

Again it is hard to resist the temptation to see this awesome directive as anything but a comic set-up: "You want meat? Of course I'll give you meat. And not just tomorrow but meat and meat and meat . . . until it comes out of your noses. That's what I'll give you for meat." But if this is comic, it carries a deadly serious undertone. Before his bitterly ironic reversal, God's prefatory statement that the Israelites had "wept in the hearing of the Lord" directly recalled God's reason for returning to the Israelites after four centuries' absence, "And God heard their moaning, and God remembered His covenant. . . . And God saw the Israelites and God knew."[21] Whatever God knew then, he knew now that he was enraged at this stiff-necked people.

Moses now knew this too. And he knew something more. God's rhetorical twist of the knife from his gift of meat to the cursed glut of meat was not directly stated to the Israelites; God directed Moses to deliver this message. How could Moses not suspect that this bitter message was also aimed at him, for his outburst to God, "From where shall I get meat to give to all this people, when they weep to me?" This outburst also directly recalled Moses's first encounter with God in the burning bush, with his explicit protestations of his own incapacities and his implicit doubts about the strength of God's professed commitment.

Moses himself might have heard this resemblance and apologized that the stress of the Israelites' persistent demands had led him back to his first introduction to God before their long intimate association had resolved all doubts for him. But Moses didn't do this. He might have appreciatively noted God's offer to speak to the elders about sharing his burden, but he said nothing about this; instead Moses responded only to God's bitter message directed at the Israelites, and he responded with a weak attempt at irony himself: "And Moses said, 'Six hundred thousand foot soldiers are the people in whose midst I am, and You,

You said, 'I shall give them meat and they will eat a month of days?' Will sheep and cattle be slaughtered for them and provide for them? Will all the fish of the sea be gathered for them and provide for them?"[22]

This sounds as if Moses were renewing his complaint rather than taking comfort from God's response, as if he were saying, "You claim to be 'in the midst' of this weeping people but you don't seem to understand my situation—you're up there and I'm down here and 'six hundred thousand foot soldiers are the people in whose midst I am.' How do you realistically, reliably propose to lift the burden you have imposed on me?" God's response to Moses was, "Will the Lord's hand be too short? Now you will see whether My word will come about or not."[23] God was not pleased with Moses's riposte.

God was not then prepared to abandon Moses or the Israelites. Even so, the first seeds of doubt about Moses's leadership were exposed in the next chapter of Numbers—doubts raised by his siblings, Miriam and Aaron. God overheard them complaining, though Moses himself apparently did not hear. God convened the three of them and reiterated his confidence in and intimacy with Moses—"Mouth to mouth do I speak with him, and vision, and not in riddles, and the likeness of the Lord he beholds."[24] God then punished Miriam in particular for her presumptuousness in challenging Moses, God's anointed. In the Numbers chapters that follow, God directed Moses to send scouts into Canaan, the land he had promised to the Israelites. The scouts returned with reports of giants living there, to which the Israelites responded with weeping and recriminations—"why is the Lord bringing us to this land to fall by the sword?"[25] God again reacted angrily at the Israelites' lack of faith and, as he had done earlier, proposed to destroy them all and make Moses "a nation greater and mightier than they." But again Moses dissuaded God from this course—relying significantly on God's earlier compassionate portrayal of himself. God tempered his forgiveness, however, with a directive that none of the Israelite adults would ever enter his promised land but would instead wander in the wilderness for an additional forty years.

The next five chapters of Numbers cover familiar territory: God dictated additional commandments on various matters to Moses for him to convey to the Israelites (chapter 15); a small group of Levites rebelled against Moses's authority and God assisted him by opening the earth to swallow the rebels (chapter 16); the Israelites generally complained at the harsh treatment of the rebels and God proposed to destroy them all except for Moses and Aaron; at Moses's direction, they atoned to God and he relented (but not until after he sent a scourge that killed 14,700 people) (chapter 17); and God resumed dictation of various commandments, first to Aaron alone (chapter 18) and then to Moses and Aaron together (chapter 19).

Chapter 20 seems to continue in this same vein. In the middle of this chapter an event occurs that is narrated in five short verses with the same flat reportorial tone as the immediately preceding chapters, and yet the event is altogether extraordinary. The chapter begins with the same old dance: the Israelites complained that they had no water and wished they had never left Egypt; Moses, accompanied by Aaron, appealed to God. God told Moses to take his staff, stand before the Israelites with Aaron, and "speak to the rock," which would yield water that God "shall bring forth." So far, just an ordinary day at the campsite.

Moses then did as God "had charged": he and Aaron gathered the assembly and Moses "said to them, 'Listen, pray, rebels! Shall we bring forth water from this rock?' And Moses raised his hand and he struck the rock with his staff twice and abundant water came out."[26] God then spoke to Moses and Aaron in the same routine tone that he had just used in chapter 15 to dictate instruction about how fringes should be tied on garments. But God's message was anything but routine. God said to Moses and Aaron, "Inasmuch as you did not trust Me to sanctify Me before the eyes of the Israelites, even so you shall not bring this assembly to the land that I have given them."[27] That's it. No parting of the earth, no fire and brimstone. Just a matter-of-fact announcement to Moses and his brother that God's relationship with Moses was at an end. And Moses said nothing in response to this announcement—no protest, no apology, not even an acknowledgment that an important event had just occurred. Though Moses's dealings with God would persist for some time, the divorce had been decreed.

This account raises two questions. The first, obvious question is: what was so wrong about Moses's conduct here that led God to bar him from entering the promised land along with the Israelites whom he had led? The second, less obvious question is: why did the biblical narrator present this decree in such an off-handed, seemingly casual way?

There is a conventional answer to the first question. Moses did not do exactly what God directed. God told him to "take the staff [and] speak to the rock," but instead Moses struck the rock with his staff twice and told the assembled people that "we"—apparently referring to himself and Aaron—would "bring forth water" from the rock, whereas God had clearly instructed Moses, "I shall bring forth water." Thus according to the conventional interpretation, Moses not only ignored God's specific directive but usurped God's rightful authority.

Strictly speaking, this is an accurate indictment. But it seems trivial nonetheless. When Moses stood at the Red Sea with the Egyptian army in fast pursuit, and the Israelites "cried out to the Lord" in fear, God said to Moses, "Why do you cry out to me? Speak to the Israelites, that they journey onward. As for you, raise your staff and stretch out your hand over the sea and split it apart."[28] At this critical moment, God was willing to have Moses appear as the active force in accomplishing miraculous events with water, events that saved the lives of the Israelites. On a later occasion, when "the people murmured against Moses" and complained of thirst, God was again willing to have Moses claim credit for its miraculous appearance: "Look," God said, "I am about to stand before you there on the rock in Horeb, and you shall strike the rock and water will come out from it and the people will drink."[29] In these instances, so far as the witnessing Israelites were concerned, God's authority and Moses's leadership were inseparably intertwined. God himself had envisioned this when he had originally proposed to Moses that he would convey divine instructions to Aaron, who would then speak to the people. "He," God said, "he will be a mouth for you, and you, you will be for him like a god. And this staff you shall take in your hand, with which you will do the signs."[30]

Perhaps Moses should have been alert to the variation in God's instructions to him on this later occasion, but it surely would have required extraordinary attentiveness for Moses to grasp that God was not reiterating his previous arrangement about striking the rock and claiming credit for the water's appearance but was instead rescinding that arrangement. This fact, moreover, that God's new directive was a reversal of his prior instructions is an important clue toward answering the second question, about the back-handed way that God's punishment of Moses suddenly appeared in the text. God had already rescinded his previous relationship with Moses in the very instruction he had issued. The reason for this rescission thus could not arise from the fact that Moses violated the new directive. The new directive was the rescission, regardless of whether Moses complied with it or violated it.

Something had already occurred, therefore, which led God to end his prior relationship with Moses, including the intimate intertwining of Moses's authority with his in the eyes of the Israelite people. I believe that God decided to rescind his relationship with Moses during their extended, dramatic encounter described in chapter 11 of Numbers—nine chapters before God announced his decision to Moses. (Indeed, Moses's violation of God's specific instructions in chapter 20 might have been purposeful, to reflect his own understanding that his intimate relationship with God had already been ended.)

The breach occurred in chapter 11 when Moses, for the first time, protested to God that the constant complaints of the Israelites had become "too heavy" for him to bear "alone" and that God had done "evil" to him in putting "the burden of all this people" on him. Before this, there had been a recurrent pattern of Moses complaining about the Israelites and seeking support from God, and responding to God's complaints about this intolerably stiff-necked people with pleas for restraint. But this time, Moses did not ask for God's support. He complained that God had failed him, had inflicted "evil" on him. He concluded, "if thus You would do with me, kill me, pray, altogether."[31] At the time, God seemed to ignore this request when he promised Moses that he could enlist the assistance of the seventy elders of the people.

Notwithstanding this sympathetic response, it is difficult to see how God would view Moses's hyperbolic wish for death as anything but an insult. He had already suggested an alternative that would have relieved Moses of the burdensome Israelites—that they might all be destroyed and Moses made the progenitor of a new, great (and presumably more pliant) nation. Moses had declined this offer. He had even insisted that he be killed if God decided to kill all the Israelites. This insistence, however, was clearly in the service of preserving the relationship with God both for himself and for the Israelite people. In Numbers chapter 11, however, Moses turned away from any continuing relationship with both God and the Israelites. Indeed, God subsequently renewed his offer of a new nation for Moses, in Numbers chapter 14, and Moses again refused it.[32] God thus was willing to commit himself to a continuing relationship with Moses, but Moses did not reciprocate.

This was a direct violation of the commandment that mankind "shall love the Lord your God with all your heart and with all your being and with all your might." But this commandment did not appear as such until Moses's speech to the Israelites at the very end of his life, as recorded in Deuteronomy.[33] Even so, God might have used Moses's renunciation as the occasion for announcing this command as the basis for Moses's punishment. He did not do so, and the reasons for his reticence are implicitly conveyed in the brief explanation that he did provide for barring Moses from the promised land—"inasmuch as you did not trust Me to sanctify Me before the eyes of the Israelites." Moses's offense was thus portrayed not as withholding love from God but as withholding "trust" and failing "to sanctify" him in public. Neither of these attributes depends on Moses for its existence; God can be trustworthy without Moses's acknowledgment of this trait, God can be holy though Moses refuses to sanctify him. But God cannot be loved by Moses unless Moses loves him.

The conventional account thus has a strong basis, that Moses's offense was acting as if he had as much power as God by following his own path, rather than God's instruction, to extract water from the stone. But this conventional account proves more than its pious proponents would like. The fact is that Moses's disobedient course for extracting water actually succeeded. "Abundant water" did emerge from the rock after Moses struck it twice with his staff rather than speaking to it as God had commanded.[34] The pious might say that this occurred only because God willed it, notwithstanding Moses's arrogant pretension. But why would God have permitted this?

Here is one possible reason. There were two audiences for Moses's deed, the Israelite people and Moses himself. The public audience could not know that Moses had obtained water in defiance of God's commands; indeed, Moses's conduct exactly followed his previous practice, much earlier in their wanderings, when he had struck the rock and water flowed. Moses alone would know that he had violated God's instructions, and his success might have surprised him, because it showed that he was as powerful as God in his capacity to extract water from a stone. And Moses would indeed be more powerful than God, if God wanted love from him and Moses withheld it.

God's subsequent formulation of an obligation, a command, to love him does not convey any acknowledgment of superior power in those who choose to violate this command. The commandment conveys only that God will punish violators; it does not imply that he needs their love or is in any way diminished by their disobedience. But God wanted unforced love from Moses. Strolling in the Garden of Eden, it seemed that he wanted unforced love from Adam and Eve when he called out for their company but was disappointed. When he considered destroying Noah along with the rest of humanity, and then found that he took pleasure in the fragrance of Noah's offering, God may have come to a clear acknowledgment in his own mind of his wish for a continuous relationship with humans. This was the implication of his vow to himself never again to destroy all humanity; he didn't reveal this vow to Noah, however, but only offered the qualified assurance that he would never again bring destruction by flood. God may have withheld his private thoughts from Noah in the same way that Noah didn't want his sons to see him naked and vulnerable. But the very fact that he made any promise at all to Noah—that he purported to bind his own future freedom of action—was a sign, clearer than the rainbow, that he was prepared to diminish his own power in order to sustain a relationship with humanity for the future.

In his dealings with Abraham God expressed this same convoluted goal of binding himself in order to sustain a future relationship—by making promises and then living by those promises. God subordinated himself to human judgments of his justice and righteousness (in his exchange with Abraham about the destruction of Sodom and Gomorrah) while at the same time he withheld any explicit acknowledgment that he was binding himself and thereby diminishing his power (so that Abraham remained uncertain to the end of his life about whether God had saved Lot and Ishmael or whether his own paternal relationship with Isaac survived the ordeal that God had inflicted on them both). Isaac and Jacob were unlikely candidates for God's amorous designs—the former was too passive and needy himself, the latter too narrowly focused on self-aggrandizement.

But Moses was different. In his relationship with God, Moses coupled fearless honesty with companionship, even intimacy, but he never offered unquestioning obedience. And God reciprocated by displaying his willingness to defer to Moses's independent judgment more openly than he did for anyone before or after him in the entire corpus of the Hebrew Bible. The impetus for this shift can be readily deduced from the gradual evolution of God's relationship with Moses. The intimacy between God and Moses was not self-sustaining. For reasons that were never clearly stated, God persisted in offering intimacy to Moses. But Moses did not reciprocate with unconditional love. At various times in their dealings, Moses made clear to God that his loyalty depended on whether he approved of God's conduct—not toward himself (and this absence of self-seeking may have been one of the traits that attracted God's wish for intimacy with him), but toward the people of Israel.

God did not initially find it burdensome to comply with Moses's conditional loyalty and the implicit judgments underlying that conditionality. Moses's insistence that God's essence was loving kindness was intrinsically attractive to God. He appeared to accept Moses's invocation of this trait not as an external constraint on his conduct but instead as a prized depiction of himself—in the way that a lover's admiration can enhance the self-esteem of the beloved. This is what it can mean for one lover to be made "in the image" of the other as the first creation put it, or for two lovers to "become one flesh" as in the second.

At the beginning of their engagement, God was more interested than Moses in forging a relationship. The exact terms of the relationship that God wanted were not, however, clear. He wanted a human agent to lead the Israelites from Egypt, and Moses's upbringing and character seemed to equip him for this role. God may have also seen the possibility of intimate companionship with Moses from the beginning, but if he did, God also appeared deeply ambivalent about whether he wanted this. There is no other way to explain his murderous assault on Moses immediately after he had exerted such effort in persuading/imploring/demanding that Moses accept his mission. The ritual that saved Moses—"a bridegroom of blood by the circumcising," as Zipporah described it—conveyed intimacy, violence, and deference to God in the same gesture. But if God was appeased by this apparent act of obeisance by Moses's wife on his behalf, and if he was pleased by the intimate companionship that he and Moses subsequently experienced, and if some measure of acknowledged equality was a defining element of the relationship that they came to—if all this were true, nonetheless God was not ultimately satisfied with their relationship.

Perhaps in response to Moses's outburst about the "evil" inflicted on him by the burdensome leadership of the Israelites, God concluded that Moses's explicit wish for release through death was a unilateral breach of their relationship. God's mollifying response to Moses's outburst conveyed that God was eager to sustain their relationship—more eager than Moses, who was prepared to welcome death instead; and perhaps, as God reflected on this misfit between their motives, he concluded that he had come to need Moses more than Moses needed him, that he had become dependent on Moses in a way that was intolerable to him.

But if God was troubled that Moses had threatened to abandon him and then troubled in turn at his own disturbance, Moses himself seemed to have had the same picture of his relationship with God. Moses had not simply complained that the weight of leadership was too much for him; the "evil" that God had inflicted was to bestow the leadership on him and then leave him "alone" to bear its burdens. Thus Moses was feeling abandoned by God. From his perspective, his death wish was not an abandonment of God but a response to God's withdrawal from him.

As in any failing marriage, blame for the dissolution is shared between the partners, and the origins of the difficulties are buried in minutely accumulating grievances and misunderstandings. Regardless of who initiated the breach between God and Moses, it was ultimately clear that, from God's perspective, continuation of his relationship

with Moses had become an affront to him, a diminution of his stature
that he was not prepared to accept.

God's subsequent command to the people of Israel, through Moses
as his conduit, of an obligation to love him "with all your heart and
with all your being and with all your might," arose from the experience
of the failed intimacy between him and Moses. Their close companionship was not based on God's command that Moses was obliged to
love him—nor did it occur to Moses that God was obliged to love him.
Their companionship was voluntary and reciprocal; this was its core.
God's subsequent shift to commanded love looked on its face like exercise of his unquestioned power and consequent entitlement. But at its
core, it was not a display of power; it was a reflection of the limits of
God's power over mankind, an implicit admission of God's incapacity
to obtain from mankind what he truly wanted.

In issuing this command as such, God appears to have anticipated
Machiavelli's advice to his Prince, that "it is much safer to be feared
than loved, if one has to lack one of the two. . . . [S]ince men love at
their convenience and fear at the convenience of the prince, a wise
prince should found himself on what is his, not on what is someone
else's."[35] This may be a wise maxim. From God's perspective, reflecting
on his extended relationship with Moses, it is a sad one.

The pattern that we have seen in the evolution of God's relationship
with Moses and, through him, with the Israelites precisely traces the
narrative arc that we have already identified in the difference between
the first and second creations in Genesis. In the first, the question
of God's authority over humanity was essentially moot; it made no
sense to describe humanity as either obedient or disobedient to God's
wishes. Instead there was such seamless harmony between them—each
in the image of the other—that the question of authority was meaningless as such. The question of authority only arose in the loneliness
and barrenness of the second creation and was not appeased by God's

planting of Eden but was reinforced because his first negative commandment was inextricably rooted there.

From the beginning of his dealings with Moses, God sought to return to the relationship he had enjoyed with humanity (recalling that it was "very good") in the first creation. God did not command Moses to lead the Israelites from Egypt. He tried to persuade him to accept this offer—and neither promised anything in return if Moses did accept nor threatened any punishment if Moses refused. God became angry at Moses's persistent reluctance but contained his anger and responded only with additional offers of assistance (through Aaron's ministrations). Thus God laid the groundwork for the ultimate intimacy that he achieved with Moses—their face-to-face relationship.

It was as if God's hope for an intimate relationship with Adam and Eve, his expectation of their companionship as he strolled through Eden enjoying the evening breeze, finally came to fruition with Moses. God had not found that intimacy in Eden itself. But this failure was not because Adam and Eve had disobeyed his commandment; the failure came from the structure of the relationship that God himself had previously dictated. God could not obtain the intimacy that he had enjoyed in the first creation because, in the second, he had issued an explicit negative commandment. This act in itself fundamentally transformed the relationship. Whether mankind responded with obedience or disobedience to God's commandment, the question of dominance or submission immediately became the core issue in the relationship. Loving intimacy has no space to unfold in this context.

God's pleasure in the intimacy he had attained with Moses apparently led him to make the same offer to the Israelite people when he invited them—but pointedly refrained from coercing them—to become his "treasure among all the peoples" despite the many indications that this unruly populace was an unlikely source of satisfaction for God (or for Moses). Perhaps God thought that he could relate to the entire people of Israel with the same loving intimacy that he had experienced in the first creation and seemed at last to have recreated with Moses. But if God had even momentarily entertained this idea, he was quickly disabused of it.

God had made a quick transition from the first to the second creation accounts when he issued his commandments, coupled with threats of punishment for disobedience. As with the abrupt transition between the two creations, the underlying reason for God's sudden shift to impose a command-and-punish relationship on the Israelite people is unexplained. This same transition occurred in the relationship between God and Moses—from an initial offer by God that mankind should voluntarily accept intimacy followed by God's disappointed retraction and his imposition of a new command-based relationship coupled with the punitive threat of withdrawing entirely from any relationship. This transition occurred much more gradually with Moses than with the Israelites generally, but in both cases, the transition was triggered by human beings coming to the conclusion that God had already abandoned them or had failed to keep his promises to them. (Recall that the Israelites turned to the Golden Calf because they felt bereft and abandoned after a forty-day hiatus when God and Moses conferred alone on Mount Sinai; and Moses himself subsequently felt abandoned by God after some two exhausting years of service as God's intermediary in fending off the bitter complaints of the Israelites.)

The conclusion that God had abandoned either the Israelites or Moses may not have been reasonable; it may only have been a reflection of their fear of abandonment, based on their knowledge of their vulnerability—the fear that first appeared among mankind at the beginning of the second creation. But even if God considered the charge of abandonment to be unjustified and even if he responded to the complaint by reaffirming his commitment (as he initially did in response to Moses), mankind's fearful conclusion brought the question of abandonment into a relationship where this possibility had previously seemed inconceivable. And once the question of abandonment was raised, the further question presented itself, "Who was likely to abandon whom?"

This question itself was like a serpent intruding on a previously conflict-free relationship, and in response to this newly visible question, both partners (God and mankind) become tempted to make preemptive strikes. On God's side, the initial temptation is to forbid withdrawal, to command love that had previously been voluntarily offered and to threaten abandonment if love is not forthcoming; on mankind's side, the initial temptation is to demand love and protection as the price of continued loyalty. And so both parties have moved, without quite knowing why this has happened, from the irenic harmony of the first creation to the calculated, and ultimately failed, effort in the second to satisfy mankind's vulnerable sense of loneliness and God's concern (his vulnerable concern?) that mankind would not persist in honoring his wishes.

We can speculate about the causes for this dramatic shift in the terms of the relationship between God and mankind. The biblical account, however, rigorously withholds any attempt at causal explanation, and for our purposes, it is not necessary to fill in this blank space. The important message that the biblical narrative conveys is that this cycle of initial seamless intimacy followed by mankind's fear of abandoned vulnerability and God's punitive response appears again and again in the relationship between God and mankind. In the Hebrew Bible, at least, the cycle never ends, but it is equally significant that the effort to break this cycle, on God's part or mankind's, also never ends—though often the will to engage it lapses for long stretches of time.

The Bible's failure to identify crisply the underlying causes for this cycle may arise because its authors, even with divine inspiration, didn't know the answer. Or it may arise because the biblical authors believed that the cycle could not be broken and yet were unwilling to accept the permanent breach in relationship between God and mankind that this acknowledgment might provoke. Whatever the reasons for its reticence in offering causal explanations, the crucial point is that, by the biblical account, this repetitive cycle of intimacy and withdrawal is the template for identifying the terms of the relationship between God and mankind. Accordingly, the fundamental question for the political theory of the Bible is how to respond to this recurrent phenomenon in the relationship between ruler and ruled. If in the biblical account it was not clear who was abandoning whom, it also became unclear who was ruling whom.

CHAPTER SEVEN

Grief and Grievance

Moses and Job

EUTERONOMY, THE LAST of the Five Books of Moses collectively known as the Torah, ends unhappily. Its account of Moses's death is suffused with grief. From the top of Mount Nebo, God "let [Moses] see" the entire panorama of the land that the children of Israel were about to enter. God said to him, "This is the land that I swore to Abraham, to Isaac, and to Jacob, saying, 'To your seed I will give it.' I have let you see with your own eyes, but you shall not cross over there." The narrator continued, "And Moses, the Lord's servant, died there in the land of Moab by the word of the Lord. And he was buried in the glen in the land of Moab opposite Beth-Peor, and no man has known his burial place to this day."

Following the austere example of the previously recorded deaths of the patriarchs in Genesis, this would have been a fitting place for the account to end. But the narrator cannot seem to let go of Moses. The text continues: "And Moses was one hundred and twenty years old when he died. His eye had not grown bleary and his sap had not fled. And the Israelites keened for Moses in the steppes of Moab thirty days, and the days of keening in mourning for Moses came to an end."

Here, too, would be another natural place to end. But the narrator persisted: "And Joshua son of Nun was filled with a spirit of wisdom, for Moses had laid his hands upon him, and the Israelites heeded him and did as the Lord had charged Moses. But no prophet again arose in Israel like Moses, whom the Lord knew face to face, with all the signs and the portents which the Lord sent him to do in the land of Egypt to Pharaoh and to all his servants and to all his land, and with the strong hand and with all the great fear that Moses did before the eyes of all Israel."[1]

Finally, then, we come to the end of the account of Moses's death. It is notable, however, that the final sweeping sentence of Deuteronomy is a mixed evocation of Moses's intimacy with God ("whom the Lord knew face to face") and the "strong hand and . . . great fear" that Moses, at God's direction, inflicted on Pharaoh and the people of Egypt "before the eyes of all Israel." In one sense, the grief of the Israelites at Moses's death expressed their fear that they had lost their direct access to God and his protection against their enemies. In his extended final charge to the Israelites, Moses tried to reassure them; "before the eyes of all Israel," he said to Joshua, his anointed successor, "Be strong and courageous, for you will come with this people into the land which the Lord swore to their fathers to give to them. . . . He will be with you and will not forsake you. You shall not fear and you shall not be terrified."[2]

The prospect of armed conflict against Israel's enemies living in the promised land was not, however, the only issue for which Moses tried to offer reassurance. A considerable portion of his lengthy valedictory was concerned with the prospect of terrible punishment that would befall the Israelites if they abandoned their covenant with God. On and on, Moses recited the terrors. The likely impact on the Israelites listening to Moses's recitation can be appreciated by lengthy (even though only partial) quotation:

> And it shall be, if you do not heed the voice of the Lord your God to keep and to do all His commands and His statutes that I charge you to-day, all these curses will come upon you and overtake you. Cursed you will be in the town and cursed you will be in the field. Cursed your basket and your kneading pan. Cursed the fruit of your womb and the fruit

of your soil, the get of your herds and the offspring of your flock. Cursed you will be when you come in and cursed you will be when you go out. The Lord will send against you blight and panic and disaster in all that your hand reaches, that you do, until you are destroyed and until you perish swiftly because of the evil of your acts, as you will have forsaken Me. . . . The Lord will strike you with consumption and with fever and with inflammation and with burning and with desiccation and with emaciation and with jaundice, and they will pursue you till you perish. . . . And you will be a horror to all the kingdoms of the earth. And your carcass will become food for the birds of the heavens and for the beasts of the earth, with none to make them afraid. . . . The Lord will strike you with madness and with blindness and with confounding of the heart. And you will grope at noon as the blind man gropes in darkness. . . . A woman you will betroth and another man will bed her. A house you will build and you will not dwell in it. . . . Your sheep will be given to your enemies and you will have no rescuer. Your sons and your daughters will be given to another people with your own eyes seeing and wasting away on them all day long, and your hand will be powerless. . . . And you will be crazed by the sight of your eyes that you will see. . . . And you will become a derision, a byword, and an adage among all the peoples where the Lord will drive you. . . . Inasmuch as you will not have served the Lord your God in joy and with a good heart out of an abundance of all things, you will serve your enemies whom the Lord will send against you in hunger and in thirst and in nakedness and the lack of all things, and he will put an iron yoke on your neck until you are destroyed. . . . And you will eat the fruit of your womb, the flesh of your sons and your daughters whom the Lord your God gave you, in the siege and in the straits in which your enemy will press you.[3]

If all this were not enough, after twenty more verses of horrors (including "the Lord will make your plagues and the plagues of your seed astounding, great and relentless plagues, evil and relentless illnesses"), Moses concluded as if for good measure:

And your life will dangle before you, and you will be afraid night and day and will have no faith in your life. In the morning you will say, "Would that it were evening," and in the evening you will say, "Would that it were morning" from your heart's fright with which you will be afraid and from the sight of your eyes that you will see. And the Lord will bring you back to Egypt in ships, on the way that I said to you, "You shall not see it again," and you will put yourselves up for sale there to your enemies as male slaves and slavegirls, and there will be no buyer.[4]

This was hardly a reassuring valedictory. There is an especially ironic twist to Moses's brief mention, in the middle of his recitation, that all these curses would come because the Israelites had not "served the Lord your God in joy and with a good heart." This was an echo of God's commandment to love him with all one's heart and soul, but embedded in threats of the most horrific catalogue of punishments imaginable—designed to induce compliance but hardly "in joy and with a good heart." After these endless inflictions of torture, the final indignity that Moses mustered seems almost comical (though gallows humor, to be sure): the disobedient Israelites will offer themselves for sale to their enemies, "and there will be no buyer."

Surely three or four or maybe even a dozen of the threatened punishments would have been enough to make Moses's point. Imagine if you had been not merely reading this speech several thousand years (and many plagues) later, but actually present while Moses recited it. At some point, this declamation must have seemed gratuitous, best explicable as an act of sadism on Moses's part—or even more to the point, on God's part, since when Moses had completed his catalogue Deuteronomy recites that "these are the words of the Covenant that the Lord charged Moses to seal with the Israelites."[5]

What might have provoked this endless, relentless assault on God's part? One hint is provided in the so-called Song of Moses, which Moses subsequently chanted to the assembled Israelites and in which he directly quoted God's words:

> The Lord saw, and He spurned,
>   from the vexation of His sons and His daughters.
> And he said, "Let Me hide My face from them,
>   I shall see what their end will be.

For a wayward brood are they,
   children with no trust in them.
They provoked Me with an ungod,
   they vexed Me with their empty things.

I would have said, 'Let Me wipe them out,
   let Me make their name cease among men,'
Had I not feared the foe's provocation,
   lest their enemies dissemble,
     lest they say, 'Our hand was high,'
     and not 'the Lord has wrought all this.'"[6]

God makes clear reference here to the Israelites' worship of the Golden
Calf and his consequent inclination to destroy the entire populace. At
the time, Moses offered God two reasons to relent from this destruction: it would make God appear weak in the eyes of the Egyptians, and
it would violate God's prior promises to Abraham, Isaac, and Jacob. In
the event, God relented, but now, through Moses's recitation, God asserts that his motives were entirely self-seeking, without any regard for
his previous promises. Even more chillingly, God invokes by implication the second time when, in response to Moses's pleading, he revoked his intention to destroy the Israelites because of their vexatious
conduct. On that occasion, Moses offered God a third reason: that the
destruction would be inconsistent with God's proclaimed vision of
himself on Mount Sinai: "The Lord, the Lord! A compassionate and
gracious God, slow to anger, and abounding in kindness and good
faith, keeping kindness for the thousandth generation, bearing crime,
trespass, and offense." The endless accumulation of horrors that Moses
recited at God's direction would make clear to the Israelites that they
should not be misled by God's apparent prior willingness to forgive offenses against him. No more Mr. Nice Guy.

    Moses himself might have had the same motive in piling up God's
threatened curses. When the Israelites had worshiped the Golden Calf,
Moses had not told them that God had resolved to destroy them all

and had relented only in response to his pleading. Moses came down from Mount Sinai, expressed fury on his own behalf, and launched a bloody civil war among the Israelites. But to the survivors, he then promised to return to God to ask forgiveness for their idolatry. In Deuteronomy, by contrast, Moses now understood that God no longer appeared interested in seeing himself as "compassionate and gracious." Indeed, immediately after Moses concluded his recitation of horrors, he was explicit in his warning to the Israelites that if any of them "turns away" from God, "the Lord shall not want to forgive him . . . and the Lord shall wipe out his name from under the heavens."[7]

The question remains, however, why it was not enough for Moses simply to say this much, on his own behalf or speaking as God's intermediary, that the Lord would not forgive any offense against him. It may be that both God and Moses wanted a more elaborate listing of retaliatory punishments in order to establish what lawyers call an *in terrorem* effect, to threaten such dire consequences for even seemingly minor offenses that the populace would steer a wide path away from any transgression. But it may also be that God was in no mood to appear even minimally conciliatory and that Moses not only understood this rigidly unforgiving stance but viewed it as an excessive, even sadistic, impulse from God that Moses wanted to share with the Israelites.

This is, of course, speculation on my part. But I find some support for this interpretation in the unusual format of Deuteronomy. Unlike the three preceding books, Exodus, Leviticus, and Numbers, which recount extended conversations between God and Moses, Deuteronomy records no verbal exchanges between God and Moses.[8] The format of Deuteronomy implies that some considerable unaccustomed distance had come between God and Moses—in a way reminiscent of the absence of any conversation between God and Abraham in Genesis after Abraham had been saddled with the climactic test of his loyalty by God's command that he sacrifice Isaac.

The interpersonal distance between God and Moses also appears tinged with some anger on Moses's part at least. Support for this possibility can be found in the fact that Moses never acknowledged the justice of God's punishment against him—that he would die in sight of, but without crossing over into, the promised land. God's stated reason for this punishment was that Moses's act of striking a rock to obtain water rather than speaking to it, as God had specified, was an affront—"you did not trust Me to sanctify Me before the eyes of the Israelites."[9] At the time, Moses said nothing in response to this charge, neither admitting nor denying it nor pleading for mercy; as we have seen elsewhere in the biblical text, silence in response to God's word is a sign of disbelief. Near the end of Deuteronomy, God repeats his accusation to Moses, with somewhat greater emphasis: "die on the mountain . . . as Aaron your brother died . . . because you two betrayed Me in the midst of the Israelites through the waters of Meribath-Kadesh . . . because you did not sanctify Me in the midst of the Israelites."[10] Again Moses remained silent—a stony silence, it seems to me.

Moreover, on two occasions when Moses explained to the Israelites why he would not accompany them into the promised land, he said nothing about God's stated grounds. Instead, he told them that they had not trusted God to protect them in the promised land, as he had done in the flight from Egypt and in the wilderness thereafter. As a result, God "was furious" and forbade the entire original generation of freed Israelite slaves to enter the promised land. Moreover, "against me, too, the Lord was incensed because of you, saying 'You, too, shall not come there.'"[11] On the second occasion, Moses told the Israelites that he had asked God to let him "cross over [to] see the goodly land which is across the Jordan. . . . And the Lord was cross with me because of you, and He did not listen to me."[12] Nowhere else in the biblical text does Moses shift blame from himself to others, and nowhere else does Moses ascribe motives to God that are flatly contradicted by God's own words elsewhere in the text. Perhaps Moses was too ashamed of his wrongdoing to admit it to the Israelites. But it seems at least plausible,

and I would say more likely, that Moses could not provide any coherent justification to the Israelites for the real reason that God gave for
his punishment, and, even conceding that there had been something
offensive in his conduct, he regarded God's death sentence against him
in sight of the promised land as wildly out of proportion to his supposed offense.

It is thus not surprising that Moses was prepared to convey God's
threats of endlessly escalated punishments. It is as if Moses were saying, "This is the character of your God, as I have come to understand
him. Don't expect mercy from him if you vary from his wishes even by
a millimeter. I have learned that this God is quick to take offense and
relentlessly cruel in response." At the same time, the mounting, ob-
sessively repetitive inflictions of terror and pain that Moses recited
seemed almost calculated to inspire not just fear but revulsion among
the Israelites. It is as if Moses's depiction of God's vindictiveness were
not only a warning but an indictment of God himself. At the least, Moses's portrayal provides a measure of how far God had moved away
from being receptive to any plea for mercy based on an appeal, as Moses had previously made on behalf of the stiff-necked Israelites, that
God should "forgive, pray, the crime of this people through Your great
kindness and as You have borne with this people from Egypt till now"
because God himself had "spoken, saying, 'The Lord is slow to anger
and abounding in kindness, bearing crime and trespass.'"[13]

It may seem too extravagant to portray Moses as indicting God for
his infliction of an undeserved punishment. But this was the basis for
Job's indictment, and the folk tradition that the book of Job was written by Moses himself takes on plausibility from the premise that Moses
regarded himself as aggrieved, as unjustly punished. Moses did not suffer, and did not claim to suffer, the cataclysmic horrors that befell Job.
But it is illuminating to imagine that Moses, perhaps as he stood on
Mount Nebo gazing into the unattainable distance of the promised
land, momentarily set aside his writing of the last chapters of Deuter-

onomy (as folk tradition has it, Moses was the author of the entire Torah) and turned to writing a parable, a kind of roman à clef, reflecting
on the vicissitudes of his relationship with God.[14]

In this just-so story, Moses might have imagined (or we can imagine
for him) that he had not remained silent in response to God's accusation of infidelity and the imposition of his punishment, but that he
had openly protested—and imagined further what might have come
of such protest. In reading the book of Job as a counterfactual account
of Moses's relationship with God, we can see the way that Job func-
tions first as a reflection on the reasons this extraordinarily intimate
relationship—the most intimate between God and man in the entire
Hebrew Bible—ultimately was not able to sustain itself, and second as
an imagined alternative of a way that the breach in their relationship
could have been addressed and even ultimately healed.

This approach to the book of Job places it in the context of the question posed at the end of the preceding chapter—that if the biblical narrative relates a recurrent pattern of breach in the relationship between
God and humanity, does the Bible also point to the possibility of rem-
edies for that breach? This much is clear from the biblical presentation
of these recurrent breaches—that the possibility of a permanent remedy is contradicted by the biblical narratives, that the goal of complete
harmony, however much repeatedly pursued by God and humanity, is
never attained within the narrative structure of the Hebrew Bible. The
book of Job can be read, however, as a reflection on these repetitive
failures—a reflection specifically on whether God and humanity are
simply stuck in a perpetual cycle of approach and breach of harmonious relations or whether some different way of framing their relationship and some different means toward that end are possible and desirable. In this sense, the book of Job asks the question that Amartya Sen
posed, as discussed in the first chapter of this book—that is, whether
there is a better alternative to the pursuit of perfect justice in political
relations generally.

The book of Job was written sometime after the first five books of the Hebrew Bible.[15] It is the most extraordinary episode in the Hebrew Bible. Its story line is simple, but the indictment of God's conduct that leaps from the events of this story and from Job's mouth directly is both unprecedented and compelling. The book begins with a description of Job—directly endorsed by God himself—as "innocent, up-right, and God-fearing."[16] Satan, the Adversary, then appears and challenges God, claiming that Job's apparent virtue is based wholly on the good fortune that God has bestowed on him. Take all this away, Satan asserts, "and watch him curse You to Your Face!"[17] God instantly takes the bait and authorizes Satan to take everything from Job, but not to inflict direct bodily harm on him. Immediately, in a spare, chilling recitation, Job loses everything: first all his animals and servants and then his seven sons and three daughters. Job throws himself to the ground in despair and says, in words customarily reiterated in Jewish funeral orations to this day, "Naked I came from my mother's womb and naked I return there. Yahweh has given and Yahweh has taken. Blessed be the name of Yahweh."[18]

God then tells Satan, triumphantly but with some chagrin, that Job had persisted "in his innocence, though you prevailed upon me to ruin him for no reason."[19] But Satan was undeterred. Mankind, he says, is basically concerned with self-preservation; if you "strike his flesh," then he will "curse You to Your face." Once again, inexplicably, God swallows the bait. "He is in your power," God says to Satan, "but see that you preserve his life." Now Satan covers Job with open sores, and Job's wife makes her only appearance in the book. "Are you still persisting in your innocence?" she challenges him. "Curse God and die."

As Job sits on a pile of ashes, scratching himself with a shard of pottery, three Friends join him. Appalled at his appearance, they sit silently with him for seven days. Job then breaks this silence with an extended lament, and an extensive dialogue between him and the Friends ensues, in which the Friends increasingly berate Job for his lack of faith and Job in turn scorns the Friends for their lack of sympathy and aims an increasingly adamant indictment at God for the injustice of his actions. Finally God appears to Job from within a Whirlwind but offers no apology nor explanation for his conduct; instead he seems to deride Job for his presumption in challenging God. Job makes a final speech to God, which, as we will see, is virtually impossible to decipher—is it a capitulation by Job, an even more angry indictment of God, or a simple withdrawal from any dependency on God? The book ends with a sudden shift: God criticizes the Friends for failing to speak truth about him as Job had done, and God doubly restores Job's fortune and gives him once again seven sons and three daughters.

From this rapid outline of the book, it is clear that the portrait of God—erratic, easily swayed by Satan toward infliction of obvious injustice, unrepentant when he finally deigns to show himself to Job— is hardly flattering. On its face, there is a deep puzzle about why this book was accepted into canonical status in the Hebrew Bible. I believe, however, that the book of Job is not an anomaly within the narrative arc of the Hebrew Bible. It is, rather, a culmination and explicit avowal of the human critique of God that has percolated throughout the biblical text, sometimes just below the surface of that text and sometimes on its surface, though always somewhat muted or reticently presented. But there is no muting, no reticence, in Job's escalating indictment of God—except perhaps, as we will explore, at the very end of this text.

Many elements in the book of Job point to connections between Moses and Job. Moses's social stature, for example, is similar to Job's initial depiction as "the greatest of the men of the East." The Prologue's description of Job's isolation from his children as they feasted among themselves and his concern for their welfare because they "might have cursed God in their hearts" resonate with Moses's injunctions to the children of Israel as they proceed without his protective presence into the promised land. The calamities inflicted on Job also mirrored the punishments that Moses warned against in his catalogue of horrors in Deuteronomy chapter 28:

> The Lord will strike you with boils and with scabs . . . Your ox will be slaughtered . . . Your sheep will be given to your enemies . . . Your sons and daughters will be given to another people . . . and your hand will be powerless . . . And you will become a derision, a byword and an adage among all the peoples [as Job himself complained, "[O]usted from the world of men—now I am their mocking song, the topic of their gossip! They scorn me, they shun me, they spare my face no spit."[20] . . . You will have no faith in your life. In the morning you will say, "Would that it were evening," and in the evening you will say, "Would that it were morning," from your heart's fright [exactly as Job laments, "[T]roubled nights have been my lot. When I lie down, I say, 'How soon can I get up?' . . . My days . . . end when the thread of hope gives out."[21]].

From this last lament of his hopelessness, both day and night, Job seems to long for death not only for its own sake but so that God could not find him: "Remember," Job says, "My life is just a breath, my eye will never again see pleasure. The questing eye will not detect me; Your eye will catch me—just!—and I'll be gone. . . . In no time, I'll be lying in the earth, when You come looking for me, I'll be gone."[22] It is possible to read this threat as a direct parallel to Moses's request that God kill him because of the "evil" burden of caring for the Israelites that God had inflicted on him. God could well have been angered by Moses for two reasons: his allegiance was not unconditional but would be forfeited if God failed to make matters comfortable for him; and he wanted to die, which God could plausibly view as a threatened abandonment. God, of course, said none of this at the time. But, as noted, several chapters later God's anger flared unexpectedly about a matter that seemed trivial on its face but led to Moses's death sentence. This fulfilled Moses's previously expressed wish to die but was administered so distant in time from that expression that few would suspect that God had been offended by that wish or by the implication that Moses didn't love him unconditionally. God's punishment would appear an act of strength, an assertion of his raw power to define offenses and inflict punishment for any reason or for no reason—rather than a reflection of his dependence on Moses's loyalty and his sensitivity to Moses's apparent act of *lèse-majesté*.

But if no one knew God's true motive in punishing Moses (even though Moses might have silently suspected), Satan knew God's vulnerability when he taunted him to instigate Job's ordeal. In response to God's boast about Job's allegiance to him ("no one like him on earth . . . God-fearing, and keeping himself apart from evil"), Satan taunted him: "Is Job God-fearing for nothing? Look how You have sheltered him on all sides . . . But reach out with Your hand and strike his property, and watch him curse You to Your face!"[23] (There may even be a veiled reference here to Moses's ostensible sin: after being instructed to speak to the rock to obtain water, "Moses raised his hand and he struck the rock. . . . And the Lord said to Moses . . . 'Inasmuch as you did not trust Me to sanctify Me . . .'"[24] Is this God's retaliatory infliction on Moses/Job: "Because I suspect that you did not trust me when you raised your hand and struck the rock, I will raise my hand and strike you and your property for the same reason"?)

Moses responded to his inflictions in the same way that Job initially reacted—continued protestations of faith in God followed by prolonged silence about what had befallen him, a silence broken by expressions of suicidal despair (which for Moses had preceded rather than followed his punishment). But then Job's path departs from Moses's; Job mounts an increasingly adamant, outraged denunciation of God's injustice that Moses never expressed. If in the biblical accounts, Moses is real while Job is fictional, it is quite easy to read the book of Job as a fictional account of a pathway that no actual man, even as strong and sanctified as Moses, would dare to take. And like all fantasies, Job can easily be seen as a wish on the part of real people to alter the disappointing reality of their lives.

After all his comforts and family had been stripped from him, Job's anger toward God first emerged when, following his seven days of silence, he cursed all of God's creation and wished that he himself had never been born. Job's wish for non-existence took a darker cast in his response to the first speech of Eliphaz, in which he sympathetically urged Job to hold to his faith and God would ultimately protect him. Job angrily dismissed Eliphaz as a false friend offering false comfort, and he then turned to speak directly to God. "Why should I restrain my mouth?" he asked. "I'd rather choke—death is better than this misery. I've had enough! I will not live forever! Let me alone, my life is just a breath. What is man that You make so much of him, and think about him so, examine him each morning, appraise him every moment. . . . But what have I done to You, keeper, jailer of men? Why should You make me Your target, a burden to myself?" Then came Job's climactic conclusion, implicitly linking injury to himself and to God: "In no time, I'll be lying in the earth; when You come looking for me, I'll be gone."[25]

Job may have envisioned his own suicide here rather than, as Moses did, asking God to kill him. But both Job and Moses displayed the same bitterness, the same sense of abandonment, and the same consequent wish to die, thereby threatening to reject any future relationship with God. Job, moreover, gave voice to exactly the question that God seemed to have asked himself after he had made his initial commitment to Moses and immediately sought to kill him: "What is man that You make so much of him, and think about him so?"

Job in effect offered an answer to this question in his final speech before God appeared to him in the Whirlwind. In Job's responses to the Friends' escalating condemnation of him, Job moved from suicidal despair to an increasingly self-confident insistence on his own righteousness and a bold demand that God directly respond to his charges, to justify himself and even to submit to an arbiter who would stand impartially between them. Job thus, with increasing adamance, portrayed himself as a judge of God's conduct and envisioned the possibility of subordinating God either to his moral condemnation or to the judgment of an arbiter hierarchically superior to them both. God, however, remained silent throughout these complaints and accusations from Job—as if God maintained, in lawyer's language, that Job's claims to impose external judgment on him failed for lack of jurisdiction, that no one had authority to compel God to justify himself.

Why, then, did God ultimately relent and appear in Job's court? The closest parallel to God's submission to such an appearance was when he "stood before" Abraham and invited judgment about whether he should destroy Sodom and Gomorrah.[26] God's appearance in that instance was, however, entirely voluntary. Abraham had no advance knowledge of God's plans; God decided to bring Abraham into his confidence because he "will surely be a great and mighty nation" and should be able to instruct his dependents "to keep the way of the Lord to do righteousness and justice."[27] When Moses convinced God to abandon his plan to kill the idolatrous Israelites, God never clearly explained his willingness to accept Moses's judgment about the wrongfulness of this course. God's appearance before Job was thus the first instance in the biblical text when God acceded to a specific demand for accountability, a demand that he justify his conduct in response to an indictment from an allegedly injured human being.

This legalistic interpretation of God's appearance before Job is not, however, the full story—and indeed may not be any part of the story, from God's perspective. Job repeatedly demanded God's appearance. But God did not in fact appear until a new element had entered Job's complaint, an element that had not been heard in any of Job's alternately despairing and angry outbursts. To understand the impasse between God and Job at the end of the Hebrew Bible, and by extension the impasse between God and humanity, we must turn to this question of why God chose to appear to Job from the Whirlwind.

At the beginning of Job's last speech before God's appearance, Job repeated his basic claim as if he were speaking directly to God: "Never will I call you right, never deny my innocence until the day I die! I insist I am right. I will not yield."[28] But his mood then mellowed and he mused, "But wisdom—where can it be found? Where is the place of true knowledge? No man knows how to reach it, for it is not found in the land of the living."[29] Job then continued, "If only I could be under the moons of old again, back in the days when the god watched over me! When He held His lamp so it shone about my head, and I could walk by the light in darkness. If I could be again as I was in my daring days, with the god above my tent, protecting; when Shaddai was still with me."[30] Until this moment, Job had not permitted himself to remember these happily intimate days "when Shaddai was still with me."

Job then repeated his complaint about God's silence: "I cry to You— no answer; I stand—You stare at me, You harden yourself to me, spurn me with Your mighty hand."[31] But at this moment, Job's complaint had a different tone; it carried the echo of longing for return of their past intimacy more than angry recrimination at God's abandonment. If God were listening all the while, if he were continuously and minutely examining this man as Job himself had asserted, God might now himself recall the answer that he would have given if he had responded to Job's earlier question, "What is man that You make so much of him, and think about him so?" This answer was foreshadowed in the pleasure God had found in Noah's burnt offering after he had rescued Noah from the Flood waters. This pleasure at human companionship found its fullest flowering in the intimacy of his relationship with Moses—an intimacy now recalled for God when he heard Job's final words: "If only I had someone to hear me! Here is my desire: that Shaddai answer me, that my opponent write a brief; I swear that I would wear it on my shoulder, bind it on me like a crown. I would . . . come before Him as before a prince."[32]

This new theme from Job of blissful recollection and correlative longing for intimacy is interrupted by an interlude preceding God's appearance when a fourth Friend, Elihu, suddenly appears in the narrative as if from nowhere and declaims the longest uninterrupted speech in the book of Job. No one speaks to Elihu, however, or even acknowledges his presence, and God himself in the Epilogue omits any recognition of him.[33] The strange disconnection between Elihu and the rest of the book of Job has led some philologists to conclude that Elihu's speech was a later interpolation into the book, another meaningless cut-and-paste job.[34] Perhaps it was, but there is a narrative logic to the insertion of Elihu's speech between Job's newly explicit yearning and God's appearance. Elihu's lengthy diatribe directed at Job in one sense anticipates God's dismissive rant toward Job when he finally does appear. At the same time, however, Elihu's speech implicitly highlights the question of why God bothered to appear before Job, why he didn't simply rely on proxies such as the three Friends and Elihu to countermand Job's insistence that God appear directly to him. Elihu's incomprehension and isolation are epitomized in his final declaration: "Shaddai: We cannot find Him out . . . He will never answer. Therefore, mortals, fear Him whom even men of wisdom cannot see."[35] Immediately after this declaration, the narrator states: "Yahweh answered Job from the storm."[36] Elihu obviously misread God and missed something that had implicitly transpired directly between Job and God—something that God's actual appearance brings to the fore.

The text does not clearly tell us what motivated God to appear, why he did not simply remain remote and unavailable, as Elihu had predicted. The overt message that God delivered when he did appear—his mocking tirade against Job—might seem to suggest that he had found something lacking in the indictments that Job had already obtained from the three Friends and Elihu and that God accordingly wanted to deliver his denunciation in person. But there is a covert message underlying God's appearance that his blustery tirade cannot entirely conceal—a message that something from Job attracted God, softened his resolve to dismiss him entirely. I would say that the sudden appearance of Job's blissful memory of their past harmonious relationship and his open pleading for a resumption of this harmony are the new element in Job's address that prompted God to want a face-to-face encounter, to reciprocate Job's wish for renewed intimacy.

But even if it were Job's recollection of their former intimacy that brought God into the open, there was no appearance of tenderness in his address to Job. God's first words were, "Who dares speak darkly words with no sense?"[37] From this unpromising beginning, God proceeded to parade his vast power before Job: "Where were you when I founded the earth?" "Have you ever reached the depths of the sea and walked around there, exploring the abyss?" "Can you loose the lightning, and have it say, as it goes, 'Your servant!'?" "Does the eagle soar at your bidding, building his nest up high?"[38] Throughout his lengthy diatribe—the longest continuous speech delivered by God anywhere in the Hebrew Bible—God never responded to Job's insistence on his innocence and his complaint against God's mistreatment of him. Instead of justifying his conduct, God boasted of his awesome power as if to say that no one could compel him to explain anything, no one would dare.

And yet, underlying this tirade and almost totally obscured from view, a different message can just barely be discerned, a message that tempers and even contradicts God's arrogant self-depiction. The fact is that God did appear in response to Job's complaint. If God's message apparently belittled and mocked Job, the fact that he was delivering any message—no matter what its content—conveyed some contrary implication. Amid his self-promotion, moreover, God paused and demanded an action from Job that paradoxically enhanced Job's stature.

"One who brings Shaddai to court should fight!" God said. "He who charges a god should speak."

But at this point Job declined: "You see how little I am. I will not answer You. I am putting my hand to my lips." On its face Job's response was self-deprecatory. But God didn't treat it this way. His rage flared at this response, as if Job's silence was itself a power play. God demanded: "Is your arm as mighty as God's? Does your voice thunder like His?" This was an odd retort. Job had not claimed that his voice had any thunder in it; he had vowed to remain silent in the face of God's assault.

God's diatribe then reached a rhetorical peak. Before he demanded that Job speak, God had boasted of his power in creating the earth, the seas, the stars, and assorted creatures (lions, ravens, antelopes, buffalos, ostriches, stallions, eagles). After Job's refusal to speak, God mustered the great mythological beasts Behemoth and Leviathan. But with these vastly powerful creations, a small suggestion of pathos emerged as if God's redundant self-inflation betrayed a defensive quality. Thus regarding Leviathan, God challenged Job, "Can you draw [him] with a hook . . . string him through the nose with a reed? . . . Would he beg you for mercy, gentle you with words? Would he deign to be your ally? Could you make him a slave for life?"

Job did not have the raw strength to do any of this with Leviathan. But something in Job's indictment had hooked God and pulled him (by the nose?) into Job's presence. God certainly didn't beg Job for mercy or gentle him with words. Even so, his insistence that Job could not enslave Leviathan suggested that God was not content with the self-evident strength of his own independent power. God felt compelled to insist that no one could enslave him. The very existence of his compulsion was itself a limitation on God's independent power.

This compulsion might be internally generated without regard to any external force. But even though entirely self-induced in its origins, this compulsion was a limitation on God's freedom of action because he was internally in conflict, at war with himself. He was, in himself, an irresistible force confronting an immovable object. Perhaps this internal force was God's conscience pricked by Job's complaint (as Moses had spoken to God's conscience, his sense of compassion and mercy, in pleading against his plan to destroy the Israelites). In this sense, Job— even more uninvited than Moses—was taking on the function of the mnemonic rainbow.

God had originally devised the rainbow to remind himself of his resolve not to destroy humanity. The rainbow role that Abraham and Moses assumed also had a propositional content, to remind God (in Abraham's case) of his commitment to justice and (in Moses's case) of his commitment to mercy and forgiveness. (Abraham himself might have played this mnemonic role without understanding that he was reminding God of his prior commitment to doing justice, but God's motive in enlisting Abraham's opinion about the destruction of Sodom and Gomorrah was based on his own resolve "to do righteousness and justice."[39] Moses, by contrast, clearly knew what he was doing when he reminded God of his own self-characterization as "abounding in kindness and good faith."[40])

Job's blissful memory of "the moons of old" when he and God were intimately harmonious had a different valence. Job's memory was not a propositional resolve but an emotionally deeper commitment. Job's memory was in effect a recollection of the complete harmony that God and humanity had enjoyed in the first creation described in Genesis chapter one. Moreover, Job invoked this memory to bring it to God's attention; after recalling "when Shaddai was still with me," this was the import of his subsequent complaint, "I cry to You—no answer ... You harden Yourself to me."

Even if God was prompted to appear by Job's memory of their previous intimacy, in the act itself God was not noticeably soft-hearted nor conciliatory toward Job. In his speech from the Whirlwind, God ostentatiously declared to Job that he was not constrained by any moral standards, his own or others', and that he needed no human beings but was content with the vast array of other animals he had created. But notwithstanding his eruption, God appeared to be protesting too much. In his memory of blissful days together, Job may have reminded God of his own pleasure in Job's company—which in turn spoke to the possibility of God's internally derived need for a continued relationship with Job and a consequent dependence on him that offended God's cherished sense of his own stature, of his omnipotence. God's own memories of their prior intimacy may have prompted him to speak once again to Job, but by the time he actually spoke, God seemed more intent on reducing Job's importance, on humiliating him. God might have said, "I miss you too, Job." Instead he said, "Who dares speak darkly words with no sense?"

Three aspects of his speech from the Whirlwind give credence to this possibility that God was recoiling from any suggestion that he might need Job's company and that Job therefore could exert some power over him. First, the structure of God's speech followed the initial Genesis roadmap for his creation of the universe, from establishing the foundations of the earth, to constraining the sea, to fashioning the heavens and stars, to creating abundant animal life. God appeared to be remaking the universe in response to Job's first speech, which undid the Genesis order of creation. It thus seemed as if Job had been able to destroy what God had originally made, so that God needed to repeat the process (as, indeed, appeared to have occurred while God rested at the end of the first creation account).

Second, in this restorative process in God's speech from the Whirlwind, there was no mention of his creation of humanity, as if God were claiming that in this reiterated world, he had no need for stiff-necked human beings. But the fact is that God performed this recreation in front of a human being, Job. When God paraded each of his animal creations before Job, in the supposed service of inspiring awe, it was as if God were repeating what he had done with Adam in the second creation, bringing the animals to him for naming and, more important, remedying Adam's loneliness. In this recreation from the Whirlwind, God named the animals himself and did not offer control over them to Job as he had offered Adam. But if this was not to remedy Job's loneliness, it seemed nonetheless that loneliness was in the air—and that the recreation of the animals this time was God's response to the possibility of his own loneliness in Job's potential absence.

Third, God's speech was filled with questions directed at Job. The questions were scornful on their face, and they seemed to be merely rhetorical flourishes. But they nonetheless recalled God's earlier questions to human beings which were similar in form but more clearly implied that God was actually asking for something that he didn't already possess, something that he wanted from humanity. Thus God's opening question from the Whirlwind, "Who dares speak darkly . . . ?" was a challenge but also suggested that he did not recognize Job—"who is this who dares to speak?" God's failure to recognize Job confirmed the implication in the question that God had put to Satan at the very beginning—"Have you noticed my servant Job?"—as if God had lost contact with Job and was wondering where he might be and whether Satan might have some information on this score. This reading of God's question to Satan is reminiscent of his question to Adam and Eve, "Where are you?" and his question to Cain, "Where is your brother Abel?" All of these questions carried condemnation with them, but they also conveyed a wish on God's part for human companionship— a wish that he consistently refused to acknowledge because it constituted a limit on his unquestioned power.

This hint of a wish on God's part may explain why it is plausible to translate the last words of Job's final speech, after God had completed his oration from the Whirlwind, as some do, "I knew You, but only by rumor; my eye has beheld You today. I retract. I even take comfort for dust and ashes."[41] Using "dust and ashes" as a metonym for the mortality of human beings, the sense of this rendering is that God's underlying wish for human contact is ultimately comforting to Job. Job had previously referred to himself as "dust and ashes" to signify his vulnerable mortality.[42] But "dust and ashes" was also Abraham's self-description when he was challenging the morality of God's plan to destroy Sodom and Gomorrah. Job's invocation of these same two words in his final speech readily conveys the same sense as Abraham's—a deferential gesture, an apparent self-abasement, but contradicted by his dominant message insisting on justice. Job's references to "dust and ashes" may seem incidental to a casual reader of the text. But God would surely have recalled the allusion to this defining moment of his relationship with Abraham, the first time that he indicated his willingness to submit himself to human judgment.

The contradictory overtones conveyed by "dust and ashes" were amplified by multiple contradictory meanings of the Hebrew word *nacham*, which appears at the end of Job's final speech. *Nacham* can be translated as "comfort," but it can also mean "abhor," "reject," or "shudder at." The conventional translation of Job's speech not only opts for "abhor" but also supplies a referent—"I abhor myself"—that is entirely absent in the sentence itself. It is a common characteristic of biblical Hebrew that the subject and object of verbs are omitted; even if we accept "abhorrence" as the preferred meaning of *nahmen* in this speech, it is not at all clear whether Job is abhorring himself or his abject state or God. The author of Job provides no context that could guide our choice in understanding this utterly ambiguous statement; the conventional translators rely on their prior attitude of piety and import it into the text.

This does not mean that the conventional translation is erroneous; it is, however, only one possibility among many. Job's last words can be variously understood as a proclamation that he "repents" or "retracts" his previous criticism of God or that he is "comforted" by what he now understands from God's speech or that he "hates, rejects, or shudders at" what he has now seen in God's performance. It is equally plausible to construe Job's final words as being "I knew You, but only by rumor; my eye has beheld You today. I retract. I even take comfort for dust and ashes";[43] or, as the Jewish Publication Society version would have it, "I recant and relent, being but dust and ashes"; or, as the New Oxford Bible Revised Standard Edition says, "I despise myself, and repent in dust and ashes"; or, as a recent translator (Jack Miles) puts it, "now that my eyes have seen you, I shudder with sorrow for mortal clay";[44] or, as an even more recent translator (Leslie Wilson) says, "now my eye has seen you. And so I reject [you] and I feel sorry for all humanity."[45]

Hebrew readers of the text could not help hearing the contradictory interplay in the sentence. Moreover, another play on the word *nahem* is readily accessible to Hebrew readers, including God himself—that is, the phonetic play on the name Noah, which lacks only the final *mem* of *nahem*. When Lamech, the notorious murderer in the initial lineage from Adam, named his son Noah, he observed, "This one will console us for the pain of our hands' work from the soil which the Lord cursed."[46] The last sentence of Job's final speech thus brings together references to Noah and to Abraham—to Noah who had provided consolation from God's curse and was left adrift in the Flood for an extended period, uncertain whether God had promised protection or had retracted that promise; and to Abraham at the moment when he had insisted that God was obliged to honor norms of righteousness and justice in his dealings with humanity.

If, despite all the contrary evidence I have cited, Genesis can be read as a hymn to God's reliability and a justification for human obedience to him, the predominant (though not univalent) reading of Job is exactly the opposite. Job takes the doubts and protests against God that were submerged in Genesis and brings them into such high visibility that they almost overwhelm the claims for the legitimacy of God's authority put forward elsewhere in the Bible.

The best way of comprehending these mixed messages is to treat them exactly as that—as contradictions that are purposefully embedded in the text. The proper way to translate from Hebrew into a modern language would be to preserve the contradictions, not to resolve them one way or the other, to insist on Job's self-abhorrence and recantation or on his abhorrence of God's misconduct. To this end, the best translation into English that I can imagine is as follows: "I had heard of you with my ears; but now my eyes have seen you. Of all that I have said to you with my mouth I am appalled. Therefore in dust and ashes, I withdraw."

The virtue of this translation, as I see it, is its uncertainty. Was Job appalled at his own presumptuousness in what he had said to God in charging him with injustice? Or was he appalled at God's injustice which he had described as such? Was Job withdrawing his indictment? Or was he withdrawing from further relations with God?

If we continue with the premise that Moses was the author of Job and that he wrote it with God as his primary intended audience, then we can understand the multiple contradictory meanings expressed in Job's final words to God as a mirror for the inconsistent messages God himself conveyed in his extended speech from the Whirlwind—his anger, arrogance, and boastfulness joined with hints of loneliness and disappointment at being spurned. This much is clear, however, in Job's final words; the Hebrew can convey only this meaning: "I had heard of you with my ears, but now my eyes have seen you." There can be no mistake in this reference; who else besides Moses had seen God with his eyes, since no one "in Israel [was] like Moses, whom the Lord knew face to face"?[47]

Moses's actual experience, as recorded in Deuteronomy, ended where Job's final speech ended—with a calmly resigned acceptance of God's punishment, but only because of God's overwhelming power, not with a clear acknowledgment of the propriety or legitimacy of the punishment that had been inflicted on him. But writing the book of Job would have permitted Moses to imagine an alternative ending—an ending in which he did in fact proceed into the promised land. And following Job's final speech, this is where the Epilogue to the book of Job takes us—to a new place, a place where God seems willing to honor his promises.

The Epilogue begins with God speaking to Eliphaz, the leader and most eloquent of the Friends. God suddenly reverses course from his angry dismissal of Job's challenge (and his mockery of Job for even daring to complain about God's conduct). "I am very angry," God says to Eliphaz, "at you and your two Friends, for you have not spoken rightly about me as did my servant Job."[48] The Friends, of course, had spoken in support of God, claiming that Job must have been guilty of something because God was always just, and in any event that Job was not entitled to question God's actions. If Job had seemed to retract his complaint at the end of God's tirade from the Whirlwind, God immediately thereafter in the Epilogue rescinded his attack on Job. Unlike with Job's final words, however, there was no ambiguity, no difficulties in comprehending or translating God's intended retraction in his observation to Eliphaz: "you have not spoken rightly about me as did my servant Job."

The only uncertainty in translating this sentence from Hebrew is whether God said that the Friends had not "spoken rightly" to him rather than about him.[49] This alternative is still a condemnation of the Friends, but for failing to speak truly about their own attitudes toward God's justness and reliability—for failing to admit, that is, their own hidden doubts, as compared with Job's honesty. By this translation, the Friends would have been guilty of cursing God in their hearts, whereas Job was open and forthright.

However we define God's observation to Eliphaz, that Job had spoken rightly to him or about him, this is a virtually explicit acknowledgment by God of the truth expressed in Job's protestations of his innocence and his complaint that God had treated him unjustly. In Job's bold remonstrance to God, we have come to the apotheosis of the rainbow function in the Hebrew Bible: Job reminds God of his past in-timacy with humanity and provokes the thought in God's mind that the current breach in their relationship is not what God himself truly wants and that some reparative action is needed.

At the beginning of God's speech from the Whirlwind, he had said to Job, "I will put questions, and you will inform me." At that moment, this invitation seemed to mock Job for his presumptuousness. In Job's final speech after God had spoken from the Whirlwind, Job repeated God's opening remark, "I will put questions, and you will inform me."[50] Job might have been mocking himself in this repetition, but it is at least equally plausible that Job was now offering to answer God's questions, to "inform" him as Abraham and Moses had done.

God's recognition of his wish for Job's company was implicit in his directive to Eliphaz that he and his two Friends should go to Job, and that only if Job prayed for them would God refrain from punishing them (for "not speaking rightly about me as did my servant Job"[51]). The Friends did go to Job, and he did in fact pray for them. In response to Job's prayer, God then not only remitted the Friends' punishment but also "restored Job's fortunes after he prayed for his Friends, dou-bling everything Job had."[52] This double payment seems to refer to the rule God propounded in Exodus, that a thief was obliged to pay double damages to his victim.[53]

This is as close to an open admission of guilt from God as we can find anywhere in the text of the Hebrew Bible. In his earlier exchanges with Abraham and with Moses, God had refrained from taking action in response to their moral criticism; here, however, God had already acted. He couldn't quite bring himself to an explicit acknowledgment of wrongdoing, but his comparison of Job's truthfulness to the Friends' untruths and his payment of a thief's penalty in restoring Job's fortune amount to an almost direct confession.

God similarly could not bring himself directly to ask Job's forgive-ness. But just as God had veiled his confession of guilt in his angry

outburst toward Eliphaz, so too he disguised his request for forgiveness in his instruction to Eliphaz. God said that he would forgive the
Friends' falsehoods if, but only if, Job would pray to him on their behalf. This directive had two implications. It was first of all a test of Job's
willingness to forgive the Friends for the calumny and suffering they
had imposed on him. When Eliphaz informed Job that God would
punish the Friends unless Job acted for them, would Job feel vindicated
and take pleasure in the prospect of these divine inflictions? Would Job
conclude that, unlike his suffering, the Friends' punishment was deserved? Or would Job see the terrible irony that the Friends would be
punished for believing in God's goodness and justice, as Job himself
had believed prior to his ordeal?

Would Job, in other words, be willing to protect the Friends—and
thereby forgive them for their inflictions on him—in order to forestall
an unjust imposition by God on them? By making Job the central actor
in determining whether God would forgive the Friends, God would
learn whether Job was willing to forgive the Friends for their unjust actions toward him.

The second implication of God's directive was that God would learn
whether Job was prepared to speak to him again. In the midst of God's
tirade from the Whirlwind, he demanded that Job speak to him but
Job declined, apparently from humility ("I see how little I am. I will
not answer You. I am putting my hand to my lips."[54]). This refusal
seemed to enrage God further, and Job finally did reply at the end
of God's oration. Whatever meaning God extracted from the complicated, contradictory content of Job's final speech—self-abasement, defiance, comfort—it was not clear at its conclusion that Job was prepared to speak to God again. Job's reference to Abraham in his last
words, "dust and ashes," carried the suggestion that, like Abraham after
coming down from his near-sacrifice of Isaac, he might never again
speak to God. Like Abraham, Job never again spoke to his wife. In the
Epilogue, though God gave Job twice his previous fortune, he did not

resurrect Job's dead children but provided him with ten new children —the identical number, not a twofold increase. And though Job's brothers and sisters came to his restored house and comforted him "for all the harm that Yahweh had brought upon him," there is no mention in the Epilogue of Job's wife. Perhaps she had killed herself, as she had urged on Job in the Prologue; perhaps she had died of grief, as the rabbis said that Sarah had done believing that her child, Isaac, had been killed. Perhaps Job had a new wife to match his new children. It is striking, however, that the Epilogue refers to Job's siblings and his new children, and indicates at the very end that Job lived "to see his sons and grandsons to the fourth generation"—all without any mention of Job's former or new wife. Was this silence meant to reflect some lingering sense of loss that afflicted Job, notwithstanding the abundance of family and fortune that surrounded him for the rest of his life, another 140 years from the end of his ordeal? Would this lingering grief at the loss inflicted on him lead Job, like Abraham, to have no contact with God for the rest of his life? Job's willingness to pray to God on the Friends' behalf would also answer this question.

In his brief directive to Eliphaz, it seemed clear that God was eager to have Job speak to him. He referred to Job four times in three sentences—"you have not spoken rightly about me as did my servant Job . . . go to my servant Job . . . make sure that Job my servant prays for you; for only him will I heed not to treat you with the disgrace you deserve for not speaking rightly of me as did my servant Job."⁵⁵ But it was not clear that God's eagerness for contact was directly conveyed to Job. The Epilogue records that the three Friends "did exactly what Yahweh told them to do"—presumably to plead with Job on their own behalf but not necessarily to tell him how urgently and repeatedly God spoke of "his servant Job." The Epilogue, moreover, says nothing about Job's own deliberations whether to support the Friends or to speak to God. There is only a brief elliptical notation, "and Yahweh accepted Job's prayer"—as if the narrator was unwilling to acknowledge that Job was the central decision-maker in this interaction with both the Friends and God.

It is also striking that the Epilogue says nothing about the content of Job's prayer. This silence in itself invites imaginative speculation. Might Job have prayed to God as Moses did when pleading for the Israelites: "Remember your promises, remember that you are a God of compassion and mercy"? Might Job have prayed as Abraham did before the destruction of Sodom and Gomorrah: "Do not punish innocent people; should not the judge of all the earth act justly?" Or might Job have devised some prayer of his own: "You punished me although I trusted and believed in you. Now you plan to punish the three Friends although they trusted and believed in you. What kind of god are you?" We readers, moreover, know more than Job knew about the origins of his punishment in God's wager with Satan; from this knowledge, we might imagine a script for our own prayer to God: "Almighty God, you singled Job out for punishment *because* he trusted and believed in you and now you plan to punish the Friends *because* they told Job to have faith in you instead of speaking the truth as he did, the truth that you were not trustworthy. Is this the kind of faithless god that you are?"

These imagined prayers by Job and by us on his behalf bring us to a central distinctive characteristic of the political theory of the Bible. The Bible differs from the dominant strand in modern political theory in presuming the prior existence of a relationship between ruler and ruled. Modern theory, for its part, is preoccupied with the initiation of a relationship. Moreover, modern theory attempts to identify the terms on which a permanently stable relationship can be constructed whereas the biblical theory assumes that the relationship is recurrently and inevitably unstable because of the mutually contradictory demands to which ruler and ruled are driven, each for their own reasons. Biblical theory thus directly confronts a problem that modern theory essentially ignores—how to resume the relationship after breach, always assuming that both ruler and ruled for their own reasons want a resumption. From this perspective, the central political virtue in the biblical theory is not obedience to a ruler or respect for the rights of the ruled but the capacity for forgiveness on both sides following a breach of the relationship.

The book of Job invokes this virtue, though only in a veiled way. On Job's side, his willingness to pray to God in order to avert the Friends' punishment clearly implies his willingness to forgive the Friends for their abuse and at least to speak to God again rather than terminating all relations. On God's side, the Epilogue says only that God "accepted Job's prayer." God did not ask Job to forgive him. He did not thank Job for choosing to speak to him again. But might God have construed this prayer as Job's willingness to forgive God himself? All that we are told about God's thinking is that after Job "prayed for his Friends," God "restored Job's fortunes . . . doubling everything that Job had."[56]

Imagining that God might have asked and been grateful for Job's prayer might seem to be an intolerable act of impiety because it portrays God as humbling himself before a man. But in the implicit message conveyed about God's conduct in the Epilogue, we can see a deep connection with God's first encounter with Moses: the humble appearance of the burning bush and, even more notably, God's repeated willingness to solicit Moses's assistance, his virtual pleading for such assistance in the face of Moses's persistent refusals. We have already construed Moses's refusals as a reflection of his lack of trust toward God because of God's prolonged inactivity during the suffering of the Israelites in Egypt. In his initial confrontation with Moses, God requested but did not command Moses's concurrence; if God were intent on pursuing forgiveness from Moses, he could only ask rather than command it. So, too, in the Epilogue to Job, God did not command Job to pray to him; using the Friends as his proxy, his matchmaker, God only asked. Both Moses and Job were thus free to choose whether to forgive or to withhold forgiveness from God.

Job was most explicit in demanding an admission of wrongdoing from God. Job did not approach God deferentially; he was not a supplicant. In fact, he actually disdained the gestures toward this posture displayed by Abraham and, to a lesser degree, by Moses. Before God appeared in the Whirlwind, Job remained stubbornly presumptuous as if to demand that God satisfy the criterion of a fit ruler and apologize to him.

When God finally did appear in the Whirlwind, he adamantly dismissed this demand. And yet beneath this resistance were two small hints of a more accommodating impulse. The first hint was in God's initial question, "Who dares speak darkly words with no sense?" On their surface, these words are hostile and dismissive. But there is a contrary suggestion in God's question—a suggestion that he does not recognize Job for the same reason that the Friends initially did not recognize him. The Prologue recorded that "Job's three Friends heard about all the trouble that had come upon him, and . . . [t]hey agreed to meet to go and to mourn with him and comfort him. Peering from the distance, they could not recognize him. They raised their voices and wept and each tore his robe, and all put dirt on their heads . . . none saying a word to him, for they saw that his pain was very great."[57] When the Friends did speak, they were ultimately as hostile and dismissive toward Job, as offended by his disrespect, as God himself was in his speech to Job from within the Whirlwind. But the initial shock of nonrecognition at Job's pained transformation may have affected God with the same visceral empathy as the Friends felt—before God, like the Friends, refused any sympathy to Job in order to defend themselves from the impact of his pain.

The second hint of some compassionate regard beneath God's assaultive anger appeared in his challenge immediately following his question, "Who dares speak darkly words with no sense?" God then said, "Cinch your waist like a fighter. I will put questions, and you will inform me."[58] I noted earlier that these words on their face also appear mocking and dismissive—an impression underscored by the rhetorical questions that God immediately propounded to Job, "Where were you when I founded the earth?" "Who set its measurements, if you know?" and so on. But there is a contrary impulse in the challenge itself, as if God were saying, "Pull yourself together—and help me understand some questions that I cannot answer by myself." After God had concluded his lengthy oration, Job restated God's opening challenge to him in his final speech, "Listen now and I will speak. I will put questions, and you will inform me."[59] This restatement can be read not only as Job's acknowledgment of God's mockery and his retraction of his presumptuousness but also as a simple declaration that God had asked to be informed and Job would now proceed to inform him.

The content of this information from Job is, as we have repeatedly seen, difficult to grasp and contradictory on its face. But if we assume that God was himself alert to nuance and contradiction—that he did not feel compelled to paste an unambiguously pious face on Job's final words, as more deferential readers of the text have done—then we might imagine God hearing Job's message to him in all of its complexity: that Job acknowledged God's raw power and was fearful of it; that he had foolishly imagined he might compel God to accede to his demands but he now accordingly retracted these demands; that he felt diminished and abased by God's display of power over him; that he was appalled at what he had seen and shuddered in contemplating any future relationship with God; and that he took comfort in the possibility—the bare hint—that, though he was a mere mortal and God was all-powerful, God remained interested in pursuing a mutually satisfying relationship with him.

What, then, is God's question to which Job has offered this answer? It was not God's explicit questions that followed from his request—not "where were you when I founded the earth," and so on. The question that Job answered was implicit in the fact that God chose to appear in the Whirlwind—that notwithstanding the apparent arrogance of Job's demands, God still wanted a relationship with him and wanted to know from Job himself the possible terms for a continued relationship. Job's answer in his final speech was, in effect,

> If you want a relationship with mankind based on fear, you can have it by your raw display of overwhelming power. On mankind's side, this relationship will be characterized by cowering surrender and ultimately humiliated silence—as I, at times, have felt. But if you want a relationship that offers you more than this—if you want a relationship based on respect, loyalty, love, on mankind's acknowledgment of the legitimacy of your authority—then your raw power alone cannot accomplish this. Instead you must forgive mankind's presumptuousness in making demands on you, and you must admit when you have behaved unjustly, as you have toward me. The choice is yours. Mankind cannot force you to accept the relationship that we want, since we are but "dust and ashes." But if you ask me how you might have a satisfying relationship with us, this is my answer.

God's seemingly abrupt transformation in the Epilogue—his chastisement of the Friends coupled with his expressed willingness to forgive their transgression, and his apology to Job, barely discernible but implicit in his repudiation of the Friends and his doubled repayment to Job—in fact followed from the information that Job provided to him, in answering his implicit question. God affirmed that he wanted a relationship with mankind based on more than abject terror; he wanted acknowledged legitimacy, respect, loyalty, love.

These were the virtues that were displayed in the human relationships described at the end of the book of Job. After God restored Job's fortune, "all his brothers and sisters and all his former acquaintances came and ate bread with him in his house and mourned with him and comforted him for all the harm that Yahweh had brought upon him." Job's immediate family was replenished, we might say, with ten new children. We readers had not known the names of any of his earlier children, but this time we are told his new daughters' names—Dove, Cinnamon, and Horn-of-Kohl or Eye-Shadow. These are sensuous names speaking to an intimacy that Job did not seem to have had with his deceased children. Nested in this loving family, "Job lived one hundred forty years; he lived to see his sons and grandsons to the fourth generation and died in old age after a full life span."[60]

This happy portrait of Job's family and all his acquaintances had not been a consistent part of Job's life; in the depths of his suffering, his only human contacts had been with the hectoring Friends. The task for Job was to reconstruct all of his relationships notwithstanding their previous inflictions on him. Job's willingness to accept this task was itself a further answer to God's question about the possibilities for reconstructing a satisfying relationship between him and mankind. Assuming that God wanted such a relationship, the necessary terms of re-engagement were clear from Job's forgiveness of his siblings and acquaintances for their previous abandonment of him and his willingness to accept a renewed relationship with them.

Job accepted re-engagement with his siblings and acquaintances notwithstanding the possibility, and perhaps even the likelihood, that they would desert him again if tragedy struck him. And Job embraced an even more intimate involvement with his new children despite the possibility that another "great wind [would come] from across the desert" and he would be grief-stricken yet again.[61] When Job had boldly challenged God, he had put only his own life at risk and nothing more. In renewing his involvement with family and the Friends, Job displayed even greater courage in his willingness to accept the possibility that he would love and then lose all that he had loved once again.

This courage to transcend disappointment and mistrust and to renew and even deepen loving relationships is the core virtue in the political theory underlying the Bible. When this virtue is distilled into a prescriptive injunction, it reads like a flaccid homily. But this abstract distillation is not the Bible's way of teaching. The biblical lesson—the lesson that we have imagined Moses offering in writing the book of Job—emerges from cumulated narratives of interactions between God

and mankind and among mankind itself. In its depiction of these relationships, the central insight is that the participants recurrently make
mutually inconsistent demands on one another, demands that are so
diametrically opposed that no mutual satisfaction is possible. Again
and again, the Bible insists that the essential problem for shaping relationships—the central problem for an adequate theory of politics in
interactions with God or among humans—is to acknowledge the recurrent demand for and the impossibility of complete mutual satisfaction. The consequent imperative that emerges from the biblical
account is the need to choose between two inconsistent alternatives:
either to abandon any relationship because its reliability cannot be en-
sured or to identify the attributes and modalities necessary for the task
of continuously re-forming, again and again, promising relationships
that have been broken.

CHAPTER EIGHT

As We Forgive Those

*T*HE BOOK OF JOB EXPRESSES the most visible challenge by a human being to the legitimacy of God's authority in the Hebrew Bible, most openly addresses the inconsistency of the demands that God and humanity make toward each other, and most clearly sets out the difficulties faced by each in any efforts to restore their broken relationship. The format of the book of Job also differs from that of the rest of the Hebrew Bible. Unlike any other book of the Bible, Job is written in the form of a dialogue, and this format in itself speaks to both the techniques and the obstacles envisioned in the Bible in restoring relationships.

In the traditional canon of Western political theory, the work that most closely approximates the Bible's mode is Plato's *Dialogues,* where Socrates repeatedly seeks to engage interlocutors in moral discourse, is frequently challenged and sometimes powerfully so, and continuously presents himself as "knowing nothing" but nonetheless implicitly holding forth as if he knows everything. Throughout, the author of the *Dialogues,* Plato himself, maintains an apparent posture of neutral reportage, taking no clear side in the debates for or against his former teacher. Socrates is present in all the *Dialogues,* and this fact alone might seem to provide some precedence to his expressed views; in an even more insistent sense, God has an exalted status in the biblical text, and when he speaks his words appear to carry special, even over-whelming, weight. But the book of Job implicitly calls God's special precedence into question, just as Plato's studious neutrality in the *Dia-logues* raises questions about Socrates' preferred status.

The confounding quality of the dialogues in the book of Job is un-derscored by several elements. At crucial moments in the exchanges between God and Job in particular, it is literally impossible to know what Job is saying. This inability to comprehend Job's meaning is not an issue restricted to those of us who are unable to read Job in the original language of its composition. Translating Job does indeed pre-sent special problems because the book was written in an Aramaic ver-nacular and contains more unique words than any other book of the Bible. But the problem of comprehension is more profound than this; unintelligibility is virtually coded into the book.

There are two moments in Job when this unintelligibility is particu-larly vivid, so much so that it is most plausibly understood as an au-thorial choice rather than as a mishap. The most important moment occurs in Job's final speech to God, at the end of God's tirade from the Whirlwind, and is mirrored in a crucial aspect of the very beginning of the book.

In the Prologue, Job, Satan, and Job's wife all spoke of "cursing" God; Job feared that his children had cursed God in their hearts, Satan pre-dicted that Job would curse God to his face, and Job's wife urged him to curse God and die. In all these instances, the Hebrew word used was *b'ruch*—a word that ordinarily translates as "bless." This is a strange reversal of terms—to write "bless" when the context clearly means to convey "curse" (for how, after all, would it have been sinful, as Job feared, if his sons had said a *b'rucha*, a blessing, for God?). This strange reversal has a conventional explanation in biblical commentary: for the author(s) of the book of Job to have written the words "curse God," and for the countless generations of scribes to copy those words, would have been intolerable acts of impiety. And so the written words are "bless God," though the obvious meaning is the opposite.[1]

This reticence is not limited to the depiction of Job's sons. The same strange use of "bless" when the obvious meaning is "curse" appears multiple times in the first two chapters of Job. Thus in chapter 1, verses 10 and 11, Satan tells God that Job is "innocent and upright" only because God "has blessed *(b'ruch)*" him with riches, but that if all his good fortune is taken away then "watch him curse *(b'ruch)* You to Your face." How should the Hebrew reader sort out these two immediately juxtaposed uses of the word *b'ruch?* Might Satan have meant that the riches God had previously bestowed on Job were actually a curse? This reversal of ordinary meaning gains plausibility when we consider that it is precisely Job's great good fortune that provokes Satan's taunt and God's immediate agreement that Job's world should be stripped from him.

Then comes another *b'ruch.* Immediately after the death of his children and destruction of his livestock, Job "tore his robe, and cut off his hair" and famously exclaimed, "Naked I came . . . and naked I return . . . blessed *(b'ruch)* be the name of Yahweh." Hebrew readers (and the English translators) thus encounter another problem. Should *b'ruch* be understood in this sentence as "blessed" or as "cursed be the name of Yahweh"? The book's narrator appeared to anticipate this question by appending an explanation: "In spite of everything, Job did not sin and did not attach blame to God." But might Job have "cursed *(b'ruch)* God in his heart" as Job himself had previously speculated about his sons?

Then Satan induced God to authorize direct inflictions on Job's body, with the renewed wager that Job would "curse *(b'ruch)* You to Your face," and Job's wife made her cameo appearance to taunt Job, "Curse *(b'ruch)* God and die." Job appeared to resist this injunction, but the narrator immediately observed, "In spite of everything, Job did not sin with his lips," provoking the suspicion that Job may have cursed God in his thoughts, though he did not say the words.

This conflation of blessing and cursing is by now almost inextricably intertwined by the repeated use of the Hebrew word for "bless" six
times in two chapters. Four of these clearly imply "curse"—Job's worry
about his sons' attitude toward God, Satan's two wagers about Job's
likely response to his misfortunes, and his wife's challenge that Job
should kill himself. The other two uses are more ambiguous but even
so convey ambivalence about whether "blessing" or "curse" is intended:
Job's initial thought about "blessing" God after he has both given and
taken away doesn't appear to sustain itself after his second affliction;
and Satan's observation that God had "blessed" Job with worldly success turns out to be a "curse" insofar as this success marked him for
Satan's special attention.

Is this conflation and confusion of blessing and curse restricted to
the first two chapters of the book of Job? Is it restricted only to the
book of Job? God was willing, by his own admission, to inflict suffering
on Job "without cause." Is this revelation of God's unpredictability and
vulnerability to Satan's temptation grounds for uncertainty about the
meaning of "blessings" throughout the entire text of the Bible? Must
we readers search for context every time the word "bless" appears to
make sure that it doesn't mean "curse"? Or should we assume, after
reading the book of Job, that blessings and curses are always intricately
interwoven?[2]

In one sense, this interpretive puzzle arises because of the author's
unwillingness to speak directly of cursing God even when the context
obviously called for it. This reticence produced the paradoxical result
that the author disabled himself from ever "blessing" God without
prompting the reader to wonder whether "curse" was truly intended.
Blasphemy thus creeps in from ostentatious piety. Perhaps, however,
this was not unintended. Perhaps this was quite purposeful—a sly suggestion that, for an alert reader, nothing about God in the Bible is simply what it first appears, that praise of God can also imply disguised
criticism, and even that the most extravagant praise (when mankind

rises to the presumptuous height of "blessing" God) conveys the most damning criticism.

This confounding use of language violates ordinary rules of logic— and it points to one considerable difficulty in reading the Bible as a uniformly coherent work. How can A also mean *not-A?* There is, however, a possible logic to this apparent illogic embedded in the biblical text. The logic is in the juxtaposition without resolution of diametrically contradictory ideas.

This is exactly what is conveyed by the overall structure of the book of Job. There is no resolution at the end of the conflict between God and Job. Moreover, this conflict is the climactic expression of the battle between Job and the Friends, a kind of preliminary sparring before the championship bout.

There is an apparent lull in this conflict when Job and the three Friends fall silent and Elihu, a fourth character, appears. Elihu seems to have witnessed the previous arguments between Job and the Friends and offers his own judgment against Job's claims. But no one seems to listen or respond to Elihu or even to acknowledge his existence. God himself in the Epilogue only mentions three Friends, also apparently ignoring Elihu's lengthy harangue. As noted, biblical philologists conclude from this silent reception that Elihu's speech is a later addition to the original, authentic text of the book of Job. As I see it, however, the silence and social isolation that surround Elihu have an important place in the overall structure of Job. This silence and isolation are a marker for the utter failure of social relations, the dead end to which the book of Job has come at this point in its narrative. Elihu resembles Socrates in his final extended oration directed at Callicles in the *Gorgias.* Notwithstanding his promise to Socrates that he would persist in dialogue no matter how deeply divided they might appear, Callicles had disdainfully fallen silent, and Socrates then violated his own principle by addressing his views to no conversational partner at all. The possibility of a satisfactory social relationship had come to an impasse in the *Gorgias* just as this possibility had vanished in the book of Job when Elihu spoke alone.

This destruction of the social world, denoted in both the book of Job and the *Gorgias* by the end of discourse, the mutually unintelligible silence that falls upon the actors, marks another similarity underlying an apparent difference between the biblical text and paradigmatic modern works of political theory. The biblical account never imagines a moment when humans stand outside relationships, whether with God or with other human beings. (For a brief time in the second creation account Adam related only to God, but even then he was born into a relationship.) Paradigmatic modern thinkers do imagine such a moment, at least regarding other human beings—a state of nature outside organized social relationships. Sometimes the state of nature is posited as a heuristic fiction, other times as an actual historical event. For modern thinkers, this conceptual stance outside social relation establishes a base line for positing reasons that humans join in relationship. It also opens the possibility of reserved rights as a condition for coming together. The biblical account, by contrast, regularly speaks of pre-existing relationships between God and humans or among humans which, for one reason or another, break apart. Job is the quintessential expression of this biblical paradigm—the apparent dead end of the relationship between humanity and God, between ruler and ruled. The irresolution at the end of the book of Job about that relationship, about whether it is resumed and, if so, on what terms, is the challenge presented to its readers.

This indeterminacy points to perhaps the most notable difference between biblical and modern political theory. The paradigmatic modern theorists insist on singular meanings; they are constructing authority from nothing, and nothing less than determinate authoritative meaning will do the job. By contrast, in withholding definitive resolutions, biblical politics differs from modern theory but is at once, we might say, both premodern and postmodern. Many different explanations are possible for this difference. If, as I contend, a close reading of the Bible reveals a consistent strain of criticism toward God—a strain that erupts into clear visibility in the book of Job—then it is no surprise that, in a pious society kept together by its piety, the authors and redactors of the holy book for this society would frame their critique of God's authority in veiled fashion. Leo Strauss has famously called this the literature of "persecution . . . in which the truth about all crucial things is presented exclusively between the lines."[3]

The "persecution" need not be imposed from outside. The authors and redactors of the Bible may have been struggling with contradictory ideas and ideals in their own thinking—struggling, in Freud's terms, with unconscious meanings (of longings, of rage, of guilt) in tension with their conscious perceptions of personal and social needs. Multiple contradictory meanings of words can give expression to these tensions in the same way that condensations serve in what Freud calls our "dream-work."[4] Contradiction does not necessarily connote incoherence. As Freud observed, the logic of dreams is conveyed by "thoughts which are mutually contradictory [and] make no attempt to do away with each other, but persist side by side."[5] Dreams thus illuminate unconscious thought processes that coexist in every individual alongside conscious thinking bent toward the rules of linear rationality. In this sense the politics of the Bible may be more faithful to the complexities of social life—to the inevitable admixtures of rational and irrational thinking, of conscious and unconscious meanings—than the rigid rationalizations of modern political theorists.

The fundamental difference with the biblical account of political relations is that modern political theorists typically strive to identify some resolution to the recurrent instability in the relationship between ruler and ruled. This resolution is usually offered as a normative principle which—so the argument goes—would gain the adherence of both ruler and ruled based on persuasive rational considerations, on "right reason." By contrast, in the Bible—and most explicitly in the book of Job—even if neither God nor humanity could do without the other, they nonetheless could not find mutually satisfactory terms for their continuing relationship.

In modern political thought, it may seem at first glance that the People have won through the establishment of constitutionally limited government. But this, too, is an oversimplification. The abiding and essentially unsolved problem of constitutional theory is in identifying the limits of the People's authority over one another. To put it another way, the abiding problem is discerning the legitimacy of the authority that some of the People can invoke to override the claims of others among the People. Or, to put it yet a third way, the abiding problem arises from the attempt to find some master principle for adjudicating mutually inconsistent claims for popular sovereignty (whether the legitimacy of popular sovereignty means acceding to majority rule or, contradictorily, to vested individual rights). The biblical narrative never abandons this same pursuit of a master principle that would restore harmony between God and humanity; though it never reaches this goal, it persistently tries different paths to its attainment. In the Bible these different paths persistently lead back to rupture.[6]

On the surface of its narratives, the Hebrew Bible never breaks this recurrent cycle but instead repeats it over and over again. In this way, the Bible enacts the proposition that Amartya Sen has put forward that the pursuit of "perfectly just social arrangements is inherently problematic" and always doomed to fail.[7] The Bible does not abandon this pursuit, but it shifts attention from the effort to actually arrive at perfect justice toward a more chastened but more realistic goal—that of seeking ways to repair the ruptured relationship between ruler and ruled, of prescribing paths toward forgiveness for the inflictions of injustice.

Rather than relentlessly insisting on the attainment of perfect justice, characteristically expressed in secular Western political theory, the biblical account identifies the central role of forgiveness as the transcendent political virtue precisely because of the inevitable cycle of the pursuit and unattainability of perfect justice. The possibility of forgiveness provides the motive force in the biblical account for the recurrent pursuit of justice notwithstanding the inevitable failure of this pursuit. As the biblical narrative proceeds, moreover, the exploration of the possible means toward forgiving injustice becomes a central organizing theme. The substantive ideal of justice as perfect harmony between God and humanity remains the same throughout; the effort to identify the means to attain this ideal is intensively explored and, for one or another reason, the best bets—on humanity's side by unquestioning obedience to God's will and on God's side by keeping his promises to humanity—are repeatedly found wanting. But reflecting back on the biblical narratives we have explored thus far, we can see how the theme of forgiveness gradually came into prominence, in effect as a response to the impasse continually encountered in the recurrent pursuit of perfect justice.

The central focus of this theme as the narratives unfold is the possibility of God's forgiving humanity for its wrongdoing. This possibility was not, however, prominent or even acknowledged at the outset. Both Adam and Eve tried to excuse their wrongful conduct by shifting blame, but neither acknowledged wrongdoing nor sought forgiveness. Similarly Cain, though devastated by his punitive exile, did not admit guilt or seek forgiveness. The issue of forgiveness emerged as a subliminally organizing theme in Abraham's hope that God would end his exiled wandering, and the theme comes dramatically into view in Moses's successful pleading on behalf of the idolatrous Israelites.

There is, by contrast, almost no exploration of the possibility of God's asking or receiving forgiveness from humanity. There are some hints in Jacob's more or less successful wrestling with God and extraction of promises from him and in Moses's resistance to God's injunction to lead the Israelites from slavery. The presumptuous possibility of humanity's forgiving God comes more to the forefront in the book of Job, but even there the proposition is not openly avowed.

The question of forgiveness for injustice is, however, much more extensively explored in the biblical narratives of relationship between human beings. Two instances in particular involve injustice inflicted by superiors on subordinates—and accordingly they can be read as proxies for the relationship between God and humanity. These two instances, moreover, explore the essential nature of forgiveness—in particular, whether forgiveness requires an admission of wrongdoing by the offender or whether unilateral forgiveness is a coherent and valued proposition.

The idea of unilateral forgiveness anticipates a theme that is central to the Christian Bible—the virtue of "turning the other cheek" to one's adversary. In the Christian Bible, this practice is enjoined not only on human beings in their own relations but on the relations generally between God and humanity. The link between confession of sins and forgiveness is by no means abandoned in the Christian Bible, but it is not a *sine qua non*. Consideration of two instances where unilateral forgiveness is extolled in the Hebrew Bible will help us to understand the significance of this practice when it reappears in the Christian Bible and assumes greater prominence. These instances are Judah's forgiveness of the wrongdoing of his father, Jacob, and David's forgiveness of Saul's wrongdoing toward him.

Judah and Jacob

As Jacob was about to die, he assembled his sons and rendered a final accounting on each of them. He was bitterly critical and dismissive of his three eldest sons, but when he reached Judah, the fourth, he said, "Judah, you, shall your brothers acclaim ... your father's sons shall bow to you.... The scepter shall not pass from Judah ... that tribute to him may come and to him the submission of peoples."[8] This was a momentous choice for the future lineage of the children of Israel; it is the reason that Jacob's descendants are known today as Judahites, as Jews. By appointing Judah his heir as patriarch, Jacob bypassed Joseph, the eldest son of his beloved second wife, Rachel. Jacob's ostentatious favoritism toward Joseph had been the cause of his brothers' hatred of him and their vengeful attack that led to his disappearance into Egypt. Judah had played a leading role in this plot, convincing his brothers to sell Joseph into slavery rather than killing him outright, not to save Joseph's life but to realize some financial gain from the brothers' deed.[9] Moreover, Judah had acted in concert with his brothers in lying to their father that his favored son had been killed by a wild beast. Why, then, did Jacob single out Judah to elevate above all his brothers, including Joseph?

Jacob's final speech gave no clear answer but only announced his conclusion. But Jacob based his rejection of Judah's elder brothers on their conduct in prior episodes recounted in Genesis, and that is where we must look to find the grounds for Jacob's anointing of Judah.

The saga of Joseph's kidnapping begins in Genesis chapter 37 and resumes in chapters 39 through 50, where Genesis ends. But immediately after Joseph's brothers sell him into slavery at the end of chapter 37, the narrative suddenly breaks away to an apparent digression, an intricate narrative in which Judah is the principal actor. Genesis chapter 38 relates that Judah married a Canaanite woman and had three sons; his eldest son married but soon died without children, and Judah instructed his second son to "do [his] duty as brother-in-law" and to impregnate his brother's widow, Tamar. But the second son, Onan, refused to honor this legal obligation. He slept with Tamar but withdrew before ejaculation so as to "waste his seed on the ground" (hence, the origins of "onanism"). This action angered God and Onan died. By rights, the obligation to impregnate Tamar should then have proceeded to Judah's third son, but Judah was unwilling to risk the possibility that this son, too, might die in the effort. He misled Tamar, however, telling her to remain as a widow in her father's house until Judah's third son had grown. "A long time passed." Judah's wife died and Judah's third son grew into manhood, but Tamar remained without husband or children in her father's house.

Finally Tamar decided to take action on her own. She disguised herself as a prostitute and stationed herself alongside a road where she knew that Judah would pass. Judah did not recognize Tamar and immediately propositioned her, promising to send her a lamb for payment; Tamar agreed but demanded Judah's identifying instruments— as Robert Alter puts it, the equivalent of Judah's driver's license and credit card—as sureties for the ultimate payment. The transaction was consummated and Tamar became pregnant, but Judah could not subsequently locate this roadside prostitute to convey the lamb and reclaim his identifying instruments. Three months passed. Tamar's pregnancy became apparent, Judah was informed and immediately directed that she be killed, as decreed by biblical law: "Out she was taken, when she sent to her father-in-law, saying 'By the man to whom these belong I have conceived,' and she said, 'Recognize, pray, whose are this seal-and-cord and this staff?' And Judah recognized them and he said, 'She is more in the right than I, for have I not failed to give her to Shelah, my son?'"[10] So Judah remitted the punishment and Tamar received her just due, giving birth to twins.

This extended tale is Judah's second appearance in Genesis after the account of his role in Joseph's abduction. The narrative then abruptly shifts to Joseph's time in Egypt, and Judah does not reappear until four chapters later, after Joseph had completed his passage from house slave to Pharaoh's grand vizier and the famine that Joseph predicted had spread across the land. In chapter 42, Jacob sends his ten elder sons down to Egypt to seek provisions but keeps with him his youngest son, Benjamin (Joseph's only full brother). The elder sons encounter Joseph decked in grandeur but don't recognize him; the brothers identify themselves as ten of the twelve sons of one man, adding that "the youngest one is now with our father, and one is no more." Joseph, however, recognizes them, gives them food, but treats them harshly and demands that they not come to him again unless accompanied by their younger brother. The brothers then return to Jacob. Through all this narrative, no specific mention is made of Judah.

The provisions that the brothers had brought back from Egypt were soon exhausted, but the famine persisted, and now Judah explicitly reappears in the narrative. Jacob instructs the brothers to return to Egypt for more food, and Judah tells him of "the man's" requirement that they must bring Benjamin with them. Jacob responds, "Why have you done me this harm to tell the man you had another brother?" The brothers together explain that "the man" had questioned them closely about their family and that they had no idea he would demand to see their younger brother. Judah then specifically promises that he will personally take responsibility for Benjamin's safety. "If I do not bring him to you and set him before you," he told his father, "I will bear the blame to you for all time."[11]

The brothers return to Egypt with Benjamin in tow, still not recognizing Joseph, and Joseph arranges an elaborate hoax to justify imprisoning Benjamin. As this hoax unfolds on the unsuspecting brothers, Judah steps forward to become the voice for all of them. He pleads with Joseph to take him rather than Benjamin, and in explaining the devastation that would otherwise fall on his father, he quotes Jacob's misgivings about releasing Benjamin for their return to Egypt: "Our father said to us, 'You know that two did my wife bear me. And one went out from me and I thought, O, He's been torn to shreds, and I have not seen him since. And should you take this one, too, from my presence and harm befall him, you would bring down my gray head in evil to Sheol.'"

The previous narrative had mentioned Jacob's reluctance to release Benjamin, but Judah's account to Joseph is the first time that we readers learn the specific content of Jacob's statement to his elder sons. That statement, as relayed by Judah, conveys an extraordinary indictment of Jacob. He was not only willing to subject his elder sons to risks that he would not contemplate for Benjamin, but he had spoken as if he had only one wife, Rachel, and two sons, Joseph and Benjamin, the children of Rachel. Jacob simply obliterated his eight elder sons conceived with his first wife, Leah, and two slavegirls in Jacob's household. Jacob's favoritism toward Joseph had been the basis for the elder brothers' hatred and vengefully destructive acts. Jacob, with almost astounding insensitivity, had thus set the stage for a repeat performance.

But though Judah's direct quotation of his father's sentiments might have been galling to him and his full brothers, this is not the conclusion that Judah drew. Instead he reminds Joseph of their earlier meeting when the brothers had informed him of Benjamin's existence— and here, too, Judah elaborates on the narrative that Genesis had previously provided. Judah now recalls that they had told Joseph, "We have an aged father and a young child of his old age, and his brother being dead, he alone is left of his mother and his father loves him." In this extended account, Judah frankly acknowledged his father's favoritism toward his two half-brothers. He continued,

> And so, should I come to your servant, my father, and the lad be not with us, for his life is bound to the lad's, when he saw the lad was not with us, he would die, and your servants would bring down the gray head of your servant, our father, in sorrow to Sheol. For your servant became pledge for the lad to my father, saying, "If I do not bring him to you, I will bear the blame to my father for all time." And so, let your servant, pray, stay instead of the lad as a slave to my lord, and let the lad go up with his brothers. For how shall I go up to my father, if the lad be not with us? Let me see not the evil that would find out my father.[12]

At this plea from Judah, Joseph "could no longer hold himself in check before all who stood on attendance upon him, and he cried, 'Clear out everyone around me!' And no man stood with him when Joseph made himself known to his brothers. And he wept aloud."[13]

Joseph then reassured his brothers that he held no grudge against them for their past conduct. Perhaps the brothers believed this, perhaps not. But the central drama that had just occurred was not about Joseph's feelings. It was about Judah's belated wish to avert a repetition of the harm to his father that he and his brothers had previously inflicted in bringing about Joseph's disappearance. Judah spoke of Jacob as "my father," though Jacob had pointedly refused to include Judah and his full brothers as his sons. And by nominating himself instead of Benjamin as a "slave," he was offering to reenact the enslavement that he had been instrumental in originally promoting as Joseph's fate. This time Judah voluntarily embraced, as a kind of penance, the wrong that he had inflicted on Joseph. That time Judah had been motivated by hatred of his half-brother and vengeful feelings toward his father. This time Judah was moved by love for his father, notwithstanding the harm that his father had inflicted—and continued to inflict—on him. On Judah's part this was an act of love—of unconditional, unrequited love.

In his interactions with Tamar, Judah had already displayed some of these moral qualities. He had done an injustice to her by withholding his youngest son for fear of the harm that might befall him. This was, of course, precisely why Jacob had refused to let Benjamin leave him for the trip to Egypt. But Tamar's actions in effect brought Judah into direct confrontation with his wrongdoing, and, without hesitation, Judah accepted the indictment. In this acceptance, Judah did what his father had never done for him—acknowledge his failure of paternal responsibility.

Judah's acceptance of responsibility for his duties as a son, notwithstanding his father's failures, was an even more generous act. Judah was not an inherently righteous man. He had been capable of terrible wrongdoing. But when confronted by evidence of his wrongdoing and its harmful consequences on others, he tried to redeem himself by his willingness to acknowledge his guilt and to accept punishment in return. Judah also showed that he was able to forgive injustices that had been inflicted on him, even when the perpetrator of the injustice refused to admit, or was characterologically incapable of admitting, his wrongdoing and asking forgiveness for it.

In his last act, finally living up to his patriarchal responsibility, Jacob saw these qualities in Judah that were apparent in none of his brothers (including Jacob's favorites, Joseph and Benjamin). Perhaps Jacob had glimpsed these qualities in his brother Esau, who embraced him and appeared to forgive him for his prior deception and consequent theft of their father Isaac's blessing. Jacob had remained wary of Esau's motives when they re-encountered each other many years after his wrongdoing, and the biblical account of their reunion leaves open the possibility that Esau was indeed toying with Jacob and was insincere in his protestations of forgiveness. But the very ambiguity in Esau's conduct might have provoked Jacob to reflect on his wrongful actions toward his brother and his own wish for forgiveness. Even if Esau had not clearly acted with the generosity that Jacob might have wanted, Jacob could recognize the genuine article when it appeared.

Judah was the real thing: a wrongdoer who was ready to admit his unjust infliction on a subordinate and to ask her forgiveness, to humble himself before her. He was a victim of wrongdoing at the hands of his father whom he forgave even though this superior authority lacked the grace to acknowledge his own transgressions and to seek forgiveness. No one in the whole of Genesis displayed these qualities with the same force and clarity as they appeared in Judah—not even God himself. If there is one hero in all of Genesis, it is Judah—whose status as such is confirmed by Jacob's blessing.

Saul and David

The same themes that we have seen between Jacob and Judah, father and son, reappear between Saul and David, king and subject (who also refer to their relationship in explicitly filial terms[14]). Saul, having been told by the prophet Samuel that he had lost the kingship, repeatedly attempted to kill David, suspecting that David had been secretly chosen as his successor. Though David had a clear opportunity to kill Saul in justified self-defense, he held back and, in effect, demonstrably forgave Saul. David's act provoked Saul's conscience, and Saul renounced his murderous intentions. He was too jealous and fearful of David to sustain this renunciation, however, and renewed his attempts to kill him. David then had a second opportunity to kill Saul but again he held back; again Saul was conscience-stricken and promised to relent before yet again breaking this promise.

This quick version of the interactions between Saul and David flattens the subtle psychological portrayal in the biblical account and omits the conflicting impulses portrayed in David's conduct. But the overall pattern nonetheless holds to the model provided by Judah's conduct toward his father—that ultimately David accepted the wrong inflicted on him and held back from retaliation. Moreover he, like Judah, was motivated by filial loyalty that was not met by a reciprocated paternal response. Saul, in one of his brief moments of moral clarity, saw this trait in David and drew the same conclusion from it that Jacob had drawn regarding Judah. After David demonstrated that he had refrained from killing Saul when he could easily have done so, Saul wept and said, "You are more in the right than I, for it is you who requited me good whereas I requited you evil. . . . and so, look, I know that you will surely be king and that the kingship of Israel will stay in your hands."[15]

There is yet another strong similarity between Judah and David and a contrast between them and Saul. All three men committed serious wrongs. David engaged in adultery with Bathsheba and then cold-bloodedly arranged for the death of her husband to conceal evidence of his liaison—an offense, if anything, more awful than Judah's participation in his brother Joseph's enslavement. But when the prophet Nathan confronted David with a moral critique of his actions, David instantly acknowledged his guilt and made no attempt at exonerating excuses.[16] Saul's offense was violating God's explicit command that he destroy all of the populace and property of the Ameleks, the historic enemy of Israel; Saul instead spared the king of the Ameleks and their best livestock, apparently for self-aggrandizing reasons, since he accompanied these actions by erecting "a monument for himself."[17] But when confronted with his violation of God's command by the prophet Samuel, Saul equivocated, saying first that he had intended to use the livestock as offerings to God and then that he had "feared the troops and listened to their voice."[18] Saul's refusal to accept personal responsibility for whatever wrong he had committed stands in sharp contrast to the conduct of Judah and David when confronted with their wrongdoing.

David's willingness to refrain from retaliation against his unrepentant superior mirrored Judah's forgiveness of his father. David was also willing to forgive his son Absalom notwithstanding the son's clear offenses—his mustering of armed rebellion against David and his sexual dalliances with his father's concubines. When David's troops sought out the rebels, David abjured them to capture but not to kill Absalom. When he learned that his instructions had not been followed and that Absalom had been killed, his grief was profound—perhaps the most wrenching, extended expression of grief in the entire Hebrew Bible: "And the king was shaken. And he went up to the upper room over the gate and he wept, and thus he said as he went, 'My son, Absalom! My son, my son, Absalom! Would that I had died in your stead! Absalom, my son, my son!' . . . And the king covered his face, and the king cried out with a loud voice, 'My son, Absalom! Absalom, my son, my son!'"[19]

The extravagance of David's grief may have arisen, at least in part, from his sense of guilt for the death many years earlier of his infant son born from his illicit liaison with Bathsheba—a death imposed by God as the punishment for David's adultery and his murderous plot against Bathsheba's husband. For the entire seven days of the infant's terminal illness, David fasted and slept on the ground. He grieved so intensely that his servants feared he would harm himself when the child died. Though he apparently recovered his composure with surprising speed, his lament over Absalom's death—"would that I had died in your stead"—might seem more an echo of his previous grief and guilt for the punishment that he deserved but that fell on his infant son instead.

In any event, David's grief at Absalom's death demonstrates that he was prepared to forgive a subordinate who had inflicted wrongdoing on him though he had demonstrated no remorse at all—just as his forbearance toward Saul showed his willingness to forgive his superior for unapologetic wrongdoing. The existence of these traits—willingness to forgive wrongdoing even if the perpetrator remained unrepentant and readiness to accept responsibility for one's own wrongdoing—thus appears as the central criterion for fitness to rule over others, for David to displace Saul as king of Israel and for Judah to assume the mantle of patriarch.

Are these traits equally characteristic of God, the marks of his fitness to rule? The short answer is that in the beginning, there was no evidence of these traits in God's character just as there was no need to find any justification for his fitness to rule. These traits emerged over time, as the Hebrew Bible's narrative unfolded, in God's attempts to find satisfactory terms for his interactions with mankind; and it was in this search for a relationship with mankind that the question of God's fitness to rule emerged as a recognizable issue. God did not initiate this question, and mankind articulated it only slowly and with considerable diffidence—from Noah's fearful uncertainty and display of naked vulnerability, progressing to Abraham's challenge in response to God's invitation before destroying Sodom and Gomorrah, to Jacob's extraction of promises in his wrestling match with God, to Moses's face-to-face insistence that God should forgive the Israelites' transgressions, and finally to Job's explicit protest at the injustice of God's inflictions.

At each step of this progression, God offered some accommodation to mankind's demands on him, but these accommodations were always tentative, and God never openly admitted that he felt compelled to defer to mankind's needs or wishes. Even so, in his interactions with David, God strongly implied that he had come to embrace a conception of himself that gave priority to forgiveness of wrongdoing rather than to punitive severance of relations with the wrongdoer. Soon after David was recognized as king, after Saul's death, God said, "I will make the throne of his kingship unshaken forever. I will be a father to him and he will be a son to me, so should he do wrong, I will chastise him with the rod men use and with the afflictions of humankind. But My loyalty shall not swerve from him as I made it swerve from Saul whom I removed before you."[20]

David did subsequently commit a terrible wrong, in arranging for the death of Uriah to cover up his adultery with Uriah's wife, Bathsheba. And God did "chastise him . . . with the afflictions of humankind." But God did not abandon his prior relationship with David as he had with Saul, and in this steadfastness, God provided a deeper understanding of the virtue of forgiveness than the ordinary usage of the word conveys.

Forgiveness, as God portrayed it in his initial commitment to David, did not imply forgoing blame or even the imposition of punishment. Forgiveness instead implied that God's basic underlying loyalty to David remained intact, notwithstanding his wrongdoing. And though David admitted his transgressions, this action was not the central premise for God's promise of loyalty. The promise was unconditional. It was based on a recognition by God of their prior filial relationship. Most notably, God's promise, "I will be a father to him and he will be a son to me," is the first time in the Hebrew Bible that God described himself, or was recognized by any human being, specifically as a father.

Between ruler and subject, relationships can be severed. But the biological connection between father and son cannot be broken as such.

The biological connection does not necessarily imply that social relations will be preserved, but God used the connection between father and son as the model for his new conception of an unbreakable bond with humanity, no matter how grievously one may offend the other. This bond does not, moreover, require reciprocal acknowledgment. One partner could unilaterally sustain this loyalty even if the other partner refused to reciprocate. This unilateral act would not, however, be an isolated expression. It would in effect be an announcement to the alienated other that the possibility always remained open for a restored recognition of their relationship. From one side or the other, from the father or from the son, the relationship was preserved intact, waiting only for the alienated party to take advantage of the offer.

God did not explain why he had chosen to change the terms of his relationship with David after he had permanently severed relations with David's predecessor, Saul. It may be that God was especially touched by David in a way that he not been by Saul. David is the most universally loved person in the entire Hebrew Bible, and he seems aware of his seductive capacities. Immediately before God swore loyalty to him, David had engaged in an ecstatic dance before God; as the biblical text described it, "David was whirling with all his might before the Lord, girt in a linen ephod." Michal, David's wife and Saul's daughter, jealously criticized David for "exposing himself to the eyes of his servant's slavegirls." But David responded, "I will play before the Lord!" Immediately afterward, David promised to build a house for God more imposing than the diminutive ark in which God had manifested his presence—an offer that God declined, saying instead, "Is it you who would build Me a house . . . The Lord declares that it is He Who will make you a house."[21] It was then that God characterized his relationship with David as filial and promised sustained loyalty.

Thus it may be that God's promise was unique to David, who had touched his heart as no human being had done before. The intimacy that God had bestowed on Moses was more a relationship looking toward equality than a father-son bond. Perhaps the closest filial love that God had previously displayed was for Adam, in whom he had breathed life. I have suggested that God may have been a shy and disappointed lover toward Adam, as Adam turned away from him toward Eve. There was no reticence, however, in God's open profession of filial love for David. God may have been struck that David felt no shame in whirling naked before him, unlike the attitude of Adam or Noah toward their nakedness. David explicitly rejected his wife's effort to shame him with his nakedness. Unlike Adam, moreover, David turned away from his wife to "play" with God—to offer him the loving companionship that he had sought as he strolled in the evening breeze in the Garden of Eden. No wonder that God was smitten. It was as if God had been waiting for this kind of love for all of humanity's life.

Even if God was not prepared to extend this filial relationship to all humanity in the Hebrew Bible, his relationship with David served as the precursor on which his relationship with Jesus was constructed in the Christian Bible, a promise of loving loyalty that Jesus extended beyond himself. God's promise of loyalty to David was apparently a unilateral commitment. The promise was prompted by David's open-hearted love for God, but once God had acknowledged the filial relationship, he described his promise as unconditional. For the first time in a relationship with a human being, God clearly announced that his loyalty could not be forfeited no matter how grievously David might sin. This promise in the Hebrew Bible is the key to the Christian Bible's conception of God's forgiveness for the persistence of sin and injustice.

CHAPTER NINE

A Renewed Testament

Mark, Matthew, and Luke

*T*HE CONVENTIONAL CLAIM is that the Hebrew Bible foretells the events narrated in the Christian Bible. But there is a deeper continuity between the two Bibles. The recurrent problem of mutual mistrust and abandonment in the relationship between God and humanity is addressed in a new way in the Christian Bible; nonetheless, the same problem ultimately reappears.

In the Hebrew Bible, the cause of the rift between God and humanity is persistently diagnosed as humanity's failure to obey God's commandments. If only humanity would obey, the breach would be healed and God would resume his protective custody: so this refrain goes from Abraham to Moses to the Hebrew Prophets to Job's Friends. As we have seen, Abraham, Moses, and Job each come to doubt this prescription as it applies to his own relationship with God, and it is not clear whether the breach that appeared in those relationships is ever fully healed. Even so, the possibility and desirability of healing remain an urgent concern, perhaps for them and certainly for readers of the biblical narrative.

Jesus saw the stalemate in this relationship and offered a new approach that promised to break through it. Put in its simplest form, Jesus identified a new goal for healing the breach—not obedience to

God's commandments but love between God and humanity. Moreover, Jesus prescribed a new means for achieving that goal: not unilateral deference to God's authority but mutual deference based on the interlocking, reciprocal authority of God and humanity. Jesus himself personified this new understanding, as the Son of God who was both human and divine. This is the core message in the Gospels of Mark, Matthew, and Luke, the so-called Synoptic Gospels. As we will see in the next chapter, this conception of shared authority was not subsequently sustained in other texts of the Christian Bible—in particular, Paul's Letters, John's Gospel, and the Revelation—but for this chapter, we will concentrate on the Synoptic Gospels in order to establish a basis for comparison with the other texts.

Jesus taught this new approach to the relationship between God and humanity in his direct preaching, but his full meaning and its novelty cannot be grasped by attending to his words alone. More important, Jesus taught through his actions, and, like his parables, these actions are often difficult to decode. These difficulties are increased by the fact that different Gospel authors often give different accounts of Jesus's statements and actions. As in our exploration of the Hebrew Bible, we will pay especially close attention to these apparent inconsistencies—with an intent not to resolve them, to identify the "one true version," but to identify the reasons behind the inconsistencies and why they remained unresolved in the Gospels and other canonical accounts in the Christian Bible.

First Act: Jesus's Baptism

Mark's Gospel was the first of the Synoptic Gospels; Matthew and Luke subsequently took Mark's Gospel as a baseline that they elaborated and occasionally contradicted in various ways.[1] Mark's Gospel opens with these dramatic introductory words: "The beginning of the Gospel of Jesus Christ, the Son of God." Matthew's Gospel has a much more prosaic beginning: "The Book of the Genealogy of Jesus Christ, the son of

David, the son of Abraham"; and Luke's begins somewhat pedantically with a letter addressed to the "most excellent Theophilus," explaining why he was drawing on previous narratives "to write an orderly account" of Jesus's life.

Mark's account of the beginning is anything but orderly. He defies conventional narrative technique by seeming to start in the middle of things. Matthew begins more conventionally with a twenty-eight-generation genealogy leading to Jesus's birth (after the style of the Hebrew Bible lists of "begats"), and Luke begins with John the Baptist's conception and then moves to Jesus's birth. Mark, by contrast, starts his narrative with a quotation from Isaiah, "Behold, I send my messenger . . . the voice of one crying in the wilderness: Prepare the way of the Lord." Mark continues: "John the Baptist appeared in the wilderness, preaching a baptism of repentance for the forgiveness of sins." Mark then briefly depicts a multitude of people who come to John for baptism in the river Jordan, and he quotes John's observation that after him "comes he who is mightier than I," he who will baptize not with water but "with the Holy Spirit." And then, abruptly, Mark proclaims: "In those days Jesus came from Nazareth of Galilee and was baptized by John in the Jordan."

Jesus thus first appears in Mark as an adult, with no indication that he had a past, much less a past relevant to an understanding of his immediate appearance or what followed from it. And Jesus's first act after his abrupt appearance, as if from nowhere, was to accept baptism from John. Mark thus opens with a dramatic puzzle: what does it mean that "the beginning of the Gospel of Jesus Christ, the Son of God," announces Jesus's "baptism of repentance for the forgiveness of sins"? The narration of Jesus's baptism implies that he joined with the others who received John's baptism in "confessing their sins." What sins might the Son of God need to confess at the outset of his ministry?

Mark proceeds to relate that immediately after Jesus's baptism "he saw the heavens opened and the Spirit descending on him like a dove; and a voice came from heaven, 'Thou art my beloved Son; with thee I am well pleased.'"² God may have been speaking generally about his pleasure in Jesus, but the immediate juxtaposition of God's encomium with Jesus's baptism suggests that God was particularly pleased with this act. Might he be pleased with his beloved Son's humility in openly acknowledging his shortfalls? Or pleased that his Son had acted as his proxy to confess God's own sins against humanity? Or simply pleased that his Son feels an empathic identification with human sinners? Mark offers no explanation for Jesus's act of baptism or for God's response to it. But the very absence of any adornment that might qualify its apparent meaning conveys the implication that Jesus and/or God had some reason to repent and to seek forgiveness, or identified with those who had sinned. So it would seem at least to the multitudes of people crowded around John to seek their own baptisms.

The other Gospel writers, however, were not comfortable with this implication and struggled against it. Matthew revealed his discomfort in his elaboration of Mark's account. Jesus's baptism appears in Matthew's Gospel only after an extended account of Jesus's illustrious genealogy from Abraham through David to Jesus's conception as "child of the Holy Spirit," the "wise men's" recognition of Jesus's divinity immediately after his birth, and the Holy Family's flight into Egypt to avoid Herod's death decree. Having established Jesus's claim to divine origin and authority, Matthew proceeds to Jesus's adulthood and his first public act of baptism. But, unlike Mark, Matthew records resistance to this act. Here is his account:

> Then Jesus came from Galilee to the Jordan to John, to be baptized by him. John would have prevented him, saying, "I need to be baptized by you, and do you come to me?" But Jesus answered him, "Let it be so now; for thus it is fitting for us to fulfil all righteousness." Then he consented. And when Jesus was baptized, he went up immediately from the water, and behold, the heavens were opened.³

Mark, of course, had said nothing of John's attitude, much less his resistance, toward Jesus's accepting baptism from him. In Matthew's account, the Baptist voices discomfort, as if it were inconceivable that Jesus, the Son of God, would have any sin to confess—as if the very idea of God's committing sin was self-contradictory. Matthew then follows this account with another variance from Mark's version. Matthew reports that when the heavens opened after Jesus's baptism, the "Spirit of God" descended on Jesus and a voice from heaven said, "This is my beloved Son, with whom I am well pleased." By Mark's account, the heavenly voice had said, "You are my beloved Son"—seemingly a private communication between God and Jesus, whereas Matthew's heavenly voice refers to Jesus in the third person, as if God were addressing others who thereby witnessed confirmation of Jesus's divine status. There is, however, an odd grammatical lapse in Matthew's account. When the heavens opened, Matthew records that "he [Jesus] saw the Spirit of God descending"; when this sentence ends, there is no indication of a shift in audience from Jesus, who alone saw the Spirit, to others besides him who heard the heavenly voice. Matthew seems to have followed Mark's account of Jesus's solo witnessing, but later in the same sentence he confusingly shifted the narrative from Jesus alone hearing God's praise to the general public hearing the heavenly voice with him.

Matthew seems compelled in this account to reassure his readers that Jesus was truly divine even though he appeared to confess his own sinfulness. Mark doesn't acknowledge anything strange in Jesus's acceptance of baptism, though his readers would almost certainly be perplexed; this is one instance of Mark's repeated pedagogic strategy of embedding puzzles in his compressed narratives. Although Matthew could not eliminate the puzzle without repudiating Mark's account, he tries to soften its abrasive edge by insisting that the Baptist understood that Jesus didn't need to be baptized, and, to the same effect, that every witness to this baptism was immediately and unquestionably informed that Jesus was the Son of God.

Luke deals with Jesus's baptism in yet another way that reveals discomfort. Similarly to Matthew, Luke begins his Gospel with an ex-

tended account of Jesus's birth and youth, during which many people
(the "shepherds out in the field," the "righteous and devout" Simeon,
the "prophetess, Anna") recognize his divinity. Luke then describes
John's baptizing of multitudes of people with much more detail than
Mark or Matthew provided, and he comes to Jesus's baptism almost
backhandedly: "Now when all the people were baptized, and when Jesus also had been baptized and was praying, the heaven was opened,
and the Holy Spirit descended upon him . . . and a voice came from
heaven, 'Thou art my beloved Son; with thee I am well pleased.'"[4] Luke
seems to calculate that no one would notice Jesus's baptism or ascribe
special significance to it if it were related quickly and buried in a subordinate clause in a sentence devoted to the awesome appearance
of God. Moreover, though Mark and Matthew both indicated that Jesus alone saw the heavens open and the Holy Spirit descending, Luke
does not indicate who saw these grand events, thus leaving open the
possibility that the multitudes had overheard God address Jesus, even
though he refers to him in the first person.

These variations among the Synoptic Gospel accounts are so stark
that they must be filled with meaning, and the most plausible meaning
is that, unlike Mark, Matthew and Luke were reluctant to acknowledge
the most obvious explanation for Jesus's willingness to accept baptism,
and they actively sought to downplay its significance. (As we will see in
the next chapter, John's Gospel went even further and refused to acknowledge that Jesus was ever baptized.) As strange as it might seem by
ordinary conventions to say that God or his corporeal embodiment or
representative on earth can sin (or feels an identification with sinners),
that is exactly what Mark appeared to say (and what Matthew, Luke,
and John struggled against acknowledging). Mark's seemingly simple
statement that the first act of Jesus's public ministry was to seek "a baptism of repentance for the forgiveness of sins" thus might be a stunning ratification of the hints sprinkled through the Hebrew Bible that
God is subject (or has chosen to subject himself) to extrinsic norms of
good conduct in his dealings with humanity.

Second Act: Jesus in the Wilderness

Whatever meaning we might ascribe to Jesus's acceptance of baptism as his first public act, something in the transaction appeared to trouble God himself. He acknowledged Jesus as his Son and expressed pleasure in him at the conclusion of this act. But then, according to Mark, "The Spirit immediately drove [Jesus] out into the wilderness. And he was in the wilderness forty days, tempted by Satan; and he was with the wild beasts; and the angels ministered to him."[5] As abruptly as this event in the wilderness intruded, Mark says nothing more about it; he simply resumes his narrative account of John's arrest and Jesus's preaching in Galilee, almost as if nothing had happened after John baptized Jesus and the heavenly Spirit initially embraced him.

We might, however, find clues to the meaning of this intervening event in the few details that Mark provides about it, which are directly evocative of several episodes in the Hebrew Bible. The fact that the Spirit acknowledges Jesus as his Son and then drives him "out into the wilderness" recalls Abraham's expulsion and effective abandonment of his son Ishmael into "the wilderness of Beersheba."[6] The forty days' length of Jesus's stay in the wilderness apparently corresponds to Noah's forty days drifting in the Flood waters, after which he began to fear that God had abandoned him to the same fate that had fallen on the rest of humanity. This time specification also appears to evoke the "forty days and forty nights" that elapsed between Moses's ascent on Mount Sinai and the Israelites' turn to the Golden Calf (because "Moses lagged in coming down from the mountain [and] we do not know what has happened to him").[7] Just as Noah and the Israelites feared that God had abandoned them after forty days' absence, so it appears that Satan was tempting Jesus to believe that God had abandoned him during his forty days in the wilderness.

The abrupt, unexplained narrative intrusion in Mark in which God drove Jesus out into the wilderness recalls another narrative break in Exodus "on the way at the night camp" when God "encountered [Moses] and sought to put him to death." God's assault on Moses at the first moment after the beginning of their joint enterprise suggests a direct link with God's infliction on Jesus immediately following his paternal embrace. In Exodus, God was about to embark on a more intimate relationship with a human being than any in his experience throughout the Hebrew Bible; his sudden, though momentary, eruption of violence toward Moses suggested powerful misgivings—perhaps doubts about Moses's reliability (especially in light of his reluctance to enter the relationship), perhaps an ambivalence about the constraints imposed on God himself by the prospect of his intimate attachment to Moses. We can only infer from the stark presentation of his attempt to kill Moses that God thought briefly of withdrawing from the relationship. Mark's equally stark account of God's driving Jesus into the wilderness conveys the same inference.

These parallels from the Hebrew Bible point to a connecting pattern of deep significance among the events at the beginning of Jesus's ministry: his baptism, God's proclamation of love for him, and God's immediate banishment of him to the wilderness, where he was tempted by Satan. In these three events, Jesus admits to personal vulnerability (his need to be baptized for the forgiveness of sins); God responds by acknowledging his love for Jesus—which in turn makes him vulnerable should Jesus refuse to reciprocate or subsequently withdraw his love; and God immediately withdraws from Jesus, as if to preemptively abandon him before Jesus can take advantage of God's vulnerability toward him.

This pattern of relations between God and humanity repeatedly occurred throughout the Hebrew Bible, with each turning toward the other while at the same time wary of the possibility of abandonment. The first act of Jesus's public ministry brings this recurrent pattern into stark visibility. This pattern encapsulates the central problem in the politics of the relationship between God and humanity in both the Hebrew and the Christian Bibles—the problem of a mutual wish for a harmonious relationship repeatedly undermined by fear on both sides of vulnerability and the prospect of abandonment.

To state this problem as "political" may seem a misapplication of the term. This might appear to be a problem among lovers, a ("merely") personal domestic issue. In fact, however, the core problem in relations between government and the citizenry is the need on both sides for sustained allegiance. Government depends on the loyalty of its citizens (though there are many ways of trying to secure this loyalty, from soliciting consent to outright coercion and subordination); citizens in turn are dependent on the supportive loyalty of the government (and there are many ways of trying to ensure this loyalty, from flattering pledges of fealty to threats of rebellion and transferred attachment to some other governor).

Jesus's constant appeal to love on both sides employs an unconventional vocabulary for political relationships. But this shift is his way of trying to address the political problem that had continuously been presented in the Hebrew Bible through the more conventional vocabulary of command and submission. In this vocabulary the problem had been cast in univalent terms, with God issuing commands and humanity regularly failing to obey them. But Jesus recast the problem as a mutual failure—a failure on each side to rely on the other's continued allegiance, to trust that each would not abandon the other. Jesus's ministry was an effort to show both God and humanity that, at the core of their relationship, each wanted to remain faithful to the other and to overcome the legacy of mutual mistrust that had accumulated since the end of the first creation in Genesis.

Mark enacted this legacy in his depiction of the first acts of Jesus's ministry, the baptism, the expulsion, and Jesus's return from the wilderness after Satan's temptations. The starkness of his depiction, the absence of any explanation for these actions, intensifies their puzzling character and, in itself, breaks with the command modality of God's interaction with humanity since its second creation in Genesis. By Jesus's account, as Mark portrays it, humanity must actively engage itself in repairing its relationship with God rather than passively deferring to God's commands. Mark's puzzles in themselves demand active engagement rather than passive acquiescence from his readers. This is his "beginning of the Gospel of Jesus Christ, the Son of God."

Matthew and Luke were, however, uncomfortable with Mark's presentational strategy. They wanted to provide more reassurance (and, one senses, to obtain more reassurance for themselves). Beyond their reluctance to acknowledge the vulnerability implied by Jesus's baptism, both Matthew and Luke spell out the specific terms of the temptations that Satan presented to Jesus and demonstrate that Jesus successfully resisted them—a reassurance that Mark refused to provide, at least explicitly.

According to both Matthew and Luke, Satan put three temptations to Jesus. When Jesus was hungry after "forty days and forty nights" of fasting, Satan taunted him to prove he was the Son of God by commanding stones to become loaves of bread; he dared Jesus to throw himself down from the pinnacle of the Jerusalem temple to show that God's angels would rescue him; and he offered Jesus "all the kingdoms of the world" if Jesus would "fall down and worship" him.[8] Each of these temptations alluded to tests in the Hebrew Bible that God had put to humans because he suspected or had concluded that they had abandoned him. The most direct allusion was Satan's dare that Jesus should endanger himself and rely on God to protect him. This was the same taunt that Satan—in his only appearance in the Hebrew Bible— aimed at God, insisting that Job appeared faithful only because God "had sheltered him on all sides."[9] God then tested Job to assure himself that, if he withdrew protection, Job would not abandon him. Jesus, however, refused to test whether God would protect him. "You shall not tempt the Lord your God," he said, thus apparently chastising Satan for his temptation of God in Job and assuring God (who presumably was overhearing the transaction) that his loyalty was unconditional.

Satan's temptation that Jesus should slake his hunger by commanding stone to turn into bread apparently alludes to Moses's failure of God's test when he struck rather than spoke to the rock to extract water from it; as I suggested in Chapter 6, the impetus for God's test was Moses's threat to abandon God when he asked God to kill him to relieve him of his burden—the "evil" God had inflicted on him—in leading the stiff-necked Israelites. And Satan's temptation that Jesus should "fall down and worship him" was a direct invitation to abandon God, evocative of the Israelites' worship of the Golden Calf.

The message that Jesus conveyed in turning away from Satan's temptations was that he would not abandon God no matter what the provocation might be, even if it came from God himself, as when he appeared to abandon Jesus to Satan and the beasts in the wilderness. This message denied the existence of any disharmony between Jesus and God, but it did not rebut the implication that God had feared the possibility of disharmony and had devised a test of Jesus's loyalty that, as God saw it, he might well fail.

We could reject this implication by asserting that God knew Jesus would resist the temptations but set out the tests to demonstrate to humanity the unconditional loyalty that his Son gave to him and that he equally expected from everyone. This evasion of the plain meaning of the biblical text would be similar to the attempts to acquit God of endangering Isaac's life by testing Abraham's willingness to sacrifice him on the ground that God knew Abraham would pass the test and would be rescued from it at the last moment. In both cases, we can't know God's motive, but the biblical texts in both cases do not require this reading and thus ostentatiously leave open the possibility that God did not know how Abraham or Jesus would respond to his tests of their loyalty. The possibility remains open, that is, that God wants unconditional loyalty but is unsure whether his wishes will be fulfilled. Put another way, God does not want to be abandoned, and he repeatedly tries to reassure himself against this possibility by abandoning, or appearing to abandon, humanity in order to see if we will retaliate in kind. By

Matthew's and Luke's accounts, Jesus offered reassurance to God of his unconditional allegiance by disdaining Satan's temptations; but more significant, in their accounts, Jesus urged God to refrain from ever again testing his or anyone else's loyalty.

In Matthew and Luke, Jesus explicitly posed this lesson both to humanity and to God himself. Matthew recounts that in the Sermon on the Mount, Jesus told humanity, "Pray then like this: Our Father who art in heaven ... lead us not into temptation, But deliver us from evil."[10] (The Revised English Bible translation is more direct for our purposes: "do not put us to the test, but save us from the evil one.") The plea from humanity that Jesus dictated might have implied that God should refrain from testing because humanity feared that it might not pass, but this is hardly an attractive basis for any exemption from testing. A more plausible reading is that Jesus, on behalf of humanity, was asking God to withhold temptation because it was unnecessary, and perhaps even self-defeating, for him to act on the premise of mistrust implied by his recurrent testing of humanity. As Jesus put it earlier in this prayer: "forgive us our debts, as we also have forgiven our debtors" (or, in the Revised English Bible translation, "forgive us the wrong we have done, as we have forgiven those who have wronged us"). If, as Jesus's experience in the wilderness suggested, humanity feared abandonment by God and God resented even the possibility of abandonment by humanity, the prayer to God that Jesus recommended was a plea for mutual forgiveness between God and humanity.

Third Act: The Secret of Jesus's Authority

Having assured God of his unconditional loyalty despite being tested in the wilderness, Jesus then turned toward humanity—a turn that became the focus of his efforts until virtually the end of his ministry, when, in his agony in the garden of Gethsemane and then ultimately on the Cross, he once again directly addressed God. For both humanity and God, however, Jesus's message remained the same: that their fear of abandonment was misplaced, that the mistrust that had arisen from this fear could be surmounted by a promise of unconditional allegiance, and that the key to this reconciliation was that loyalty could be obtained not by a coercive demand on one side or the other but only by a consensual pledge on both sides. This was the underlying signification of Jesus's teaching in Matthew's Gospel that "if any one strikes you on the right cheek, turn to him the other also," and in Luke's, that you should "love your enemies, and do good, and lend, expecting nothing in return."[11] As applied to relations between God and humanity, the message was that previous injuries should not be met with retaliatory punishment or withdrawal but with purposefully sustained vulnerability to further injury, with "love . . . expecting nothing in return."

In the Synoptic Gospels generally, however, Jesus taught this lesson to humanity much more by his silences than by what he said. In Mark's Gospel, Jesus was virtually always silent—that is, he taught principally in actions (or in puzzling parables) whose meanings were not self-evident but had to be actively extracted by engaged listeners. In Matthew and Luke, Jesus was less demanding and seemingly more accessible; nonetheless, in these Gospels, too, Jesus remained silently elusive at centrally important moments.

In Mark's account, Jesus's first move toward humanity after leaving the wilderness was to select a few disciples. In this process, Jesus set the essential pattern for all his subsequent appeals for adherents. We can see this pattern by asking why Jesus chose as he did and why the denominated disciples decided to follow him. Here is Mark's entire description of the enlistment process:

> And passing along by the Sea of Galilee, he saw Simon and Andrew the brother of Simon casting a net in the sea; for they were fishermen. And Jesus said to them, "Follow me and I will make you become fishers of men." And immediately they left their nets and followed him. And going

on a little farther, he saw James the son of Zeb'edee and John his brother, who were in their boat mending the nets. And immediately he called them; and they left their father Zeb'edee in the boat with the hired servants and followed him.[12]

Mark offers no reason that Jesus selected these men for any special status (except, perhaps, because of the pun that their occupation as fishermen would offer him). But the very absence of distinction in these men may convey precisely the message that Jesus intended, that his adherents required no special prior qualification but that they became special by the fact that they chose to adhere to him.

But why did they exercise this choice? What did Jesus offer them? At this point in Mark's narrative, Jesus had performed no miraculous works, nor had anyone but Jesus heard God's paternal recognition from the heavens. The disciples' immediate, unquestioning acceptance of Jesus's offer might appear reminiscent of Abraham's instantaneous acceptance of God's injunction to follow him "to the land I will show you." But in that instance, God promised to make Abraham "a great nation"; in any event, some biographical details were provided about Abraham's relationship to his younger brother that suggested a further motive for Abraham beyond blind obedience to God or the possibility of self-aggrandizement.[13] By contrast, Jesus's disciples left their homes to follow this itinerant preacher though they had heard no heavenly voice investing him with clear authority, and Jesus's own capacity to make them "fishers of men," whatever that might have meant to them, was hardly demonstrated. The disciples literally took Jesus on faith.

The disciples' motives for following Jesus appear more explicable in Luke's account. According to Luke, Jesus first encountered Simon Peter and the others only after he had attracted widespread notoriety from his preaching and healing activities. And Jesus filled their nets with "a great shoal of fish" though they had "toiled all night and took nothing." They were accordingly "astonished"; Simon Peter then "fell down at Jesus' knees, saying 'Depart from me, for I am a sinful man, O Lord.'"

But Jesus responded, "'Do not be afraid; henceforth you will be catching men.' And when they brought their boats to land, they left everything and followed him."[14]

Matthew's account of Jesus's first meeting with the disciples more closely follows Mark's cryptic account; according to Matthew, Jesus saw them and called out, "'Follow me, and I will make you fishers of men.' Immediately they left their nets and followed him."[15] But Matthew differs from Mark in one crucial way. When Jesus was publicly baptized, "a voice from heaven" had said, "This is my beloved Son, with whom I am well pleased."[16] In Mark's account of this event (as well as Luke's), the heavenly voice referred to Jesus in the second person, "You are my beloved Son," strongly implying that Jesus alone heard this communication. Matthew's use of the third person suggests that the assembled multitude heard this description of Jesus.[17] Moreover, unlike Mark, both Matthew and Luke begin their accounts with Jesus's infancy, and, according to them, many people recognized his divine stature before he met the disciples. Thus by Matthew's and Luke's accounts, Jesus's fame may have preceded him and prepared the disciples for their instant acceptance of his invitation.

Notwithstanding the difference in their details, however, these three accounts in the Synoptic Gospels are not necessarily in conflict with one another; they may indeed complement one another if read together. Thus by my reading of Matthew, the fishermen might have heard about Jesus's extraordinary reputation, were surprised to see him in person, and were dazzled that he should explicitly invite them to follow him. Luke's more extensive gloss suggests that Simon Peter spoke for all of them in expressing his pre-existing sense of guilt and his expectation that Jesus would spurn him ("Depart from me, for I am a sinful man, O Lord"). Jesus's overflowing gift of fish, of nurturing sustenance, and his offer of a special affiliation might have seemed to Simon Peter and the others like the antidote to their sense of unworthiness and the fulfillment of their long-standing wish. Mark's stark account, precisely because it provides no clearly indicated motive, conveys a heightened sense that the fishermen had been waiting for something though they knew not what, and that Jesus's sudden appearance and unexpected invitation struck them like a lightning bolt, giving clarity and structure to their previously inchoate desires, and this was the reason they immediately succumbed.

Mark's account thus amplifies the implication of the other Gospel accounts—that the disciples instantly accepted Jesus's authority because, like Eve toward Adam, they "longed" for him and therefore agreed that he "shall rule over them." But unlike Matthew or Luke, both of whom suggest some clear rational motives and some external impetus for the disciples' conduct, Mark conveys a surge of internally generated feeling that goes beyond rational calculation. Mark, more than the others, suggests that the disciples fell in love with Jesus, and that it was love at first sight. Jesus did nothing more, however, than gesture toward them; it was the disciples who gave their own signification to this gesture. "Follow me"—his initial invitation to his disciples—demanded much more independent effort from them (and from us, following along in the disciples' footsteps and struggling to understand their motives) than any command to fall in line behind a leader.

If Jesus had said to Simon Peter and the others, "Follow me because I love you" or "Follow me because you and I both already know that you love me," the proclamation would have seemed contrived. The force of the event would have been diminished if the Gospel text itself proclaimed that "love" moved the disciples to follow Jesus. Use of that word as such would have conveyed its conventional meaning and provoked considerable skepticism: how could Jesus have "loved" these men whom he had never met and saw only from a distance in their fishing boats? Why should these fishermen "love" this stranger? But Jesus invoked an unconventional concept of love. His concept was a connection of such intense intimacy that it deepened and even transformed the ordinary usage of "love." His love could not be captured by the ordinary word; it could be comprehended only in action—as when the fishermen instantly left all other attachments to become his devoted disciples.

Fourth Act: Miraculous Cures

After the small group of Jesus's disciples were assembled, Jesus proceeded in his ministry from town to town performing what were generally perceived as miraculous cures. But careful attention to the details of this healing activity reveals the same qualities that Jesus had exemplified in attracting his disciples. As with his disciples' choice to follow him, Jesus taught that unconditional faith must precede the sufferer's cure, not that faith would or could arise from that cure.

According to the conventional view of Jesus's healing powers—both among most of the direct witnesses in the Gospel accounts and among many believers today—Jesus was exercising hierarchically superior authority over disease and thereby taking charge to cure the passive beneficiaries of his healing power. But close attention to paradigmatic examples of Jesus's healing activities in the Synoptic Gospels reveals the error in these accounts. His healings are not conventional invocations of punitive command authority, but instead rely for their success on mutual dependency and trust between Jesus and suffering human beings.

Consider this example from Mark chapter 5. Jairus, "one of the rulers of the synagogue," feared that his daughter was near death and pleaded with Jesus, "Lay your hands on her, so that she may be made well, and live." Jesus set out for Jairus's home and on the way heard several people tell Jairus that his daughter had died, but Jesus said to him, "Do not fear, only believe." When Jesus arrived at the home, he found "a tumult, and people weeping and wailing loudly"; he assured them that the girl was only sleeping, "and they laughed at him." But Jesus "put them all outside" and proceeded into the house with only the girl's parents and his disciples. Jesus then took the girl's hand and, according to Mark, said in Aramaic, "Tal'itha cu'mi." Mark then translated this phrase: "which means," he said, "'Little girl, I say to you, arise.'" Mark continued, "And immediately the girl got up and walked (she was twelve years of age), and they were immediately overcome with amazement. And he strictly charged them that no one should know this, and told them to give her something to eat."[18]

This vignette is touching in its domestic simplicity. Everything that Jesus does is calculated to heighten its intimacy. He leaves the tumultuous, weeping crowd outside the elder's house and proceeds inside only with his disciples and the girl's parents. And although everyone else had concluded that the girl was dead beyond recall, Jesus spoke simply and directly to her. He did not command that demons leave her or even that she should return to life. He simply invited her to arise.

Mark, moreover, conveyed a special quality about this invitation. All of Jesus's statements in Mark's Gospel were made in Aramaic; this was the vernacular used by Jesus and virtually everyone around him. Mark wrote in Greek, but almost nowhere else in his Gospel did he call attention to the fact that every quotation he ascribed to Jesus was a translation from the Aramaic. In this instance, however, Mark's quotation of the Aramaic and his immediate translation for the reader's benefit convey the sense that the readers are overhearing an intensely intimate transaction between Jesus and the girl, so intimate that we cannot understand it at first and it must be translated for us. The girl "immediately" responded; she "got up and walked"—rather like, I would say, the immediate response of Jesus's disciples to his invitation that they should walk with him. And, of course, his disciples were the only other witnesses to this transaction besides the girl's parents.

It was only after she arose that Mark inserted a parenthetical observation that the girl was twelve years old. This is a peculiar ordering of the information about her. In an ordinary journalistic narrative, we would expect to have learned the girl's age at the outset of the story.

For all we knew when Jesus entered Jairus's home, the daughter could have been middle-aged. It was Jesus who first referred to her with the intimate diminutive "little girl"; and it is only when she awoke and arose that we learn that she was in fact a young girl, whose very youth heightened the poignancy of her parents' impending loss and added a surge of relief to Mark's narrative observation that everyone was "immediately overcome with amazement." The intimacy of this event was then underscored by its conclusion: Jesus told her parents "to give her something to eat." Jesus in effect said to the young girl's parents, don't be "overcome with amazement," but have compassion for your child. She has been confined to her bed for a while and she is probably hungry. "Give her something to eat." He thus restored this household to its prior state of intimate, protected domesticity.

Another aspect of the ending of this episode conveys a further sense of intimacy. Immediately before telling the parents to feed their daughter, Jesus "strictly charged them that no one should know this." What could this injunction for secrecy have meant? Jesus could not have intended that the girl should be hidden in her parents' house and that none of the weeping crowd outside should know that she was alive. But what did Jesus not want the crowd to know? Presumably, he meant that they should not know how it came about that she arose from her bed, they should not know that Jesus spoke to her or what he said. But why not?

This question goes to the heart of the nature of Jesus's healing power, and ultimately of his authority generally. The injunction for secrecy is a recurrent trope in the Synoptic Gospel accounts when Jesus appeared to perform miraculous healing. Again and again Jesus immediately enjoined the healed beneficiaries to tell no one.[19] His directives were often disobeyed, and his popular fame spread. But Jesus was dismissive, even annoyed, at this popular appeal. He repeatedly complained that this acclaim was based on a misunderstanding of his power, that "this generation requires signs" to prove his God-given authority but that these external signs are inconsistent with the nature of that authority.[20]

We can draw out the reason that Jesus enjoined secrecy about his healing activities from an episode that Mark recorded in the middle of his account of Jairus's daughter. As Jesus proceeded toward Jairus's house, still surrounded by a large crowd, a woman who had suffered from bleeding for many years approached him from behind. Without Jesus's knowledge, the woman touched his garments, saying to herself, "If I touch even his garments, I shall be made well." Immediately she was cured, and Jesus, "perceiving in himself that power had gone forth from him," asked who had touched him. His accompanying disciples were puzzled at this question: "You see the crowd pressing around you," they said, "and yet you say, 'Who touched me?'" But the woman knew Jesus was referring to her and "came in fear and trembling and fell down before him." The woman apparently expected Jesus to chastise her, but instead he said, "Daughter, your faith has made you well; go in peace, and be healed of your disease."[21]

There is an intimacy in this interaction that is mirrored in the account of Jairus's daughter. In both cases a healing power went out from Jesus, but its effective force seemed to rest in a reciprocal affirmative responsiveness from the individual sufferer. The bleeding woman did not cure herself, but Jesus did not cure her on his own. Similarly, Jesus did not cure Jairus's daughter based on his own efforts alone; he enlisted her action by taking her hand and inviting her to rise up. In both cases, the healing occurs through a reciprocal interaction—not, as the conventional conception of the healer's art posits, a unilateral imposition of the healer's power and authority to command the disease.

There are numerous instances in the Synoptic Gospels where Jesus did embody the conventional conception of the authoritarian healer, but all of these involved his commands to demons that they leave the bodies of suffering people.[22] The difference between Jesus's relationship to demons and to suffering people was vividly illustrated by the episode of the father and the epileptic boy in Mark chapter 9.[23] As Jesus was surrounded by his disciples and a large crowd, a father complained that his son was possessed by a "dumb spirit" that he had asked Jesus's disciples to cast out "and they were not able." Jesus "answered them, 'O faithless generation, how long am I to be with you? How long am I to bear with you? Bring him to me.'" Jesus did not seem to limit his reply to the father alone, and his remonstrance appeared to be clearly heard by both the crowds and his disciples; it is, however, unclear whether he exempted his disciples from the charge of "faithlessness." In any event, as soon as the boy was brought before Jesus, the spirit "convulsed the boy" and he fell into a seizure. The boy's father said to Jesus, "if you can do anything, have pity on us and help us." Jesus responded to the father, "'If you can!' All things are possible to him who believes." The boy's father immediately cried out, "I believe; help my unbelief." Jesus then directly addressed the "unclean spirit," saying, "I command you, come out of him and never enter him again." At that directive, the spirit "came out, and the boy was like a corpse, so that most of them said 'He is dead.' But Jesus took him by the hand and lifted him up, and he arose."[24]

As with Jairus's daughter, it might appear on the surface of this account that Jesus was solely responsible for restoring the epileptic boy to health and life. Careful attention to the details of the episode, however, also shows the interactive quality of that restoration—that Jesus intimately "took him by the hand and lifted him up," but that the boy then of his own accord "arose." Jesus's interaction with the dumb and unclean spirit was starkly different; Jesus "commanded" this spirit and the spirit passively obeyed, whereas Jesus invited the boy to rejoin life and the boy actively accepted the invitation. Moreover, Jesus's response to the boy's father recapitulated his interaction with the bleeding woman whose faith in him cured her. The father appealed to Jesus, "if you can do anything"; Jesus turned this plea around, "'If you can!' All things are possible to him who believes." Immediately the father cried out, "I believe; help my unbelief." As with the bleeding woman, the reciprocal bond—the virtual dissolving of separate identities—between Jesus and the sufferer was the key to curative power.

In these microcosms, we can see the two different modes of authority wielded not only by Jesus but by God himself in both the Christian and the Hebrew Bibles. In the Synoptic Gospels, Jesus's interactions with human beings are instructive, inviting, inspirational—but not punitively commanding. In the Hebrew Bible, God restricted himself to this collaborative mode of authority only at the very beginning, in the first Genesis creation. God's invitation there to man and woman together "to be fruitful and multiply" had the identical import of Jesus's urging Jairus's daughter and the epileptic boy to rise up and walk. In the first creation, God in effect said to humanity, "I have endowed you with the capacity to be fruitful and multiply; but this capacity will come into realization only if you choose to exercise it." Jesus offered the same instruction to sufferers; he gave them the capacity to overcome their suffering, but their use of this capacity depended on their active choice.

If these instructions from God and from Jesus had been commandments in the conventional sense, then punishment would follow from mankind's nonobservance. But there is no punishment as such in these instances. If humans refused to procreate or if Jairus's daughter or the epileptic boy refused to rise up, they would have turned away from bounteous gifts. By thus depriving themselves, they might be self-punitive. But this punishment would not be externally imposed on them. By the same measure, if God had forced humans to accept progeny or if Jesus had forced the young girl or boy to accept relief by threatening punishment as the alternative, the result would not have been experienced as a gift. Its worth would have been diminished both for the human recipients and for the benefactors, Jesus and God.

In its essential structure, Jesus's healing recapitulated the relationship between God and humanity that had existed in the first Genesis creation—a relationship that had become immediately fractured in the second creation and remained in eclipse, except for brief illuminations throughout the rest of the Hebrew Bible. Jesus's intimate bodily contact with his beneficiaries suggests a complete harmony, even a dissolving of boundaries between them—a shared identity that was the defining characteristic of the first account of creation when there was no separation between male and female or between God and humanity. Jesus's healing activity is accordingly a specific enactment of the overall goal of his ministry—to restore the relationship between God and humanity to its primal unity in the first Genesis creation before the breach that occurred in the second.

Jesus's mission is thus to remind both God and humanity of the conflict-free intimacy they had originally enjoyed and, by evoking this memory, offer both the possibility of renewed intimacy—a possibility that had been lost or forgotten between them in the heated exchanges about betrayal and abandonment that had afflicted their relationship since their falling out in the Garden of Eden. In this sense, Jesus is extending the rainbow function that we have already seen at work in God's mind after the Flood and in the increasingly bold promptings offered to God by Abraham, Moses, and Job. Jesus's extension addresses both God and humanity, commanding neither but instead recalling both to the possibility of mutual love if only each would renew their original vows.

In the Synoptic Gospels, Mark is the clearest place to see the relationship between Jesus's substantive message and this pedagogic style. This is not because Mark himself is clear on this score; quite the contrary, it is because his text is so difficult to unravel. Mark's format in itself demands the intimate interaction between his readers and Jesus that is the hallmark of the revised style of divine authority that Jesus offered.

We can see this in the continuation of Mark's narrative that follows the episode of the epileptic boy. That episode had begun with the boy's father complaining to Jesus that his disciples "were not able" to cure the boy. Immediately after the boy was healed through Jesus's ministrations, Mark relates that "his disciples asked him privately, 'Why could we not cast [the spirit] out?'" Jesus responded obscurely: "he said to them, 'This kind cannot be driven out by anything but prayer.'" (In Matthew's retelling of this episode, Jesus informs the disciples that they did not succeed "because of your little faith."[25]) Mark continues:

> They went on from there and passed through Galilee. And he would not have anyone know it; for he was teaching his disciples, saying to them, "The Son of man will be delivered into the hands of men, and they will kill him; and when he is killed after three days he will rise." But they did not understand the saying, and they were afraid to ask him.
> And they came to Capernaum; and when he was in the house he asked them, "What were you discussing on the way?" But they were silent; for on the way they had discussed with one another who was the greatest. And he sat down and called the twelve; and he said to them, "If any one would be first, he must be last of all and servant of all." And he took a child, and put him in the midst of them; and taking him in his arms, he said to them, "Whoever receives one such child in my name receives me; and whoever receives me, receives not me but him who sent me."[26]

This narrative distilled the lessons of the immediately preceding episode with the father and the epileptic son. The disciples had not been able to cure the boy, and they revealed in their dispute among themselves that they held onto the conventionally hierarchical conception of authority—"who was the greatest" among them? The disciples did not understand that this conventional notion in itself obstructed their capacity to cure the boy. Jesus responded to their misconception by instruction—the first "must be last"—and by example, embracing a child "in the midst of them," as he had "lifted up" both Jairus's daughter and the epileptic boy, both of whom could then "arise" through their own efforts.

Interwoven in this lesson, Jesus drew a parallel with his own predicted fate, that he himself would be killed and "after three days he will rise." The disciples were confounded by this statement and too fearful to reveal their lack of understanding. This sudden narrative appearance of Jesus's prediction and the disciples' fearful incomprehension seems on its face to be an artless sequence, as if Mark were simply reporting the random events and conversations as they occurred while Jesus and his disciples traveled from the home of the epileptic boy to Galilee and then on to Capernaum. But this narrative sequence should be as arresting to us readers as it must have been to Jesus's disciples; by accepting the challenge to work out the intricate puzzles for ourselves, guided only by the hints that Mark's Gospel gives us, we too can join Jesus and his disciples in an intimate relationship.

Jesus's refusal to identify himself as the Messiah and his demand for silence from those who recognized him as such are another expression of his pedagogic strategy for conveying his utterly unconventional conception of his authority. At a pivotal moment in each of the Synoptic Gospels, Jesus asked his disciples, "'Who do men say that I am?' And they told him, 'John the Baptist; and others say Elijah; and others one of the prophets.' And he asked them, 'But who do you say that I am?' Peter answered him, 'You are the Christ.'"[27]

There are differences among the Synoptic Gospels about Jesus's reaction to this recognition. In Mark's account, Jesus says nothing in direct response to Peter's identification; according to Mark, he simply "charged them to tell no one about him." Luke's account is identical to Mark's.[28] But according to Matthew, Jesus appeared to confirm Peter's statement ("[Y]ou are favored indeed! You did not learn that from any human being; it was revealed to you by my heavenly Father."). Even so, Matthew confirms that Jesus then told "the disciples to tell no one that he was the Christ."[29]

Jesus similarly refused to identify himself as the Messiah when challenged to do so by hostile interlocutors. Thus when Jesus was "teaching people in the temple," the chief priest, scribes, and synagogue elders demanded to know "by what authority you are acting like this; who gave you this authority," and Jesus refused to answer.[30] After Jesus's arrest, when the high priest directly challenged him, "I charge you to tell us, are you the Messiah, the Son of God?" Jesus neither affirmed nor denied this but said only, "The words are yours."[31] He said the same thing when subsequently challenged by the Roman governor, Pontius Pilate, whether he was "king of the Jews." Jesus responded, "The words are yours." Pilate pressed him, "'Do you not hear all this evidence they are bringing against you?' but to the governor's great astonishment he refused to answer a single word."[32]

The conventional explanation for these specific refusals was Jesus's caginess, his refusal to give his detractors a clear ground for accusing him of blasphemy. But in Jesus's seemingly evasive repetition of the very words that his accusers aimed at him—"the words are yours"—I see another dimension. Consistent with his general pedagogic strategy, Jesus was insisting that his authority arose not independent of his followers' understanding but from shared faith. By responding to his accusers' challenges that the words were theirs when they asked if he was the Messiah or the king of the Jews, he ironically told them in effect that their words could invest him with this authority—and indeed, that if only they understood what they had just said, they had already acknowledged his authority.

In the climactic confrontation with Pilate, the three Synoptic Gospels give the same account. But in Jesus's dealings with the high priest, Mark's account differs significantly from the others. According to Mark, when the high priest asked Jesus, "Are you the Messiah, the Son of the Blessed One?" Jesus directly replied, "I am."[33] This clear self-identification by Jesus is especially striking because it appears in Mark's Gospel. Though there are a few instances in the other Synoptic Gospels where Jesus ambiguously refers to himself as the Son of God, Mark rigorously excludes any such account except for this one striking encounter with the high priest—quickly followed by Jesus's interchange with Pilate, when, according to Mark as well as to the other Synoptic Gospels, Jesus reverts to his customary pattern of refusing to identify himself.

This is not a meaningless or even a small detail. Jesus's self-identification as the Messiah to the high priest is a unilateral assertion of superiority over him rather than an invitation that the high priest should believe in him, as in all of Jesus's other exchanges with human interlocutors. In Mark's Gospel, Jesus virtually never assumes that anyone is unavailable for a loving relationship with him. Even Pontius Pilate is graced with Jesus's invitation to believe in him, however ironically extended when he tells Pilate, "the words are yours." The high priest is, however, rigidly close-minded—not surprisingly so, in light of his exalted conventional status, and Jesus's direct assertion that he is the Messiah is inconsistent with the possibility that the high priest could ever recognize him as such. In effect, Jesus's willingness to demand obedience from the high priest is another instance of his paradoxical pedagogy. Mark's readers would understand that a high priest, more than any other personage, would be utterly blind to Jesus's appeal; Jesus accordingly knows that he has nothing to offer the high priest because nothing will be offered by him in return.

This identical lesson, in equally paradoxical form, appeared in one other encounter that Mark describes. Immediately after the healing interactions with the bleeding woman and Jairus's daughter, Mark relates that Jesus "went away from there and came to his own country." Once there "he began to teach in the synagogue; and many who heard him were astonished, saying, '. . . Is not this the carpenter, the son of Mary and brother of James and Joses and Judas and Simon, and are not his sisters here with us?' And they took offense at him." Jesus chastised them, saying, "A prophet is not without honor, except in his own country, and among his own kin, and in his own house." Mark immediately adds this observation: "And he could do no mighty work there, except that he laid his hands upon a few sick people and healed them. And he marveled because of their disbelief."[34] Jesus's allusion to himself as a "prophet" is a more veiled claim for exalted status than in his response to the high priest, but it is such a claim nonetheless. And Mark draws out the implications of that claim, that "he could do no mighty work there . . . because of their disbelief."

Here in highly compressed form is the key to Jesus's authority regarding human beings—that he could do nothing mighty unless his interlocutors believed in him, but that with their belief nothing was impossible. Thus when the father of the epileptic boy pleaded for his assistance "if you can do anything," Jesus responded, "'If you can!' All things are possible to him who believes."[35] Thus Jesus told Jairus, "the ruler of the synagogue, 'Do not fear, only believe.'"[36] Thus Jesus told the bleeding woman, "Daughter, your faith has made you well."[37]

This description of divine authority is radically different from any direct account in the Hebrew Bible, but it draws out and makes explicit a theme that quietly pervaded this older text. This theme is that God and humanity are engaged in a reciprocal relationship and that each needs the other. The Hebrew Bible is quite explicit that this relationship is broken when human beings turn away from God or, similarly, when humans assert some unilateral superiority over God, either by turning toward other deities or by relying on their own authority. The Hebrew Bible does not openly admit that God's authority is diminished when he asserts unilateral command over humanity or turns away from us. But this lesson can be read between the lines of Moses's sly taunt to God that if he killed all the Israelites because of their disloyalty to him in worshiping the Golden Calf, "What would the Egyptians say?"[38] On a second occasion when he threatened to kill them all, Moses even more pointedly challenged God, "And the nations who have heard rumor of You will say, saying, 'From the Lord's inability to bring this people to the land that He swore to them, He slaughtered them in the wilderness.' And so, let the Lord's power, pray, be great."[39]

But why should God care what the Egyptians think or whether other nations believe that he was unable to accomplish what he wanted or to keep his promises? More generally, why should God care, as much as he obviously and repeatedly does care, whether human beings believe in him or remain loyal to him? God doesn't need others to believe in his powers if he is truly omnipotent. He is what he is, whether human beings recognize this or not.

Jesus brings into visibility this implicit lesson about the limits of God's effective power—in effect, his weakness in dealing with humanity. It is not that humanity has practical power to force God to do anything, but that God cannot force humanity to do what he wants without our active collaboration. Ultimately the only power God can exert over humanity is utterly to destroy us. This catastrophic destructive power might appear to make God all-powerful in relation to humanity, but this would be true only if God were willing to do without us. God indeed contemplated this possibility during the prolonged period when Noah, the last survivor of all humanity, remained engulfed in the Flood waters. But God "remembered" Noah and resolved not to destroy him, the last remnant of humanity, notwithstanding that "the devisings of the human heart are evil from youth."[40]

When Noah had been saved from the Flood waters, he built an altar and made burnt offerings and God "smelled the fragrant odor"— a pattern of conduct that recurs throughout the Hebrew Bible, as mankind repeatedly tries to please God and thereby ensure its safety. The Hebrew Bible thus appears to convey the explicit message that this propitiation is necessary to cajole God into keeping his protective promises toward us. But the implicit, though never openly acknowledged, message in the Hebrew Bible is that God prizes our existence regardless of what we do to heighten or diminish his pleasure in our companionship. Whatever his reasons, God's wish for our continued existence is a considerable, though self-imposed, limitation on his power over us. God recurrently struggles against this self-imposed limitation throughout the Hebrew Bible, but he never breaks free from it (though at times, he seems to come perilously close—as when he taunted Job about his puny insignificance in the great scheme of God's creation, yet even so he instructed Satan to spare Job's life despite the escalating inflictions of torment that he authorized).

The great innovation of the Christian Bible is that God appears to overcome his ambivalence about the power he has bestowed on humanity. Jesus signified this momentous step in two ways: through his preaching that God loves us unconditionally and wants nothing more from us than unconditional love in return; and, more dramatically, through his very presence on earth and his willingness as the Son of God to accept suffering inflicted on him by humanity. Jesus's transcendence of his physical death on the Cross was a literal return to the blissful state before any conflict had appeared between God and mankind —to the first Genesis creation when the entire universe was harmonious and God saw that it was "very good." But God cannot force us back to that initial harmony any more than humanity can force this harmony on him. We must both willingly return in order to recreate the perfect justice of the first creation. To force this result is to destroy. This is the unacknowledged paradox in Emperor Ferdinand's proclamation noted in the first chapter, "Fiat justitia, et pereat mundus"—"Let justice be done, though the world perish."

Jesus's return to this seamless harmony with God is signaled by Paul's depiction of him as a direct reincarnation of Adam—"the last Adam," as Paul says in his First Letter to the Corinthians.[41] This last Adam, unlike the first, was not dissatisfied with his initial, exclusive relationship with God. While the first Adam longed for Eve's company, Jesus explicitly spurned all human familial attachments in favor of a direct, all-encompassing relationship with his Father in heaven. Thus Matthew records:

> While [Jesus] was still speaking to the people, behold, his mother and his brothers stood outside, asking to speak to him. But he replied to the

man who told him, "Who is my mother, and who are my brothers?" And stretching out his hand toward his disciples, he said, "Here are my mother and my brothers! For whoever does the will of my Father in heaven is my brother, and sister, and mother."[42]

Thus Jesus rescinded the directive after Eve's appearance, in the second Genesis creation, that "therefore does a man leave his father and his mother and cling to his wife and they become one flesh."[43] Jesus, this last Adam, took no wife but instead returned to primal unity with his father.

Jesus's ultimate return came with his death, and in the terms of the Christian Bible, eternal life after death appears to be a permanent harmony with God, a permanent peace. The plot line of the Hebrew Bible is a recurrent search for, breach of, and renewed search for harmonious relations between God and humanity. The possibility of eternal life after death plays no role in this drama. In the Hebrew Bible, an individual's death is the cessation of his relationship with both God and the rest of humanity. In the Christian Bible, the prospect of this post-mortem relationship is a central concern, perhaps even the central concern. Indeed, it appears that Jesus himself believed that the complete end of humanity's life on earth was imminent, even within a generation's time.[44] Even so, life on earth was not thereby made irrelevant or without importance. Quite the contrary, life on earth is understood within the terms of the Christian Bible as preparation for death. In this sense, both the Hebrew and the Christian Bibles pursue the same fundamental goal—a totally harmonious relationship between God and humanity, whether in this life alone (as the Hebrew Bible envisions) or in this life and the next (as the Christian Bible sees it).

It is not clear whether the Hebrew Bible provides an illustrative example of any human being who actually achieves this goal on earth. Many people pursue the goal, but, as we have explored in previous chapters, the traditional listing of those who purportedly succeed— Noah, Abraham, Moses, Job (after his final speech)—turns out to be misleading. In the Christian Bible, Jesus clearly succeeds. He begins in harmony, recognized by God as his beloved Son; he wavers in this harmony, as evidenced by his agony in the Gethsemane garden and on the Cross; and he succeeds in recapturing this harmony, as evidenced by his resurrection.

But in the terms of the Christian Bible, is it possible for others to succeed as Jesus has done? Jesus urges humanity to follow him, and this invitation apparently conveys the implication that everyone could potentially succeed in this effort. But the canonical texts of the Christian Bible provide no illustrative example of anyone other than Jesus who does succeed. The question is thus left open, if not openly advertised, whether the pathway that Jesus traversed is so difficult that very few, if any, subsequent successes will be possible.

Indeed, an even more fundamental question is left open: whether Jesus is so unique, in combining both divine and human attributes, that no mere human can reach the total harmony with God that he achieved. If this is the case, then the Christian Bible would convey the same message that we have drawn from the Hebrew Bible: that the pursuit of harmony between God and humanity is a compelling ideal, that both God and humanity are repeatedly impelled to pursue it, but that this pursuit will always fail—although then, on one side or the other, the pursuit will always be renewed.

CHAPTER TEN

The Same Old Testament

Paul and Jesus

*A*LL THE AUTHORS OF THE canonical texts in the Christian Bible struggle with the question whether human beings can actually achieve a restoration of the original harmony with God in the first Genesis creation. Some even suggest that Jesus himself was troubled by doubts on this score. But Paul and John grapple with these questions in ways that are radically distinct from their treatment in Mark, Matthew, and Luke.

Paul: The Exemplary Man

After Jesus, Paul is the most consequential figure in the development of Christianity. Without Paul, Christianity might have survived, if at all, as a variant sect within Judaism; with Paul's passionate vision and abundant proselytizing energy, Christianity was carried beyond the Jews to the Gentile population throughout the Roman world and the groundwork laid for its ultimate expansion across the globe. Unlike the Jerusalem-based disciples committed to conveying Jesus's mission, Paul had no personal contact with Jesus during his presence on earth. But Paul's Letters to promote and guide the nascent Christian congregations outside the Jewish world have canonical status in the Christian

Bible. In addition to highlighting aspects of Jesus's teachings and the significance of his death and resurrection, the Letters also illuminate Paul's conduct and character.

From the evidence of his Letters, Paul illustrates the paradoxical problems within the terms of the Christian Bible for anyone (other than Jesus) to achieve permanent reconciliation with God. In his two Letters to the Corinthians, most notably, Paul describes himself as standing on the edge of the two styles of authority derived from the difference between the first and second Genesis creations that I have identified at the core of Jesus's teaching. Paul said to the Corinthians, "[T]he kingdom of God does not consist in talk but in power. What do you wish? Shall I come to you with a rod, or with love in a spirit of gentleness?"[1]

Paul's preference for love as the basis for all his relationships is apparent in the most sustained and eloquent paean in all of the Christian Bible, unsurpassed even by Jesus's own words in the Gospel accounts. In his First Letter to the Corinthians, Paul wrote,

> If I speak to you in the tongues of men and of angels, but have not love, I am a noisy gong or a clanging cymbal. And if I have prophetic powers, and understand all mysteries and all knowledge, and if I have all faith, so as to remove mountains, but have not love, I am nothing. . . . Love is patient and kind; love is not jealous or boastful; it is not arrogant or rude. Love does not insist on its own way; it is not irritable or resentful. . . . Love never ends . . . For our knowledge is imperfect and our prophecy is imperfect; but when the perfect comes, the imperfect will pass away. . . . For now we see in a mirror dimly, but then face to face. Now I know in part; then I shall understand fully, even as I have been fully understood. So faith, hope, love abide, these three; but the greatest of these is love.[2]

But Paul did not sustain this attitude. In response to challenges to his own authority, he fell away from his reliance on freely offered love and moved toward an increasingly adamant command for unquestioning deference. Thus immediately after his hymn to love in First Corinthians, Paul said, "If any one thinks that he is a prophet, or spiritual, he should acknowledge that what I am writing to you is a command of the Lord. If any one does not recognize this, he is not recognized."[3] Was Paul coming to the Corinthians "with a rod, or with love in a spirit of gentleness"? The answer appears to be both.

Paul's ambivalence on this score seems to mirror his own difficulty in establishing his good faith in claiming apostolic status. Paul's entry into the ranks was an exceedingly divisive event for the apostolic enterprise. We can see this first of all from Acts of the Apostles, written by Luke as a companion book to his Gospel narrative of Jesus's life. Luke's account can be essentially divided into two parts: before and after Paul's appearance. Luke's portrayal of relations among the apostles in the first, pre-Pauline part of his narrative is essentially irenic. The apostles were gathered in Jerusalem, comprising some 120 people at the beginning of Acts; the core group had known Jesus personally and the rest had been directly enlisted by them.[4] The Jerusalem apostles were subjected to harsh punishment and a few even put to death by the local authorities, but they were united among themselves: "all who believed were together and had all things in common; and they sold their possessions and goods and distributed them to all, as any had need. And day by day, attending the temple together and breaking bread in their homes, they partook of food with glad and generous hearts, praising God and having favor with all the people."[5] According to the Gospel accounts, Jesus left his disciples with one instruction, "that you love one another as I have loved you," which could be understood as a prescription for practicing unconditional love among themselves that would prepare them to realize the unity and eternal life that Jesus had attained with God.[6] The blissful relationship that Luke depicts among the pre-Pauline apostles seemed to embody Jesus's instruction.

Paul makes his first appearance in Acts as an aggressive oppressor of the apostles. Then known by the Hebrew name of Saul, he was apparently in charge of the stoning death of the apostle Stephen. According to Luke, witnesses to Stephen's death "laid down their garments at the feet of a young man named Saul . . . And Saul was consenting to his death." Immediately afterward, "a great persecution arose against the church in Jerusalem . . . [and] Saul was ravaging the church, and entering house after house, he dragged off men and women and committed them to prison."[7] Sometime later, "still breathing threats and murder against the disciples of the Lord," Saul obtained permission from the high priest in Jerusalem to continue his pursuit in Damascus. But on the way, Luke continues, "suddenly a light from heaven flashed about him. And he fell to the ground and heard a voice saying to him 'Saul, Saul, why do you persecute me?' And he said, 'Who are you, Lord?' And he said, 'I am Jesus, whom you are persecuting; but rise and enter the city, and you will be told what you are to do.'"[8]

This was the beginning of Paul's mission for Christ. But the apostles in Jerusalem were, not surprisingly, intensely suspicious of Paul's credentials. Paul, moreover, did not return to Jerusalem until three years after he had commenced his missionary activity for Christ; according to his own account, in his Letter to the Galatians, on this return visit Paul remained in Jerusalem for only fifteen days and saw only two of the disciples, Cephas and James, Jesus's brother. Paul then left to continue his missionary work in Syria and Cilicia, and didn't return to Jerusalem for another fourteen years.

Paul put an upbeat spin on this prolonged separation from the Jerusalem apostles: "I was still not known by sight to the churches of Christ in Judea; they only heard it said, 'He who once persecuted us is now preaching the faith he once tried to destroy.' And they glorified God because of me."[9] But Luke offered a different reading of the disciples' attitude toward Paul. Luke recounted that after Paul's fourteen-years absence, "when he had come to Jerusalem he attempted to join the disciples; and they were all afraid of him, for they did not believe that he was a disciple." But one among them, Barnabas, vouched for his "bold teaching" in the hinterlands, and he was apparently accepted to pursue his preaching in Jerusalem.[10] Even so, suspicions remained among the disciples, and these suspicions ultimately grew into open conflict.

The specific cause of controversy was whether male circumcision should be required to gain acceptance into the Christian brotherhood. According to Luke, there was "no small dissension and debate" on this issue; Paul and Barnabas participated in this debate, having come from their preaching activity in Antioch, and they both wanted to encourage conversion among the Gentiles by waiving the requirement for circumcision.[11] In good bureaucratic fashion, decision was postponed in favor of sending two "leading men within the brethren" to accompany Paul and Barnabas back to Antioch in order to speak to the congregation there. A letter was drafted that these two "leading men"—Judas known as Barsabbas and Silas—were instructed to read to the congregation; the letter began, "since we have heard that some persons from us have troubled you with words, unsettling your minds, although we gave them no instructions, it has seemed good to us, having come to one accord, to choose men and send them to you with our beloved Barnabas and Paul."[12] It is easy to read between the lines of this letter that "our beloved Barnabas and Paul" were being brought back under some supervision.

After Barsabbas and Silas had "spent some time" in Antioch "exhort[ing] the brethren with many words and strengthen[ing] them . . . they were sent off in peace by the brethren to those who had sent them there." This send-off also has a suspicious ring to it, a hint that all was not truly peace and harmony in Antioch. These suspicions were amplified by Luke's immediately subsequent account that Barnabas and Paul, who had previously been united, suddenly parted ways. The stated cause for their separation was that Paul asked Barnabas to accompany him to cities other than Antioch, where they had previously preached together, but Barnabas also wanted "John called Mark" with them and Paul refused, on the ground that he "had withdrawn from them in

Pamphylia, and had not gone with them to the work." Luke records, "And there arose a sharp contention, so that they separated from each other; Barnabas took Mark with him and sailed away to Cyprus, but Paul chose Silas and departed . . . [for] Syria and Cilicia, strengthening the churches."[13] On its face, this reason for Paul and his strongest ally among the other disciples to separate, after "sharp contention," seems insufficient.

One other element in Luke's account also casts doubt on Paul's credentials. Luke describes Paul's conversion on the Damascus road in two different places in his narrative; in the first telling, Luke speaks in his own voice as narrator while in the second, Luke quotes Paul directly. These two narratives differ, however, in a small but significant way. In the first account, Paul's traveling companions "stood speechless, hearing the voice but seeing no one."[14] In the second account, in which Luke quotes Paul verbatim, "those who were with me saw the light but did not hear the voice of the one who was speaking to me."[15] This inconsistency might seem inconsequential. But there is a distinct oddity here. We don't have different versions of this event from different witnesses, as we have often encountered in various versions of the same event among the Gospel authors. This inconsistency is in the narrative written by the same author, Luke. Acts of the Apostles is not a lengthy document, and it is hard to believe that Luke failed to notice the discrepancy in his two versions of the crucial event on which Paul relied to establish his transformation from an oppressor to an apostle of Christ. If we might imagine a modern-day trial challenging Paul's credentials, this discrepancy would undoubtedly have been used to great effect on cross-examination.

How did Paul deal with these doubts about his status? He made ever-escalating claims to the sanctity of his own authority and increasingly belittled his opponents. Paul might have followed Jesus's example in the Synoptic Gospels, pursuing his ministry not only undaunted by others' failure to recognize his authority but purposefully enjoining silence on those who might ratify his credentials. As Jesus had insisted in the Synoptics, so too Paul might have sought to ensure that others' recognition of him would not come in response to an external command but would arise from within, from an inner-generated enlightenment.

Paul, of course, did not have the texts of the Gospels available to him for guidance; they had not been written during his lifetime. But Paul's paean to love in his First Letter to the Corinthians displays an eloquent appreciation of this imperative. At other places in this Letter, however, Paul implicitly acknowledges the existence of challenges to his status among other disciples and defends himself in various ways. "Am I not an apostle?" Paul asks rhetorically. "Have I not seen Jesus our Lord? Are not you my workmanship in the Lord? If to others I am not an apostle, at least I am to you; for you are the seal of my apostleship in the Lord."[16] Later he returns to this theme more extensively:

> [Christ] was raised on the third day [and] he appeared to Cephas, then to the twelve. Then he appeared to more than five hundred brethren at one time, most of whom are still alive, though some have fallen asleep. Then he appeared to James, then to all the apostles. Last of all, as to one untimely born, he appeared also to me. For I am the least of the apostles, unfit to be called an apostle, because I persecuted the church of God. But by the grace of God I am what I am, and his grace toward me was not in vain. On the contrary, I worked harder than any of them, though it was not I, but the grace of God which is within me. Whether it was I or they, so we preach and so you believed.[17]

There is a striking mixture of humility and pride in Paul's self-defense: I am "unfit to be called an apostle," but "I worked harder than any of them," though my work was "not I but the grace of God which is within me." In Paul's Second Letter to the Corinthians, this mixture is more explicitly in evidence, and even virtually acknowledged by Paul himself: "[E]ven if I boast a little too much of our authority, which the Lord gave for building you up and not for destroying you, I shall not be put to shame. . . . But we will not boast beyond limit, but will keep to the limit God has apportioned us, to reach even to you. For we are not overextending ourselves, as though we did not reach you; we were the first to come all the way to you with the gospel of Christ." Paul then continues in a different, almost pleading vein: "I wish you would bear with me in a little foolishness. Do bear with me! I feel a divine jealousy for you, for I betrothed you to Christ to present you as a pure bride to her one husband. But I am afraid that as the serpent deceived Eve by his cunning, your thoughts will be led astray from a sincere and pure devotion to Christ. . . . (What I am saying I say not with the Lord's authority but as a fool, in this boastful confidence . . .) But whatever any one dares to boast of—I am speaking as a fool—I also dare to boast of that." Paul then sets out an extensive list of his suffering—imprisonments, beatings, "danger at sea, danger from false brethren"—to establish his priority over other preachers to the Corinthians. "Are they servants of Christ?" he asks. "I am a better one—I am talking like a madman—with far greater labors, far more imprisonments, with countless beatings, and often near death."[18]

Paul's unguarded confession—"talking like a madman"—calls to mind an exchange between Jesus and his original disciples that Mark subsequently recorded, when Jesus instructed them, "If any one would be first, he must be last of all and servant of all."[19] In his Second Letter to the Corinthians, Paul appears both to embrace this instruction and to violate it. By his reckoning, he was indeed the "last of all" because he claimed to have been the last among the apostles to see the risen Jesus. In Paul's telling, this seemed a basis for pride not humility—except that he immediately insisted that "he was not fit to be an apostle" because of his prior oppression of the church; except that he worked harder than any of the other disciples in spreading Jesus's teachings; except that, speaking as a "fool" or a "madman," he was better than any of them because he had suffered more. And somehow it followed for Paul from this contradictory web of self-appraisals that if anyone else "thinks that he is a prophet, or spiritual, he should acknowledge that what I am writing to you is a command of the Lord. If any one does not recognize this, he is not recognized."

Paul thus emerges from the doubts that others have about his status with some doubts of his own. His response to this congeries of uncertainty is self-abasement inextricably connected to self-inflation of his suffering and his consequent authority to command others' allegiance. Paul thus presents the difficulties that we will see among the subsequent Gospel writers in dealing with their own doubts about the significance of Jesus's death and resurrection. In their struggles with these doubts, the Gospel writers answer Paul's question, "shall I come to you with a rod, or with love in a spirit of gentleness?" by increasingly favoring the rod in order to suppress doubts and finally to eliminate all doubters.

Jesus: Betrayals and Abandonments

The move in the Hebrew Bible from unconditional love to a regime of punitively enforced commands was driven by the belief that God and humanity had repeatedly betrayed and abandoned each other. Paul's struggle about his own acceptance into the ranks of the elect presents a version of this progression, enacted in the immediate context of his relationship with other human beings but ultimately as a marker of his success in achieving forgiveness from and reconciled unity with God.

On a much grander scale, Jesus himself struggled with these same underlying issues of betrayal, abandonment, and forgiveness as he approached the end of his life on earth. There was a virtual cascade of actual and suspected betrayals among Jesus, his disciples, and God in Jesus's final days. The recurrent problem in the relations between God and humanity thus emerged into high visibility—almost as if the Gospel writers were giving intense dramatic expression to this problem in order to demonstrate (and perhaps even to test) the effectiveness of Jesus's novel solution to it. Would he sustain "love in a spirit of gentleness" both with his disciples and with God despite his own suffering and isolation, his belief that he had been abandoned by them both?

As he and his disciples took their last supper before his crucifixion, Jesus specifically foresaw that his disciples would betray their promises and abandon him. As they sat at the table, Jesus said to them, "One of you will betray me, one who is eating with me." Each of them in turn asked Jesus, "Is it I?" But Jesus did not answer directly. Instead, after they had finished eating and gone out to the Mount of Olives, Jesus said, "You will all fall away . . . but after I am raised up, I will go before you to Galilee." Peter was most adamant in denying this prediction. "Even though they all fall away," he said, "I will not." But Jesus responded, "Truly, I say to you, this very night, before the cock crows twice, you will deny me three times." Mark recounts that Peter responded "vehemently. 'If I must die with you, I will not deny you.' And they all said the same."[20]

In the event, as Jesus had predicted, all of the disciples did abandon him. Judas's betrayal was most notorious; he kissed Jesus as a sign identifying him to the armed mob that had come to seize him. But the other disciples abandoned him in different ways. At Gethsemane, Jesus left them with an injunction to remain on guard while he retreated alone in the garden to contemplate his fate, but he returned to them three times to find that they had all fallen asleep. He chastised them "and they did not know what to answer him."[21] When the mob finally seized Jesus after Judas had identified him, all of the disciples "forsook him, and fled."

Peter, apparently alone among the disciples, "followed him at a distance, right into the courtyard of the high priest; and he was sitting with the guards, and warming himself at the fire." One of the maids of the high priest then recognized Peter, saying, "You also were with the Nazarene, Jesus." But Peter denied this. "I neither know nor understand what you mean," he said. The maid repeated her charge two more times, and each time Peter repeated his denial. Then, Mark recounts, "immediately the cock crowed a second time. And Peter remembered how Jesus had said to him, 'Before the cock crows twice, you will deny me three times.' And he broke down and wept."[22]

Thus all of Jesus's disciples betrayed him, Judas for material gain and the others from self-protective fear. Peter's abandonment, in denying that he knew Jesus, was contrary to his assurances and his best intentions—but even so he, too, betrayed Jesus. Then he was apparently overwhelmed by guilt: "And he broke down and wept."

Jesus had seemed reconciled to these betrayals before they occurred. After predicting to the disciples that they would "all fall away," he reassured them that he would go before them to Galilee after he had been "raised up," as if to promise that he would forgive their betrayals and return to them when, as he also predicted, he would be resurrected from death. Indeed, the disciples might themselves have felt abandoned by Jesus's insistence that he would do nothing to avert his own death. When Jesus first revealed to them that he "must suffer many things . . . and be killed," Peter "took him, and began to rebuke him. But turning and seeing his disciples, he rebuked Peter, and said, 'Get behind me, Satan! For you are not on the side of God, but of men.'"[23]

Peter must have been stung and unsettled by the ferocity of Jesus's retort. So far as Peter was concerned, Jesus's prior assurance that his death would not terminate their relationship but that he would be raised from the dead must have seemed a hollow promise, even an unintelligible one—and a promise instantaneously revoked by Jesus's accusation that Peter had somehow taken Satan's side against God in wishing that Jesus would not die. It is thus plausible to infer from Mark's spare account that the disciples, and especially Peter, felt abandoned by Jesus's embrace of death, and their abandonment of him as the moment of his death approached can be understood as a retaliatory preemptive strike.

I stress this possibility because we saw it many times in humanity's attitude toward God in the Hebrew Bible, most notably when the Israelites felt abandoned by Moses and turned away from God to worship the Golden Calf. Whatever the disciples' motives for their betrayal of Jesus, he made clear to them in advance that notwithstanding their betrayals of him, he would be resurrected and return to them—a promise of forgiveness that came much more readily to him than it had come to God on Mount Sinai in the Hebrew Bible.

This struggle between Jesus and his disciples about who was betraying whom, and what consequences might follow, was vastly amplified in the relationship between Jesus and God as the end of Jesus's earthly mission approached. The harshness of Jesus's riposte to Peter, in which he identified him as Satan for urging that Jesus should not accept death, suggests that Jesus saw Peter's plea as an additional impetus to abandon his unquestioning faith in God beyond those Satanic temptations that Jesus had previously spurned. Matthew characteristically gives more detail than Mark in describing this encounter with Peter, and thereby offers added meaning to it. In Matthew's version, "Peter took him, and began to rebuke him, saying, 'God forbid, Lord! This shall never happen to you.'"[24] The words "God forbid" have become so commonplace that we easily miss their significance here, but Peter's usage clearly implies a prayer, even an exhortation, directly to God: "God," he says, "[should] forbid . . . This [should] never happen to you." Peter's rebuke, in Matthew's account, is not so much to Jesus for wanting to die (though it does carry this implication) but more powerfully to God for failing to forbid this event. Matthew also added another detail to Jesus's reprimand of Peter. According to Matthew, Jesus said, "Get behind me, Satan! You are a hindrance to me; for you are not on the side of God, but of men."[25] Jesus's accusation that Peter was a "hindrance" or a stumbling block to him suggests that, like Satan, Peter was tempting Jesus to fall away from his own resolve, to withdraw his unconditional, unquestioning faith in God's protective intentions toward him. Peter may have cultivated doubt in Jesus's mind, but the seeds for that doubt must have been immanently present there beforehand.

At the beginning of his ministry, Jesus appeared to have had little difficulty in turning away from Satan's temptations to test God. As the end loomed, however, Jesus's resolve seemed shaken. He confessed this difficulty to his disciples at Gethsemane: "[H]e took with him Peter and James and John, and began to be greatly distressed and troubled. And he said to them, 'My soul is very sorrowful, even to death; remain here, and watch.' And going a little farther, he fell on the ground and prayed that, if it were possible, the hour might pass from him. And he said, 'Abba, Father, all things are possible to thee; remove this cup from me; yet not what I will, but what thou wilt.'"[26] He then immediately returned to his disciples "and found them sleeping, and he said to Peter, 'Simon, are you asleep? Could you not watch one hour? Watch and pray that you may not enter into temptation; the spirit is willing, but the flesh is weak.' And again he went away and prayed, saying the same words." Jesus then returned and again found his disciples sleeping, and he repeated this cycle yet again. This third time, he said, "Rise, let us be going; see, my betrayer is at hand."

Jesus's apparent reference here was to Judas, who immediately appeared in Mark's narrative. But in fact Jesus was surrounded by betrayers at this moment—and none more powerfully revealed than in his prayer to Abba, his Father. Jesus's injunction to Peter—"pray that you should not enter into temptation"—directly invoked his original prescription for prayer to God, lead us not into temptation, do not test us. In his own prayer to God in Gethsemane, Jesus appeared to suspect not only that he might betray God by refusing the suffering and death that awaited him but that God was betraying him by subjecting him to this test. So far as Jesus was concerned, something unaccustomed had intruded into his previously intimate and harmonious relationship with God—some distance between them, some mistrust. Jesus was, moreover, left wholly on his own in struggling with this matter. God previously had a few direct communications with Jesus, recognizing him as a "beloved Son" after his baptism and again at the transfiguring epiphany witnessed by his disciples on the mountaintop. ("A voice came out of the cloud, 'This is my beloved Son; listen to him.'"[27]) But this time God said nothing to Jesus, offered him no reassurance nor even recognition, as Jesus suffered alone and struggled with his conflicting impulses.

God remained silent, saying nothing to Jesus or anyone else, throughout Jesus's ordeal beginning at Gethsemane and ending with his crucifixion. By Mark's account (echoed by Matthew), Jesus's sense of utter abandonment intensified until the very end, when, after suffering for nine hours on the Cross, "Jesus cried with a loud voice, 'E'lo-i, E'lo-i, la'ma sabach-tha'ni?' which means, 'My God, my God, why hast thou forsaken me?' . . . And Jesus uttered a loud cry, and breathed his last."[28]

Mark's rendering of Jesus's words in Aramaic followed by his translation for the uncomprehending reader has an even greater impact than his account of Jesus's life-offering words to Jairus's daughter. We overhear but cannot immediately understand the intimate plea from Jesus to God, yet when Mark translates it for us, we are still unable to understand it. How can it be that Jesus felt abandoned by his Father? Could it be that God had been offended when Jesus asked him for release in the Gethsemane garden? Might God have heard in Jesus's prayer the same wish that God had construed as abandonment when Moses asked for death in order to forsake the mission to lead the Israelites for which God had enlisted him? Even though Jesus had immediately appeared to withdraw his plea—"yet not what I will, but what thou wilt"—his distress seemed to indicate that he had lost his previously unconditional faith in God's protective intentions toward him.[29] Might God retaliate by barring Jesus, as he had done to Moses, from entering the promised land—which for Jesus meant not simply a home overflowing with milk and honey but eternal life at God's right hand? Mark's unadorned account of Jesus's despairing last words on the Cross forces these doubts into high visibility and leaves them unresolved.

Mark's account of the events following Jesus's death on the Cross are even more extraordinary and disturbing. Jesus was wrapped in a shroud and placed in a tomb that had been hewn from rock, and a large stone was rolled against the door of the tomb. On the third day after the crucifixion, three women who had ministered to Jesus on the Cross went to the tomb with spices to anoint his body:

> And they were saying to one another, "Who will roll away the stone for us from the door of the tomb?" And looking up, they saw that the stone was rolled back—it was very large. And entering the tomb, they saw a young man sitting on the right side, dressed in a white robe; and they were amazed. And he said to them, "Do not be amazed; you seek Jesus of Nazareth, who was crucified. He has risen, he is not here; see the place where they laid him. But go, tell his disciples and Peter that he is going before you to Galilee; there you will see him, as he told you." And they went out and fled from the tomb; for trembling and astonishment had come upon them; and they said nothing to any one, for they were afraid.[30]

The original text of Mark's Gospel ends here. In the canonical text of Mark as it ultimately came to appear in the Christian Bible, however, several verses were added. In one version, the text continues, "But they reported briefly to Peter and those with him all that they had been told." This version apparently tries to mask its contradiction in the immediately preceding sentence that the women "said nothing to anyone" by asserting that, nonetheless, they spoke only "briefly" to the disciples.[31] In another version, the preceding observation about the women's silence is ignored. The added narrative simply asserts that Jesus subsequently appeared to the three women, that they then told the disciples but were not believed, and that Jesus himself then appeared to the disciples and "upbraided them for their unbelief and hardness of heart."[32] According to widespread scholarly consensus, these two versions are later appendages to the original text of Mark's Gospel, which ended with the women fleeing from the empty tomb "in trembling and astonishment" and telling no one, "for they were afraid."[33]

Why might Mark have ended his Gospel in this unbelievable way—
so extraordinary and disturbing that it could not be canonically acknowledged until a more comfortable ending had been pasted on? In
my view, the original, unresolved ending is consistent with Jesus's entire self-presentation throughout Mark's Gospel. Mark's Jesus purposefully refrains from offering comforting assurances about his own authority or others' success in following him. The women who fled telling
no one about his empty tomb were acting just as he had enjoined all of
the others who had seen even more direct evidence of his divinely
given powers. Mark's Jesus, moreover, consistently derides "this generation's" need for concrete signs of his divinity. Providing direct eyewitness evidence of his resurrection would have been yet another such
concrete sign, and reliance on these external indicators would have
been inconsistent with the lesson that Mark's Jesus repeatedly taught,
that his followers must discover their belief in him, their faith in him,
from within themselves and not in deference to externally imposed authority either from him or even from the surface evidence provided by
their own eyes of his miraculous cures and great works.

At the inception of his account, Mark stated that what followed was
"the beginning of the Gospel of Jesus Christ, the Son of God."[34] Mark
does not, however, purport to provide indisputable proof that Jesus
was Christ, the Son of God. Mark's concluding observation—that the
women fled in terror from Jesus's empty tomb and told no one—presents a difficult puzzle for any reader who returns to Mark's opening
words. How is this the "good news" of his Gospel? How has Mark
shown us that Jesus is Christ, the Son of God? Mark refuses to answer
this puzzle. He leaves us, as he began his Gospel, with his own declaration of faith, and he challenges us—just as Jesus did in all of his teaching, according to Mark—to find the same faith for ourselves, guided by
the knowledge that others had followed Jesus's invitation to this destination before us. Perhaps Mark meant that his entire account was only
"the beginning of the Gospel" and that for authentic belief, each reader
must reach the conclusion on his own that Jesus was the Christ.

Mark does not, however, leave his readers entirely without resources, without any road map, for following Jesus's path toward a reconciled relationship with his God, who had apparently abandoned him. Jesus's last words, according to Mark—"My God, my God, why hast thou forsaken me?"—contain within them a hint, but only a hint, that his despair was a first step on a path that ultimately led toward renewing his faith in God's love. The hint arises from the fact that these last recorded words of Jesus are identical to the opening words of Psalm 22, traditionally attributed to David: "My God, my God, why hast thou forsaken me?"

From this bleak beginning, David proceeded to give full voice to his despair: "Why are thou so far from helping me, from the words of my groaning? O my God, I cry by day, but thou dost not answer; and by night, but find no rest."[35] But from within this despair, David worked his way slowly, even haltingly, so that by the end of his psalm he has found in himself a belief that God "has not despised or abhorred the affliction of the afflicted; and he has not hid his face from him, but has heard, when he cried to him."[36] David then concluded with praise for God, that "men shall tell of the Lord to the coming generation, and proclaim his deliverance to a people yet unborn, that he has wrought it."[37]

God did not speak to David at any point in this psalm. Nothing but David's inner faith impelled him from his initial despair to his ultimate reconciliation with God. Jesus's last words of terror and despair are David's first words in Psalm 22, which ends with David's profession of confidence in God's protection. The women who fled the empty tomb were similarly in despair, similarly terrified by Jesus's death and his absence from the tomb. They had only the barest hope from the assurance of the white-robed youth that Jesus had risen from the dead, that he had kept his promise to return to his disciples in Galilee. Mark implies that their small hope might blossom into confident conviction if, but only if, they could find the resources within themselves to follow Jesus's path, if they could move from Jesus's despairing final words to the first words of David's psalm and then onward to David's ultimate destination as he recaptured his loving relationship with God.

This is the same challenge, the same necessity, that Jesus presented in his miraculous curative practices—that he could point the way toward healing but could not accomplish it unless the terrified, despairing sick person could find the resources in herself to follow his lead. Jesus could not keep his promises to cure desperately ill people or to return to his despairing disciples if the potential recipients remained passive. The promises could only be kept, the fear of abandonment could only be overcome, by a mutual act of trust—not as a consequence of the restored relationship but as a necessary prelude to it.

Accordingly, Mark's Jesus could not assuage the terror of the fleeing women by proving uncontrovertibly to them that he had risen from the grave and returned to them. The women must find him for themselves, they must search for him with an inner confidence that he will be searching for them. Mark's Jesus could not effectively command the women to trust him, to have faith in him, to believe in him. They cannot find him unless they first offer trust to him. This is the reason that Mark's Gospel authentically ends as it does.

In this ending, we can find the basic resolution that Jesus offers, according to Mark, to the recurrent problem in the Hebrew Bible of the relationship between God and humanity. From humanity's perspective, the central question had been whether God would keep his protective promises or abandon us. From God's perspective, the reciprocal question had been whether humanity would abandon him and, if so, whether he should keep his promises to us. The basic theme of Jesus's teaching is that the relationship between humanity and God had repeatedly foundered because of mistrust on both sides, so that both felt continually driven to test the other's confidence in and love for them.

This mutual mistrust first appeared in the interval between the first and second creations in Genesis, and Jesus taught that humanity and God could find their way back to the goal that each desired—the goal of the harmonious communion that was actualized in the first creation—only by an initial act of transcending mistrust, only by a wholehearted prior offer of unconditional love and loyalty. The demand for definitive proof of love and loyalty as a precondition for repairing the broken relationship was precisely the demand that caused the breach. The demand for prior proof is thus self-defeating; it locks both humanity and God into an endlessly recurring cycle of approach and abandonment.

To feel abandoned and yet to remain trusting is a hard task to accomplish. Jesus's injunction that "if any one strikes you on the right cheek, turn to him the other also" is a specific application of this discipline, a way of continually rehearsing it in the context of relationships among human beings.[38] But Jesus did not restrict this practice to human relations; he directly linked it to the relationship between God and humanity: "love your enemies, and do good, and lend, expecting nothing in return, and your reward will be great, and you will be sons of the Most High; for he is kind to the ungrateful and the selfish. Be merciful even as your Father is merciful."[39] Jesus cannot implement this teaching by threatening punishment for failure to observe it; he can only promise, as he does, a reward for observance.

In this promise, Jesus has returned to the same hortatory style that God invoked for all creatures in Genesis chapter one, an exhortation to "be fruitful and multiply" that appealed to their inner nature rather than an attempt to impose a commandment from outside. But the Christian Bible encounters the same difficulty in sustaining this appeal that we have seen in the Hebrew Bible from Genesis chapter two onward.

CHAPTER ELEVEN

Eliminating Doubts and Doubters

John

*T*HE HEBREW BIBLE CONTAINS many puzzling omissions and apparent contradictions. But the text is nonetheless organized on the premise that, taken together, its narratives have an underlying coherent unity. The format of the text essentially makes this claim, especially for the first five books, the Torah, reputedly written by one author, Moses. The format of the Christian Bible conveys the opposite implication. The central subject of all the Christian texts is Jesus Christ; on its face, this seems to imply that there is only one Christ, and whatever puzzles might appear in the various descriptions of him must be harmonized into a single, internally consistent portrait. But the early Church fathers could have endorsed this implication as the anonymous redactors of the Hebrew Bible had done centuries before—that is, by taking the various available texts and weaving them together into a single authoritative version. The Church fathers chose instead to retain the separate identities of the various Gospels, describing each of them as the work of different men, notwithstanding that all of them spoke to the same subject-matter, the person and teachings of Jesus Christ. Accordingly, when we see apparent variations among the Gospel accounts, it is always plausible to conclude that a so-called Rashomon effect is at work, that different people viewed the same events differently and that no one version necessarily possesses a privileged status over the others. The different versions are just that—different—and we must somehow learn to cope, either by resolving disparities by appeal to some meta-principle or, if this is not possible, by living with the unresolved variations.

The portrait I have sketched of the conception of Jesus's authority in Mark's Gospel is, in broad outlines, consistent with the other Synoptic Gospels by Matthew and Luke. Nonetheless, these later writers were uncomfortable with some elements in Mark's account and struggled against them. In John's Gospel, the fourth of the canonical texts, this discomfort grew into an outright rejection of the essentials of Mark's account replaced by a dramatically different conception of Jesus as exercising unilateral, hierarchically superior authority over humanity. In stark contrast to the Synoptic Gospels, John never records that Jesus enjoined silence on any beneficiaries of his healing. To the contrary, in John's account, unlike the others, Jesus repeatedly asserted in public and in private that he was the Son of God and as such invested with divine authority. For example, to a group of Jews who "persecuted" Jesus because he healed a man on the sabbath, Jesus said, "My Father is working still, and I am working. . . . The Father . . . has given all judgment to the Son, that all may honor the Son, even as they honor the Father. He who does not honor the Son does not honor the Father who sent him."[1] On another occasion, a crowd of hostile Jews asked Jesus, "Who do you claim to be?" He responded, "[I]t is my Father who glorifies me, of whom you say that he is your God. But you have not known him; I know him . . . Your father Abraham rejoiced that he was to see my day; he saw it and was glad." The Jews then challenged him, "You are not yet fifty years old, and have you seen Abraham?" Jesus replied, "Truly, truly, I say to you, before Abraham was, I am."[2] On yet another occasion, a crowd of Jews "gathered around him and said, 'How long will you keep us in suspense? If you are the Christ, tell us plainly.' Jesus answered them, 'I told you, and you do not believe. The works that I do in my Father's name, they bear witness to me ... [E]ven though you do not believe me, believe the works, that you may know and understand that the Father is in me and I am in the Father."[3]

This stark contrast between the Synoptics' Jesus, who withheld direct claim to divine authority, and John's Jesus, who seems to seize every opportunity to make such a claim, suggests that they cannot both be correct accounts. In my opinion, however, there is no basis for choosing one view over the other as *the* authentic teaching or character of Jesus. On close examination, there is more of a continuum from Mark to Matthew and Luke to John than sharp contradictions among the Synoptic Gospels as a whole. Among the Synoptic Gospels, Mark is most relentless in withholding direct claims for Jesus's divine power; Matthew and Luke follow the general outline of Mark's reticence but at various times reveal some discomfort with its implications. These two thus anticipate, to some extent, the confident assertiveness in John's account of Jesus. Even so, the difference among the Synoptic authors is only a matter of degrees of emphasis, while John appears fundamentally to disagree with all of them in kind. The progression from Mark through Matthew and Luke to John reiterates the shift between the first and second Genesis creation accounts, from seamless harmony between God and humanity to God's assertion of punitive command over humanity. Four specific instances involving Jesus's claim to authority reveal this progression among the Gospel writers.

The first concerns Jesus's baptism. As we've seen in Chapter 9, Mark presents Jesus's acceptance of the Baptist's ministration as conveying Jesus's own belief that he had committed some offense that required confession and repentance, whereas Matthew struggles against this implication by portraying the Baptist as insisting that Jesus did not need baptism and only reluctantly acceding to Jesus's insistence. Luke tries to slide past the issue by mentioning almost unnoticeably that the act had occurred and, within the same sentence, quickly changing the subject. In John's Gospel the possibility that Jesus's baptism might in any way diminish his perfection and consequent claim to divine authority is eliminated by a simple expedient. By John's account, Jesus's baptism never occurred. Jesus first appears in John's narrative when the Baptist is ministering to the multitudes, as in Mark's account. But according to John, the Baptist saw Jesus only from a distance and immediately proclaimed to all those around him that he had previously seen "the Spirit descend [on Jesus] as a dove from heaven" and that the Spirit had spoken directly to the Baptist, identifying Jesus as "he who baptizes with the Holy Spirit." The Baptist concluded, "I have seen and have borne witness that this is the Son of God."[4] Thus at the first moment of Jesus's appearance in John's Gospel, a reliable third party testified to having witnessed clear evidence of his exalted status. It is not simply that, in John unlike the Synoptic accounts, Jesus was only a baptizer and was not baptized, but that the Holy Spirit had publicly embraced Jesus as the Son of God rather than privately acknowledging their filial relationship to Jesus alone.

Matthew and Luke also struggled with a second aspect of Mark in his account of Jesus's incapacity in his own hometown, where he was known and belittled as the "carpenter's son." Mark asserted that Jesus could not do, whereas Matthew claimed that Jesus chose not to do, "mighty work" there.[5] Luke avoided the issue by quoting Jesus, "Truly, I say to you, no prophet is acceptable in his own country," but providing no behavioral context to illustrate that proposition.[6] John, however, turns Jesus's observation on its head; he notes that "Jesus himself testified that a prophet has no honor in his own country," but continues that when he actually went to Galilee, this prophecy was disproven: "So when he came to Galilee, the Galileans welcomed him, having seen all that he had done in Jerusalem at the feast, for they too had gone to the feast."[7] John then records that Jesus performed a miraculous healing there. Unlike in Mark's account, Jesus's powers were unimpaired in Galilee; unlike in Matthew's account, Jesus chose to exercise those powers "in his own country"; unlike in Luke's account, Jesus's general observation that prophets are not honored at home was refuted by the welcome Jesus actually received, all according to John.

The third instance in which Luke differs in emphasis from Mark, and in which John simply contradicts them both, is in their accounts of Jesus's final moments on the Cross. In both Mark and Matthew, the last words of Jesus express despair that God had forsaken him; Matthew appears simply to have copied Mark's version, including the direct quotation of Jesus's statement in Aramaic followed by the explicit translation as such into Greek.[8] In Luke, Jesus's last words are "Father, into thy hands I commit my spirit."[9] Luke's account also seems to draw on David's Psalm 22, but he invokes its later portions where, after his initial despair, David had continued, "In thee our fathers trusted; they trusted and thou didst deliver them. . . . Yet thou are he who took me from the womb; thou did keep me safe upon my mother's breast. . . . Be not far from me, for trouble is near and there is none to help. . . . O thou my help, hasten to my aid!"[10] Thus Jesus's last words in Luke's rendering seem to express confidence that God, who had given him birth, would continue to keep him safe: "Father, into thy hands I commit my spirit."

There is, however, also an echo of doubt, of testing God's benevolence, in Luke's last words of Jesus. Satan's final temptation in the wilderness was that Jesus should "throw himself down" from the "pinnacle of the temple in Jerusalem" and that "if you are the Son of God . . . He will give his angels charge of you, to guard you, and on their hands they will bear you up." Jesus refused, saying, "You shall not tempt the Lord your God."[11] But in his final words on the Cross, according to Luke, Jesus seems to do just that—to test whether God will raise his hands to receive the spirit that Jesus has committed to him, at the same time expressing confidence that God will indeed save him as if he were falling from the pinnacle of the temple in Jerusalem.

In John's account, however, Jesus's last words on the Cross convey neither despair nor even any wish to be protected by God's hands. "It is finished," is all that Jesus said, according to John.[12] There is nothing but calm resolve and self-possession in these words. (The Revised English Bible underscores this implication with its translation of these last words, "It is accomplished!") John also, alone among the Gospels, records that Jesus's immediately preceding words were "I thirst." But as if to contradict the suggestion that Jesus was actually thirsty, that he needed some external sustenance, John's full account was "Jesus, knowing that all was now finished, said (to fulfil the scripture), 'I thirst.' A bowl full of vinegar stood there; so they put a sponge full of the vinegar on hyssop and held it to his mouth."[13] John's scriptural reference is to Psalm 69, verse 21: "They gave me poison for food, and for my thirst they gave me vinegar to drink." The other Gospel writers noted that vinegar was given to Jesus on the Cross, but none of them explicitly mentioned the scriptural basis for this drink. John, however, sets this in a parenthetical observation not only to show that Jesus's death was a fulfillment of prophecy in the Hebrew Bible but also, it seems, to contradict the possible impression that Jesus had any weakness on the Cross. That is, Jesus wasn't truly thirsty; he said "I thirst" only "to fulfill the scripture." He was in command of himself to the very end.

What, then, does John make of Jesus's agony in the Gethsemane garden? Mark and Matthew agree that Jesus was "greatly distressed and troubled" when he prayed that God "should remove this cup from me."[14] Luke does not characterize Jesus's mood, but he records the same prayer as Jesus withdrew in solitude, "Father, if thou are willing, remove this cup from me; nevertheless not my will, but thine, be done."[15] For John, however, there was no solitary prayer, no anguished second thoughts, in Gethsemane; Jesus went to this garden "knowing all that would befall him" only because Judas was familiar with this meeting place and would lead the mob there.[16] The only hint that Jesus was "troubled" at the prospect of his death came, by John's account, in an earlier speech to a large crowd. Jesus said,

> "Now is my soul troubled. And what shall I say? 'Father, save me from this hour'? No, for this purpose I have come to this hour. Father, glorify thy name." Then a voice came from heaven, "I have glorified it, and I will glorify it again." The crowd standing by heard it and said that it had thundered. Others said, "An angel has spoken to him." Jesus answered,

"This voice has come for your sake, not for mine . . ." He said this to
show by what death he was to die.[17]

In this account, we are far removed from Jesus's solitary agony, from
his prayer that this cup should pass from him and his immediately
subsequent submission to God's will. In John's account, Jesus explicitly
refuses to ask God for any release. His acknowledgment of a "troubled
soul" seems almost hypothetical, as if to say, "Even if I were troubled,
I would not want anything except to glorify God's name and purpose."
If anyone in this crowd might misunderstand Jesus's mention of his
troubled soul, his immediate dismissal of any such trouble is instantly
rewarded by an approving voice from heaven. There is, moreover, no
suggestion that this voice is reassuring Jesus. He needs no reassurance;
the voice from heaven spoke to the crowds, not to Jesus—"for your
sake, not for mine"—to confirm his authority over them.

The fourth instance where the Gospel writers differ is in their treatment of Jesus's resurrection. Unlike the other examples, in which the
Synoptic Gospels differ in degrees of emphasis among themselves but
John stands apart and starkly opposed, this issue represents a more
continuous spectrum of views among all the Gospel writers. Mark
stands on one extreme of this spectrum; as we have seen, the resurrected Jesus makes no appearance in Mark's original account, and we
have only the word of the mysterious young man dressed in white that
this promised event has actually taken place.

The subsequent Gospels offer more eyewitness accounts of Jesus's
resurrection, each in turn increasing the specificity of their observa-
tions and even the amount of time that the resurrected Jesus remained
on earth. Thus Matthew related that the angel told the women that Jesus had risen, and "with fear and great joy" they ran to tell the disciples
but were met by Jesus on the way. He said "Hail" to them "and they
came up and took hold of his feet and worshipped him." Jesus then instructed the women to tell the disciples "to go to Galilee, and there they

will see me." The eleven disciples then went to a mountain in Galilee and saw Jesus, "but some doubted" and he then spoke directly to them, saying, "All authority in heaven and on earth has been given to me. Go therefore and make disciples of all nations . . . teaching them to observe all that I have commanded you; and lo, I am with you always to the close of the age."[18]

Luke's account is even more extensive. Jesus appears first to two men walking along the road and engages them in conversation, but they don't recognize him; the men "look[ed] sad" and told this apparent stranger of Jesus's death and their dashed "hope . . . that he was the one to redeem Israel." Jesus then chastised them, "O foolish men, and slow of heart to believe all that the prophets have spoken." Without revealing his own identity, Jesus then gave them an extended disquisition "interpret[ing] to them in all the scriptures the things concerning himself." This touching domestic scene then unfolded: "[T]hey drew near to the village to which they were going. He appeared to be going further, but they constrained him, saying 'Stay with us, for it is toward evening and the day is now far spent.' So he went in to stay with them." As they sat together at the dining table, Jesus broke bread, blessed it, and gave it to them; "their eyes were opened and they recognized him; and he vanished out of their sight." The men then recalled, "Did not our hearts burn within us while he talked to us on the road, while he opened to us the scriptures?" They then ran to find the disciples, and as they spoke, "Jesus himself stood among them. But they were startled and frightened." Jesus then reassured them, "See my hands and my feet, that it is I myself; handle me, and see." Jesus then clinched the proof in this prosaic detail: "And while they still disbelieved for joy, and wondered, he said to them, 'Have you anything here to eat?' They gave him a piece of broiled fish, and he took it and ate before them."[19]

John, not surprisingly, exceeds the other Gospel writers in the detail and extensiveness of his eyewitness accounts confirming Jesus's resurrection. Thus, according to John, at the very moment that Mary

Magdalene stood weeping at the empty tomb, Jesus appeared and
spoke to her; then "on the evening of that day," Jesus appeared and
spoke to the disciples. Eight days later he came again to the disciples
and, after some indeterminate lapse of time, yet a third time. But even
these repeated encounters are not enough for John. He adds: "Now Jesus did many other signs in the presence of the disciples, which are not
written in this book; but these are written that you may believe that
Jesus is the Christ, the Son of God, and that believing you may have life
in his name."[20] And yet again, in twenty-five additional verses, John
adds more proof. Moreover, he asserts that his account was based on
"the disciple whom Jesus loved, who had lain close to his breast at the
[last] supper"; this, John says, "is the disciple who is bearing witness to
these things, and who has written these things; and we know that his
testimony is true." Yet even with this, John cannot constrain himself
from a final over-the-top claim: "But there are also many other things
which Jesus did; were every one of them to be written, I suppose that
the world itself could not contain the books that would be written."[21]

The increasingly numerous affidavits in the Gospel accounts of Jesus's resurrection, rising to a crescendo in John, point to a core difficulty in the entire Christian Bible. According to Jesus's diagnosis, the
central problem in the relationship between God and humanity in the
Hebrew Bible was a failure of trust on both sides. This failure could not
be remedied by God's testing humanity to see if his commandments
would be obeyed, or by humanity's testing God to see if he were truly
committed to protecting it. The problem could be remedied only by a
genuine offer of unconditional trust on both sides—although one side
or the other might take the initiative to break the deadlock and move
toward this ideal goal (as God had done, by sending his beloved Son to
live, suffer, and die among humanity).

Mark holds firm to this diagnosis and prescription by offering no
direct proof that Jesus kept his promise to humanity that he would
return from the dead. But this rigorous stance was not acceptable to

the other Gospel writers, nor even to the subsequent readers of Mark's text who added direct proof claims to his unadorned account. The three other elements where I have identified differences among the Gospel accounts—Jesus's baptism, his capacities in his hometown, and his resoluteness in accepting death, including his final words on the Cross—all spoke to possible doubts about Jesus's independent strength. Mark not only acknowledged these doubts but embraced them, whereas the other Gospel writers were increasingly uncomfortable with this acknowledgment and finally, in John's account, rejected it altogether. The underlying premise fueling this dispute is whether Jesus was strong enough to protect humanity. Unquestioned strength had been the predicate for the conditional trust that humanity had offered to God in the Hebrew Bible, and when that protection failed to appear, this was the basis for humanity's charge that God had violated his promise. The differences in the Gospel accounts of Jesus's resurrection reflect a dispute about the strength of the proof that they themselves are willing—or feel compelled—to provide that Jesus was strong enough to overcome death and thereby keep his promise to return.

By purporting to provide incontrovertible proof of Jesus's resurrection, whether because of their own felt needs or because they acceded to public demand for such proof, the Gospel writers other than Mark became ensnared in exactly the dead end that Jesus had identified in the prior relationship between God and humanity. The added gloss to Mark's Gospel starkly identified the problem without appearing to acknowledge or perhaps even to understand it. In this gloss the resurrected Jesus "upbraided [the disciples] for their unbelief and hardness of heart, because they had not believed those who saw him after he had risen." Jesus then proceeded immediately to enjoin these unbelieving and hard-hearted disciples to "preach the gospel to the whole creation [that] he who believes and is baptized will be saved; but he who does not believe will be condemned."[22] Perhaps Jesus meant that the disciples should base their teachings on what he said but not on what they did. Unless the disciples realized, however, that their behavior violated Jesus's instruction, they were unlikely to be effective propagators of his message. Even with this realization, they would hardly offer an effective demonstration that Jesus's difficult admonition could be followed.

John seemed to grasp this problem in his disapproving portrayal of Thomas, the disciple whom John effectively saddled with the epithet of "Doubting Thomas." In fact, however, John's treatment of Thomas indirectly impeached his own efforts. According to John, Thomas was not present among the disciples when Jesus first appeared to them, and he subsequently refused to believe their eyewitness accounts. He said to them, "Unless I see in his hands the print of the nails, and place my finger in the mark of the nails, and place my hand in his side, I will not believe."[23] Eight days later, Jesus again appeared to the disciples, now including Thomas, and subjected himself to Thomas's test: "Put your finger here, and see my hands; and put out your hand, and place it in my side; do not be faithless, but believing." Without any indication that he actually touched Jesus, Thomas immediately responded, "My Lord and my God!" And Jesus replied, "Have you believed because you have seen me? Blessed are those who have not seen and yet believe."[24]

Though John conveyed condemnation of Thomas for his failure to believe without seeing, John apparently did not see that he was also disqualified from earning Jesus's blessing by dint of his repeated insistence that he was providing copious proof of Jesus's resurrection, that he had special access to Jesus's most beloved disciple, "who is bearing witness to these things."[25] Even worse, John's elaborate parade of authoritatively visible proofs creates a stumbling block for those who aspire to Jesus's blessing because they believe though they have not seen.

If John's Gospel becomes self-contradictory by its piling up of proofs, by its extensive elaboration of the mistrustful gloss that was added to the original text of Mark's Gospel, then it might appear that Mark alone offers the path to an authentic grasp of Jesus's message. This may be true, but only in a paradoxically confounding way. The best way to understand Mark's indirection and ambiguity is as a reflection of the core ambiguity in Jesus's message that Mark does not, and cannot, resolve. In the same way that Job's final speech to God cannot be definitively translated because it is inherently ambiguous, so Jesus is inherently ambiguous in confronting the fundamental question posed by the Hebrew and Christian Bibles—the question whether permanent reconciliation is possible between God and humanity.

Both Bibles ultimately offer the same paradoxical answer to this question: permanent reconciliation is not possible but, though unattainable, must nonetheless constantly be pursued. This obligation to pursue reconciliation is not a moral prescription emanating from some external source of authority. It is an internally generated compulsion that comes from the wish or the need that both God and humanity, both ruler and ruled, have for unity with each other. Whatever its ultimate source, this wish or need is the driving impulse in the politics of the two Bibles. Both the Hebrew and the Christian Bibles find their way to this answer by explicitly addressing this underlying question: Can the mutual mistrust between God and humanity that appeared in the second Genesis creation ever be surmounted so as to return to the complete harmony that obtained in the first creation—or is there some internal dynamic in the relationship between God and humanity that ineluctably leads from the harmony of the first creation to the disorder of the second?

The text of the Hebrew Bible does not answer this question but merely states it, most graphically in the unexplained, contradictory transition between the first and second creations. While God rested on the seventh day, what happened to shatter the complete unity that had initially existed between him and humanity? How did the Satanic serpent of mistrust take hold in God's mind that led him to issue commandments to humanity and that tempted humanity in turn to disobey? Jesus clearly saw this transitional moment as the central problem to be remedied, and he himself remedied it in his own person. But could others who were mere humans successfully follow the path that he had traveled?

Mark's account is utterly ambiguous about all these questions. In his Gospel, God and humanity reach toward mutual, unconditional trust through Jesus's intermediation, but we never know for certain whether anyone reaches this goal (including Jesus himself). Then in the Gospels immediately following Mark's account (indeed, even pasted onto Mark itself by later glossators), we find ourselves falling back into the world of the second Genesis creation, where, like God in the Hebrew Bible, Jesus issues commandments and threatens punishment (invested with increasingly explicit authority from God). Among the Gospel writers, John is at the furthest end of this transition from the first to the second Genesis creation. But within the canonical texts of the Christian Bible, John's Gospel is itself only a waystation toward increasingly harsh exercises of Christ's divine authority that retrace the steps in the Hebrew Bible from a loving to a vengeful, punitive God. By the time we reach the final book in the Christian canon, the Revelation to John, we have been drawn relentlessly toward a Divine Authority intent not merely on punishing the disobedient so that they relent from evil and seek redemption but also on destroying all evil-doers—a goal whose own internal dynamic, according to the overall text of the Hebrew and Christian Bibles, presses toward the destruction of all humanity.

We can see the impetus toward this end when we re-examine the strategies that Jesus himself pursued in addressing his own doubts about God's beneficence toward him. At various moments in the Synoptic Gospels, Jesus displayed considerable difficulty in maintaining his unquestioning belief that God was committed to him. Jesus deployed two strategies in these Gospels for dealing with his doubts— strategies that anticipated the techniques for eliminating doubt that became central, and increasingly elaborated, in the subsequent Christian texts. In the Synoptic Gospels, both of these strategies were ultimately revealed as failures.

The first technique was Jesus's effort to project his own doubts onto Peter and then to castigate Peter for having those doubts. This occurred at the crucial moment in the Synoptics when Peter explicitly recognized Jesus as the Christ and then "rebuked" Jesus for predicting his suffering and death. In Matthew's account, Peter exclaimed, "God forbid, Lord! This shall never happen to you." On its face, Peter's wish that God should protect Jesus against suffering and death seems reasonable and even praiseworthy. Although Jesus had also predicted that he would rise on the third day after his death, surely Peter's misunderstanding about the possibility and cosmic significance of this event would deserve some sympathetic explanation and reassurance. Jesus responded, however, with some ferocity: "Get behind me, Satan. You are a hindrance to me; for you are not on the side of God but of men."[26] Rather than gently correcting Peter and explaining that because these extraordinary events were part of God's plan, Peter should trust God with the same confidence that Jesus himself possessed, Jesus accused Peter of being a "hindrance" or a "stumbling block" to him.

But why would Peter's wish for what he thought was Jesus's welfare be an obstacle for Jesus—unless he was struggling with his own doubts and felt undermined when Peter, however ill-informed or well-intentioned, gave voice to those doubts. Thus Jesus literally demonized Peter and tried to expel him from consciousness: "Get behind me, Satan." This is a classic psychological defense maneuver of disowning one's unwanted thoughts by projecting them onto another and then condemning that other as if he were the instigator of the forbidden, disavowed thoughts. By this circuitous logic, we can understand Jesus's accusation that Peter hindered him by giving voice to the thoughts that Jesus was struggling to suppress in himself.

The second defensive maneuver that Jesus deployed to deal with his own doubts about God's beneficence was a simple act of repression. This occurred in Gethsemane when Jesus told his disciples that his "soul was very sorrowful, even to death" and then privately expressed the wish to God that, since "all things are possible" for him, he should "remove this cup" from Jesus. But having said this, and this time directly expressing his own doubts about God's plan for him, Jesus immediately retracted the wish: "yet not what I will, but what thou wilt."[27]

In the Synoptic Gospels, these two defensive efforts by Jesus to deny his doubts clearly, even spectacularly, failed. On the Cross, Jesus gave full expression to the deepest imaginable doubts: "My God, my God, why hast thou forsaken me?" (As noted, Luke's formulation was a more modulated expression of this same fear, when Jesus in his final words tested whether God had in fact abandoned him by falling into God's hands.) In the event, Jesus's resurrection demonstrated that God did not forget him—though the Synoptic Gospels leave unclear, like the uncertainty about God's "remembering" both Noah afloat in the Flood and the children of Israel who cried out after (and presumably during) their four hundred years of enslavement in Egypt, whether God had never forsaken Jesus or had instead reconsidered his previous abandonment. The Synoptic Gospels also leave unclear whether Jesus had recaptured his faith in God's benevolence toward him before or as a consequence of his reception at God's right hand and resurrected presence on earth.

The other canonical Christian texts deal with this uncertainty more resolutely than do the Synoptic Gospels. All of them deploy the same defensive maneuvers of projection and repression that Jesus assayed, but unlike their deployment in the Synoptic Gospels, these defenses do not visibly fail. John's Gospel maintains a confident stance throughout, both by Jesus and about Jesus. John uses the defense of repressing doubts by a wholesale revision of the many places in the Synoptic Gospels where Jesus expressed doubts about his own power, his authority, and God's beneficence toward him. John could, of course, maintain that his revisions were in the service of truth, and that his informants were more reliable—especially the best-beloved disciple—than those who informed the authors of the Synoptic Gospels. (None of the Gospel writers purported to be direct eyewitnesses to Jesus's ministry, but all relied on hearsay testimony.) But repression of discomforting evidence is not the same as falsification; the evidence might be repressed because it is misleading or inflammatory and therefore likely to move away from the truth.

This could be said in John's defense; the fact remains, however, that John is utterly relentless in excising from his narrative even the smallest doubts that appear in the Synoptic Gospels. As we've seen, Matthew and Luke struggle to downplay many of the doubt-inspiring aspects of Mark's narrative, but their struggles do not lead them to John's repeated recourse to flat-out traversals of any doubt-provoking elements. Matthew and Luke engage, we might say, in attempted repression of uncomfortable elements in Mark's Gospel, but as with Mark, all the efforts at repressing doubts ultimately and explicitly fail with Jesus on the Cross. In John's account, however, no doubts are explicitly admitted anywhere.

At the very end of John's Gospel, however, doubts do emerge—and at the same time are emphatically disavowed. Doubts are initially ascribed to Thomas. After Jesus appeared to Thomas and submitted to his test, Jesus sharply rebuked him, "Have you believed because you have seen me? Blessed are those who have not seen and yet believe."[28] Jesus thus pointedly withheld blessing from Thomas because he had demanded physical proof of his resurrection before believing it—because he insisted on testing whether Jesus had fulfilled his promise that he would return from the dead rather than trusting that he would keep that promise.[29]

John also took aim at Peter's reception of Jesus's resurrection, though his criticism was not as direct as his treatment of Thomas. John records that Peter and "the other disciple, the one whom Jesus loved," went together to the empty tomb, and that even though the beloved disciple "outran" Peter and arrived at the tomb first, he didn't enter.[30]

When Peter arrived, according to John, he went into the tomb and saw the linen clothes that had been wrapped around Jesus and the napkin that had been on his head. The beloved disciple, "who reached the tomb first, also went in, and he saw and believed."[31] The clear implication of this narrative is that Peter, though surrounded by proof that Jesus had risen, did not "see and believe" as the beloved disciple had done—and, moreover, that the beloved disciple could have entered the empty tomb ahead of Peter, whom he had "outrun," but he did not need to enter in order to confirm his belief that Jesus had risen from the dead.

John underscored Peter's devaluation in his account, unique to his Gospel, of a conversation that occurred on the third occasion when the resurrected Jesus appeared to his disciples. According to John, Jesus asked Peter three times, "Do you love me?" and "Peter was grieved because [Jesus] said to him the third time, 'Do you love me?'"[32] Jesus's third questioning of Peter, as if he disbelieved Peter's prior avowals of love for him, seems to recapitulate his prediction before his arrest that Peter would deny him three times before the cock crowed. John's account of this interaction between the resurrected Jesus and Peter implies that Jesus believed that Peter would deny him three times again. No wonder Peter was "grieved."

Thus John excludes Peter from the company of the elect, just as he had excluded Thomas, because of his failure wholeheartedly to trust Jesus. The exact nature of Peter's offense is not clear from this account, but the offense can be deduced from John's juxtaposition of Peter's initial failure to believe in Jesus's resurrection with the beloved disciple's unquestioning faith, Thomas's disbelief and consequent chastisement by Jesus, and Jesus's implicit accusation that Peter had insufficient love for him.

But if the measure of sufficient love for Jesus is willingness to put your faith in him and to believe wholeheartedly and without doubt that he loves you, then there is a problem—an internal tension—in

John's Gospel. The problem arises in John's calculation of the proofs he needs to adduce in order to persuade his readers that Jesus was in fact resurrected and thereby kept his promise to return to his grieving disciples. John considered Thomas's demand for unequivocal proof disqualifying, and he implied as much in his treatment of Peter. And yet John piles proof upon proof at the end of his Gospel to persuade readers that Jesus's resurrection truly did occur.

As if what he had already written were not enough, John describes a third, and the most extended, occasion when Jesus reappeared to his disciples. This time seven of the disciples were fishing without success when Jesus appeared on the beach and suggested that they cast their net on the right side of the boat; none of them recognized Jesus, but they followed his suggestion and came up with a vast quantity of fish. At that, "the disciple whom Jesus loved" suddenly appeared and told Peter, "It is the Lord!" Peter jumped into the sea and swam toward Jesus while the other disciples struggled to bring the boat back to shore; and with Jesus they all feasted together on the fish. John then interpolates this observation: "This was now the third time that Jesus was revealed to the disciples after he was raised from the dead"—as if the readers could not count the occasions in John's narrative for themselves, as if John were building a case to prove that Jesus really, but really and truly, had been resurrected and returned in the flesh to the disciples.

There is an unacknowledged paradox in this effort. If we readers apply Jesus's rebuke to ourselves, if we, like Thomas or Peter, demand concrete evidence of his resurrection, what are we to do with John's assurance that his account "is true" because it is based on the testimony of the preeminent beloved disciple who was "bearing witness to these things" from his own personal observation? What are we to do with John's multiplication of occasions when the resurrected Jesus appeared to large numbers of people, an aggregation far in excess of the other Gospel accounts? In this effort to pile up indisputable proofs of Jesus's resurrection, has John made himself a hindrance, a stumbling block, to our capacity to believe in Jesus, to follow his path, on the basis of things "not seen" and yet believed?

We can see this situation as an early catch-22: in order to achieve harmony and eternal life with God, we must believe that Jesus rose from the dead. But if we demand proof of Jesus's resurrection before we are willing to believe, we are disqualified from achieving harmony and eternal life with God. Those early readers who insisted on adding the gloss to Mark's spare account fell into this disqualification. Matthew and Luke similarly could not resist offering their own accounts of eyewitnesses to Jesus's resurrection, and John indulged in an unrestrained escalation of proof, all the while condemning Thomas (and to some extent, Peter) for insisting on direct evidence.

None of this provides any basis for questioning the truth of the Gospel accounts that Jesus did indeed rise from the dead. To question this truth would involve standing outside the Christian texts in order to criticize them; it would violate the methodology that I have followed throughout this book of remaining inside the biblical texts while identifying internal tensions or contradictions within the terms of the texts themselves. The only truth that I assert regarding the resurrection is that John, as well as Matthew, Luke, and the glossators of Mark's Gospel, create a conundrum for themselves by insisting that no true believer should demand proof of Jesus's resurrection and then proceeding to pile up proofs of Jesus's resurrection. The result is an inherent instability in the text itself. This instability undermines the possibility that anyone who reads these narratives can achieve what the texts purport to enjoin—a fully harmonious relationship with God according to the pathway designated by Jesus Christ. Thus Paul's inconclusive struggle for complete recognition as an apostle, as one of the saved elect, turns out to be more than a personal difficulty for him. His struggle represents the conundrum that emerges from the full text of the

Christian Bible—that it may not be possible for mere humans to accomplish what Jesus appeared to promise.

This same conundrum, this internal instability, was also at the core of the Hebrew Bible in its depiction of the recurrent efforts and recurrent failures of God and humanity to attain a harmonious relationship. In the Hebrew Bible, this instability was conveyed by repeated narratives of breaches in the relationship between God and humanity, of perceived and actual betrayals and abandonments on both sides. The Christian Bible offers a different narrative; Jesus experiences and then surmounts betrayals and abandonments—and appears to offer an example that any of us could follow. But this more optimistic message conveying the possibility for all humanity to achieve ultimate harmony with God is undermined by the conundrum that the Gospel writers present, though without acknowledgment as such.

Paul's struggle and the instability that it reveals in the text of the Christian Bible are magnified in the final canonical book, the Revelation to John, also known as the Apocalypse. In this book, Jesus appears in a vision and reveals that he will imminently destroy the "first heaven and the first earth," and in their place a new heaven and earth, "a new Jerusalem [will come] down out of heaven from God." This will be the ultimate reconciliation between God and humanity: "He will dwell with them, and they shall be his people, and . . . he will wipe away every tear from their eyes, and death shall be no more, neither shall there be mourning nor crying nor pain any more."[33] This beatific vision will, however, be achieved only through a massive act of destruction: "nothing unclean shall enter it, nor any one who practices abomination or falsehood, but only those who are written in the Lamb's book of life."[34] Those sinners who are not inscribed in the book of life will be "thrown into the lake of fire . . . and tormented day and night for ever and ever."[35]

This vengefully violent Jesus appears difficult to reconcile with the

Jesus who chastised his disciple for assaulting and "cutting off the ear" of his captor: "Put your sword back into its place; for all who take the sword will perish by the sword."[36] But more than this, Revelation seems to contain an inner contradiction regarding the numbers that will ultimately be saved and destroyed. The criterion for making this differentiation seem clear enough: all who "did not repent . . . of their murders or their sorceries or their immorality or their thefts" will be excluded and condemned to eternal hellfire.[37] But who will be included? This group might be twofold: those who did repent and those who had no need to repent. For the first category, however, how do we calculate the last moment when repentance is still available to them? And for the second category, who among us is without sin? The clear answer given in the Gospel texts is that there is no one in this second category, no one "without sin" who is entitled to "cast the first stone."[38]

Accordingly, Jesus in the book of Revelation may contradict his earlier teachings. But if this is true, on what basis do we choose between the earlier and the later instruction?

Revelation presents itself as a vision vouchsafed to one man; is this a firm enough basis for rejecting the teachings that all four of the Gospels present, based on testimony of those who knew Jesus on earth? But why is this apparent contradiction presented in the biblical canon without any acknowledgment as such? Is Revelation another example of Jesus's pedagogic technique of paradoxically self-contradictory instruction—in this case, because the categorical distinction he propounds between those saved and those condemned in the final Apocalypse cannot be drawn, that its impossibility follows from his core meaning that he intends for us to discover for ourselves rather than supinely accept on the basis of his superior authority?

In the Hebrew Bible, we also encountered the paradoxical teaching that the sinner and the righteous must be treated differently even though it is impossible to distinguish between them because everyone is a sinner. God himself embraced this proposition when he first decided to destroy all humanity because "the evil of the human creature was great on the earth," with the exception of Noah, a "righteous man . . . blameless in his time," and subsequently vowed never again to "strike down all living things . . . [because] the devisings of the human heart are evil from youth."[39] Jesus's proclamation that when the world is entirely destroyed all unrepentant sinners would be eternally condemned is less openly paradoxical than God's syllogism after the Flood, but the reasoning is the same in both cases. And Noah's uncertainty and fear that God had abandoned him as he floated indefinitely on the Flood waters are an apt portrayal of the predicament of all humanity in trying to discern Jesus's meaning in Revelation: Who deserves to be saved? Is even Noah "blameless" enough?

As the last book of the Christian Bible, the Apocalypse in Revelation appears to depict the final triumph of good over evil that will lead to perpetual harmony, a restoration of unity, between God and humanity. And yet a careful reader cannot avoid concluding that uncertainty remains—the persistent instability in the relationship between God and humanity recurs—even in this account. (Perhaps this reader is being too careful, but the stakes are high here, and Noah's example teaches that humanity must read God's proclamations with exceeding caution before relying on any promise of salvation.)

We thus reach the final accounting of the internal politics of the Bible: There is no permanent resting place, no ultimate achievement of unity between God and humanity, but a persistent wish on both sides for this achievement, an episodically repetitive effort initiated on one side or the other to reach this goal, and an occasional harmonization ineluctably followed by a sense of betrayal and abandonment on one side or the other. And then this process repeats itself, without end.

The reasons for humanity's captivation by this endless process are easier to grasp than God's. On humanity's side, we are aware of our vulnerability and long for God's protection. On God's side, we know from the biblical account only that he appeared to cherish union with humanity from the very beginning. In the first iteration, he "created the human in his image, in the image of God He created him, male and female He created them."[40] In the second creation, he sought out human companionship as he was "walking about in the garden in the evening breeze . . . and the Lord God called to the human and said to him, 'Where are you?'"[41] And God was bitterly disappointed; his disappointment increasingly mounted in Genesis until he reached the conclusion that he had made a mistake in creating humanity, and he "was grieved to the heart."[42] He thus resolved to destroy all of us except for Noah, seemed to waver even about saving Noah, but then "remembered" him and made dry land for him.[43] Noah responded by "making burnt offerings on the altar. And the Lord smelled the fragrant odor and the Lord said in His heart, 'I will not again damn the soil on humankind's account.'"[44]

We don't know what pleased God about the fragrance of Noah's offering and, by extension, the continued prospect of humanity's existence—whether we appeased his loneliness or flattered his vanity or fulfilled some other wish. We know only that God's hope for us is never finally fulfilled, that he is repeatedly disappointed or angry or "grieved to the heart" or some mixture of emotions about us, and that nonetheless he has always appeared willing, though sometimes after some considerable hesitation, to renew his efforts to obtain from us what he wants.

We also know that this biblical cycle of approach and withdrawal between God and humanity has shown two overall patterns: a movement from unconditional love on both sides to escalating commands for obedience on both sides. This was the pattern of the relationship in the Hebrew Bible, from the seamless unity in the first creation, to the doubts in God's mind that led him to test humanity by commanding its obedience in refraining from the forbidden fruit, and the doubts in Adam's mind that God would appease his loneliness. Just as God's commandments and threatened punishments increased exponentially in his subsequent relations with humanity, so too Adam's expectations of benefits from God increased among humanity as we insisted that God keep the promises that he repeatedly made to us in his efforts to reward and to secure our allegiance.

It is in this sense that humanity attempted to command God's obedience just as he attempted to command ours. In the course of this progression in the Hebrew Bible, we see that God has vast brute force to impose his will that humanity lacks, but humanity does have at its disposal the weapon (for whatever it's worth) of shunning God by refusing to engage with him. This refusal can lead ultimately to punitive self-destruction by humanity so that, as Job dramatically put it to God, "When You come looking for me, I'll be gone."[45] God's repeated wish to find humanity for whatever purpose—for a companionable evening's stroll in the garden or for the fragrance of our offerings to him—is thus the force that we can exercise to command his attention.

This same pattern in the Hebrew Bible repeats itself in the Christian Bible, with the progression from unconditional love to reciprocal commandments as the basis for the relationship between God and humanity. This progression is evident in the successive depictions of Jesus's teachings from the Synoptic Gospels, starting with Mark and gradually moving through Matthew and Luke (a progression apparent in the internal conflict in Paul's Letters) until we reach a virtual transformation to a punitively enforced command-based relationship in John and its apotheosis in Revelation. On God's side, this progressive transformation is as apparent in the Christian as in the Hebrew Bible. On humanity's side, the increasingly explicit command that God is bound to comply with his promises is less starkly presented in the Christian Bible, but it arises implicitly nonetheless from Jesus's promise that faith in him will lead to the reward of eternal life.

CHAPTER TWELVE

The Insoluble Problem of Politics

*A*CCORDING TO SECULAR theory, the central problem framing all political relationships is the scarcity of resources. All politics, therefore, is about the allocation of scarce resources. Some theorists focus their attention on identifying the substantive principles that should govern such allocations—who gets how much of what (not only material but spiritual resources such as honor, deference, love). Others are more directly engaged in specifying the social processes that might yield the most appropriate allocations. Whatever the mix of substantive and procedural concerns in their various theories, all political thinkers in the Western tradition—from Plato to the modern era—aim to solve the problem presented by the scarcity of resources.

The conviction that the scarcity problem is soluble reflects the grip on Western political thought generally of the driving impulse in the Christian Bible—the possibility of a permanent return to the blissful unity of the first creation in Genesis, when all needs were satisfied and there was no want. The Christian Bible does its best to sustain this belief, even though it cannot stop the narrative impetus toward contradicting the possibility of its realization. The Hebrew Bible is, by contrast, much more explicit in its portrayals of the persistent grip and equally persistent failure of this irenic ambition. The Hebrew Bible effectively acknowledges that scarcity is inescapable and insoluble because of the inconsistency and insatiability of the reciprocal demands that God and humanity make on each other. The Christian Bible implicitly admits this in spite of itself. But this lesson is lost on the canonical modern political theorists who imagine that some satiation, some stable resting point is attainable—some version of Justice that depends on finding fixed points of accommodation among conflicting demands, a definitive ranking of some claimants' desires as hierarchically superior to others'.

The closest approximation in modern political theory of the biblical lesson of mutually insatiable demands can be found in Sigmund Freud's thinking. Though he is not conventionally understood as a political theorist, Freud saw the repeated cycle of longing and angry disappointment in human relationships that we have seen in the biblical account of relationships between God and humanity; he traced the origins of this compulsively repetitive pattern to the earliest relationship between infant and caretaker, when love inevitably transforms itself into hostility. "It is as though our children had remained for ever unsated," Freud said, "as though they had never sucked long enough at their mother's breast. . . . Such is the greed of a child's libido. Perhaps the real fact is that the [infant's] attachment to the mother is bound to perish, precisely because it was the first and was so intense . . . [T]he attitude of love probably comes to grief from the disappointments that are unavoidable and from the accumulation of occasions for aggression."[1]

Freud also saw the repeated resurgence of this infantile longing to satisfy insatiable needs in adult political relationships. "A group," he said, "is clearly held together by a power of some kind; and to what power could this feat be better ascribed than to Eros, which holds together everything in the world?"[2] This erotic power, this loved and loving force, holds everything together not only in the psychology of groups but for each of us individually.[3] Within the terms of the Hebrew and Christian Bibles, this Eros is God himself. No wonder we are drawn continuously to him, notwithstanding our repeated disappointments and even hostility toward him because he has failed yet again to satisfy our insatiable needs.

Of all the theorists whose work has been enshrined in the Western canon of political philosophy, Thomas Hobbes most clearly anticipated Freud's conclusion in acknowledging the psychological premise of human insatiability and the consequent insolubility of the scarcity problem. Hobbes's "war of all against all" in the pre-political state of nature derives from this premise. Hobbes may have believed that this state once actually existed, or he may have only posited its existence as the inevitable alternative in the absence of a supreme authoritarian ruler. But Hobbes believed that human beings were necessarily so hostile to one another, so insatiable in their competitive demands for scarce resources, that no overarching substantive principle could ever be identified that might resolve this warfare. The only alternative he saw to endless warfare and consequent perpetual insecurity was that all human beings would rationally be driven to mutual surrender and the establishment of an absolute ruler over all of them. This absolute ruler, the Leviathan, would allocate resources as he alone saw fit; his unquestioned authority would not satisfy his subjects' neediness but would simply suppress any conflict among them.

Hobbes's Leviathan was itself modeled on his understanding of God's authority in the book of Job, and it does indeed appear to track the claim that God put forward in his diatribe against Job from the Whirlwind. As we have seen, it is not at all clear that Job acquiesces in God's claim or that God sustains this claim in the Epilogue, where he appears chastened and eager for a renewed relationship that Job has the practical power to withhold. There is, moreover, an even more crucial difference between Hobbes's conception and the biblical account. For Hobbes, the Sovereign's authority arises from a mutual agreement among warring subjects, but he is not party to this agree-

ment. Hobbes's Sovereign stands outside and above political relationships; he wants nothing from his subjects but exercises absolute authority over them solely on the basis of what they want from one
another (that is, respite from endless warfare). In the book of Job, however, God wants to remain in a relationship with Job.

Indeed, at one point in his catalogue of complaints against God, Job
explicitly called for "an arbiter between us to lay his hand on both of
us."[4] Job seemed to envision some superior authority who would "lay
his hand" on God. By the end of the book of Job, no one appears to
take on this role, but that does not mean that God, like Hobbes's Sovereign, stands outside and above a relationship with Job or with humanity generally. Unlike Hobbes's Sovereign, God wanted something from
Job on his own account. The entire impetus for the book of Job, in fact,
arose from God's desire to refute Satan's taunt that Job's allegiance
to God was merely contingent on his good fortune from God. God
wanted unconditional loyalty from Job—just as he wanted from everyone. Of the Ten Commandments that God issued to the children of
Israel in Exodus, the first four were about himself—about the loyalty
that he demanded; he even described himself as a "jealous God" in the
Second Commandment.[5] (God's Fifth Commandment, to honor one's
father and mother, might also be counted as self-referential.)

Hobbes's Sovereign was not jealous, and he sought nothing on his
own account; he was merely occupying a role that his desperate subjects thrust on him because of their aggressively insatiable demands on
one another. The perpetual warfare that Hobbes sees among humans
in his state of nature is what the book of Job sees at the core of the relationship between God and humanity, precisely why Job wished for an
arbiter to stand over him and God. This warfare also arises from the
same root cause: the unquenchable character of the demands that God
and humanity make of each other.

The Hebrew Bible—not only in the book of Job, but throughout—
is virtually explicit in depicting the insatiability of humanity's de-

mands on God. The endless demands of the Israelites after their Exodus from Egypt are the clearest instantiations. Jacob is not far behind
them, and the inability of Adam and Eve to restrain themselves from
eating the one forbidden fruit among Eden's abundance signifies humanity's insatiability from the outset. Of all the figures in the Hebrew
Bible, Moses came closest to occupying the arbiter's role that Job envisioned, but he had only fleeting success in both leading the children of
Israel to temper their demands on God and prompting God to restrain
his equally insatiable demands on them. In the end, Moses himself became the victim of God's demands. God resented Moses's attempt to
withdraw as his intermediary with the children of Israel and so would
not allow Moses to enter the promised land. Moses, that is, found himself caught between God's boundless demands for the Israelites' obedience and the endless appetite of the Israelites.[6]

This was the "evil," as Moses characterized it, from which he sought
release when he asked God to kill him. Recall Moses's complaint to
God: "Why have You done evil to Your servant . . . to put the burden of
all this people upon me? Did I conceive all this people, did I give birth
to them, that You should say to me, 'Bear them in your lap, as the
guardian bears the infant' . . . From where shall I get meat to give to all
this people when they weep to me, saying, 'Give us meat that we may
eat'? I alone cannot bear this people, for they are too heavy for me. And
if thus You would do with me, kill me, pray, altogether."[7] It was God, of
course, who conceived "all this people," who gave birth to them; in this
passage, Moses implicitly referred to the infantile insatiability of the
Israelites to support his accusation that God had foisted an impossible
burden on him. Recall, too, God's initial response to Moses, instructing
him to tell the Israelites, "The Lord will give you meat and you will eat.
Not one day will you eat and not two days and not five days and not
ten days and not twenty days, but a full month of days, till it comes out
of your noses and becomes a loathsome thing to you, inasmuch as you

have cast aside the Lord Who is in your midst and you have wept before him, saying, 'Why is it we have come out of Egypt?'"[8]

God thus mocked his children because of their greediness, but it is not clear that the glut of meat that he proposed to inflict on them would indeed slake their hunger. Thus this episode ends with God's sweeping quail from the sea, "about a day's journey in every direction all around the camp and about two cubits deep on the ground. And the people arose all that day and all that night and all the next day and gathered the quail. . . . The meat was still between their teeth, it had not yet been chewed, when the Lord's wrath flared against the people, and the Lord struck a very great blow against the people. And the name of the place was called Kibroth-Hattaavah, for there the people buried the ones who had been craving."[9] The translation of this Hebrew place-name is "Graves of Desire (or Lust)."[10] God thus sought to bury, to expunge, the insatiable lusting of his children (as indeed, three of his Ten Commandments sought to limit adultery [Seven], theft [Eight], and "covet[ing] . . . anything that is your neighbor's" [Ten]). The entire trajectory of the Hebrew Bible testifies to the persistence of God's effort to restrain human desires and his repeated failure to achieve this goal.

In the Christian Bible, Jesus confronted the insatiability of human demands by drawing on an apparently endless resource: God's boundless love for humanity. God's willingness in the Christian Bible to satisfy humanity's limitless hunger is signified in two episodes, directly contrasting with God's angry glut of quail in the Hebrew Bible, when five loaves and two fish were multiplied to feed more than five thousand, who "all ate and were satisfied," and then again when seven loaves "and a few small fish" became enough to feed more than four thousand, who "all ate and were satisfied."[11] God's loving nurturance could, however, satisfy human neediness only if it were unconditional, truly without bounds.

Jesus conveyed this understanding in his promise that no sinner was beyond the reach of God's love. But in his own life on earth, Jesus enacted the difficulty of holding to the belief in this promise. His final words from the Cross in Mark and Matthew proclaim that even he was vulnerable to believing that God had abandoned him. His success in surmounting these doubts points the way for humanity to follow. But Paul's difficulties in persuading others that he was a true disciple and in believing himself that his sins had been forgiven dramatically represent the considerable difficulties that mere humans encounter in trying to follow Jesus's path.

We have seen this same struggle in the Hebrew Bible. Job displayed it in his initial fear that his "sons have sinned by cursing God in their hearts."[12] Abraham even more vividly revealed this difficulty. God may have concluded that Abraham satisfied all his tests of loyalty. But from Abraham's perspective, these repeated tests—culminating in God's command to sacrifice Isaac when it already seemed to Abraham that Lot and Ishmael had died—appeared to signify that God would never be convinced of Abraham's worthiness, since God's reassurances were always followed by a renewed (and even more onerous) test. Perhaps Abraham thought that these escalating tests were undeserved, as Job concluded; perhaps Abraham believed that his guilt was so great (as I have speculated) in his profit from his younger brother's death that God would never forgive him.

The possibility of God's willingness to forgive sins moves to the center of the relationship between God and humanity in the Christian Bible. But human beings' capacity to sustain belief in the boundless character of this promise is increasingly tested in the unfolding narrative of the Christian Bible. Moreover, the promise appears undermined as sharp boundaries ultimately emerge in Revelation, the final book of the Christian Bible.

Secular political theorists have dealt with the problem of human insatiability in radically different ways, but the ultimate goal of the canonical modern theorists has been virtually identical to the goal pursued in both the Hebrew and the Christian Bibles. Whereas the two Bibles speak of the wish to return to the harmonious relationship, the seamless unity, between God and humanity (as represented in the first creation account in Genesis), modern theorists seek to create the functional equivalent of a perfectly harmonious regime of relationships among human beings. This harmony may be coercively imposed, as in Hobbes's vision of a mutual agreement among humans to end their warfare by total, mutual self-subjugation. This harmony may be understood to arise from self-interested deliberation about the social contract in John Locke's society of property-holders or from disinterested reflection about the demands of Justice (from behind a "veil of ignorance") in John Rawls's polity. This harmony may be understood to arise with apparent spontaneity as the mutually agreed reflection of the General Will in which each individual sees himself fully realized in the communal relationship, as Jean-Jacques Rousseau envisioned. This harmony may be understood to come from the dialectic struggle of material forces that Karl Marx portrayed as ultimately leading to a "withering of the state" and a society in which each individual gives "according to his capacity" and receives "according to his needs."

The routes to the ideal vary among these political thinkers. The specific terms of the social relationships that obtain in their polities are radically different. But in all these arrangements, the ideal remains the same: to respond to human demands that exceed the available supply, to solve the problem of apparent insatiability. The premise of all these efforts is that human insatiability is only apparent—that rational deliberation either in advance of establishing a scheme of political relationships or as part of an ongoing process of deliberations within a political relationship can solve this problem.

When Job momentarily imagined the possibility that an arbiter could be found who would lay his hand impartially on both him and God, he succumbed to the same temptation that has lured modern political theorists in their quest for some fixed overarching principles that could be used to adjudicate disputes by someone standing outside the relationship between the disputants. In the book of Job, no such arbiter ever appears. The closest approximation is Elihu, who suddenly emerges from nowhere after Job and the three Friends have fallen silent and before God appears from the Whirlwind. But Elihu delivers his lengthy declamation—the longest speech in Job—to no one; neither Job nor the three Friends respond to him or even acknowledge his existence, and God subsequently also entirely ignores him.

Elihu's speech itself is filled with windy platitudes. As noted, some scholars have been led by its "inferior" literary quality—"prolix, labored, and somewhat tautologous," as one put it—to conclude that Elihu's speech was a late addition to Job written by a different author and can indeed, as another concluded, "be removed from the book without any sense of loss."[13] But this critique is like the philological claim that the contradictions between the first and second creation accounts in Genesis prove their separate authorship and thus have no substantive significance. This critique misses the point that Elihu is full of wind and is ignored by all parties because he is attempting to occupy a role that does not exist; he is attempting to stand outside of the contested relationship both between Job and the three Friends and between Job and God, and to render disinterested judgment regarding who among them was correct, who deserved to prevail.

I began the quest for the political theory of the Bible by noting that the Bible differed from standard works of political theory because its lessons were not stated in abstract syllogistic principles but were instead embedded in extensive narratives about relationships between God and various people and among different people themselves. We can now see that these narratives are not simply disguised ways of presenting abstract principles that stand above the parties' disputes. The narrative format graphically depicts the political theory of the Bible. The biblical conception of political relationships cannot be expressed as disembodied propositions addressed to a generalized, anonymous audience. Its conception can be depicted only in intensely engaged interactions between God and humanity (and also between humans themselves)—persistently contentious interactions, afflicted by betrayals and abandonments, often falling into prolonged silence but then resumed with offers of reconciliation and sometimes with apologies.

This narrative format signifies that in any dispute touching the fundamental question of how the parties should relate to each other—who owes what to whom—the disputants are ultimately and inevitably making incommensurate demands on each other. The demands are incommensurate because they arise from the insatiability of the neediness with which each party confronts the other. Each party may insist that the other curb its appetite—relying on the logical force of the proposition that an insatiable demand can never be satisfied and that some point of accommodation must be found; or relying on the greater coercive strength that one party can muster against the other, so as to endlessly appease one's own neediness at the perpetual expense of the other. A third party, standing outside the dispute, can make the same moves—claiming greater persuasive force or justifying greater coercive force on the ground that he has no personal stake in the outcome. But the dispute can never be conclusively settled, by the parties themselves or by an outside adjudicator, because the disputants inevitably remain locked in the conundrum of mutually inconsistent, inherently insatiable demands. Temporary truce lines can be drawn in this dispute. But the warring parties cannot easily walk away because of the need each has for the other.

There is, however, always the threat that the loser will be driven to walk away because his loss is so total, so overwhelming, that he can gain nothing close to adequate compensation and is nothing more than the aggrieved object of his opponent's insatiable appetite. This is the conclusion that Job came to, when he threatened suicide and thereby fell back on the only weapon at his disposal in combating God's heedlessly insatiable need for proof of his allegiance. Faced with this prospect of irrevocable breach (and possibly encouraged by Job's fleeting memory and longing for past times when God "was still with me"), God chose to appear before Job, ostensibly to berate him but ultimately to search for some basis for a continued relationship with him.[14]

The book of Job thus distills the entire underlying political theory of the Hebrew Bible. It accomplishes this first of all, as we have already seen, by giving explicit voice to humanity's complaints about God's reliability, about the satisfactions that we can expect from remaining in a relationship with him—complaints that were muted but nonetheless discernible throughout the rest of the biblical text. The second distillation in Job is implicit in its dialogic format. An external narrator appears briefly in the Prologue and Epilogue to the book, but the heart of Job is an unmediated exchange of complaints and recriminations, charges and countercharges, among the aggrieved parties themselves. This format encapsulates the structure of the political arrangements, the procedural terms of the relationship, between God and humanity that follows from the biblical premise that although permanent reconciliation cannot be achieved, both God and humanity are nonetheless constantly impelled to seek it.

This interactive format is virtually unprecedented in the rest of the Hebrew Bible. The only other book that comes close to this format is the Song of Solomon, a passionately erotic love poem sometimes spoken in a woman's voice and sometimes in a man's but each almost indistinguishable from the other; indeed, they seem to melt seamlessly into each other throughout the text. In the ordering of books in the Hebrew Bible, the Song of Solomon appears immediately after Job; the erotic merging and separately re-emerging voices in the Song thus serve as a commentary to Job, a depiction of the goal that was sought but never clearly achieved in the dialogues between Job and the Friends or between Job and God. As in the Song, erotic love between a man and a woman served briefly in the second Genesis creation to recall the prior initial harmony in the first creation. Immediately after Eve appeared in the second creation to appease Adam's loneliness, the narrator suddenly intruded to proclaim, "Therefore does a man leave his father and his mother and cling to his wife and they become one flesh."[15]

The goal in the book of Job is that all of the contesting parties come to a mutual understanding, become "one flesh," so as to satisfy their endless need and longing for one another. Job instructs that this goal can be approached, the insatiable longing for it can be appeased, by continuous dialogic engagement between God and humanity, even if this goal is never achieved and is never actually achievable. In the Christian Bible, Jesus conveys the same instruction through his use of parables as the central instrument of his pedagogy. Jesus's disciples were puzzled by his reliance on parables, and Jesus offered this apparent explanation to them: "To you has been given the secret of the kingdom of God, but for those outside everything is in parables; so that they may indeed see but not perceive, and may indeed hear but not understand; lest they should turn again, and be forgiven."[16]

This is, however, a puzzling explanation, as if Jesus were purposefully using parables to obstruct rather than to promote understanding among the uninitiated.[17] His reassurance to his disciples, moreover, that they were blessed with comprehension was apparently contradicted by their inability to decode the parables and their need to ask Jesus for specific explanations.[18] Mark presents this paradox with characteristic sharpness: after telling his first parable, regarding the sower and the seeds, Jesus remonstrated against his disciples, "Do you not understand this parable? How then will you understand all the parables?"[19] Jesus followed this rebuke with an extended explanation to his disciples of that parable, but they gave no indication that they understood this (to my eyes and ears, at least, quite obscure) exposition.

If, however, we take at face value Jesus's explanation that he uses parables to confound rather than clarify understanding among both the masses and his disciples, we can see a parallel with the pedagogic use of narrative in the Hebrew Bible generally and the reliance on dialogue in the book of Job specifically. In all cases, the goal is not to promote comprehension as such—not to produce a meeting of the minds—but to impel, to lure, to seduce opposing parties to enter into direct interchange with each other. The goal is to seek mutual understanding, even though ultimate agreement is not achieved and, indeed, can never be reached because of the insatiability of the demands that each makes of the other. The crucial distinction is not between success and failure in comprehension but between interaction and disengagement. Persistent interaction, in biblical terms, means that each party acknowledges his need for the other, even if that need can never be satisfied. Disengagement means denial of that neediness, a false claim of self-sufficiency. This is the normative distinction that underlies the politics of the Bible.

Neither the Hebrew nor the Christian Bible directly acknowledges the inconsistency of the demands that God and humanity make on each other. Neither text admits the insatiability of both God and humanity toward each other. Neither explicitly identifies the consequences that follow from this insatiability: that is, the inevitable failure of both God and humanity to arrive at a permanently satisfactory relationship. But both the Hebrew and the Christian Bibles implicitly acknowledge these dispiriting propositions by their narrative depictions of the persistent efforts toward attaining perfect harmony between God and humanity and the equally repeated failures on both sides to reach this goal.

These biblical narratives also convey a deeply disturbing message about the consequences of the pursuit by God or humanity of perfect harmony. That is, because it will inevitably be disappointed, the determined pursuit of this relationship can readily lead to an undesired conclusion, the destruction of any relationship. We have seen this paradox most graphically in God's avowedly regretful decision to "wipe out the human race" in the Genesis Flood because of its "perpetually

evil" scheming—a decision that almost led him to universal destruction by abandoning Noah and the other inhabitants of the ark. We have
seen it in the vision in Revelation of Christ's return in order to eradicate sinfulness from the world by destroying all sinners—without any
clear assurance that there would be any non-sinners available for survival, much less to cast the first stone in this holocaust. On humanity's
side we have seen this paradox in the repetition of angry disappointment and sense of abandonment leading to a repudiation of any relationship with God—among many examples, as when the Israelites
turned to the Golden Calf after Moses's prolonged absence in Sinai or
when Jesus's disciples disavowed him and fled after his arrest notwithstanding their prior pledge of undying loyalty.

Just as the biblical narratives don't explicitly acknowledge these insoluble problems but repeatedly portray them, so too the texts don't
explicitly identify ways to address these problems with the recognition
that they cannot be definitively solved. Nonetheless, the texts do point
—characteristically in narrative format—toward some possibilities of
an ameliorative response to these problems in the relationship of God
and humanity.

In the Hebrew Bible, this possibility is most extensively essayed in
the book of Job. In demanding justice from God, Job envisioned the
continuance or resumption of their relationship, but based on different terms that were more satisfactory to Job's conception of himself. In
secular terms, litigation is an accepted means for pursuing such a rede-
fined relationship: the aggrieved litigant takes his demand to an independent judge, an impartial third party, with acknowledged authority
to adjudicate the dispute between the parties. There is, however, no
such impartial adjudicator available in the Hebrew or Christian Bibles
for disputes between humanity and God. The search for such an adjudicator itself might appear blasphemous in its implication that someone somewhere could exercise binding authority over God himself.

Even so, at one point in their direct interchange when God appeared before Job in the Whirlwind, God spoke as if he were a defendant in a lawsuit that had been initiated by Job. In the middle of his tirade against Job, God paused and said, "One who brings Shaddai to court should fight! He who charges a god should speak."[20] There was, of course, no judge in sight to make his confrontation with Job into a regular courtroom proceeding. Nonetheless, in its essential structure, the book of Job mimics the modalities of a courtroom confrontation. This is the implication of the unique dialogic format of the book.

For most of the proceeding, we might say, God was represented by advocates on his behalf (the Friends and Elihu) while Job appeared throughout on his own behalf (*pro se,* as the lawyers style it). The pleadings are interrupted when Job and the Friends break off conversation and when no one even acknowledges Elihu's wordy presence. But the disputation resumes when God steps forward to advocate on his own behalf. At the end of his diatribe, it again appears as if the proceedings are terminated by Job's final speech (in which he apparently withdraws his complaint with an apologetic self-abasement or despondent and dismissive anger). But yet again, in the Epilogue, the proceedings resume as God contrives to have Job speak to him on the Friends' behalf and Job does indeed respond.

At the conclusion of the book, there is no clear end to the dialogue, and the possibility is left open that God and Job might have many more such interchanges. The substantive dispute between God and Job is never conclusively resolved. But the persistence of their dialogue is not simply a descriptive detail. This persistence implies a normative proposition favoring the continuation of a relationship through the dialogue as such between God and Job. This preference for dialogic interaction does not arise from any external normative judgment that the disputants should have a continued relationship, should be mutually dependent on each other. The fundamental biblical premise is that God and humanity do in fact need each other, that they are psychologically constructed to need each other—and yet both God and humanity resist acknowledging, and often entirely lose sight of, this fact about themselves.

Thus at one point in his lamentations, Job appears to plead with God to turn away from him. "Let me alone," Job says. "My life is just a breath. What is man that You make so much of him; and think about him so, examine him each morning, appraise him every moment? What have I done to You, keeper, jailer of men? Why should You make me Your target, a burden to myself?"[21] Similarly, God appears to spurn any continuing relationship with Job in his diatribe from the Whirlwind, when he boasts of his immense powers in creating all of the animal kingdom but pointedly omits any mention of his creation of (or presumed dominance over) humanity. Each side accordingly shows a strong inclination to turn away from the other, to insist on self-sufficiency. And yet some internal force continuously draws each side back toward interaction with the other—not happily, often angrily, but nonetheless persistently.

Before God appeared to him in the Whirlwind, Job clearly hoped that God wanted some future relationship with him. Job's desire for this result was palpably stronger than his wish to be left alone. This was the clear import of his climactic expression of longing in his last speech before God actually appeared.[22] We can see a similar impetus on God's side in his declamation from the Whirlwind. In his apparently boastful and dismissive parade of animal life before Job, we can glimpse a reminder of God's original action in creating animals without offering Adam a human companion to remedy his loneliness—as if God were holding fast to the possibility of some exclusive relationship that he wanted from Adam alone. It is also notable that Job's wife never reappears in the book after her initial injunction that Job should "curse God and die."[23] By withholding any mention of a wife who gave birth to Job's new children, the book of Job strives to hold back any interference with the possibility of Job's resumed intimacy with God. Even if God avoided the necessity for a new wife by resurrecting Job's original

children—as some *midrashic* commentators have imagined—his elim-
ination of her could testify to the same impetus on his part toward an
exclusive relationship with Job.

The ultimate lesson of the book of Job is that perfect satisfaction,
permanent harmony, is always beyond reach. This fact recurrently
drives God and humanity apart in angry recriminations about broken
promises, betrayals, and abandonment. This anger on each side cannot
be avoided; but direct, continuous confrontation about the causes and
possible (even if temporary) solutions for these recriminations provides the most likely course by which each party can come to a more
satisfying outcome than if they permanently retreat from each other.
When God and human beings are in conflict, and making inconsistent
demands on each other, both of them would best serve their own desires and interests by remaining in direct conversational interaction.
The underlying goal of this continuous interaction—this extended
trial proceeding, to use lawyers' language—is to provide a forum in
which the disputants are likely to be led to acknowledge (each to himself as well as to the other) their need for each other and their consequent mutual dependency.

This preference for continuous dialogue is thus itself not based on a
moral norm that stands outside or above the wishes of the disputants
themselves. It is not a norm that is externally imposed on either humanity or on God himself by some higher authority. The preference
for continuous interaction arises from the disputants' own neediness,
from the self-interest of each party—although neither God nor humanity, in the heat of bitter mutual recriminations, is likely to see the
wisdom of this course. The fundamental problem that the biblical narratives present, as distilled by the book of Job, is how to design a format for interaction, for continuous disputatious dialogue, that illuminates for both God and humanity the fact that their need for each other
transcends their anger over their inability to satisfy each other's need.

In Genesis, no satisfactory format was ever found for pursuing this goal. Throughout Genesis, the format for interaction was direct dialogue between God and specific human beings. All of God's direct addressees in Genesis—Adam, Eve, Cain, Noah, Abraham, Sarah, Abimelech, Isaac, and Jacob—were free to tell others about their conversations with God, but this was not an explicit aspect of God's arrangement with them. By the end of Genesis, direct dialogue between God and humanity had disappeared; indeed, in the final fourteen chapters of Genesis, narrating the story of Joseph and his brothers, God never speaks directly to any human being, except briefly to Jacob before his trip to rejoin Joseph in Egypt.

God did not break his extended silence at the end of Genesis until four centuries later, when, according to Exodus, "God heard their moaning, and God remembered His covenant with Abraham, with Isaac, and with Jacob. And God saw the Israelites, and God knew."[24] Thus God had no interaction with the Israelites for four hundred years; if he had any need for their companionship or any human contact, he had not said so. He apparently had not seen, heard, or remembered them; he had been deaf, blind, and dumb to the plight, and even to the very existence, of the enslaved Israelites. What, then, did God suddenly "know" after four hundred years that he had not realized before? Exodus doesn't tell us.

But when God "remembered" the children of Israel for whatever reason and resumed his engagement with them, he introduced a striking procedural innovation. He reinstated dialogue with one human being, Moses. But God did not choose Moses simply to have a conversational partner. In contrast to his discourse with human beings in Genesis, God explicitly directed Moses to serve as an intermediary between him and the Israelites. There was one instance when God directly spoke to the tribal elders to offer the Sinai covenant to them, and "all the people" responded affirmatively. But aside from this constitutional moment, God's relationship with the people was carried out entirely through Moses's mediation. (God did also speak directly to Miriam and Aaron, Moses's elder siblings, but only to tell them that Moses remained his chosen medium and that they should refrain from trying to undermine him.[25])

This novel use of Moses in Exodus blossomed into an entirely different modality by which God exercised his authority, and it had a consequence that God may not have anticipated. In his intermediary role, Moses stood between God and humanity, aspiring to act as a trusted teacher who could enunciate moral judgments about their conduct, instruct them about their own deepest longings and needs toward one another, and advise them about the most instrumentally effective way of honoring those feelings.

In the Christian Bible, Jesus occupied a similar role. The Gospel accounts in the Christian Bible understand Jesus to have a more exalted status than Moses; whereas Moses spoke on God's behalf to humanity, Jesus was the direct embodiment of God himself. In the Christian Bible, moreover, God more fully embraced the lesson that Moses had tried to teach him earlier—the virtues from God's own perspective of acknowledging his vulnerability toward, his dependence on, and his love for humanity, and to forgive humanity for its trespasses against him. God's direct appearance in the Christian Bible through his Son and the visible suffering of his Son at the hands of human beings can be understood as a dramatic endorsement of Moses's lesson to God in the Sinai desert.

Christ's appearance can also be seen as God's acknowledgment of the lesson that Job tried to offer when he wished for "an arbiter between us to lay his hand on both of us." If we more closely attend to Job's wish, we can see that it was not—as it initially appeared—for some judge who would adjudicate the dispute between him and God, who would somehow invoke superior authority over both to impose on them the correct result, the just outcome. Job's wish was more limited than this: "[A] man like me cannot just challenge Him, 'Let's go to court together!' Now if there were an arbiter between us to lay his hand on both of us, to make Him take His rod away, so that His terror would not cow me, then I could speak without this fear of Him, for now I am not steady in His presence."[26]

Job thus wished for an arbiter to promote the possibility of a constructive dialogue between him and God, of an interchange in which both sides would speak their true feelings and articulate their full demands. But Job complained that God's vastly superior power and status would render him speechless and therefore, in particular, unable to express his anger at God's betrayal of his past promises. Correspondingly, God's vast effective power and presumed status would tempt him to ignore his own vulnerability toward Job and to disdain him. Accordingly, neither Job nor God would be likely to speak truth to each other, about their mutual anger or their mutual neediness—at least in the absence of an arbiter who might calm and guide them toward acknowledging their true attitudes toward each other.

In fact, when God finally appeared in the Whirlwind, their unmediated confrontation produced exactly this pattern that Job had anticipated. When God had demanded that Job should speak because he had brought "Shaddai to court [and he] who charges a god should speak," Job had responded fearfully, "I see how little I am. I will not answer You. I am putting my hand to my lips."[27] At the end of God's tirade, Job did speak again, but, insofar as he appeared to recant, Job's self-abasement was not what God wanted in his wager with Satan. As Satan had seen, God wanted unconditional love from Job, not self-serving love based on gratitude for gifts bestowed or forced love based on fear of punishment. But Satan was not interested in modulating God's anger; he wanted to win his wager that Job would curse God to his face. If in his final speech Job did repudiate his past angry complaints against God, this seemed to be a prologue for the same consequence that Abraham and Moses had drawn from their anger toward God and inability to obtain satisfaction from him—that is, life-long subsequent silence.

But after his rant from the Whirlwind, God seemed to regret his belittling of Job. In the Epilogue, he berated the Friends because they had "not spoken rightly about me [or to me] as did my servant Job." Moreover, God enlisted the Friends in trying to induce Job to speak to him again. God did not want the frightened, pious Friends as conversational partners; he instead seemed to realize that honest interchange was the only way that he might obtain what he truly wanted from human beings and that he himself had disserved this goal, as Job indeed had anticipated, by brandishing his rod, by trying to inflict terror so that Job could not "speak without this fear of Him."

It may be that Job had steadied himself and was not fearful in his last speech to God; it may be that God understood Job's last speech not as a retraction but as renewed direct criticism—that Job did not "abase himself" but "shuddered for humanity's sake [after] my eye has beheld You today." If God then realized that he wanted an honest, continuous interchange with human beings rather than their reflexively fearful bowing and scraping in response to his vast power, it is nonetheless possible that he had come to this realization too late to rehabilitate his relationship with Job. We don't know what Job said to God in response to the Friends' entreaty that Job pray to him on their behalf, but it is possible that Job fearlessly spurned all future relationship with God, in exasperated anger at his threat to punish the Friends because of their piety.

If God did fail in his wish for a continued relationship with Job, it appears in the Christian Bible that God resolved to try again—and this time, as Job had pleaded, God withheld any display of his vast destructive powers. As we have seen, by the end of the Christian Bible, in the book of Revelation, God resumed his angry, destructively threatening diatribe against sinful humanity. But even if the biblical texts provide no clear accounts of successfully sustained relationships between God and humanity, these texts do testify to the inescapable persistence on both sides of a wish for reconciliation, and the texts lay out a procedural road map by which this wish might most fruitfully be pursued.

As the book of Job makes most explicit, this road map must involve not only continuous confrontation between God and humanity, as if they were in a courtroom, but also an intermediary such as Moses or Jesus to stand between God and humanity—offering moral judgments, interpreting one to the other, and guiding each of them toward deeper knowledge of their own needs and wishes regarding the other. In carrying out this role, moreover, the intermediary must somehow find a way by which God, the most ostentatiously powerful disputant, can be induced to "take His rod away, so that His terror would not cow" the weaker party, so that both disputants might thereby be led to see and openly acknowledge their mutual dependence on each other. The intermediary's goal, in effect, is to obtain a kind of rough equality in the disputants' perceptions of each other, notwithstanding the vast differences between them in stature and effective power in their initial confrontations.

This is the ideal that Moses and Jesus approached and that Job urgently invoked. God sometimes acquiesced in this ideal, but more frequently, in the Hebrew Bible generally and in the Christian Bible beyond the Synoptic Gospels, he recoiled from it, fell back on his Genesis-based unmediated command-and-punish modality, and insisted that his authority could not legitimately be questioned or limited by anyone. But God's resistance to this ideal does not mean that the biblical texts reject it in deference to his command-and-punish authority. In fact, the texts themselves illuminate its benefits for both God and humanity—the way that the intermediary, Moses or Jesus, is able to render God more approachable and steadier, by appealing to his more loving and lovable qualities, which God himself was inclined to repress.

The first appearance of Moses as an adult—the appearance that presumably sparked God's interest in Moses as a possible intermediary to help revive his relationship with the children of Israel—was when Moses instinctively felt an empathic connection with the Hebrew slave and, at some risk to himself, protected this vulnerable man against the overseer's inflictions. This action set the pattern for Moses's repeated interventions against God to avert his destructive retaliatory rage against the Israelites. (When Moses had challenged the Hebrew brawler, "Why should you strike your fellow?" the man replied, "Who set you as a man prince and judge over us?"[28] One could readily imagine God responding to Moses in the same terms.) Jesus's first recorded act as an adult, in the Synoptic Gospels, was to seek baptism from John, thus signaling his identification with sinners. Throughout his ministry Jesus reinforced this empathic connection by his willingness to "receive sinners and eat with them."[29] Specifically, he made a point of protecting prostitutes and adulterous women ("Let him who is without sin among you be the first to throw a stone at her"[30]).

Thus in his intermediary role between God and humanity, neither Moses nor Jesus was neutral; both were inclined to favor the vulnerable party against inflictions from the powerful one, whether that power was social or divine in character. In this effort, neither Moses nor Jesus attributed characteristics to God that he did not already possess; they brought these loving qualities to the forefront, not only for humanity to see but more important for God himself to acknowledge. Both Moses and Jesus had ample ground for discerning these qualities based on the fact that, for Moses, God had chosen to reappear after four centuries' absence and that, for Jesus, God had sent him, his beloved Son, to earth in human form. As Exodus recorded, God already "knew" that he wanted to return to a relationship with the children of Israel. He didn't need Moses to tell him this, but as it turned out, he did need Moses to remind him continually of this original motivation. When God threatened to destroy all the Israelites because of their idolatry in worshiping the Golden Calf, Moses did not base his objection on an external norm that should govern God's conduct (as Abraham had done when he urged God to save Sodom so as to avoid killing innocent people, or as Job had done when he complained that God should not punish righteous people). Moses instead evoked God's own vision of himself as compassionate and merciful—a self-conception that he had disregarded because of his retributive anger against the Israelites. Moses did not argue that God's anger was unjustified, much less that God was obligated by some superseding principle of forgiveness. He appealed to God in a way that brought into focus God's own preference for compassionate conduct, his underlying empathy for the wrongdoers. Thus Moses took on the role that God had devised for the rainbow—the role of reminding God of his own preferred vision of himself.

This same pedagogic methodology was apparent in Jesus's parable of the Good Samaritan. In Luke's narrative of this parable, we can see the same strategy that we have seen in Moses's interventions with God—that is, Jesus refused to announce or to command a definitive moral norm to his interlocutor but instead demonstrated to him that they were already committed to the same norm, though the interlocutor had not seen this until Jesus showed it to him. In the parable, Jesus's interlocutor was a human being, but the pedagogic methodology that Jesus employed could also be seen in his few interchanges with God the Father.

Luke records that "a lawyer stood up to put [Jesus] to the test, saying 'Teacher, what shall I do to inherit eternal life?'" Jesus did not answer this challenge but turned the question, "the test," back on the lawyer. "What is written in the law?" Jesus asked him. "How do you read?" If the lawyer's initial question was a hostile test, an attempt to trap Jesus into uttering some sacrilege, Jesus skillfully stepped aside. Much more than self-protection, however, Jesus's response implies an attempt to engage the lawyer, to take his question not as a hostile act but as a truly personal concern that the lawyer had on his own behalf. In the event, the lawyer did not respond in an adversarial mode, as he might have done. He accepted Jesus's invitation at face value and offered this answer: "You shall love the Lord your God with all your heart, and with all your soul, and with all your strength, and with all your mind; and your neighbor as yourself." Jesus responded, "You have answered right; do this, and you will live."[31]

The first portion of the lawyer's answer is drawn directly from Moses's valedictory address to the Israelites in Deuteronomy 6:3–4, but the instruction "and [you shall love] your neighbor as yourself" does not appear there. In Luke's rendering, this additional instruction suggests some equivalence between love of God and love of neighbor—an implication that is carried forward in John's version of Jesus's final admonition to his disciples, "A new commandment I give to you, that you love one another; even as I have loved you, that you also love one another."[32] It is as if love of fellow humans is a rehearsal for or a reenactment of love between God and humanity.

When we explored the Deuteronomy command to love God in Chapter 6, we noted the oxymoronic implication of compulsory love. John's version of the obligation that Jesus imposed on his disciples to love one another conveys this same oddity. But Luke's account of this directive has a very different implication; the lawyer, to be sure, was looking for a command (as conventional lawyers are wont to do), but Jesus turned away from the role of law-giver and instead asked the lawyer how he read the law. Jesus then ratified the lawyer's reading, and thus it might appear that he retained final authority. But this appearance was directly contradicted by the next set of exchanges between the lawyer and Jesus.

After Jesus had articulated the obligation to love "your neighbor as yourself," the lawyer persisted in his challenge. "And who is my neighbor?" he continued. But Jesus again refused to give a direct answer. Instead he recited a parable about a man "going down from Jerusalem to Jericho" who was set upon and beaten by thieves. From the specific geographic detail, it seemed that this man was a Jew, and the lawyer's first impression of Jesus's meaning was most likely that the tribal affiliation he shared with this Jewish victim was both the defining and the limiting boundary of their obligation to love one another as neighbors.

But the parable immediately undermined this implication. As Jesus continued the tale, three men encountered this half-dead Jew on the road. The first two were themselves Jews—a "priest" and a Levite—and both crossed over to the other side of the road and passed him by. The third man stopped "and when he saw him, he had compassion." He treated his wounds, "brought him to an inn, and took care of him," going so far as to return the next day to reimburse the innkeeper for any expenditures on the injured man's behalf.

This third man was a Samaritan. Not only did he lack any tribal affiliation with the wounded man but, as the lawyer would vividly know, a powerful history of animosity existed between Jews and Samaritans based on differences in their religious practices. Indeed, Jews were forbidden to marry Samaritans and even warned against travel in Samaria because of a belief that contamination would arise from any direct encounter with them. Listening to the parable, we don't know if this particular Samaritan had somehow previously transcended the hostility between his tribe and the Jews. We are told only that the Samaritan saw the injured man as had the two Jews before him, but the Samaritan instantly "had compassion" for him "and went to him and bound up his wounds." Having told this story, Jesus then put a second question to the lawyer: "Which of these three, do you think, proved neighbor to the man who fell among the robbers?" The lawyer said, "'The one who showed mercy on him.' And Jesus said to him, 'Go and do likewise.'"

There may be a command implied in Jesus's parting injunction to the lawyer. But if it is a command, it is not in a conventional command-and-punish format. Jesus had shown the lawyer what was already in his mind and in his heart. Jesus did not dictate the abstract rules about deserving eternal life. In response to Jesus's question, the lawyer revealed that he already knew the rules. Nor did Jesus instruct the lawyer about which of the three men in the parable was the true neighbor to the wounded Jew. One could imagine a legalistic response that the lawyer might have made to Jesus's second question: that notwithstanding the Samaritan's kindness, he nonetheless lacked the crucial criterion for recognition as a neighbor because he was not Jewish. The lawyer might have said that the priest and the Levite violated their obligation to love their neighbor, but that the Samaritan had no neighborly obligation because the Samaritan was disqualified from being a neighbor or from loving the wounded Jew as such. But the lawyer did not tangle himself up in these legalisms. Though he began his hostile questioning of Jesus apparently intent on demonstrating that there was no true neighborly affiliation between them—because Jesus held views that were anathema to truly observant Jews—Jesus did not try to dominate the lawyer but instead offered to help him discover what was already in his heart. The lawyer's instant conclusion that the Samaritan was the true neighbor was derived from the same compassion for Jesus that the Samaritan had shown toward the wounded Jew. Jesus's concluding injunction "Go and do likewise" was not an externally imposed command; it was an instruction, an invitation that the lawyer should now act on the basis of his own instinctive empathy, which he had not recognized in himself until Jesus led him to see it.

In his remonstrances with God, Moses had relied on this same gambit, appealing to God's own instinctive empathy. This reliance arose not from Moses's normative preference to respect God's autonomy but from his own incapacity to control God. We might say that in Moses's hands, the rainbow function was a weapon for the weak. Jesus was not similarly afflicted—or so it might seem. In fact, however, notwithstanding his divine stature, Jesus was inherently limited in his power to direct humanity toward his preferred goal just as much as Moses was unable to command God. The limitation on Jesus's power arose from the fact that he wanted voluntary, unconditional love from humans—love for God, for himself, and for neighbors. Jesus clearly understood that coerced love was unsatisfactory, a contradiction in terms. In the book of Job, Satan taunted God with this contradiction by wagering that Job loved God only because God had paid him so well. God's authorization of aggression against Job suggested his frustration and fury at his inability to command unconditional love. At the end of the book of Job, God may have reconciled himself to this inherent limitation in his power. In the Synoptic Gospels of the Christian Bible, Jesus appears aware of this limitation and accordingly embraces a pedagogic methodology toward humanity.

From these two styles of God's authority—command and punish versus the rainbow function—we will turn in the next chapter to the lessons that might be drawn for the deployment of secular authority as specifically illustrated by the United States Supreme Court in its constitutional adjudications.

CHAPTER THIRTEEN

Justice, Justice Shall You Pursue

*W*E ARE NOT FINAL because we are infallible, but we are infallible only because we are final." So Justice Robert Jackson observed about the United States Supreme Court.[1] Jackson presumably meant to contrast divine and secular authority. In the course of this book, we have encountered many instances in which the biblical text portrays God as neither infallible nor final, except for his possession of overwhelming destructive power. It may be that God's authority and the U.S. Supreme Court's authority have more in common than the conventional accounts admit. Jackson's witticism points to one overarching similarity. Both God and the Supreme Court are understood and publicly present themselves as the ultimate, unreviewable authority. In God's case, his claim is universal and irrevocable, while the Supreme Court's claim to supremacy as the interpreter of the U.S. Constitution is apparently more limited since the Court's authority can be overridden by a popularly enacted constitutional amendment. It is, however, so difficult to amend the Constitution that the Supreme Court's interpretive authority makes it for all practical purposes irreversible and therefore infallible—God-like in its authority to command obedience and punish disobedience.

There is, however, a different biblical conception of authority that can be applied to the Supreme Court—the rainbow function that evolved from the Flood to Abraham, Moses, and Jesus in their challenges to God. In this conception, Abraham, Moses, and Jesus did not understand themselves as possessing superior practical power over God, but they did contest his moral authority and appealed to his conscience to obtain compliance with their directives. When the Supreme Court undertakes to protect minority rights by invalidating a statute enacted by a majority of the elected officials in Congress or state legislatures or an action of popularly elected federal or state officials, the Court has no practical coercive force at its disposal. The Court has control of neither "the sword" nor "the purse," as Alexander Hamilton observed to support his conclusion that the Supreme Court was "the least dangerous branch."[2]

The Court rarely admits its institutional weakness and its dependence on voluntarily offered, conscience-based compliance, and it almost never approaches popularly elected officials with the same elaborate display of deference with which Abraham, Moses, and Jesus encircled their moral critiques of God. Nonetheless, there have been notable occasions when the Court has admitted its vulnerability in spite of itself. These occasions highlight not only the descriptive differences between the two biblical styles of authority but also the normative differences in choosing between these two styles. In this chapter, we will examine three exemplars of Supreme Court jurisprudence— the race segregation cases, the abortion cases, and the *Nixon Tapes Case*. With this examination, we will set the stage to consider in the final chapter how God himself comes to understand the weakness of his command-and-punish authority and to admit the normative superiority of the rainbow function in the political theory of the Bible—not simply for his vulnerable human subjects in confronting him, but even for his own exercise of authority in confronting them.

The Race Segregation Cases

The most vivid example of this struggle between the two different modes of biblical authority is the Supreme Court's decision in *Cooper v. Aaron*. In that case, Orval Faubus, the governor of Arkansas, declared that he was not obliged to obey the Supreme Court's ruling four years earlier in *Brown v. Board of Education* requiring the dismantling of public school segregation. The Supreme Court responded to this frontal assault with a unanimous opinion laying out the most adamant insistence in its history for its ultimate command-and-punish authority. The operative passage in the Court's opinion is worth quoting at some length, for the same reason that extended quotation from biblical text illuminates internal conflicts within the text more than do flattened abstract summaries:

> Article VI of the Constitution makes the Constitution the "supreme Law of the Land." In 1803, Chief Justice Marshall, speaking for a unanimous Court, referring to the Constitution as "the fundamental and paramount law of the nation," declared in the notable case of *Marbury v. Madison,* 1 Cranch 137, 177, that "It is emphatically the province and duty of the judicial department to say what the law is." This decision declared the basic principle that the federal judiciary is supreme in the exposition of the law of the Constitution, and that principle has ever since been respected by this Court and the Country as a permanent and indispensable feature of our constitutional system. It follows that the interpretation of the Fourteenth Amendment enunciated by this Court in the *Brown* case is the supreme law of the land, and Art. VI of the Constitution makes it of binding effect on the States "any Thing in the Constitution or Laws of any State to the Contrary notwithstanding." Every state legislator and executive and judicial officer is solemnly committed by oath taken pursuant to Art. VI, cl. 3, "to support this Constitution." Chief Justice Taney, speaking for a unanimous Court in 1859, said that this requirement reflected the framers' "anxiety to preserve it [the Constitution] in full force, in all its powers, and to guard against resistance to or evasion of its authority, on the part of a State . . ." *Ableman v. Booth,* 21 How. 506, 524.

No state legislator or executive or judicial officer can war against the Constitution without violating his undertaking to support it. Chief Justice Marshall spoke for a unanimous Court in saying that: "If the legislatures of the several states may, at will, annul the judgments of the courts of the United States, and destroy the rights acquired under those judgments, the constitution itself becomes a solemn mockery. . . ." *United States v. Peters,* 5 Cranch 115, 136. A Governor who asserts a power to nullify a federal court order is similarly restrained. If he had such power, said Chief Justice Hughes, in 1932, also for a unanimous Court, "it is manifest that the fiat of a state Governor, and not the Constitution of the United States, would be the supreme law of the land; that the restrictions of the Federal Constitution upon the exercise of state power would be but impotent phrases." *Sterling v. Constantin,* 287 U.S. 378, 397–98.[3]

This is a battlefield declaration—"war against the Constitution"; "anxiety to preserve it"; "destroy the rights acquired"—and if the Supreme Court did not take arms to affirm its own status, then the Constitution would be "a solemn mockery," "impotent phrases." A difficult problem for the Court, however, lay behind this militant declamation: the Court had no practical enforcement power directly at its disposal. A year earlier, President Dwight Eisenhower had sent armed forces to Little Rock, Arkansas, to enforce the desegregation decree entered by the federal district court there and, at the same time, had nationalized the Arkansas state militia, thereby depriving Governor Faubus of the troops he had deployed to block implementation of the court order.

The justices knew, however, that they had no authority to order the president to enforce their decrees; the Constitution itself reserves decisions about the disposition of the military to the president as commander in chief. Moreover, Chief Justice Warren had a personal encounter with the president just before the Court decided *Brown* in 1954 during which Eisenhower had urged Warren not to force "sweet little girls . . . to sit in school alongside some big overgrown Negroes."[4] Warren undoubtedly informed his colleagues that the president was not a reliable ally in this fight. In September 1957, when Eisenhower decided to send troops to Little Rock, he publicly justified his action as required to enforce judicial orders regardless of his personal views about the correctness of those orders. But the justices knew that Eisenhower could have left them and *Brown* undefended.

In their militant manifesto in *Cooper v. Aaron,* the justices purported to exempt themselves from anyone's moral judgments. This was the implicit lesson conveyed by their reliance, in the passage that I've quoted, on the prior judgments of Chief Justice Charles Evans Hughes in 1932 just before his Court struck at the New Deal and Chief Justice Roger Taney in his 1859 opinion defending *Dred Scott* and the institution of slavery against an abolitionist state court. The message was clear: even Supreme Court decisions that violate basic moral principles must be obeyed.

To support this demand, the Court pulled out all of its rhetorical stops in a way reminiscent of God's declaration of moral exemption in his speech from the Whirlwind. Thus the Court invoked the formative years of the Republic for the establishment of judicial supremacy as a "permanent and indispensable feature of our constitutional system." (*"Where were you when I founded the earth?"*[5]) The Court declared that "every state legislator and executive and judicial officer is solemnly committed by oath" to obey its constitutional rulings. (*"Do you know the laws that rule the sky, and can you make it control the earth?"*[6]) The Court, moreover, framed its demand for obedience in an esoteric language with citations mystifying to ordinary readers—1 Cranch 137 . . . 21 How. 506 . . . 5 Cranch 115. (*Tell me if you know everything!—Where is the path to where light dwells, and darkness, where does it belong? . . . You must know, you were born long ago!"*[7])

The justices in *Cooper v. Aaron* were clearly aware of the extravagance of their rhetorical performance. Justice William Brennan prepared an early draft opinion in which he stated that the principle of judicial supremacy first enunciated in 1803 by Chief Justice John Marshall "was not without its critics, then and even now, but it has never been deviated in this Court." Brennan's colleagues objected even to this mild acknowledgment of Court critics. In his response to Brennan's draft opinion, Justice Hugo Black urged the inclusion of "more punch and vigor" in the supremacy claim, and Justice Tom Clark similarly called for more "hoopla."[8] *("Does your voice thunder like [Mine]? Just dress up in majesty, greatness! Try wearing splendor and glory!"*[9]) Brennan's mention of Court critics was deleted from the final opinion. Hoopla indeed.

But just beneath the surface assurance of the Court's rhetoric, doubts intrude almost unintentionally—also like God's declamation from the Whirlwind. In their striving for extraordinary impact, the justices in *Cooper v. Aaron* took two unprecedented steps that they obviously viewed as enhancements of their authority; carefully viewed, however, these two steps could just as readily be understand as diminishing their authority.

The first step was in the justices' attribution of the Court's opinion. Since John Marshall's tenure, the Court had spoken only in corporate format. The typical formula for attribution was "the opinion of the Court was delivered by the Chief Justice" or by some other individual justice; less typically, the opinion of the Court was described as "per curiam" without any recognition of an individual source.

In *Cooper v. Aaron*—for the first and, to date, the last time—all justices were listed individually by name as the joint authors of the Court's opinion. In one sense, this was an unusually powerful opening gambit: the separate justices were not only unanimously in agreement; they were *very* unanimously agreed. In another sense, however, the separate listing of each justice made visible that the institution as such was under assault, and the nine individuals who together constituted the institution were, after all, just nine individuals. (There is some resemblance here to Dorothy's ultimate discovery in Oz that the Wizard was just a diminutive man from Kansas concealing himself in an enormous contraption that amplified a huge disembodied voice.)

The second unprecedented step came at the very end of the Court's opinion. Having made its claim for unquestioning obedience, the Court then turned specifically to its ruling four years earlier in *Brown v. Board of Education:*

> The basic decision in *Brown* was unanimously reached by this Court only after the case had been briefed and twice argued and the issues had been given the most serious consideration. Since the first *Brown* opinion three new Justices have come to the Court. They are at one with the Justices still on the Court who participated in that basic decision as to its correctness, and that decision is now unanimously reaffirmed. The principles announced in that decision and the obedience of the States to them, according to the command of the Constitution, are indispensable for the protection of the freedoms guaranteed by our fundamental charter for all of us. Our constitutional ideal of equal justice under law is thus made a living truth.

This is a stirring epilogue, but there is an unacknowledged oddity in it. No one had asked the Court to revisit its prior decision in *Brown.* If, as the Court had proclaimed earlier in its opinion, "the interpretation of the Fourteenth Amendment enunciated by the Court in the *Brown* case is the supreme law of the land," why was it necessary or even appropriate for the justices to reaffirm *Brown?* Why were the "three new Justices who have come to the Court" not bound by the prior supreme authoritative decision of the Court? If these new justices were entitled to disobey that prior decision, who else is equally authorized to disobey: the president, who, after all, had authority to appoint the new justices? The senators, who confirmed them? The Congress generally, which controls the size of the tribunal and sets its jurisdiction? Are the dissents of these other institutional actors limited only to selecting new justices who might speak on their behalf, or does their clear authority to select such justices imply that these other actors are entitled to dissent in other ways as well?

In ending their opinion in *Cooper v. Aaron* with this grand perora-
tion, the justices clearly did not intend to feed doubts about their authority. But the very fact that they were drawn to reaffirm *Brown* reveals their own sense of institutional vulnerability. In this unintended
revelation, the justices echoed God's opening gambit in his speech
from the Whirlwind: "*Who dares speak darkly words with no sense?*
Cinch your waist like a fighter. I will put questions, and you will inform
me."[10] Is this dismissive mockery or does the mocking tone disguise
God's genuine appeal, even his self-subordination, to Job—"I will ask
questions. Will you inform me?"

Even more fundamentally, God's very act of appearing to Job was
a form of self-subordination. Immediately before God's appearance,
Elihu had predicted that he would never appear: "We cannot find Him
out—sublime in power and judgment; great master of justice. He will
never answer. Therefore, mortals, fear Him whom even men of wisdom cannot see."[11] Elihu was a poor predictor of God's conduct, but he
was correct in seeing that God's refusal to appear in response to Job's
pleading would be a more sublime assertion of his "power and judgment" than permitting himself to be drawn into argument with Job, no
matter what God might say to reaffirm his claim to supremacy. So, too,
the Supreme Court's reaffirmation of *Brown* in response to Governor
Faubus's disagreement was an unacknowledged concession to him.

The Court's bombast in *Cooper v. Aaron* might be understood as the
justices' attempt to rhetorically elevate themselves to God-like status,
to present themselves as if they commanded the same independent
force that God obviously possesses. But the parallels between the
Court's oratorical effort and God's tirade from the Whirlwind suggest
a shared vulnerability. God is not afflicted as the Court is by practical
limitations in raw coercive power. But as we have seen, insofar as God
wants voluntarily offered, unconditional love from humanity, he disabled himself from any possibility of using his vast coercive power to

accomplish his goal. Closer attention to the Supreme Court's original decision in *Brown* shows how the justices found themselves in the same bind.

The first hint of this bind appeared in the justices' effort among themselves to forge a unanimous ruling in the case. The operational rule of the Court was clear that a five-person majority was sufficient to justify action. But all of the justices sensed that this rule was inadequate for a case like *Brown*. This sense may have arisen from nothing more than a political calculation by the justices—an awareness of the extraordinary ambition of any judicial attempt to remake the social structure of race relations in the South, the likely resistance of white Southerners in part impelled by the still-vivid memories of forcible abolition of slavery and recognition of racist attitudes among white Northerners as well as Southerners. The idea that unanimity among the justices themselves in invalidating race segregation would overcome these obstacles was too extravagant to maintain. It was, however, quite plausible that division among the justices—especially if that division pitted Northern and Southern justices against one another—would dramatically diminish the Court's effective authority.

The justices' commitment to unanimity vastly increased the power of each of them individually as against the others and greatly complicated their deliberations and mutual maneuvering. But this private act of individual self-disempowerment in the Court's internal deliberations was both mirrored and amplified by a virtually unprecedented disclaimer of coercive power, a public act of self-sacrifice in the *Brown* decision itself. The conventional rule for judicial conduct is that enforcement follows automatically and immediately from any substantive decision. The convention is apparent in the customary conclusion to a judicial opinion: "it is so ordered."

In *Brown v. Board of Education,* the Court ostentatiously severed the conventionally seamless connection between a judicial ruling and judicial enforcement of that ruling. In 1954, the Court ruled unanimously that racial segregation of public schools violated the Constitution. But at the conclusion of its opinion announcing this principle, the Court withheld any enforcement order and instead explicitly separated the enforcement question for consideration in the following term. The Court's stunning 1954 ruling was demoted to *Brown I*. In 1955, after hearing additional argument from the parties, a unanimous Court issued its enforcement ruling, *Brown II*.

If *Brown I* was a bang—an apparently frontal assault on the deeply entrenched system of racial subordination—then *Brown II* was a whimper, a judicial commitment that this racist system should be eradicated . . . whenever. The catchphrase adopted by the Court in *Brown II* was that enforcement of the principles enunciated in *Brown I* should proceed "with all deliberate speed." A decade later, the Court characterized what had followed from this invitation as "entirely too much deliberation and too little speed."[12] In 1968, the justices finally rescinded the invitation; "[T]he burden on a school board today," a unanimous Court held, "is to come forward with a plan that promises realistically to work, and promises realistically to work now."[13]

Much had happened between 1954 and 1968 to transform the social context in which the justices were working. In 1954, the Court had stood essentially alone in confronting race segregation. In national institutional terms, congressional action was entirely stalemated by the effective power of the segregationist South in the Senate. Southern senators were routinely re-elected by state constituencies from which blacks were barred from voting (by devious local registrars backstopped by violent retaliations against any prospective black voter). These senators had greater seniority than any others and consequently monopolized committee chairmanships and the effective power in the institution. Even beyond these advantages, Senate rules permitted unlimited debate (known as filibusters) terminable only by a two-thirds vote of the entire Senate—a result that had never been obtained for a civil rights bill in the Senate during the preceding seventy-five years.

In the Southern state governmental institutions, racial segregation was apparently impregnable. And among Northern white voters, the oppression of blacks in the South was hardly noticed and passively tolerated when it occasionally became visible in a lynching or some other racial depredation.

The justices saw their isolation and consequent weakness in 1954 and clearly tried, in their short opinion in *Brown II*, to disguise necessity as a virtue by invoking the administrative complexity of transforming segregated public school systems as the justification for enforcement delay. The Court did, however, offer one glimpse of political reality in its *Brown II* opinion: "But it should go without saying," the Court said, "that the vitality of these constitutional principles cannot be allowed to yield simply because of disagreement with them." If it should go without saying, then why bother to say it?

By 1968, when the Court annulled the "deliberate speed" formula, many Southern states continued to resist desegregation, but the Court was no longer alone in making this demand. In 1964, two-thirds of the Senate had come together to end the iron grip of the filibuster and thereby to enact the first Civil Rights Act since Reconstruction; this act forbade race segregation in all public facilities, such as hotels, restaurants, and theaters, and penalized any segregated school district with loss of all federal funding. (The practical impact of this new federal penalty is revealed by the fact that in 1964, only 2.3 percent of black children in the South attended majority white schools while that number had increased to 12.5 percent in 1966 and to 44 percent in 1971.[14]) In 1965, the Southern filibuster was once again defeated on the way toward enactment of the Voting Rights Act, which opened voter rolls to blacks in the South by replacing local with federal government registrars and thereby changed the political structure of the region.

As demonstrated by their persistent intransigence in the Senate, white Southern officeholders were not generally transformed by 1968 into offering obedience to the Supreme Court's desegregation mandate. But in 1968, the segregationist white South stood alone. The Supreme Court now had been joined by the national Congress and the Executive, with broad-based electoral support in almost all the rest of the country. Moreover, the Supreme Court itself had been joined in 1967 by its first black justice, Thurgood Marshall, who had been the lead attorney on behalf of the plaintiff schoolchildren in *Brown v. Board of Education.*

Marshall's symbolically resonant passage from petitioner to justice was not the only significant difference in the status of blacks between 1954 and 1968. In 1954, open protest against their subjugation was far from the norm, especially in the South, where blacks' fear of whites' retaliatory violence was realistic and pervasive. The Court's decision in *Brown I* emboldened blacks, especially in the South, to rise up in protest on their own behalf. It cannot have been coincidental that 1955 was the date of the opening salvo in the modern black Civil Rights Movement, when Rosa Parks refused to yield her seat in the white section of a Montgomery, Alabama, public bus.

The resulting bus boycott in Montgomery brought Martin Luther King, Jr., forward as leader of the new movement, and he acknowledged the significance of the *Brown* decision in his first sermon upon assuming that role. "If we are wrong," he said, "the Supreme Court of this nation is wrong. If we are wrong, God Almighty is wrong."[15] A year later, when the Court invalidated the Montgomery municipal ordinance requiring segregated seating in public buses, King drew the equivalence even more tightly; in response to the ruling, he said, "God Almighty has spoken from Washington, D.C."[16] If the Supreme Court was invested with divine authority, as King claimed, this was not God in his irresistible command-and-punish mode; King knew, as the justices also knew, that the Court could issue orders to Southern officials but could not readily enforce them. King's Supreme Court was acting in the rainbow mode, as I have depicted it. Like Abraham, Moses, and Jesus, this Supreme Court was engaged in confronting the overwhelming practical power of the government and the populace, both South and North, with a moral norm, a conscience-based appeal to acknowledge a shared sense of justice on behalf of a vulnerable petitioner complaining of public abuse.

Using the template we have applied in understanding the book of Job, we can say that the Supreme Court was acting as the arbiter that Job had sought in his contestation with God. Recall that Job asked for "an arbiter between us to lay his hand on both of us, to make Him take His rod away, so that His terror would not cow me, then I could speak without this fear of Him, for now I am not steady in His presence."[17] After the Supreme Court had spoken in *Brown I,* Rosa Parks suddenly could remain seated without fear, Reverend King and his parishioners could rise up in protest without fear because they were no longer alone but had found a morally salient witness and advocate to stand beside them and keep them "steady in [the] presence" of their powerful abusers.

The Supreme Court had no formal power to order the Congress to enact the Civil Rights Act of 1964 or the Voting Rights Act of 1965. The Court had no formal power to order oppressed blacks to rise up on their own behalf or to order media coverage of this uprising and the violently repressive response of Southern white officeholders. The Court had no formal power to order substantial numbers of Northerners to change their sense of themselves from disengaged bystanders to sympathetically engaged witnesses of the oppression of Southern blacks. But the Court had unique advantage to foster these events through its capacity to command attention to grievances that had previously been inflicted with impunity by their perpetrators and ignored by passive bystanders.

Critics of the enforcement delay in *Brown II* maintain that the Court was obliged to do more than command attention, that it had formal authority to order immediate remedial action even if it lacked practical capacity to enforce that action. But this criticism misses the significance of the Court's weakness and the importance of the Court's visibly admitting this weakness rather than covering it over by confident invocation of its command-and-punish mode. The Court's enforcement weakness was not a regrettable political reality. Its weakness was at the core of the substantive right granted by the Equal Protection Clause of the Constitution.

In *Brown I*, the Court ruled that state provision of "separate but equal" public schools violated black schoolchildren's constitutional right to equal protection of the laws because separate as such was inherently unequal. In this ruling, the 1954 Court repudiated the definition of equality that had been endorsed fifty-eight years earlier in *Plessy v. Ferguson*.[18] The *Plessy* Court's definition had a mathematical plausibility. If two schools were physically identical—same furnishings, same construction and maintenance expense, same qualifications and numbers of teaching staff—then one might say the two were equal, in the same sense that separate but physically identical railway passenger cars linked together in the same train were equal. But this numerical accounting entirely ignores the human relational implications of the separation of facilities. It ignores the question, if these schools or railway cars are truly equal, then why would people insist on duplicate versions for different races?

The obvious answer is that duplication implies the absence of mutual respect among the occupants. Perhaps the disrespect was unidirectional—that is, one group claimed superiority over the other; perhaps the disrespect was itself mutual, with each group hostile toward the other; perhaps there was some mixture of these two possibilities. Whatever their specific social meaning, duplication of physically identical facilities inherently implies the absence of an engaged relationship based on mutual respect.

The duplicate facilities may rest on a demand from either or both parties of a "right to be left alone." This was the conception of social relations that the *Plessy* Court invoked and that was repeated by some prominent critics of *Brown I*, that the right at stake was "freedom of association" and that every individual should be free to refuse to enter into a social relationship with anyone else.[19] But there is a paradox embedded in this conception. If one party wants simply to be left alone but the other party wants an engaged relationship, whose wishes take priority? A quick answer to this question might be drawn from modern liberal political theory, according to which human beings come into relationship with one another only on the basis of contractual consent, and there is no obligation to give consent. The quick contrary position can be drawn from an older source asserting that we all live embedded in social relations with one another, and though we may be entitled to withdraw from relations, we are entitled to withdraw only on the basis of demonstrated good cause.

But both of these answers slide too quickly over the fundamental paradox presented when one party claims the right to be left alone and the other party insists that in their prior dealings, the first party abused the other and cannot now refuse any redress or walk away as if nothing had transpired between them. This is the nub of the dispute between whites and blacks in considering the race segregation regime. In 1896, the *Plessy* Court resolved this paradox by fiat, favoring one party's conception of its obligations without giving any credence to the other party's understanding of or claims about their prior relationship. In 1954, the *Brown* Court was accused by some critics of simply turning the tables and imposing an equally unjustified favoritism toward the perspective of one party over the other. But this is an unjustified accusation. The *Brown* Court did not resolve the paradoxical dispute one way or the other. Instead it declared that the dispute had been improperly resolved and must now be reopened—but this time, the dispute must be conducted with equal respect accorded to each side. *Brown I* reopened the dispute; *Brown II* sketched the rules for carrying out this reopened dispute.

At the least, in the conduct of this dispute each party was entitled to the presence of an arbiter (in this case, a federal district judge subject to appellate supervision) who regarded each with equal respect; this, we might say, is the minimal guarantee implied by the constitutional right to equal protection of the laws. Ideally this arbiter would guide the conflicting parties toward mutual respect as the foundation for any resolution of the dispute, whether that involved some promise of future relations or denial of any currently operative past between them. This ideal of mutual respect—of mutual acknowledgment of equal social status, whatever the outcome of specific disputes—is the core aspiration of the constitutional guarantee of equal protection of the laws.

This aspiration cannot be realized by a forced imposition on either party in any dispute. There is a limited appropriate role for coercion—that is, to arrest the impulse of one party to dominate the other by force. This coercive intervention, whether by a police action or by self-defense, can restrain active hostility or even produce a momentary truce in ongoing warfare. But neither unilateral nor mutual coercion is an instrument for dispute resolution based on mutual respect for each other's equal status.

In *Brown I*, the Supreme Court vividly portrayed the disrespect conveyed to black schoolchildren by their exclusion from attendance with whites: "To separate them from others of similar age and qualifications solely because of their race generates a feeling of inferiority as to their status in the community that may affect their hearts and minds in a way unlikely ever to be undone."[20] Is it at all credible, however, that obtaining entrance for black students into the same classrooms as white students only when accompanied by federal troops to protect them from screaming white mobs will not similarly affect "their hearts and minds"? Is it not clear that the only way that the disrespect implied by race segregation can be truly remedied is if the segregationist whites relent, acknowledge their wrongdoing, and welcome black students into a mutually respectful social relationship? Perhaps forced contact can be a waystation toward this goal. But we must move beyond this

waystation if we are to come even close to the Supreme Court's ambition that "our constitutional ideal of equal justice under law [must be]
made a living truth."[21]

This is why the Court lacks power to command the end of the race
segregation regime—not because it has no access to the "sword or the
purse" to coerce compliance with its orders but because the conventional legal mode of command-and-punish cannot achieve that goal.
The constitutional wrong inflicted by racial segregation can be remedied only if the wrongdoers themselves become conscience-stricken,
admit their wrongdoing, and ask forgiveness from those they have
harmed. The Supreme Court can appeal to the collective conscience of
the wrongdoers. It can use its power to command attention toward this
end. If, however, the judges properly understand the meaning of the
equality principle, they will also understand that they can do no more
than this to make that principle a living truth.

Though it is not customary to phrase the equal protection guarantee
in these terms, the constitutional promise of mutual respect for everyone's equal status is identical at its core to the biblical injunction to
love one's neighbor as oneself. The hostile lawyer confronting Jesus
with the question "who is my neighbor?" is in the same posture as the
white segregationists refusing to acknowledge blacks as equal participants in a communal relationship. Just as Jesus sought to instruct the
lawyer that he should transcend conventional boundaries based on
tribal or religious affiliations to see himself as a neighbor to the scorned
Samaritan, so the Supreme Court undertook to instruct the white segregationists in their relationship with blacks. The normative principle
is the same, and the imperatives of the pedagogic process are also the
same. Jesus could not force this lesson on the lawyer, and he did not attempt to do so; he turned the question back to the lawyer and implicitly appealed to the lawyer's conscience. So *Brown I* enunciated the
substantive norm of neighborly love and *Brown II* turned the question
back to the white segregationists of whether and when they would be

willing to embrace this norm and their black brothers and sisters as equals.

The justices thus left open the possibility of disobedience though they emphatically did not recommend this path. But the justices had no choice to act otherwise. The principle at stake could be vindicated only by an appeal to conscience—what I have called the rainbow function—rather than by coerced submission.

The justices' awareness of their practical political vulnerability may have led them to this pedagogic process rather than their explicit understanding of the principled imperative demanding this process. And the apparent success of their intervention by 1968 may have emboldened the justices—perhaps intoxicated by their bluster and hoopla in *Cooper v. Aaron*—to imagine that their coercive powers had done the job. During the succeeding six years, the ambitions of the Court soared, almost as if it were giddy with power. Thus in 1973, the Court unexpectedly overturned all restrictive abortion laws in *Roe v. Wade*.[22] Then, in 1974, it effectively forced Richard Nixon to resign the presidency in *United States v. Nixon*.[23] (Only three justices who had participated in *Cooper v. Aaron* remained on the Court through these later decisions —Douglas, Brennan, and Stewart.) In each of these 1970s decisions, the Court saw itself as an isolated actor disregarding any claim to independent judgment on the part of popularly elected officials and simply demanding obedience from them.

The Nixon Tapes Case

In the *Nixon Tapes Case,* the Court pointedly ignored the immediately contemporaneous actions of the Congress in moving to impeach the president.[24] Within a week after the Court ordered Nixon to disclose secret tapes of his conversations relevant to pending criminal prosecution of his aides, the Judiciary Committee of the House of Representatives voted, by a bipartisan majority, to impeach Nixon for refusing to surrender those same tapes for congressional scrutiny. As the justices well knew, the Judiciary Committee had been conducting an investigation and publicly televised hearings regarding the president's conduct in concealing evidence about the Watergate burglary. If the justices had followed their own ordinary deliberative course, the *Tapes Case* would not have reached them for judgment for several months, perhaps even longer. But the justices, seemingly impatient for a piece of the action, took the extraordinary step of granting review of the District Court's disclosure order against Nixon without waiting for any intermediate judgment by the Court of Appeals. Nixon released the secret tapes two weeks after the Supreme Court's order and three days later resigned from office.

The net result of the Supreme Court's rush to judgment was that the impeachment proceedings in the House were rendered moot and the country was deprived of the opportunity to witness whether its elected officials could transcend partisanship and unite to enforce the constitutional mandate that the president should "faithfully execute the laws." In jumping ahead of the pending impeachment proceedings, the Supreme Court was evidently (and even ostentatiously) refusing to take any risk that the Constitution might not be defended by the Congress against the president's depredations. The implicit message in the Court's action was that it alone could be trusted to do justice. The Court gave no opportunity—brooked no delay, preempted all space for publicly visible deliberations—by which elected officials in the Congress could demonstrate to the public and to themselves that they were trustworthy defenders of our national values.[25]

Roe v. Wade

In *Roe v. Wade*, the Court was equally inattentive to the active pending deliberations in state legislatures and equally disrespectful of the possibility that state elected officials might do justice on behalf of those affected by the restrictive abortion laws.[26] The Court indeed even misunderstood the central claim of the *Roe* plaintiffs' protest against the restrictive laws. The plaintiffs invoked a constitutional right to privacy to insist that no one but the pregnant woman herself could justifiably decide whether she should have access to an abortion. In its judgment, the Court gestured toward this privacy right but explicitly grounded its ruling on the proposition that "the abortion decision and its effectuation must be left to the medical judgment of the pregnant woman's attending physician."[27] The Court even reiterated this proposition as if to underscore that it did not endorse the woman's claim to self-determination: "[T]he attending physician, in consultation with his patient, is free to determine, without regulation by the state, that, in his medical judgment, the patient's pregnancy should be terminated."[28]

In retrospect, the Court's opinion in *Roe v. Wade* hardly resembles the pro-choice charter of women's liberation, of individual women's control of their own bodies, that it has come to represent. It is, however, not surprising that the nine elderly men who composed the Supreme Court in 1972 should have misunderstood the issue at stake in the case. The terms of debate regarding gender relations in general radically shifted in the late 1960s. Beginning in the mid-1950s, physicians had taken the lead in advocating more extensive legalization of abortion by broadening their discretion to construe the pregnant woman's health needs; by the late 1960s, some one-third of the states had adopted liberalized laws, some of which (like California's 1968 law) amounted in practice to abortion on a woman's demand though nonetheless concealed as an exercise of physician's discretion. The newly emergent feminist movement in the late 1960s put forward a dramatically different claim and, in 1971, perhaps surprisingly, won legislative victories for first-trimester abortions on demand in four states: New York, Washington, Hawaii, and Alaska.

In 1971, the Supreme Court took jurisdiction in the first abortion case argument in its history. District of Columbia law, like most state statutes, permitted abortions only to safeguard the woman's "health" but without providing any specific definition of that term. In *United States v. Vuitch*, a D.C. physician convicted of performing an unjustified abortion argued that the statute was too vague in its offhand reference to "health" and therefore violated the constitutional guarantee of due process of law.[29] A Court majority glibly ruled that the "health" terminology was clear enough. If the Court had endorsed the physician's vagueness claim, it would have invalidated the abortion-restrictive statutes in every state (except the four that had just endorsed abortion on demand). This would not have barred any state from re-enacting abortion restrictions; but any reenactment would require greater effort at precise articulation of the woman's interests and competing fetal or societal interests, necessarily preceded by public deliberation in the state legislative process. This deliberation would in itself amplify the voices of feminist advocates (who had been overridden or, indeed, who may not have existed as a self-conscious group when the original state laws had been enacted). Moreover, the very fact that legislative action would be required to reenact some restriction would in itself have enhanced the political power of feminist advocates, since in our system of multiple "checks and balances," it is always easier to block legislative action than to obtain it. The Court could have precipitated this popular deliberative process in *Vuitch*, but it chose otherwise.

Then, just two years later in *Roe v. Wade*, the Court grabbed hold of the abortion issue and announced a conclusive resolution that instantly applied in every state. At the time this was an utterly unexpected result, whatever one's position on the merits. Those who favored the Court's results were pleased that their claims for justice had been vindicated; those who opposed were outraged. Dispute on these terms soon escalated into the polarized pro-choice/pro-life debate that has since gripped our national politics. The expansive polarization might have occurred without any Court intervention. But the Court's claim instantaneously to resolve this dispute did nothing to encourage deliberative interaction among the opposed parties, did nothing to promote the possibility of mutual respect.

Indeed, the coherent core of the feminist complaint was not so much a derogation of women's privacy rights (since it is at least debatable that the abortion decision affects not only the pregnant woman but also the fetus, regardless of whether the fetus is a "full-fledged person" or only a "potential person"). The coherent core was the utter disrespect embedded in the restrictive abortion laws for the woman's claim to equality, her treatment as nothing more than a biological container for the fetus rather than as a full-fledged person equal to others. The *Roe* Court obviously failed to understand this claim, since it identified the primary rights-holder in the abortion dispute as the (male) physician who had a right to be "free to determine [whether] in *his* medical judgment, the *patient's* pregnancy should be terminated" (emphasis added).

More fundamentally, the Court failed to understand what it had glimpsed but then forgotten in its own extended deliberative process leading to *Brown I* and the drawn-out enforcement process endorsed in *Brown II*. In *Roe,* the Court traversed the proposition that voluntarily offered mutual respect was the only means by which the constitutional guarantee of equal justice could be made a living reality. The abortion dispute may never be resolved through mutual respect; the ongoing debate itself may never even be characterized as conducted in a spirit of mutual respect. But the *Roe* Court utterly ignored the central importance of this goal. It unthinkingly relied on its command-and-punish mode without reflecting on the inappropriateness of this mode for accomplishing its desired result.

Since *Roe,* the Court has to some significant degree retreated from the victory it had awarded to the feminist plaintiffs.[30] In the extended process of deliberation, of backing and filling about the abortion right within the Court itself since 1972, the practical weakness of the institution has been visible—especially its vulnerability to reversal through the politically driven replacement of old justices with new. But the crucial deliberations have taken place within the Court and have frequently been resolved by one vote in a five-to-four majority. In this process, the people who truly count are reduced to bystanders, passive witnesses as their fate is decided by others, and even by just one person in the entire United States by a five-to-four vote.

CHAPTER FOURTEEN

Reconciling with Injustice

THE JURISPRUDENTIAL ISSUE that we explored in the preceding chapter can be understood as the problem of delayed justice. In each of the cases—*Brown I* and *II*, the *Nixon Tapes Case,* and *Roe v. Wade*—the Supreme Court proclaimed a plausible principle of justice and relied on a plausible claim that it alone was authorized to interpret the demands of justice. I maintained, however, that the Court's claim for exclusive interpretive authority is unjustified because the very norm of justice invoked by the Court can come into living reality only if it emerges from a shared interpretative process in which the putative wrongdoer is somehow brought to acknowledge the norm and his violation of it. The jurisprudential problem raised by this position is that even if this deliberative process succeeds in reaching common ground among the Court, the putative victims, and the wrongdoers, a long time may elapse in carrying it out; in the interim, the injustice identified by the Court and experienced by the victims persists. Moreover, in a genuine deliberative process, there is no *a priori* guarantee of the outcome, and the wrongdoer may never acknowledge what others regard as an obvious injustice.

Early in our exploration of biblical text, we encountered this problem in God's deliberation about whether to destroy all humanity except for Noah "because the evil of the human creature was great on the earth and . . . every scheme of his heart's devising was only perpetually evil."[1] After bringing on the Flood and almost sacrificing Noah and the ark, God recanted, saying to himself ("in His heart"), "I will not again damn the soil on humankind's score. For the devisings of the human heart are evil from youth. And I will not again strike down all living things as I did."[2] In trying to unravel this puzzle that the very reason that led God to destroy humanity was the reason he gave for relenting from this destruction, we pointed to God's realization that his demand for perfect justice necessarily led him to the undesired outcome that he would thereby be alone in the universe, at least without human accompaniment. Throughout the text of the Hebrew Bible, we saw God struggling with this dilemma—that he repeatedly wanted to command perfect justice but that this command continually led him to vast destruction and ultimately to isolation from human companionship. We also saw this same dilemma in the Christian Bible's progression from the Synoptic Gospels through John's Gospel and ultimately to Revelations.

Thus we saw how the biblical text amplified Amartya Sen's observation that the pursuit of perfect justice can lead to Emperor Ferdinand's edict, "Fiat justitia, et pereat mundus—Let justice be done, though the world perish." According to the biblical account of the Flood, this is not only a possible but an inevitable consequence of this pursuit of perfection and thus a reason for abandoning it. In our exploration of the Supreme Court rulings, we have seen an equivalent progression from a demand for perfect justice that ultimately is inconsistent with the possibility of achieving justice. In the Court's rulings, there was nothing as obviously apocalyptic as the Flood or the destruction of all sinners in Revelations; nonetheless the rulings were dismissive of popular engagement and profoundly isolating both for members of the public because of their incapacity to debate with one another as equals and for the Court because of its avowed supremacy and infallibility. In both the Hebrew and the Christian Bibles we have also seen the persistent attraction for God of his supreme and incontrovertible isolation. If God himself regularly succumbs to this position, it is not surprising that human beings such as (but not restricted to) Supreme Court justices are routinely tempted.

The difficulties of sustaining God's commitment to tolerate injustice in the service of preserving humanity are acknowledged in paradoxical form in Jesus's Sermon on the Mount. In that extended teaching, Jesus asked God to forgive human trespasses in the same way that we forgive trespasses against us, and he set out a model for human forgiveness that is extreme and counterintuitive in its sweep.[3] Thus Jesus adjures humans "not [to] resist one who is evil. But if any one strikes you on the right cheek, turn to him the other also; and if any one would sue you and take your coat, let him have your cloak as well; and if any one forces you to go one mile, go with him two miles."[4] By implication, Jesus would apply the same extravagant model to God's forgiveness of wrongdoing. Preaching this extreme tolerance for inflictions of evil makes Jesus an easy target for mocking dismissal.[5] But the very extremity of his teaching reflects the difficulty of sustaining the basic commitment that Jesus wants to illuminate for God and for humanity. That commitment is for God and humanity to sustain mutual engagement and for humans to do the same among themselves—especially when the temptation to sever relationships feels most compelling, most just: "If any one forces you to go one mile, go with him two miles."

The most evocative expression of this teaching is in Jesus's parable about the man with two sons, popularly (but inaccurately) known as the parable of the prodigal son. The parable appears in the fifteenth chapter of Luke as the last of three parables that Jesus told on a single occasion when "the tax-collectors and sinners were all drawing near to hear him. And the Pharisees and scribes murmured, saying, 'This man receives sinners and eats with them.'"[6] Jesus then told them three parables. The first was about a shepherd with a hundred sheep who has lost one of them and "leaves the ninety-nine in the wilderness [to] go after the one which is lost, until he finds it." When he finds the one lost sheep, Jesus concludes, "he lays it on his shoulders, rejoicing. And when he comes home, he calls together his friends and neighbors, saying to them, 'Rejoice with me for I have found my sheep which was lost.' Just so, I tell you, there will be more joy in heaven over one sinner who repents than over ninety-nine righteous persons who need no repentance."[7]

There are two obvious puzzles in this parable. First, if there is more rejoicing for the sinner than for those who have remained steadfastly righteous, what good comes from avoiding the temptation to sin? Doesn't the parable set up a perverse incentive for one sheep to wander away from the flock and claim the special attention of the shepherd? And second, who takes care of the ninety-nine righteous sheep left alone "in the wilderness" while the shepherd takes himself away to hunt for the miscreant? Jesus does not answer these questions; he puts the parables to his listeners not as instruction for them—not as an injunction that if one sheep is lost, the shepherd is obliged to seek him out—but as a self-evident response for any shepherd in that situation. He began the parable by saying, "If one of you has a hundred sheep and loses one of them, does he not go after the one that is missing until he finds it?" Jesus thus both relies on his listeners' own sense of right behavior and at the same time leaves room for them to disagree with him. "No," the sinners, tax-collectors, Pharisees, and scribes might have said, "the shepherd would and should stay with his flock and forget about the solitary miscreant who has foolishly wandered off alone."

The second parable is about a woman who has ten silver coins and loses one of them. Again Jesus proceeds as if the woman's recourse is obvious to all his listeners: "does [she] not light the lamp and sweep the house and search diligently until she finds it? And when she has found it, she calls together her friends and neighbors and says, 'Rejoice with me for I have found the coin which I had lost.' Just so, I tell you, there is joy before the angels of God over one sinner who repents."[8]

This parable appears more intuitively straightforward. The woman is clearly able to put her nine coins in a safe place while she hunts for the lost one; and a trove of ten silver coins is obviously worth more than nine. It seems self-evident that the woman would and should hunt high and low for the lost coin and then invite everyone to rejoice at her restored treasure. The second parable seems to raise none of the knotty problems of the first; in the context of Jesus's narrative progression, this simple parable restores his connection with his listeners at the same time that it sets them up for the most puzzling parable of them all.

The third parable begins, "There was a man who had two sons." We can see immediately that this parable is not about "the prodigal son" but about two sons. Nowhere in the parable does Jesus indicate that his primary concern is with just one of the sons. There is thus an initial puzzle, which stands outside the text of the parable, about why it has come to be known as "the parable of the prodigal son." This is only the first puzzle in the parable, and Jesus's presentation of this story is different from his presentation of the two previous parables, in a way that underscores its puzzling character. Unlike in the two previous parables, Jesus does not claim that the various actors' behavior would be intuitively appealing to any of his listeners. Jesus thereby implies that the characters in this parable may act in ways that most of his listeners would instinctively reject.

The story in brief outline is that the younger son asked his father for his portion of the paternal estate, then left home to travel to a "far country, and there he squandered his property in loose living." Now desperate and hungry, he resolved to return home to his father, admit his sins "against heaven and before you," relinquish his filial status, and serve instead as one of his father's "hired servants." The father, however, saw his son approaching from a distance "and had compas-sion, and ran and embraced him and kissed him." He dismissed the son's self-abasement and instructed his servants to "bring quickly the best robe and put it on him; and put a ring on his hand, and shoes on his feet; and bring the fatted calf and kill it and let us eat and make merry; for this my son was dead, and is alive again; he was lost and is found."[9]

Jesus's listeners may have expected a punitive response from the fa-ther, and they almost certainly would have been surprised at his out-pouring of further riches for the son—the "best robe" in the house, the fatted calf for feasting. The son thus clearly is receiving more than his legal entitlement. Was this a reward for the son's sinful behavior? A skeptical listener might have concluded this. But the son, who abjectly confessed his sins and acknowledged his unworthiness, was more likely to see his father's act as motivated by overflowing joy at the restoration of his lost relationship—an apparently unconditional joy, without any prior demand for the son's repentance.

The father's response would most likely have seemed counter-intuitive to the sinners, tax-collectors, and disapproving Pharisees and scribes who had crowded around Jesus. Their expectation of punitive condemnation by the father would have been based on the familiar portrait of their father in heaven, of a vindictive God as he is predomi-nantly depicted in the Hebrew Bible. But Jesus calls his listeners' at-tention to a different God—or, more precisely, to different qualities of God in the Hebrew Bible. His portrait is drawn from God's self-description in Exodus—"The Lord, the Lord! A compassionate and gracious God, slow to anger, and abounding in kindness and good faith, keeping kindness for the thousandth generation, bearing crime, trespass, and offense."[10] Moses had prompted God to see himself in this light, and Jesus magnifies this conception.

Accordingly, those of his listeners who already see themselves as sin-ners can take heart because Jesus indeed willingly "eats with them," just as the stiff-necked, "murmuring" Pharisees and scribes had charged. Thus far into the parable, Jesus's message is that a good father, the father whom he recognizes as such, rejoices in sinners who have found their way back to him. But what is the force of the parable for those listeners who see themselves not as sinners but as righteous men?

There is another son in the parable, and Jesus now turns to him. In many ways, this is the dramatic heart of the parable. Following the father's joyous welcome of the younger son, here is the remainder of the parable:

> Now his elder son was in the field; and as he came and drew near to the house, he heard music and dancing. And he called one of the servants and asked what this meant. And he said to him, "Your brother has come, and your father has killed the fatted calf, because he has received him safe and sound." But he was angry and refused to go in. His father came out and entreated him, but he answered his father, "Lo, these many years I have served you, and I never disobeyed your command; yet you never gave me a kid that I might make merry with my friends. But when this son of yours came, who has devoured your living with harlots, you killed for him the fatted calf!" And he said to him, "Son, you are always with me, and all that is mine is yours. It was fitting to make merry and be glad, for this your brother was dead, and is alive; he was lost, and is found."[11]

The parable ends here, leaving the ultimate outcome in suspense. Was the elder son persuaded by his father's entreaty? Would the elder son persist in his refusal to enter his father's house? Would he agree that it was "fitting" for the father "to make merry and be glad"? Would he come home to join in the celebration? The parable offers no answer to these questions—but it does provide some clues about how the elder son should respond.

First of all, we are directly told of the depth of the elder son's resentment at the favored treatment of his younger brother. The father seems to assuage this resentment with his reassuring words, "all that is mine

is yours," but this is a disingenuous promise. In fact, since the father
had previously given his younger son the entirety of his portion of
the inheritance, the father's assurance was not an act of generosity but
a simple statement of the elder son's legal entitlement.[12] Moreover,
by bestowing valuable additional gifts on the younger son—the "best
robe" in the house, a ring, shoes, the fatted calf for feasting—the father
had obviously taken assets from the elder son's remaining share of his
estate. "All that is mine is yours" has turned into "all that is mine except
for whatever gifts from your share that I choose to give to your younger brother." From the elder son's (quite reasonable) perspective, this
brother—this "son of yours," as he says to his father—hardly appears
to be a deserving recipient, this son "who has devoured your living
with harlots." The inescapable implication is that the elder brother
has suffered a wrong at his father's hands. Why would the father think
that the elder son should view his favoritism toward the younger son as
"fitting"?

But in the elder brother's apparently justified resentment, we can
find the first clue about why he should not only acquiesce but even rejoice in his father's actions. Who is this elder brother who has suffered
from his father's inexplicable favoritism toward his younger sibling?
Jesus presents the elder along with the younger son and the father as
archetypes. But if we attend closely to the parable, we can see that the
elder brother is not an anonymous figure, not simply an archetype. We
can recognize that the elder brother is Cain, who killed his younger
brother, Abel.

The entire dramatic structure of the second half of the parable
points to this identity. At our first encounter with the elder brother, he
is "in the field." In Genesis chapter four, after God without explanation
or apparent justification favored Abel's offering of "the choice firstlings
of his flock" (an allusion to the "fatted calf" that the father in the parable had killed to fete his younger son), the elder son, Cain, was enraged.
Like the father in the parable, moreover, God gave no explanation for

his favoritism but simply urged Cain to accept his disfavored status. ("Sin crouches . . . but you will rule over it," God observed.) But Cain did not succeed in taming his anger. Instead "Cain said to Abel his brother, 'Let us go out to the field.' And when they were in the field, Cain rose against Abel his brother and killed him." God then "cursed" Cain to be a "restless wanderer . . . on the earth," a punishment that Cain lamented was "too great to bear [n]ow that . . . I must hide from Your presence."[13]

When the elder son makes his first appearance in the parable, he is "in the field," where Cain had killed Abel; he hears the merrymaking in his father's house but remains outside, a "restless wanderer." But now, in the parable, the father seeks out the elder son rather than leaving him in exile—and he conveys the almost unbelievable news that Cain's murderous act has been undone, that "this your brother was dead, and is alive," and, accordingly, the reason for his punishing exile has been erased. The dramatic question at the end of the parable is whether the elder brother could understand the significance of this good news, whether he would realize that he could end his exile, that his punishment was remitted and that he could return to his father's house if he chose to do so.

There was more good news besides this, good news paradoxically embedded in the fact that the father had given his "best robe" to the younger brother, thereby disfavoring and angering the elder. This fact provides a clue to the brothers' additional identities. The younger brother is not only Abel but is also Joseph, whose father favored him over his elder brothers with an "ornamented tunic." And Joseph was "wandering in the fields" where the elder brothers found him and "conspired to kill him" before selling him into slavery.[14] But in the parable this crime was also undone: "this your brother . . . was lost, and is found." Here is another reason for the elder brother in the parable to rejoice.

The allusion to Joseph's favored status points to another dimension of the parable—the fact, as we explored earlier in this chapter, that Jacob never admitted nor apologized for his wrongdoing in favoring the younger sons over the elders. In the parable, too, the father does not admit nor apologize for his unfairness toward his elder son. Jacob always remained obtuse to this aspect of his conduct, but the father's withholding acknowledgment or apology in Jesus's parable seems a more intentional act than for Jacob, whose silence was most likely produced by his customary self-absorption.

This aspect of the interaction between father and elder son in the parable echoes the final incident in the relations between God and Job, in the Epilogue when God refrained from offering any direct apology but instead tested whether Job was willing to forgive both the Friends and ultimately God himself for their wrongful inflictions on him. I suggested earlier that God may have withheld apology to mask his wish for forgiveness, his vulnerability. It is equally and perhaps even more plausible that God withheld any apology from Job because of his recognition that nothing he could say would compensate for or in any way excuse his previous wrongful inflictions. He wanted forgiveness, but this could not come from Job's acceptance of God's necessarily inadequate apology. God wanted reconciliation based on truthtelling, both on his part and on Job's. (This, after all, was why God threatened punishment for the Friends, because they had not been truthful with him.)

In the parable, the father makes no effort to apologize. But he holds out the possibility of reconciliation—between the elder brother, whom the younger had unjustifiably harmed, and between him and his elder son, whom he had injured without justification. Why might the father think that this prospect would be appealing to his elder son? The answer appears to be that if the elder son chose to reenter the house, he could thereby end his "restless wandering"—his isolation, his angry exile from his father's presence, which had always been too much for him to bear.

The father's offer of homecoming without any explanation of why that homecoming would be persuasively appealing to his elder son provides a clue to yet another identity of the two sons. The elder is also Abraham, who had benefited from the death of his younger brother Haran. When God offered to end Abraham's nomadic wandering and lead him to a new home in "the land I will show you," Abraham asked no questions but agreed instantly—as if, we might say, he had been waiting for this possibility ever since his younger brother had died and he had left the place of his birth to become a nomad, a "restless wanderer on the earth."[15]

All of these references are embedded in the spare narrative of the parable about the man who had two sons. Unraveling these references can solve two puzzles that I propounded at the outset of this discussion. The parable begins with a reference to two sons, but if its central subject is "the prodigal son" in the singular, choosing *the* prodigal among these two is not so easy as it first appeared. The younger son seemed to be the obvious candidate because he wasted his inheritance; but the elder son, if he refuses his father's offer to return home, may be wasting an even greater opportunity. The parable thus offers a paradoxical answer to the question of the identify of the prodigal: the prodigal son is both of them, though each in his own way.

This answer opens a pathway to the puzzle in the first parable about why the shepherd would abandon his entire flock to search for the one lost sheep. In drawing out the lesson of this parable, Jesus stated that the ninety-nine sheep left behind in the wilderness by the shepherd symbolically represented "ninety-nine righteous persons who need no repentance."[16] But who are these ninety-nine righteous persons? The paradoxical answer to this question is "no one." Like the elder brother in the prodigal son parable, these ninety-nine people mistakenly (or perhaps disingenuously) insist that they "never disobeyed [their father's] commandment." But if the ninety-nine are attentive and honest with themselves, they will realize that they are like the elder brother in the parable, they are Cain who had killed his younger brother, they are Judah who sold his younger brother into slavery, they are Abraham who benefited from his younger brother's death. The shepherd who left the ninety-nine to find the one lost sheep was not putting the ninety-nine into danger. In fact the shepherd was searching for all of them, each of whom was already lost and endangered in his own way.

Understood in this way, Jesus's three parables extend the narrative strategy of the Hebrew Bible and embrace the same underlying message. Cain reappears as Abraham, as Judah, as Saul; each of them succumbs to wrongdoing toward his younger brother and struggles with his guilt and the possibility of redemptive reconciliation. Taken together, all of these struggles portray the same underlying political problem: how can terrible breaches in relationships be resolved so that the shared longing for return to the original state of harmony can be acknowledged and pursued?

This reading of the parables appears to acquit both the shepherd and the father of any wrongdoing; the shepherd's apparent abandonment of his flock and the father's apparent disfavoring of his elder son both turn out to be actions that would provide immense benefits for them, if only they understood who they truly were and the possibilities held open for them by this recognition. By this reading, we are brought into the happy world of the second parable, about the woman and her silver coins; her success in finding the lost coin simply increased her wealth and detracted from no one. But entry into this irenic world, where justice so easily triumphed, did not come easily. From the other parables, the ninety-nine sheep who thought of themselves as righteous and the elder son who saw himself as obedient must overcome their strong, and on the face of the parables apparently reasonable, conviction that the shepherd and the father have abused them.

The stunning fact is, however, that these complainants (as well as the tax-collectors, sinners, Pharisees, and scribes who heard and presumably were sympathetic to these complaints) were not left on their own in coming to the conclusion that they had in fact been well served. In these parables, both the shepherd and the father took the initiative in seeking them out. The shepherd actively searched for his lost sheep and in this search would encounter every one of them; and the father left the festivities in his house to find his elder son in the field and to urge him to come back home. And Jesus himself ostentatiously "received sinners and ate with them," thus apparently violating norms of good conduct but in pursuit of a larger good for everyone, if only his listeners could understand this.[17]

In these exertions, the shepherd, the father, and Jesus were more gentle than God had been when he chose to seek out Job and speak to him from the Whirlwind. The shepherd and father in the parables and the teller of the parables were not, however, notably more reassuring than God had been when he spoke from the Whirlwind. None of these actors actually justified his conduct, and they all seemed to add insult to injury by this evasion. But the stunning fact remained that these figures of vast authority in the Hebrew and Christian Bibles did seek out their critics even though their justifications for their conduct or their apologies for their misconduct were veiled and indirect—or even entirely missing—rather than openly proclaimed.

Perhaps, unlike God in the book of Job, neither the shepherd, the father, nor Jesus in the Christian Bible had committed any offense that required an apology. But this possibility is not the central concern of these narratives. In all three cases, the other parties (the abandoned sheep, the elder son, the Pharisees and scribes) intensely believed that they had been wronged and that, at the least, some apology was required. Accordingly, if the avowedly abused parties remained convinced of their own righteousness and the wrongfulness of others' conduct toward them, what would they do? Would they inflict some retaliatory punishment? Would they cut off all future relations?

Jesus ends his parables without answering these questions. But the father in the parable of the two sons vividly sets out the significance of

these questions for the elder son and the continuation of his isolation—his guilt-ridden isolation and exile—if he engages in a retaliatory infliction as he had previously done to vindicate his claims against
his unjustifiably favored younger brother. The father implores the elder son to surmount his conviction of injured entitlement, however
justified it may be, and return home where his younger brother Abel
has been restored to life and his younger brother Joseph has been
found. He might thereby end his punishing exile.

The same challenge was presented to Job following God's unsatisfying response to his justifiable complaints of injustice. In the Epilogue,
Job did speak to God on the Friends' behalf, though we don't know
what he said. Job also accepted the "comfort" offered by "all his brothers and sisters and his former acquaintances . . . for all the harms that
Yahweh had brought upon him," even though they had previously
abandoned him and returned only after God had restored twice Job's
fortune.[18] Most notably, Job passionately engaged with his new children—especially his daughters, "most beautiful . . . in all the land." In
the Prologue, Job had maintained cautious distance from his children,
not attending their parties (he wasn't even invited) and worrying from
a distance that his sons had "cursed God in their hearts." None of these
children was named in the Prologue; in the Epilogue, we are told the
names of his new daughters, Dove, Cinnamon, and Horn-of-Kohl (or
Eye-Shadow). These are sensual names and imply Job's loving intimacy
with these children in sharp contrast to his remoteness from his first
children.

Job subsequently lived for 140 years and saw his "sons and grandsons
to the fourth generation." But Job's new intimacy with his children and
grandchildren was an act of considerable courage, for he knew from
bitter experience that all of them could be swept off in a moment. He
knew that none of them, himself included, were invulnerable to the
possibility of another unjust infliction by God. But Job also knew that
the only way to guarantee that he would never suffer from this injus-

tice—the only way to obtain perfect justice for himself—would be to isolate himself from any passionate relationship with his children, with any other human being, and with God himself. Job understood that this kind of perfect justice was too punishing for him to pursue.

The Past of an Illusion

I have attempted throughout this book to remain within the text of the two Bibles, rather than trying to deconstruct them historically as the philologist scholars have done or to criticize them from the outside as non-believers have done. My premise throughout has been that the texts are coherent as they stand—and even when they obviously contradict themselves, there is coherence in the contradiction. My goal has been to understand the texts in their own terms as they treat God's power and authority in his dealings with humanity.

As I come to the end of this inquiry, I want briefly to pursue a different dimension. While still remaining within the texts, I want to explore a possible psychological explanation for the narrative progression that I have described. I believe that it is potentially rewarding to read the biblical texts as expressions of psychological traits that are common to all humanity. My goal here is not to criticize the texts, not to redefine and reduce them from the perspective of a supposedly superior narrative as "symptoms" of psychological complexes or disorders. I want to set a narrative of human psychological development alongside the biblical texts, not above them, to see what illumination might emerge from the comparisons. The Bibles do not speak in these psychodynamic terms, but I believe that their narratives are not only consistent with these terms but intuitively reflective of them.

In both the Hebrew and the Christian Bibles, we have traced the repeated disappointment and sense of betrayal and abandonment on both God's and humanity's side and the equally repeated impulse to try again. There is no explicit explanation in either Bible for this endless cycle. There is, however, an implicit explanation that can be drawn from the biblical narratives—an explanation that was explicitly formulated by Sigmund Freud.

This explanation cannot be found in Freud's tone-deaf debunking of religious belief in *The Future of an Illusion*. When Freud directly thought about religious faith, he could muster no sympathy for, no empathic identification at all with, believers. But when Freud shifted attention to the psychology of human relationships, he became a much more reliable and empathic guide so that we can fruitfully apply his insights to understanding religious impulses that he did not address as such.[19]

Freud insisted that God was an illusion, a projection of human need to be protected by a powerful father. To remain within the terms of the biblical texts, we must reject this claim. There is, however, a different illusion within the Hebrew and Christian Bibles that is repeatedly identified as such in the biblical texts themselves—the illusion that perfect harmony between God and humanity is attainable. (This is virtually the last thought that God proclaimed to Moses before his death. In his valedictory address to the Israelites in Deuteronomy, Moses summarized God's extended sets of commandments, his inducements for compliance and threats of dire punishment for disobedience. God nonetheless announced to Moses that this was all in vain: "This people will rise and go whoring after the alien gods . . . and they will forsake Me and break My covenant that I have sealed with them. And My wrath will flare against them on that day, and I shall forsake them and hide My face from them. . . . I knew their devisings that they do today before I brought them into the land which I vowed."[20] God knew these devisings almost from the beginning of Genesis when he rescued Noah from the Flood; and yet he engaged in a prolonged and, by his own account in Deuteronomy, ultimately fruitless effort to attain harmony with humanity.) Freud suggested some psychological dynamic principles of human development that I propose to use as a way of explaining why this illusion of harmony was endlessly but always unsuccessfully pursued in both the Hebrew and the Christian Bibles.

Using Freud's lights, we can reexamine the relationship between the first and second creation accounts in Genesis and find in their contradictions the psychological key to this illusion in the earliest moments of humanity's infancy. In the first account, as I have repeatedly observed, there is perfect harmony between God and humanity and indeed in all of God's creation. This perfection—from humanity's perspective, this effortless satiation of any conceivable need—has a striking resemblance to Freud's account of the earliest moments of an infant's life when he and the universe were indistinguishable from each other, when the nurturing mother's breast regularly appeared as if by magic, not in response to but in anticipation of the infant's need for its warmth and succor. The infant, that is, felt no neediness but was always gratified. This blissful state even preceded birth in the protected environment of the womb; and memory traces of this state persist for everyone.

Memory is the central psychological capacity for Freud; nothing—no event, no feeling state—is ever lost. As the infant grows toward maturity, however, its innate capacity for selective attention imposes order on this flood of perception and remembered experience. Without this capacity, humans would be overwhelmed by sensory data and incapable of surviving on their own. But this survival imperative takes hold only gradually, as the mind becomes organized so that some memories are buried deeper than others. (For Freud, this is the organizational basis for the topographical distinction between unconscious, preconscious, and conscious mentation.) The most important developmental achievement that occurs in this progressive mental organization is when the maturing infant can distinguish between itself and others and correspondingly differentiate between fantasy and reality. In

Freud's terms, this is the difference between primary and secondary process thinking. All rationality is founded on these intertwined distinctions between self and other and between fantasy and reality.

In the text of the first Genesis creation account, there is no distinction between self and other. God and humanity are identical, one in the exact "image" of the other. There is no distinction between male and female. And humans, made in the image of God, "hold sway" over all animal and vegetable life without any exerted effort but naturally, omnipotently. (This is, in Freud's terms, the state of "infantile omnipotence.") Then suddenly, without any explanation or causal event identified as such, this idyllic is interrupted, and, in the text of the second Genesis account, man is alone and lonely, in need of a "help meet" or "sustainer."[21] (Robert Alter's choice of "sustainer" as the proper translation underscores the psychological difference between the two creation accounts. The traditional translation of *'ezer kenegdo* in the King James version as "help meet" is, Alter maintains, "too weak because it suggests a merely auxiliary function, where *'ezer* elsewhere connotes active intervention on behalf of someone, especially in military contexts."[22] Alter's choice emphasizes the human's isolation and need for external sustenance and protection in the second Genesis account as compared with the first account, where humans were never alone because the very conception of loneliness, of individual separateness from others, did not exist.)

In the first chapter of this book, when we initially confronted the dramatic contradictions between the first and the second creation accounts, I noted the philological explanation that the biblical redactors simply juxtaposed two inconsistent accounts drawn from different traditions, with no meaning intended from the contradictory juxtaposition. I suggested a coherent narrative possibility that the forces of chaos on which God had initially imposed order had reasserted themselves. The psychological developmental perspective suggests another kind of coherent narrative between the first and the second accounts—that they are dramatically and obviously inconsistent because they are based on radically incommensurate reasoning, the first account describing a universe in which the distinction between self and other did not exist and the second account describing a diametrically opposed conception based on this distinction. The juxtaposition without any explanation or acknowledgment of this contradiction between the two accounts thus graphically conveys the logically inexplicable and unbridgeable difference between them.

In Freud's terms, we might say that the juxtaposition of contrary conceptions of the universe in the biblical accounts corresponds to the juxtaposition of two contradictory ways of perception in the human mind, between primary and secondary process thinking. From this perspective, the existence of the two biblical accounts means not necessarily that one supplanted the other but only that they arose in succession and contradict each other.

Jesus was almost explicit in conveying this understanding of the two accounts when he traced all of the difficulty in humanity's relationship to God in the events of the second account—in God's issuance of commandments and humanity's disobedience—and offered the possibility of a return to the prior time, the first creation account, when love rather than obedience was the basis for the relationship. According to Freud's formulation, love is rooted in primary process thinking. "At the height of being in love," Freud observed, "the boundary between ego [self] and object [other] threatens to melt away. Against all the evidence of his senses, a man who is in love declares that 'I' and 'you' are one, and is prepared to behave as if it were a fact."[23]

Freud's characteristic blind spot appears in his observation that this boundary dissolution is a "threat" rather than a passionately desired state. Indeed, he virtually confessed this blindness when he admitted his inability to discover a "feeling as of something limitless, unbounded —as it were, 'oceanic'" in himself. The poet Romain Rolland had invoked this "oceanic feeling" in a letter to Freud criticizing his attack on religious belief in *The Future of an Illusion,* on the ground that Freud had failed to "appreciate the true source of religious sentiments" in this "feeling of an indissoluble bond, of being one with the external world as a whole."[24] Freud's dismissal of this way of comprehending the world was mirrored in his insistent rationalism, his hierarchical preference for secondary process thinking. As subsequent interpreters of Freud have demonstrated, however, this preference is not fundamental to his thinking—indeed, it is contradicted by a full appreciation of the significance in his own conception of the continued juxtaposition throughout every human's life of these two diametrically opposed ways of perceiving the universe.[25]

Freud would see Jesus's appeal to love as the true basis, the original basis, for the relationship between God and humanity as a psychological threat because this appeal rested on dissolved boundaries between the two; and he would thereby miss the profound appeal of Jesus's vision. This attraction is based on persistent memory traces in everyone of the earliest mode of infantile thinking, when the infant and the universe were one and every conceivable need was gratified with no effort on the infant's part, indeed even in anticipation of any conceivable need. This is the compelling attraction that fuels the persistent pursuit of perfect harmony—whether it be between God and humanity or among human beings on the basis of some transcendent ideal of perfect justice and harmony.

Even so, however, Freud's observation that this dissolution of boundaries between self and other would be experienced as a threat is a central clue toward understanding the negative dynamic coiled within the pursuit of perfect harmony. Although the infant initially experiences the world as boundlessly and effortlessly gratifying—as "very good" in the way that God himself saw the first creation—this bliss did not and could not last. The trauma of birth itself may mark the first break from the harmonious experience of life in the womb, and whatever the pleasures of earliest infancy after that initial stressful event, unsatisfied needs soon appear within the infant's purview—needs as prosaic as a persistent stomachache, or the unavailability of the mother's breast or the bottle at the moment when hunger pangs become intense, or the pain of teething. Even when these displeasures are appeased and the infant returns to the happy state of harmony with the universe, the infant not only retains memory traces of the initial bliss that attract its longing—that fuel its persistent and even desperate pursuit of renewed perfection. The infant also retains memory traces of its recurrent experience that this blissful state does not persist.

Thus one memory suggests to the infant that this time the recaptured experience will be as good as the first time when bliss seemed endlessly eternal. However, the immediately accompanying memory tells the infant that the first bliss initially seemed eternal only because it had not yet ended. After the first world-shattering event, after the first experience of pain, the infant can never again recapture the full measure of the remembered experience of eternal bliss. The remembered experience always contains within it a memory of renewed pain. The very effort to recapture initial bliss itself recalls the experience of its loss.

This endless conjunction of contradictory memories is not, moreover, the only threat that arises from the imagined return to early bliss. After the infant first learns that bliss is not a permanent state, it also learns that some kind of effort on its part can appease the loss. The infant's crying, for example, becomes associated for it with restoration of bliss because it attracts the attention of the nurturant caretaker. Just as the infant gradually comes to perceive that it and its caretaker are not fused in one undifferentiated identity—because the caretaker is not instantaneously available to satisfy need—the infant also glimpses that its independent effort can influence this caretaker's ministration to its needs. From this first glimpse of its individuated separateness, the idea emerges for the infant that there is a difference between passivity—based on the initial belief that the surrounding universe is seamlessly and effortlessly linked to the infant's satiation—and activity that has become associated with renewed satisfaction. The return to blissful memory traces of the earliest dissolution of boundaries between the infant and its caretaker thus also becomes associated with a sense of passive weakness, as a threat to the infant's learned capacity to act on its own behalf in order to obtain satisfaction. Thus the very act that is psychologically experienced as a return to bliss, to perfect harmony, is also at the same time experienced as a self-destructive act—that is, the destruction of the very idea of a separate proactive self. Freud discounted the blissful lure of the primordial "oceanic feeling," but he accurately saw the threat inevitably involved in the recapitulation of that feeling.

This continuous loop embedded in human psyches from our earliest infantile experience is the psychological dynamic that fuels the narrative pattern identified by the biblical account of the endless striving for restored unity between individuals and their surrounding universe, between humanity and God, and the equally endless failure of that pursuit. To identify this psychological dynamic is not, however, to suggest that all or even most human beings understand the dynamic or its consequences.

For much of his career, Freud himself refused to acknowledge this dynamic and attempted to use his considerable intellect to arrest it. He overstated his own and his patients' potential capacities for self-conscious exercise of rational self-mastery in order to suppress or transcend primary process thinking embedded in unconscious mental processes. This same overstatement is at the psychological core of the efforts of modern political leaders to impose unified order on unruly human behavior (often explicitly justified as the pursuit of perfect harmony and justice) and the efforts of modern political theorists to discover the philosopher's stone by which unified order (that is, perfect harmony and justice) can be recognized and attained. In psychological terms, this pursuit inevitably involves the dissolution of boundaries between self and other and thereby connotes the destruction of everyone's individual self.

As the most extreme expression of this pursuit, modern dictatorships entail the fantasy that an entire polity is understood as One Being and that state is not just symbolized but actually embodied in the One Leader. This is the destructive deformation that arises from a single-minded commitment to the hierarchical command-and-punish model of social authority. This psychological dynamic is also the driving force in the recurrent biblical narrative pattern that God's pursuit of perfect harmony with all of his creation repeatedly leads him to the edge of destroying all of his creation. In those narratives, however, God continually interrupts this destructive dynamic by acknowledging (if only to himself, as in the Flood narrative, or at the prompting of Abraham, Moses, or Jesus) that he is willing to settle for less than perfect harmony, that sinfulness and disorder cannot be permanently expunged from the universe except at the cost of destroying the universe and leaving him all alone.

Of all the biblical narratives we have explored, the interaction between God and Job most directly expresses this lesson. In the Epilogue to the book of Job, God appears chastened and, like a failed lover, eager to resume relations with Job but unable to promise that his jealous demand for unconditional love will not recur and lead him ultimately to the same abusive breach. For his part, Job seems willing to accept this tentative reconciliation. He does not shun God but talks to him again on behalf of the Friends. He appears to accept the consolation of "all his brothers and sisters and all his former acquaintances" even though they came to his house only after God had restored twice his fortune. Job lavishes love on his three new daughters and thereby makes himself vulnerable to intensified grief if God kills them too—and, of course, he has no assurance from God that this will not happen. But Job only offers the kind of passionate, unconditional love to his daughters that God had initially wanted for himself.

Was God willing to settle for less than the perfect fulfillment of his wishes that he had demanded at the outset? Was Job willing to settle for less than a promise of perfect justice for his righteousness? We know only that God permitted Job to live another 140 years, surrounded by his sons and grandsons to the fourth generation, and to die "in old age after a full life span."[26] It seems from the conclusion of this narrative that both God and Job tempered their expectations of each other.

But is this the lesson that God himself drew for his future relations with humankind? In the ordering of the Hebrew Bible, the book of Job appears virtually at the end, and God never again speaks directly to humanity. In the Christian Bible, God appears willing to forgive human sinfulness in a way that only rarely and tentatively had appeared before. But God's open lavishing of love for humanity does not sustain itself throughout the Christian Bible. At the end, God returns to his punitive vengeful modality as his renewed demand for perfect obedience explodes into a destructive rage aimed at almost all of humanity.

The biblical narratives of relations between God and humanity describe recurring cycles of passionate longing and angry recrimination, of momentary harmony always followed by accusations of betrayal and abandonment. Those who want a guide to the permanent realization of perfect harmony and justice between ruler and ruled cannot be satisfied by these narratives. But this is the best that the biblical accounts offer.

Notes · Acknowledgments · Index

Notes

1. In the Beginning

1. See, for example, any of the following three sources. Mark Lilla, *The Stillborn God: Religion, Politics and the Modern West* (New York: Knopf, 2007), 5, 8, 22: "The first modern philosophers [four centuries ago] hoped to change the practices of Christian politics, but their real opponent was the intellectual tradition that had justified those practices. By attacking Christian political theology and denying its legitimacy, the new philosophy simultaneously challenged the basic principles on which authority had been justified in most societies in history. . . . [W]e no longer recognize revelation as politically authoritative. . . . If we conceive of God as the shaper of our cosmos, which displays his purposes, then the legitimate exercise of political authority might very well depend on understanding those purposes. God's intentions themselves need no justification, since he is the last court of appeal . . . God, by creating, has revealed something man cannot fully know on his own. This revelation then becomes the source of his authority over nature and over us." Jürgen Habermas, *Between Facts and Norms: Contributions to a Discourse Theory of Law and Democracy,* trans. W. Rehg (Cambridge, MA: MIT Press, 1996), 181: "With recognized religious world pictures as a background, law originally possessed a sacral foundation. This law, usually administered and interpreted by theologian jurists, was to a great extent accepted as a reified component of a divine salvation order or of a natural world order and remained, as such, exempt from

human authority." Or see Eliot Weinberger, "Who Made It New?" review of *What Ever Happened to Modernism?* by Gabriel Josipovici, *New York Review of Books,* June 23, 2011, 42.

2. See Robert Alter, *The Five Books of Moses* (New York: W. W. Norton, 2004), 314. To similar effect, Freud noted "the peculiar importance which attaches to the *very first* communications made by patients" in analytic psychotherapy (emphasis in original). See Sigmund Freud, "Notes upon a Case of Obsessional Neurosis," in *Standard Edition of the Complete Psychological Works of Sigmund Freud,* trans. and ed. James Strachey, 24 vols. (London: Hogarth Press, 1953), vol. 10, 160n1.

3. Genesis 2:9: "And the Lord God caused to sprout from the soil every tree that is pleasant to the sight and good for food, the tree of life was in the midst of the garden, and the tree of knowledge, good and evil." It is not clear from this account whether God planted all of the trees or only the trees pleasant to look at and good for food.

4. Ancient Hebrew had a much more limited vocabulary than any modern language—and the high literary language in which the Bible was written was apparently even more limited than the Hebrew that was spoken in everyday life in the sixth century BCE. This doesn't mean that biblical Hebrew was impoverished in its capacity to convey complex thoughts. It means that, unlike more variegated languages and certainly unlike modern English with its vast vocabulary, virtually all biblical Hebrew words had multiple meanings. As one Hebrew scholar has observed, "The biblical lexicon is so restricted that it is hard to believe it could have served all the purposes of quotidian existence in [the] highly developed society" in which the Bible was composed. Angel Saenz-Badillos, *History of the Hebrew Language* (Cambridge: Cambridge University Press, 1993), quoted in Alter, *Five Books of Moses,* xxix. Modern English reflects a cultural obsession with saying exactly what one means, nothing more and nothing less, but biblical Hebrew was almost constitutionally incapable of conveying single-minded meanings.

5. See Richard Friedman, *The Bible with Sources Revealed* (San Francisco: HarperSanFrancisco, 2003). The consensus of scholarly opinion is that the "first chapter of Genesis was almost certainly written later than the second chapter of Genesis, by a different author." Robert Wright, *The Evolution of God* (New York: Little Brown, 2009), 102.

6. The philologists' reluctance to see anything more than juxtaposed contradiction from different biblical sources has not been uniformly en-

dorsed by the scholarly community. See, for example, Robert Alter, *The World of Biblical Literature* (New York: Basic Books, 1991), 7, 18: "I am . . . repeatedly impressed by the evidence in many instances of a strong synthesizing imagination that has succeeded in making once disparate voices elements of a complex, persuasively integrated literary whole. . . . [The] characteristic of biblical scholarship since the nineteenth century [is that] the text is imagined to be driven by a compulsion to report bits and pieces of tradition, with scarcely any sense that the writer might be purposefully selecting, embedding, reshaping, and recontextualizing bits and pieces of tradition in his own artful narrative. What I would argue for is a reading that takes into account the bumpiness of the text without rushing to break the text down into a series of bumps and disjunctions produced by the sheer momentum of reporting tradition."

7. Amartya Sen, *The Idea of Justice* (Cambridge, MA: Harvard University Press, 2009).

8. Ibid., 5–6, 8.

9. Ibid., 11, 15.

10. Ibid., 263.

11. Ibid., 20.

12. Ibid., 21.

13. Exodus 4:24: "And it happened on the way [to Egypt] at the night camp that the Lord encountered [Moses] and sought to put him to death"; Job 1:9.

2. The Appearance of Authority

1. Genesis 3:16.

2. Genesis 2:25.

3. Genesis 3:10.

4. Genesis 3:11.

5. Genesis 1:27.

6. Genesis 2:24.

7. Genesis 1:28.

8. See Genesis 3:6 and Robert Alter's commentary in Alter, *The Five Books of Moses* (New York: W. W. Norton, 2004), 24n6.

9. Genesis 4:7.

10. Genesis 4:13–14.

11. The anthropologist Mary Douglas points to this contradiction in atti-

tudes among the men of the Lele tribe in the Congo in the "double role" of women in their social structure—as ostensibly subject to male domination "as passive pawns" but with an implicit ability as "active intriguers" to undermine that domination. "The story of the Garden of Eden," she observed, "touched a deep chord of sympathy in male breasts. Once told by the missionaries, it was told and retold around pagan hearths with smug relish" as confirmation of the Lele men's "feeling that women are the root of all evils"—a kind of "Delilah complex, [based on] the belief that women weaken or betray" men, notwithstanding the socially sanctioned male dominance. Mary Douglas, *Purity and Danger: An Analysis of the Concepts of Pollution and Taboo* (London: Routledge and Kegan Paul, 1966), 154–155.

12. See Jack Miles, *God: A Biography* (New York: Alfred A. Knopf, 1995).
13. Jack Miles suggested this possibility to me in a personal communication.
14. 1 Samuel 8:7–10.
15. Genesis 2:14.

3. God Gives, God Takes Away

1. Genesis 4:12–15.
2. Genesis 3:21.
3. Genesis 6:6, 6:9.
4. Genesis 9:11.
5. Genesis 6:5.
6. Genesis 5:29.
7. See Robert Alter, *The Five Books of Moses* (New York: W. W. Norton, 2004), 36n29.
8. See Genesis 1:29–30: "Look, I have given you every seed-bearing plant . . . and every tree that has fruit . . . yours they will be for food"; and 2:16: "From every fruit of the garden you may surely eat."
9. Compare Genesis 1:29 with 9:3–4.
10. Genesis 8:21.
11. Genesis 6:6.
12. Genesis 8:1.
13. Exodus 2:24.
14. Alter, *Five Books of Moses*, 51n12.

15. Genesis 9:14–15.
16. In a personal communication, Amos Friedland observed that the rainbow "is an especially fragile, transient sign. It does not always appear after rainfall, it can disappear very quickly if it does appear, it sometimes is so faint you can hardly see it. It also does not ever appear in the midst of a total deluge, but only in the in-between of sun and rain, typically after the rain has ended. This adds another paradoxical, troubling element: if God is tempted to bring another deluge and flood, won't the rainbow only appear (and remind him of his covenant not to destroy humanity again) *after* it is all over?"
17. Genesis 8:22.
18. Genesis 9:11.
19. Genesis 9:21–22.
20. Genesis 8:9.
21. Genesis 8:21, 9:12.
22. Genesis 8:21.
23. Genesis 9:14–16.
24. Genesis 6:5–7.
25. Genesis 8:21.

4. God's Promises

1. Genesis 12:1, 12:2, 12:4.
2. Genesis 20:13.
3. Genesis 20:11.
4. Genesis 12:12.
5. Genesis 4:14.
6. See Genesis 24:4, 24:10.
7. Genesis 23:4.
8. Genesis 17:17.
9. Robert Alter, *The Five Books of Moses* (New York: W. W. Norton, 2004), 83n17.
10. Genesis 20:11, 13:16, 15:5, 17:2, 17:6, 17:19.
11. Genesis 15:2, 15:5–6.
12. Genesis 18:18–19.
13. Genesis 4:12: "A restless wanderer shall you be on the earth."
14. Genesis 6:5: "The evil of the human creature was great on the earth."

15. The alteration appeared in the Masoretic revision of the Hebrew Bible, prepared between the seventh and tenth centuries CE; see Alter's commentary to Genesis 18:22. Alter, *Five Books of Moses*, 89n22.
16. Genesis 18:24–26.
17. Susan Neiman has suggested that it was precisely the absence of any prospect of personal gain that qualified Abraham as a "moral hero" in daring to confront God in this episode; though Neiman did not see the personal implications for Abraham when he came to plead only for ten innocents, her account offers an explanation for his reluctance to proceed further. See Susan Neiman, *Moral Clarity: A Guide for Grown-up Idealists* (Orlando, FL: Harcourt, 2008), 82.
18. Genesis 19:27–29.
19. Genesis 21:1.
20. Genesis 15:3–4.
21. Genesis 21:11–14, 21:17.
22. Genesis 22:1–2.
23. Genesis 22:7–10.
24. See Shalom Spiegel, *The Last Trial: On the Legends and Lore of the Command to Abraham to Offer Isaac as a Sacrifice* (New York: Pantheon, 1967).
25. Genesis 24:63.
26. Genesis 37:15.
27. Genesis 24:67.
28. Genesis 26:6–7.
29. Genesis 26:3–4.
30. Genesis 28:20–22.
31. Genesis 35:2–3.
32. Genesis 28:20–22.
33. See Alter, *Five Books of Moses*, 178n10.
34. Genesis 32:25–31.
35. Genesis 11:4–6.
36. Genesis 47:9.
37. Genesis 33:3–4.
38. Genesis 33:15–16.
39. Alter, *Five Books of Moses*, 186n15.
40. Genesis 35:1.
41. Genesis 35:11.
42. Genesis 46:2–4.
43. Genesis 26:2–5, 26:23–24.

44. Genesis 27:22.
45. Genesis 45:8.
46. Genesis 46:3–7.
47. Genesis 15:13.

5. Loving Power

1. Exodus 2:3.
2. Robert Alter, *The Five Books of Moses* (New York: W. W. Norton, 2004), 313n10.
3. Exodus 2:6.
4. Exodus 2:23–25.
5. Exodus 2:22.
6. Alter, *Five Books of Moses,* 316n22.
7. Genesis 23:4; see Alter, *Five Books of Moses,* 113n4.
8. Exodus 2:13.
9. Exodus 2:14–16.
10. Exodus 3:2–4.
11. Exodus 3:5–6.
12. Exodus 3:7–10.
13. Genesis 32:30.
14. Exodus 3:14. See Alter, *Five Books of Moses,* 321n14. Harold Bloom offers the reading "I will be present whenever and wherever I will be present," which, he appropriately observes, carries "the terrible irony . . . that the opposite also is implied, 'And I will be absent whenever and wherever I will be absent,' including at the destructions of his Temple, at the German death camps, at Golgotha." Harold Bloom, *Jesus and Yahweh: The Names Divine* (New York: Riverhead Books, 2005), 27–28.
15. Exodus 4:1.
16. Exodus 3:13.
17. Exodus 6:3.
18. Exodus 4:1.
19. Exodus 7:11–12 (staff-to-snake); 7:21 (Nile River water-to-blood); 8:3 (frogs).
20. Exodus 8:14.
21. Exodus 7:1.
22. Alter, *Five Books of Moses,* 328n16.
23. Exodus 4:24–25.
24. Alter, *Five Books of Moses,* 330n24.

25. Exodus 3:6.
26. Exodus 33:11.
27. Numbers 12:6–8.
28. Numbers 12:9.
29. Exodus 24:18.
30. Exodus 32:1.
31. Exodus 32:10.
32. Exodus 32:14.
33. Exodus 32:30.
34. Exodus 32:12, 32:14.
35. Exodus 33:11.
36. Exodus 33:12–14.
37. Exodus 33:14, 33:17.
38. Exodus 34:1, 34:5–9.
39. Exodus 2:14.
40. Numbers 14:15–16.

6. Love Offered, Love Commanded

1. Paul Kahn has convincingly argued that the modern impersonal conception of relationship between state and citizen itself misses a crucial dimension of the implicit affective bond. The willingness of a citizen to surrender his life to protect the state, Kahn maintains, is best expressed as a love relationship: "The attachment to the political order is a form of love. It involves loyalty, courage, self-identification, and participation in the intergenerational project of family and community. . . . Love [is] the internal experience of power. Politics, correspondingly, is the outward face of power. The communitarians, in their argument with liberals, are reluctant to discuss power; the multiculturalists tend to see power primarily as a source of oppression. Neither sees the linked character of law, power, and love." Paul Kahn, *Putting Liberalism in Its Place* (Princeton: Princeton University Press, 2005), 228.
2. Exodus 18:13.
3. See Exodus 38:26.
4. Exodus 18:25–26.
5. Exodus 19:4–6.
6. Exodus 15:22, 16:15.
7. Exodus 19:7–8.

8. Exodus 32:26.
9. Exodus 32:30.
10. Exodus 19:5.
11. Exodus 20:3.
12. Exodus 34:16.
13. Deuteronomy 6:3–6.
14. Exodus 19:5, 19:8.
15. Numbers 11:1–2.
16. Numbers 11:5–7.
17. Numbers 11:9–10.
18. Numbers 11:11–14.
19. Numbers 11:15–18.
20. Numbers 11:18–20.
21. Exodus 2:24–25.
22. Numbers 11:21–22.
23. Numbers 11:23.
24. Numbers 12:8.
25. Numbers 14:3.
26. Numbers 20:10–11.
27. Numbers 20:12.
28. Exodus 14:15–16.
29. Exodus 17:6.
30. Exodus 4:16–17.
31. Numbers 11:15.
32. Numbers 14:12.
33. Deuteronomy 6:5.
34. Numbers 20:11.
35. Niccolò Machiavelli, *The Prince*, trans. and with an introduction by Harvey C. Mansfield (Chicago: University of Chicago Press, 1998), 66, 68.

7. Grief and Grievance

1. Deuteronomy 34:1, 34:6, 34:10.
2. Deuteronomy 31:7–8.
3. Deuteronomy 28:15–49.
4. Deuteronomy 28:59, 28:66–68.
5. Deuteronomy 28:69.

6. Deuteronomy 32:19–21, 32:26–27.
7. Deuteronomy 29:17–20.
8. The biblical scholar Abraham Joshua Heschel reports that the rabbinic sages of the early diaspora "expressed astonishment" at the omission of God's direct speech from Deuteronomy, as if this implied that Moses were speaking "on his own," without direct instruction from or contact with God. Abraham Joshua Heschel, *Heavenly Torah: As Refracted through the Generations*, ed. and trans. Gordon Tucker with Leonard Levin (New York: Continuum, 2005), 460–461.
9. Numbers 20:12.
10. Deuteronomy 32:50–51.
11. Deuteronomy 1:37.
12. Deuteronomy 3:25.
13. Numbers 14:17–20.
14. It is possible, perhaps even likely, that the book of Job was written by more than one person, but however many hands worked at it, the final result has an internal coherence and integrity that justify referring to its author in the singular. At various points in my discussion of the book, I will refer to its "narrator," by which I mean the literary character invented by the author to serve as an anonymous and apparently all-knowing rapporteur.
15. The composition date for the book is disputed. David Wolfers, for example, argues for the seventh century BCE. David Wolfers, *Deep Things Out of Darkness: The Book of Job* (Grand Rapids, MI: Wm. B. Eerdmans, 1995), 54. Leslie Wilson maintains that the second century BCE is more probable. Leslie S. Wilson, *The Book of Job: Judaism in the 2nd Century BCE* (Lanham, MD: University Press of America, 2006), 244.
16. Job 1:1. *The Book of Job*, trans., introduction, and notes by Raymond P. Scheindlin (New York: W. W. Norton, 1998). All quotations will be drawn from this translation, except where specifically noted.
17. Job 1:12.
18. Job 1:21.
19. Job 2:4.
20. Job 30:9–10.
21. Job 7:3–7.
22. Job 7:8–9, 7:24.
23. Job 1:9–12.

24. Numbers 20:11–12.

25. Job 7:11, 7:15–25.

26. Genesis 18:22.

27. Genesis 18:18–20.

28. Job 27:5–6.

29. Job 28:12–13.

30. Job 29:1–5.

31. Job 30:20–21.

32. Job 31:35–40. Here is another connection with Moses. The English translation of the last phrase—"come before Him as before a prince"—cannot convey the inherent ambiguity of the original Hebrew; because object and subject are not unequivocally identifiable as such, this last phrase could also be rendered, "I could come before Him as a prince." Thus in one sense, it is God who remains "the prince" notwithstanding Job's challenge; but in another sense, it is Job who is "the prince" and Moses who is "the prince [of Egypt]." If we take both senses together, Job's last words depict himself, God, and Moses as princes.

33. Job 42:1.

34. *The Book of Job*, trans. and with an introduction by Stephen Mitchell (San Francisco: North Point Press, 1987), 123–124.

35. Job 37:24–26.

36. Job 38:1.

37. Job 38:2.

38. Job 38:4, 38:16, 38:35, 39:28.

39. Genesis 18:19.

40. Exodus 34:7.

41. This is Raymond Scheindlin's version; similarly, Mitchell, in *The Book of Job*, 88n35, renders this as "I had heard of you with my ears; but now my eyes have seen you. Therefore I will be quiet, comforted that I am dust."

42. Job 30:19: "He conceived me as clay, and I have come to be like dust and ashes."

43. Job 42:5–6.

44. Jack Miles, *God: A Biography* (New York: Alfred A. Knopf, 1995), 325.

45. Wilson, *Book of Job*, 201.

46. Genesis 5:29.

47. Deuteronomy 34:1, 34:6, 34:10.

48. Job 42:1.

49. See Kevin Snapp, "A Curious Ringing in the Ears: Ambiguity and Ambivalence in the Conclusion of the Book of Job," *Conservative Judaism* 34 (2000), 53.

50. Job 42:4.

51. Job 42:2.

52. Job 42:10.

53. Exodus 22:6.

54. Job 40:4.

55. Job 40:2–9.

56. Job 40:10.

57. Job 2:12–15.

58. Job 38:3–4.

59. Job 42:4.

60. Job 42:11, 42:14–16.

61. Job 1:19.

8. As We Forgive Those

1. The author uses the Hebrew word *va'yikalel* for "curse" where God is not the subject, as in Job's imprecation about the day of his birth in his first extended speech. See Job 3:1.

2. I owe this insight to Benjamin Berger from discussion in our Yale Law School seminar, "The Book of Job and Injustice."

3. Leo Strauss, *Persecution and the Art of Writing* (Glencoe, IL: Free Press, 1952), 24–25.

4. Sigmund Freud, *The Interpretation of Dreams* (New York: Science Editions, 1961), 279–304. Freud also offers a way to comprehend the confusion between "blessing" and "cursing" God that I discussed earlier in this chapter. Regarding his obsessional patient who has come to be known as the "Rat Man," Freud noted the "conflict between love and hatred [that] showed itself" when, "at the time of the revival of his piety, he made up prayers for himself." These prayers, however, "took up more and more time and eventually lasted for an hour and a half [because] he found, like an inverted Balaam, that something always inserted itself into his pious phrases and turned them into their opposite." For example, "if he said, 'May God protect him', an evil spirit would hurriedly insinuate a 'not'. On one such occasion the idea occurred to him of cursing instead, for in that case, he thought, the contrary words would be sure to creep

in." In a footnote to this case description, Freud observed that there was a "similar [psychological] mechanism in the familiar case of sacrilegious thoughts entering the minds of devout persons." Sigmund Freud, "Notes upon a Case of Obsessional Neurosis," in *Standard Edition of the Complete Psychological Works of Sigmund Freud,* trans. and ed. James Strachey, 24 vols. (London: Hogarth Press, 1955), vol. 10, 193n1.

5. Freud, *Interpretation of Dreams,* 596.

6. See Robert Alter, *The World of Biblical Literature* (New York: Basic Books, 1991): "The [positivist] cognitive model for the whole modern enterprise of [biblical] commentary [going back to nineteenth-century Germany] is, I think, the textual crux. One encounters a difficult place in the text, something that does not make sense. With great patience and a little luck . . . the crux may be solved. . . . The Bible as a whole is conceived as intricate edifice of *puzzlements*—philological, compositional, historical—that one by one requires solutions and with a combination of ingenuity and serendipity will get them. What these commentators and their many modern forerunners do not readily imagine is that much biblical writing—I am, of course, not speaking of what scribes may have inadvertently interposed—might have been devised precisely not to yield a solution, or to yield multiple and contradictory solutions, and that this might be the very hallmark of its greatness" (143–144).

7. Amartya Sen, *The Idea of Justice* (Cambridge, MA: Harvard University Press, 2009), 11.

8. Genesis 49:8–10.

9. Genesis 37:26.

10. Genesis 38:25–26.

11. Genesis 43:9.

12. Genesis 44:20, 44:30–34.

13. Genesis 45:1–2.

14. See 1 Samuel 24:12, 24:17. All of the translations of 1 and 2 Samuel are from Robert Alter, *The David Story* (New York: W. W. Norton and Co., 1999).

15. 1 Samuel 24:18, 24:21.

16. 2 Samuel 12:13.

17. 1 Samuel 15:12.

18. 1 Samuel 15:24.

19. 2 Samuel 19:1, 19:5.

20. 2 Samuel 7:13–15.
21. 2 Samuel 6:14, 6:20–21, 7:2, 7:5, 7:11.

9. A Renewed Testament

1. In the canonical text of the Christian Bible, Matthew appears before Mark, but modern biblical scholars are unanimous that this ordering is historically incorrect. See, for example, "Introduction to the New Testament," in *The New Oxford Annotated Bible* (New York: Oxford University Press, 1973), 1167–1168. I follow the original ordering in my discussion of the Christian Bible, though I adhered to the historically incorrect ordering in the canonical text of the Hebrew Bible for chapters one and two of Genesis. In both instances, I am guided by the narrative coherence of the ordering rather than by the historical priority of one portion over the other.
2. Mark 1:10–11.
3. Matthew 3:13–16.
4. Luke 3:21.
5. Mark 1:12.
6. Genesis 21:15.
7. Exodus 24:18, 32:1.
8. Matthew 4:2–9; Luke 4:2–12.
9. Job 1:10.
10. Matthew 6:9, 6:13. Luke records an abbreviated version, which concludes, "lead us not into temptation." Luke 11:4.
11. Matthew 5:39; Luke 6:35.
12. Mark 1:16–20.
13. Genesis 12:1–2.
14. Luke 5:5–11.
15. Matthew 4:19–20.
16. Matthew 3:16–17.
17. This implication is blurred by Matthew's odd grammatical construction that after his baptism, "the heavens were opened and he saw the Spirit of God descending . . . on him; and lo, a voice from the heavens, saying, 'This . . . '" It is thus possible that, in Matthew's account, Jesus alone heard God's reference to him in the third person.
18. Mark 5:38–43.

19. See, for example, Matthew 12:15–16: "He healed all who were ill, and gave strict instructions that they were not to make him known"; Mark 1:43: "And he sternly charged [the cleansed leper] . . . and said to him, 'See that you say nothing to any one'"; Mark 1:34: "And he healed many who were sick with various diseases, and cast out many demons; and he would not permit the demons to speak, because they knew him."

20. See, for example, Mark 8:11–12, when the Pharisees "tested" Jesus by demanding a "sign from heaven." Jesus "sighed deeply and said, 'Why does this generation ask for a sign? Truly I tell you no sign shall be given to this generation.'"

21. Mark 5:25–34.

22. See, for example, Mark 1:23–26, 1:34, 2:11, 5:8–13.

23. See also Mark 1:31, 2:5, 2:11–12, 7:33–34; Matthew 8:13, 9:6, 9:27; Luke 19:41–43.

24. Mark 9:17–27.

25. Matthew 17:20.

26. Mark 9:28–37.

27. Mark 8:27–29.

28. Luke 9:20–21.

29. Matthew 16:16–17.

30. Luke 20:1–8.

31. Matthew 26:63–64. For an identical account, see Luke 22:66–70.

32. Matthew 27:11–14. For an identical account, see Luke 23:3.

33. Mark 14:62–63.

34. Mark 6:1–6.

35. Mark 9:22–23.

36. Mark 6:36.

37. Mark 6:34.

38. Exodus 32:12.

39. Numbers 14:15–17.

40. Genesis 8:1, 8:21.

41. 1 Corinthians 15:45.

42. Matthew 12:46–50.

43. Genesis 2:24.

44. See Mark 9:1: "Truly, I say to you, there are some standing here who will not taste death before they see that the kingdom of God has come with power." See also Matthew 16:28, 23:36.

10. The Same Old Testament

1. 1 Corinthians 4:20–21.
2. 1 Corinthians 13:1–13.
3. 1 Corinthians 14:37.
4. Acts 2:15.
5. Acts 3:44–47.
6. John 15:12. See Mark 12:30–34.
7. Acts 7:58, 8:1, 8:3.
8. Acts 9:1, 9:3–6.
9. Galatians 1:18–24.
10. Acts 9:26.
11. Acts 15:2.
12. Acts 15:24–25.
13. Acts 15:32–34, 15:37–41.
14. Acts 9:7.
15. Acts 22:9.
16. 1 Corinthians 9:1–2.
17. 1 Corinthians 15:4–11.
18. 2 Corinthians 10:8, 10:13–14, 11:1–3, 11:17, 11:21–23.
19. Mark 9:32–35.
20. Mark 14:18, 14:25–31.
21. Mark 14:40.
22. Mark 14:50, 14:54, 14:67–72.
23. Mark 8:31–32.
24. Matthew 16:22.
25. Matthew 16:23. See also Mark 8:33.
26. Mark 14:33–36.
27. Mark 9:7.
28. Mark 15:34, 15:37.
29. Mark 14:36.
30. Mark 16:3–8.
31. See note k, appended to the Revised Standard Version at the conclusion of Mark's Gospel.
32. Mark 16:9–14.
33. See Frank Kermode, *The Genesis of Secrecy* (Cambridge, MA: Harvard University Press, 1979), 65–66, and notes accompanying Mark 16:9–20 in the Revised Standard Version.

34. Mark 1:1.
35. Psalm 22:1–2.
36. Psalm 22:24.
37. Psalm 22:30–31.
38. Matthew 5:39.
39. Luke 6:35.

11. Eliminating Doubts and Doubters

1. John 5:16–17, 5:22–23.
2. John 8:54–58.
3. John 10:24–26, 10:38.
4. John 1:32–34.
5. Mark 6:5; Matthew 13:58.
6. Luke 5:24.
7. John 4:44–45.
8. Mark 15:34; Matthew 27:46.
9. Luke 23:46.
10. Psalm 22:3–4, 22:9, 22:11, 22:19.
11. Luke 4:9–12.
12. John 19:30.
13. John 19:28–29.
14. Mark 13:33, 13:36; Matthew 26:37, 26:39.
15. Luke 22:42.
16. John 18:1–4.
17. John 12:27–33.
18. Matthew 28:8–10, 28:16–20.
19. Luke 24:17–36.
20. John 20:12, 20:19, 20:30.
21. John 21:14, 21:20, 21:24–25.
22. Mark 16:14–17.
23. John 20:25.
24. John 20:27–29.
25. John 21:24–25.
26. Matthew 16:22–23.
27. Mark 14:34, 14:36.
28. John 20:25–27.
29. Elaine Pagels has concluded that John wrote his Gospel as a polemic

against Thomas's teaching and caricatured him as an unworthy doubter. See Elaine Pagels, *Beyond Belief: The Secret Gospel of Thomas* (New York: Random House, 2003), 57–58.

30. John 20:2.
31. John 20:4–8.
32. John 21:17.
33. Revelation 21:1–4.
34. Revelation 21:27.
35. Revelation 20:10, 20:15.
36. Matthew 26:52.
37. Revelation 9:20–21.
38. John 8:7.
39. Genesis 6:5, 6:9, 8:21.
40. Genesis 1:27.
41. Genesis 3:8–9.
42. Genesis 6:6.
43. Genesis 8:1.
44. Genesis 8:20–21.
45. Job 7:25.

12. The Insoluble Problem of Politics

1. Sigmund Freud, "Female Sexuality," in *Standard Edition of the Complete Psychological Works of Sigmund Freud*, trans. and ed. James Strachey, 24 vols. (London: Hogarth Press, 1953–), 21:234.
2. Sigmund Freud, "Group Psychology and the Analysis of the Ego," in *Standard Edition*, 18:920.
3. See generally Jonathan Lear, *Love and Its Place in Nature: A Philosophical Interpretation of Freudian Psychoanalysis* (New York: Farrar, Straus and Giroux, 1990).
4. Job 9:33.
5. Exodus 20:5.
6. Compare the political scientist Aaron Wildavsky's conclusion in his study of Moses's style of leadership: "Moses may expect gratitude [from the Hebrews], but what little he gets does not get him very far. Each appeasing act—water, food, whatever—is met by demands for more. What appears to Moses to be ingratitude based on insatiable appetite seems to the Hebrews a result of insatiable demands on them made by Moses

(and his God). . . . Compromise, rather than implacability, is the common Mosaic mode of resolving conflict. We can with confidence describe Moses' leadership as an endless adjustment, a tissue of evasions and compromises; Moses always prefers persuasion." Aaron Wildavsky, *The Nursing Father: Moses as a Political Leader* (Tuscaloosa: University of Alabama Press, 1984), 174–175.

7. Numbers 11:11–15.

8. Numbers 11:18–20.

9. Numbers 11:31–34.

10. Robert Alter, *The Five Books of Moses* (New York: W. W. Norton, 2004), 740n34.

11. Matthew 14:17–20, 16:34–38.

12. Job 1:6.

13. See S. R. Driver and G. B. Gray, *A Critical and Exegetical Commentary on the Book of Job* (Edinburgh, 1921), cited in *The Book of Job*, trans. and with an introduction by Stephen Mitchell (San Francisco: North Point Press, 1987), 124.

14. Job 29:5.

15. Genesis 2:23–24.

16. Mark 4:11–12. See also Matthew 13:11, 13:13, 13:16.

17. This apparent paradox is compellingly explored in Frank Kermode, *The Genesis of Secrecy: On the Interpretation of Narrative* (Cambridge, MA: Harvard University Press, 1979), esp. 23–47. For parallels in the pedagogy of the Hebrew Bible, see Robert Alter's illuminating discussion of its "narrative technique of studied reticences . . . [and] significantly patterned ambiguities" in Robert Alter, *The Art of Biblical Narrative* (New York: Basic Books, 1981), 126, 153–159.

18. Mark 4:34. See also Matthew 13:36.

19. Mark 4:13.

20. Job 40:2–4.

21. Job 7:17—21.

22. Job 29:1–5, 30:20–21, 30:26.

23. Job 2:9.

24. Exodus 2:24–25.

25. Numbers 12.

26. Job 9:29, 9:32–35.

27. Job 40:2–4.

28. Exodus 2:13–14.

29. Luke 15:2.
30. John 8:7.
31. Luke 10:25–28.
32. John 13:34. See also John 15:12–14: "This is my commandment, that you love one another as I have loved you. Greater love has no man than this, that a man lay down his life for his friends."

13. Justice, Justice Shall You Pursue

1. *Brown v. Allen*, 344 U.S. 443, 540 (1953) (concurring).
2. Alexander Hamilton, Federalist Papers No. 78.
3. *Cooper v. Aaron*, 358 U.S. 1, 19–20 (1958).
4. Earl Warren, *The Memoirs of Earl Warren* (Garden City, NY: Doubleday, 1977), 291.
5. Job 38:4.
6. Job 38:33.
7. Job 38:19.
8. Dennis Hutchinson, "Unanimity and Desegregation: Decisionmaking in the Supreme Court, 1948–1958," 68 *Georgetown Law Journal* 1, 35 (1979), 79n671.
9. Job 40:10.
10. Job 38:1–3.
11. Job 37:25.
12. *Griffin v. County School Board of Prince Edward County*, 377 U.S. 218, 229 (1964).
13. *Green v. County School Board of New Kent County*, 391 U.S. 430, 439 (1968).
14. See Geoffrey R. Stone et al., *Constitutional Law*, 6th ed. (Alphen aan den Rijn, Netherlands: Wolters Kluwer Law and Business, 2009), 475, 477, 479.
15. Quoted in Taylor Branch, *Parting the Waters: America in the King Years 1954–63* (New York: Simon and Schuster, 1988), 140.
16. Martin Luther King, Jr., "Stride toward Freedom," reprinted in *A Testament of Hope: The Essential Writings and Speeches of Martin Luther King, Jr.*, ed. J. M. Washington (San Francisco: Harper and Row, 1986), 456. The Supreme Court decision was *Gayle v. Browder*, 352 U.S. 903 (1956); King quoted this response from one of his parishioners.

17. Job 9:29, 9:32–35.
18. *Plessy v. Ferguson*, 163 U.S. 537 (1896).
19. See *Plessy*, 163 U.S. at 551: "If the two races are to meet upon terms of social equality, it must be the result of natural affinities, a mutual appreciation of each other's merits, and a voluntary consent of individuals." Compare Herbert Wechsler, "Toward Neutral Principles of Constitutional Law," 73 *Harvard Law Review* 1, 34 (1959): "For me, assuming equal facilities, the problem is not one of discrimination at all. Its human and constitutional dimensions lie entirely elsewhere, in the denial by the state of freedom to associate, a denial that impinges in the same way on any groups or races that may be involved."
20. *Brown I*, 347 U.S. at 494.
21. *Cooper v. Aaron*, 358 U.S. at 20.
22. *Roe v. Wade*, 410 U.S. 113 (1973).
23. *United States v. Nixon*, 418 U.S. 683 (1974).
24. For a more extended consideration of the *Nixon Tapes Case*, see Robert A. Burt, *The Constitution in Conflict* (Cambridge, MA: Harvard University Press, 1992), 316–327.
25. The same criticism applies to the Supreme Court's decision in *Bush v. Gore*, 531 U.S. 98 (2000), where a 5-to-4 majority resolved the electoral dispute between the two presidential candidates, ignoring the specific constitutional denomination of the Congress as the institution for deciding such disputes.
26. For a more extended consideration of the abortion cases, see Burt, *Constitution in Conflict*, 344–352.
27. *Roe*, 410 U.S. at 163.
28. Ibid.
29. *United States v. Vuitch*, 402 U.S. 62 (1971).
30. See, for example, *Planned Parenthood of Southeastern Pa. v. Casey*, 505 U.S. 833 (1992); *Gonzales v. Carhart*, 550 U.S. 124 (2007).

14. Reconciling with Injustice

1. Genesis 6:5.
2. Genesis 8:21.
3. Matthew 6:12.
4. Matthew 5:39–41.

5. For modern examples see Friedrich Nietzsche, *The Genealogy of Morals;* Sigmund Freud, *Civilization and Its Discontents,* trans. and ed. James Strachey (New York: W. W. Norton, 1961).

6. Luke 15:1–2.

7. Luke 15:5–7.

8. Luke 15:9–10.

9. Luke 15:11–25.

10. Exodus 34:1.

11. Luke 15:25–32.

12. For the source of this entitlement, see Deuteronomy 21:17 and commentary by Stephen Mitchell, *The Gospel According to Jesus* (New York: HarperCollins, 1991), 224–225.

13. Genesis 4:4–15.

14. Genesis 37:15, 37:18.

15. Genesis 12:1.

16. Luke 15:7.

17. Luke 15:2.

18. Job 42:11.

19. See Hans Loewald, *Psychoanalysis and the History of the Individual* (New Haven: Yale University Press, 1978), 57–61.

20. Deuteronomy 31:16–17, 31:21.

21. Genesis 2:19.

22. Robert Alter, *The Five Books of Moses* (New York: W. W. Norton, 2004), 22n18.

23. Freud, *Civilization and Its Discontents,* 13.

24. Ibid., 10–12.

25. See Hans Loewald who showed why Freud's prescription favoring secondary process thinking ("where the id is, there the ego must come into being") must be accompanied by the opposite prescription ("where ego is, there id must come into being again . . ."). Loewald, *Psychoanalysis,* 16.

26. Job 42:16.

Acknowledgments

I could not have written this book without the generous assistance I've received from Bruce Ackerman, Burton Alter, Aharon Barak, Ben Berger, Martin Bohmer, Lee Bollinger, Rick Brooks, Ed Burlingame, Perdida Burlingame, Jeff Burt, Linda Burt, Judy Craig, Ginny Donohue, Jess Donohue, Rebecca Engel, Anne Feuerzeig, Owen Fiss, Amos Friedland, Bryan Garsten, Jeremy Kessler, Matt Lee, Howard Lesnick, Daniel Markovits, Ted Marmor, Jack Miles, Joshua Neoh, Mark Rose, Paul Schwaber, Paul Schwartz, Bill Wagner, and Lynn Wardle.

This book would not have found its way to publication without the encouragement and substantive guidance I was offered by Elizabeth Knoll and by the careful editing of Christine Thorsteinsson of the Harvard University Press.

I am especially indebted to Jim Ponet, my friend, colleague, and teacher, and to the many Yale students, mostly from the Law School but also from the Divinity School and other parts of Yale, who joined with Jim and me at various times during the past twelve years in playful, absorbed engagement with the biblical texts. I dedicate this book to Jim and to them.

Index